Law and the Built Environment

Law and the Built Environment

Dr Jill St George

The Open University Law School, Faculty of Business and Law,
Open University, UK

Kate Ellis

London South Bank University, School of Construction Property and Surveying,
College of Technology and Environment, London, UK

Second Edition

WILEY Blackwell

This edition first published 2026

Registered Office(s)
John Wiley & Sons, Inc., 111 River Street, Hoboken, NJ 07030, USA
John Wiley & Sons Ltd, New Era House, 8 Oldlands Way, Bognor Regis, West Sussex, PO22 9NQ, UK

For details of our global editorial offices, customer services, and more information about Wiley products visit us at http://www.wiley.com.

The manufacturer's authorized representative according to the EU General Product Safety Regulation is Wiley-VCH GmbH, Boschstr. 12, 69469 Weinheim, Germany, e-mail: Product_Safety@wiley.com.

Wiley also publishes its books in a variety of electronic formats and by print-on-demand. Some content that appears in standard print versions of this book may not be available in other formats.

Library of Congress Cataloging-in-Publication Data
Names: St. George, Jill author
Title: Law & the built environment / Jill St George, The Open University Law School [and the others].
Other titles: Law and the built environment
Description: 2nd edition. | Hoboken : John Wiley & Sons Ltd, 2025. | Includes bibliographical references and index.
Identifiers: LCCN 2025034110 | ISBN 9781119907916 paperback | ISBN 9781119907930 adobe pdf | ISBN 9781119907923 epub
Subjects: LCSH: Construction industry–Law and legislation–England | Construction contracts–England | Real property–England | Landlord and tenant–England | Building laws–England
Classification: LCC KD2435 .L39 2025 | DDC 346.4204/3–dc23/eng/ 20250729
LC record available at https://lccn.loc.gov/2025034110

Cover Design: Wiley
Cover Image: © Barry Winiker/Getty Images

Set in 9.5/12.5pt STIXTwoText by Lumina Datamatics
Printed and bound by CPI Group (UK) Ltd, Croydon, CR0 4YY
C9781119907916_300126

Dr Jill St George:

For Tom, Katherine, Eliza and Henry – thank you for enabling me to indulge in a much needed distraction.

Kate Ellis:

For Kit, who encouraged me to stand on my own two feet.

Contents

Preface

This is a law book with a difference. It has been written not for law students but for those on vocational university courses studying for qualifications in property and construction professions. It aims to provide a single source of reference for students undertaking the law modules on these courses but will also be useful for those who currently work in construction industry professions to help them understand the impact of law on their roles.

Built environment students have particular needs when it comes to a law textbook. Competence in law is an essential ingredient for success in their chosen careers, but it is not the only one. They must develop competencies in a diverse range of subject areas, as well as the ability to draw effectively upon each of them in confronting real-life challenges in their professional environments.

It seeks to provide a depth of coverage of the core legal topics which are appropriate to those embarking on careers in the built environment. It recognises that they must fully understand the legal environment in which they operate and be able to discuss legal issues with their counterparts in the legal profession, whilst rarely being called upon to provide specialist legal advice themselves. Built environment professionals are not expected to be lawyers and will engage lawyers to deal with difficult legal issues. It is hoped that this text will enable those conversations.

The book introduces the key legal principles that underpin the professional and commercial lives of those who provide advice to clients in the property and construction sectors and those who must navigate commercial and contract management for construction projects. Although many of these are equally applicable to other professions, we have sought to illustrate these principles within context by reference to examples, statutes and case law which are of most relevance to the built environment. In the specialist areas of built environment professional practice – for example construction contracts and rent review – we have also gone into greater detail than would normally be encountered in a more conventional legal textbook.

The authors of the 2nd edition of this book and other lawyers teaching built environment students for many years know how difficult it can be to find a single, succinct and easily understandable textbook covering the law modules in sufficient depth and with appropriate emphasis on property and construction. With that in mind they attempted and, in our opinion, succeeded in producing a book that satisfied the demand for a specialist law textbook catering exclusively for built environment students.

This 3rd edition seeks to bring the law up to date, allowing for changes in legislation and new decisions of the courts in the ever-changing legal landscape. Two new chapters have been added, one which relates to formation and operation of construction contracts, concentrating on commonly used contract terms, whilst the other looks at dispute resolution, providing essential information regarding resolving disputes without resorting to the court system.

Building on the work of Douglas Wood, Paul Chynoweth, Julie Ashead, and Jim Mason, we have endeavoured to state the law as at 1 June 2025 and any errors or omissions are of course entirely our own.

Kate Ellis
Jill St George

Table of Cases

D

H

Q

R

V

W

Table of Statutes

U

V

W

1

The Administration of Law

CONTENTS

1.1 The Nature of Law

The law is a set of rules that define the rights and obligations of those under its jurisdiction. This book is predominantly concerned with laws that govern the built environment, which includes, at its most fundamental, land and buildings. As law is jurisdiction-specific, the law of England and Wales will be the primary focus of this book; however, comparisons may be made with Scotland and Northern Ireland, along with rights and obligations under international law. The aim of this first chapter is to provide an overview of the English and Welsh legal system, establishing a foundation for the areas of law considered in later chapters.

1.1.1 Why Regulate the Built Environment?

The importance of the built environment on society was articulated by a Government Select Committee in 2016:

> The built environment affects us all. The planning, design, management and maintenance of the built environment, and its interaction with the natural environment, have a long-term impact upon people and communities. The quality of life, prosperity, health, wellbeing and happiness of an individual is heavily influenced by the place in which they live or work and, in this way, place shapes us.[1]

1 Select Committee on National Policy for the Built Environment, Building better places, ch1, para 1.

Regulation of the built environment takes place through a combination of national and local policies and decisions, with national government providing broad frameworks and local government implementing them within their administrative boundaries. Law is integral to the overall functioning of the built environment, providing a structure under which national and local policies can be implemented.

1.2 Divisions of Law

The English and Welsh legal system distinguishes between two main types of law: criminal law and civil law.

1.2.1 Criminal Law

Criminal law is primarily enforced by the state through the Police and the Crown Prosecution Service, with proceedings brought in the name of the Crown (*R v*) against a defendant (for example, *R v St George*). The aims of criminal law are centred on the responsibility of the state to prevent and punish certain acts, alongside its obligation to protect individuals and/or society as a whole. Penalties imposed for a breach of criminal law range from community sentences to imprisonment. Although criminal law is often thought of in the context of violent offences, drug offences, offences of theft, etc., it also includes public law, which is concerned with areas governed by the state. These include health and safety regulations, environmental protections and building requirements.

1.2.2 Civil Law

Civil law governs rights and obligations between individuals, which can include businesses, companies and other forms of organisations as well as individuals. Civil law is enforced through individuals or organisations bringing actions against other individuals or organisations in order to resolve disputes (also termed private law). This is in contrast to criminal law, where the case is brought by the state, not the victim themselves. Civil law seeks to provide a recourse to those who have suffered injury or loss as a result of a breach of civil law, with remedies predominantly (but not exclusively) centred on financial compensation. In a civil case, a claimant brings a case against a defendant. As a general rule, any area of law which isn't covered under criminal law is civil law.

1.2.3 Overlaps in Criminal and Civil Law

On occasions, one set of events can give rise to both civil and criminal proceedings, and liability may be established in both. For example, a prosecution under the criminal law may be brought by the state against the driver of a vehicle under the Road Traffic Act 1988, while the question of compensation will be determined in a separate action brought by the claimant using civil law. A similar situation could arise where an employer has been negligent with regard to the health and safety of an employee, resulting in an injury at work.

The employee may bring a case under civil law against their employer, and the employer may be prosecuted under the criminal law for breaches of, or failure to comply with, the Health and Safety at Work etc. Act 1974. Where this situation arises, the two sets of proceedings are kept separate, and the matters are dealt with by different courts.

Whether a case is a criminal or civil matter, an appeal may be made to a higher court against the decision of a lower court. There must be proper grounds for appeal, and there are strict time limits within which an appeal must be made. In such circumstances, the person bringing the appeal is known as the appellant, and those against whom the appeal is brought are known as the respondents.

The law of England and Wales also governs a number of procedures, providing a legal framework under which they have to be carried out (even though there is no dispute or any matter which is contentious). The transfer of a house, making of a will or drafting of a contract are all examples. These non-contentious matters are governed by rules developed by the civil law, although there is no conflict between parties.

1.2.4 Evidence

Whether a dispute is a civil or a criminal matter, the action will not succeed unless there is sufficient evidence to support the case. In civil cases, it is for the claimant to prove the case and not for the defendant to disprove it. In criminal cases, it is for the state to prove the case, not to the defendant to disprove it. This obligation is known as the burden of proof. For criminal law, the burden sits with the state, and in civil cases, it sits with the claimant. Where either party appeals, the burden of proof sits with whoever brings the appeal. The extent to which the party bringing the action must prove their case is called the standard of proof. In a civil case, the claimant must prove their case on the balance of probabilities. In a criminal case, the standard of proof is higher, and the case must be proved beyond reasonable doubt.

An established method of pursuing or defending a case is through the use of witnesses giving evidence on oath. This is in addition to any documentary evidence which may be available, or real evidence (such as a mechanical device or a photograph of a building site where an accident has taken place). Evidence is given by a sworn statement, made on oath, known as an affidavit. Hearsay evidence is evidence which is not perceived by the witness but stated by some other person and repeated by the witness. Following the Civil Evidence Act 1995, hearsay evidence is generally admissible in civil proceedings. In criminal law proceedings, the law regarding the admission of hearsay is found in S114–136 Criminal Justice Act 2003.

1.2.5 The Common Law

Most legal systems in Europe are based on Roman law and operate under what is known as a civil law system. In contrast, the law in England and Wales operates under a common law system. The term civil law here is not concerned with the type of law (civil or criminal) but with the type of legal system.

The term common law has several meanings:

- It is used to describe the English and Welsh legal system along with other legal systems, such as those of Australia or the United States of America;
- It is used to describe the law made by judges through judgments using precedent in courts of law as opposed to law through an Act of Parliament; and
- It describes the body of law which became common or uniform to the whole of England and Wales after 1066.

Up until 1066, the laws of England and Wales varied from area to area, meaning there was no unified legal system. Each court operated in isolation, and there were no centralised institutions exercising either administrative or judicial control over the legal system as a whole. This changed with the Norman Conquest in 1066. An objective of the Normans was to establish a national system of law which would apply to all persons, regardless of where they were based geographically or their societal status (hence, the common law, common to all).

1.2.6 Equity

By the end of the reign of Edward I (1272–1307), the shortcomings of the common law were becoming apparent. Technicalities dominated common law procedures, and these had become very complex, with actions potentially failing because of minor errors in the preparation of documents required to start a case. There was also a lack of appropriate remedies to fit each set of circumstances. Claimants who were dissatisfied with the common law began to petition the King in an attempt to redress their grievances. By the end of the fourteenth century, there were so many petitions that the King began referring them to the Lord Chancellor. From this process, the courts of equity emerged, presided over by the Lord Chancellor. The Chancellor granted remedies which they thought were just and equitable depending on the circumstances of the case. This process became so popular that additional judges needed to be appointed. These Chancellor's Courts, or Courts of Chancery as they became known, provided an alternative set of courts to those of the common law.

Equity offered new remedies as alternatives to a claim for damages. Initially, the Chancellor was able to grant any remedy which they thought appropriate to the circumstances of the case. Eventually, the Courts of Equity became as formalised as the common law, with the availability of certain, specific remedies available with guidance from previous cases. Equity offered new remedies such as specific performance (a court order to compel the performance of the contract), an injunction (an order requiring a person to stop doing something or requiring them to do something) and rescission (the right to withdraw from a contract). The basis upon which equitable remedies operate is and always has been different from the availability of damages (monetary compensation) as a remedy in the common law courts. Equity is not a complete system of law, instead, it acts in conjunction with the common law by filling in any gaps. Equitable remedies are discretionary and not automatically granted even if the claimant has proved the case. In contrast, at common law, once the case is proved, the claimant is automatically entitled to claim damages irrespective of any other aspects of the case. In addition, if an equitable remedy is sought, the 'Maxims of Equity' are applicable. These are a set of rules that regulate the basis upon which remedies are granted. The conduct of the claimant, in particular, is very important where an equitable remedy is claimed.

Examples of the maxims include:

Equity Follows the Law: This reflects the notion that equity operates to mitigate the harshness of the common law. It does not deny common law rules and will only depart from common law rules where there is a good, compelling reason to do so.

Those Who Seek Equity Must Do Equity: When considering whether to grant equitable relief, the court will consider the conduct of both parties, and oftentimes requires both parties to act equitably. For example, specific performance of a contract will usually apply to both parties, not just the defendant.

Those Who Come to Equity Must Come with Clean Hands: This relates to the maximum above, and those who seek an equitable remedy from the courts must not have engaged in disreputable or dishonest conduct with regard to the issue at hand.

Delay Defeats Equity: Time limits with regard to cases brought in law are provided by statute, for example, claims relating to the quality of work in the construction of buildings are to be brought within 15 years of the fault becoming apparent.[2] Time limits for breach of contract regarding construction remain at 6 years,[3] which is the same for actions brought under the law of tort.[4] No such formal time limits exist in equity, however, equitable relief will often be denied where claimants do not act quickly. If an unreasonable, significant and/or inexcusable delay occurs, the court may determine that it is unjust to grant equitable relief.

In the nineteenth century, a number of reforms were made to the legal system, culminating in the Judicature Acts 1873–1875. To a large extent, these Acts established the system of courts as they are today. Existing court structures were reorganised, and it was established that matters governed by the common law and equity could be dealt with in the same court. Today, a court will first consider the common law position before then assessing whether equity affects the position. Although the common law and equity were fused for administrative purposes, they still retained their own individual characteristics and both aspects are present today.

1.3 Sources of Law

Most continental European countries have a legal system in which the majority of their law is in written codes which are amended as need arises (civil law systems). The Code Napoléon in France is a good example. In contrast, English and Welsh law have developed from a number of sources, each arising as the situation required, as exampled above with equity. The majority of new law is produced through an Act of Parliament (statute); however, a large part has developed from rules and principles pronounced in the decisions of courts

2 S14B Latent Damage Act 1986.
3 S14A (4) Latent Damage Act 1986.
4 S2 Limitation Act 1980.

throughout the centuries (called common law/case law). In addition to common law and statute, another source of domestic law is that of custom. Historically this was a source of law of great importance and is from where the common law originated. Its practical importance nowadays is slight, but on those occasions when a case does come to court questioning the legal validity of a custom, it tends to concern rights over land or buildings, so it is appropriate to consider it here.

1.3.1 Custom

A custom is a right or duty that has come to exist through the consent of the population. A person who wishes to prove the existence of a custom which hasn't previously been recognised by the courts must satisfy four requirements relating to the alleged right: time immemorial; continuity; peaceable enjoyment; and reasonableness and certainty.

1.3.1.1 Time Immemorial

The custom must have existed since time immemorial, which is fixed as 1189. In most cases, it is impossible for those claiming the custom to irrefutably show that it existed in 1189, so this requirement is satisfied by evidence that the custom has existed within living memory, or at least without interruption for 20 years. This was confirmed in *Mercer v Denne*,[5] where it was established that fishermen had the right to dry nets on a privately owned beach where the land had been added to by accretion. The court confirmed that 'Custom, it is argued, is a local law, which must have existed from time immemorial – that is, from the beginning of the reign of Richard I', and held that despite the accretion, the beach 'existed in and long prior to the reign of Richard I, in substantially the same condition as it does at present'.[6] The owner of the beach was prevented from building on it because to do so would interfere with the customary right to dry nets. If the custom could not have been exercised at some point since 1189, the claim will fail. In *Simpson v Wells*,[7] the appellant claimed that the obstruction of a highway with a stall set up to provide refreshments at statute sessions for the hiring of servants was a custom. However, the court held that as statute sessions were first introduced in the fourteenth century, there could be no such claim of obstructing the highway for such sessions before this time, so it was not custom by immemorial usage.[8]

1.3.1.2 Continuity

The custom must have been continuously in operation, although it need not have been exercised throughout the period, as long as the right existed. It seems a customary right cannot be lost by disuse once it is established, but failure to exercise the right may make it more difficult to prove. In *Wyld v Silver*,[9] the defendant bought a piece of land and sought to build five homes on it. The claimants brought an action to prevent the build by arguing that a custom existed allowing an annual fair to be held on the land now owned by

5 *Mercer v Denne* [1904] 2 Ch 534.
6 Cozens-Hardy LJ, Ibid.
7 *Simpson v Wells* (1872) LR 7 QB 214.
8 See case overview, judgment date 24/01/1872; *Simpson v Wells* (1872) LR 7 QB 214.
9 *Wyld v Silver* [1962] 3 All ER 309.

the defendant. The fair had not been held in living memory, and the last recorded occasion of it was 1875. Despite this, the court held that the claimants were able to prevent the landowner from building on the land owing to the fair being established as a custom. Likewise in *New Windsor Corporation v Mellor*,[10] a custom was proven which prevented a local authority from using land upon which it was established that, for many centuries, had been used for recreational purposes by the local inhabitants (even though such rights had not been exercised in recent times).

1.3.1.3 Peaceable Enjoyment

The basis of a custom is that it is exercised by common consent. If it is exercised by force or in secret, there can be no custom (Latin maxim: *nec per vim nec clam nec precario*). Similarly, if it is exercised by permission, it cannot be as of right, and, therefore it is impossible to establish it as a custom. In *Mills v Colchester Corporation*,[11] the claim of a custom entitling the claimant to an annual licence to fish for oysters failed, as the very existence of the licence prevented the fishing from being as of right.

1.3.1.4 Reasonableness and Certainty

The courts will not recognise a custom which is deemed unreasonable. In *Newcastle-Under-Lyme Corporation v Wolstanton*,[12] an attempt to claim the existence of a customary right enabling the Lord of the Manor to excavate on land without paying compensation for the damage to the owners of buildings on the land was deemed to be unreasonable.

The custom must also be certain, and those who are to benefit from a customary right must be capable of proper identification. In *Wilson v Wiles*,[13] a claim to a local custom to take turf failed because the extent of the right could not be identified. The custom must be consistent with previously established customs and must not conflict with statute or any basic principle of the common law.

1.3.2 Case Law

In a common law jurisdiction, when a judge decides on a particular aspect of the law the decision is recorded, and judges in lower courts are obliged to follow the decision in subsequent cases. This is called *stare decisis* or the doctrine of precedent. When a judge is considering the facts of a case and applying the law to the facts, it is necessary for them to look back at previous cases which have involved similar facts in the same area of law to see how those cases have been dealt with.

1.3.3 Law Reporting

The importance of case law as a source of law is dependent upon the existence of law reports, as this is where cases that establish new principles of law are published. The report

10 *New Windsor v Mellor* [1975] 3 All ER 44.
11 *Mills v Colchester Corporation* (1868) L.R. 3 C.P. 575.
12 *Newcastle-Under-Lyme Corporation v Wolstanton Ltd* [1947] 1 All ER 218.
13 *Wilson v Wiles* (1806) 7 East's Term Reports 12.

contains details of the facts of the case along with the decision of the judge (known as the judgment) and reasoning for their decision. However, not all cases of interest are reported, and the majority of decisions are unreported. Despite this, an unreported case may be taken into account by a judge when reaching a decision in a later case.

1.3.3.1 The History

The history of law reports goes back to the Year Books, which were manuscripts referring to cases that had been dealt with in a particular locality. After the demise of Year Books, a number of private reports were separately published. These were compiled primarily by lawyers for their own personal use, and their standard and quality varied greatly. Good examples include those of Coke, Dyer and Burrow, all of whom established a reputation for reporting cases accurately. The available reports of the private reporters have been reprinted in what is known as the English Reports.

1.3.3.2 Modern Law Reporting

Modern law reporting dates from the creation of the Council of Law Reporting in 1865. The 'Law Reports' comprise four series of reports: Appeal Cases (AC), King's Bench (KB) (Queen's Bench from 1952 to 2022, QB), Chancery (Ch) and Family (Fam). These reports are now supplemented by the Weekly Law Reports (WLR), which contain a report of all the decisions which will eventually appear in the more official reports. In addition to these reports there are other transcripts which are published commercially. The best known of these are the All England Law Reports (All ER), which are a general series of reports published weekly that appear in three or four volumes each year. The Times newspaper carries daily reports of leading cases, while periodicals such as the Estates Gazette and The Journal of Planning and Environmental Law publish reports of interest to their readers. Many cases are recorded in various reports and reference is made to them in a cross-section of journals. When a case is reported, after the names of the parties involved and the year it was decided, the name of the report is included along with the page where the case is to be found. For example, *Murphy v Brentwood District Council* [1991] 1 AC 398 indicates that the first volume of the AC reports for 1991 must be consulted, on page 398.

As part of the modernisation of law reporting, in 2001, a system of neutral citation of judgments was introduced. A neutral citation is a unique reference given to a judgment by the court or tribunal itself. Table 1.1 summarises some of the most common examples.

If a judgment has been reported in more than one series of law reports, the neutral citation must be given first. A good source of guidance on the use of neutral citation (as well as the citing of case law in general) is to be found in The Oxford Standard for Citation of Legal Authorities (OSCOLA).

The majority of reported cases are available through databases such as LexisNexis, Westlaw UK and Lawtel. Justis stores all unreported judgments of the Court of Appeal, Civil Division, delivered since 1980. These databases are available by subscription, but many courts and some reporting services have web pages where cases can be accessed free of charge. House of Lords opinions from 1996 are published on the House of Lords website, and many other courts make full text judgments available online (for example, the European Court of Justice and the Employment Appeal Tribunal).

Table 1.1 Example citations.

Neutral citation	Court	Example
UKPC	Privy Council	*Marr v Collie* [2017] UKPC 17
UKSC	Supreme Court	*FirstPort Property Services Ltd v Settlers Court RTM Company and others* [2022] UKSC 1
UKHL	House of Lords	*Jameel v Wall Street Journal* [2006] UKHL 44
EWCA Civ	England and Wales Court of Appeal (Civil Division)	*Wodzicki v Wodzicki* [2017] EWCA Civ 44
EWCA Crim	England and Wales Court of Appeal (Criminal Division)	*Turner v R* [2022] EWCA Crim 617
EWHC (Ch)	England and Wales High Court (Chancery Division)	*EMI Group Ltd v The Prudential Assurance Co Ltd* [2020] EWHC 2061 (Ch)
EWHC (KB)	England and Wales High Court (Kings Bench Division)	*Mathieu v Hinds and Anor* [2022] EWHC 924 (QB)

1.3.4 Judicial Precedent

Judicial precedent is an integral aspect of case law. Under the doctrine of *stare decisis* (to stand by decisions), a judge reaches a decision on a particular point through the application of rules of law contained in previous decisions (precedent) which deal with similar issues. Not every decision sets precedent, as not every case is important enough to make new law and it depends on the court giving judgment, as lower courts are bound by the decisions of higher courts. A distinction is made between the principle forming the decision, called the *ratio decidendi*, and other comments made by a judge which are not strictly relevant to the decision, known as the *obiter dicta*.

1.3.4.1 Court Hierarchy

Lower courts are bound by the decisions of higher courts. As explained by Lord Neuberger in *Willers v Joyce*:[14]

> On issues of law, (i) Circuit Judges are bound by decisions of High Court Judges, the Court of Appeal and the Supreme Court, (ii) High Court Judges are bound by decisions of the Court of Appeal and the Supreme Court, and (iii) the Court of Appeal is bound by decisions of the Supreme Court.

The court structure is discussed in greater detail at Section 1.4; however, in summary, the courts at the bottom of the court hierarchy (the Magistrates Court (primarily criminal) and County Court (civil)) are bound by decisions made in the courts above them but are not bound by their own decisions. The High Court (civil) and Crown Court (criminal) are

14 *Willers v Joyce* [2016] UKSC 44.

bound by courts above them, but not those below, and the Court of Appeal (hears both criminal and civil cases) is bound by the only court above it, the Supreme Court (which also hears both criminal and civil cases). Decisions of the Supreme Court are binding on all lower courts.

Prior to October 2009, the House of Lords was the highest appeal court, comprising of the 12 most senior judges called Lords of Appeal in Ordinary. The House of Lords was located in the legislature (the House of Lords) and could be involved in Parliamentary debate concerning Government legislation. To enable a greater separation of powers, the Constitutional Reform Act 2005 made provision for the establishment of a Supreme Court, to be situated outside of the House of Parliament. The Supreme Court is now the highest appeal court; however, House of Lords judgments made pre-2009 remain binding on lower courts unless the decision is departed from by the Supreme Court.[15] The House of Lords was confirmed as entitled to depart from its previous decisions from 1996,[16] and this right continues in the Supreme Court (although instances are rare).[17] The Supreme Court (and the previous House of Lords) is the highest appeal court for all of the UK. The position of the Privy Council in the court hierarchy is discussed at Section 1.4.3.10.

1.3.4.2 Interpretation of Judicial Precedent

Despite the importance of precedent in common law legal systems, a court will, on occasions, refuse to follow an earlier decision. It is the *ratio decidendi* of a case which is binding on subsequent courts, subject to the hierarchy rules. Before precedent has a binding effect, it must be shown to be a decision of a court within the hierarchy. *Obiter dicta* of a court, particularly the House of Lords or Supreme Court, carry weight but need not be followed by a court in subsequent cases. Similar considerations apply to the decisions of Scottish, Irish and particularly Commonwealth cases, which in recent years have been frequently cited in building disputes. Decisions of the Privy Council (see Section 1.4.3.10) also come into this category. If there are grounds for distinguishing a case from an earlier decision, then the previous decision does not have to be followed. A court may overrule a legal rule in a decision that it considers to be obviously wrong, while the decision of a lower court may be reversed on appeal if the higher court disapproves of the previous case.

1.3.4.3 Advantages and Disadvantages

There are advantages and disadvantages to the doctrine of precedent, which are summarised in Table 1.2.

1.3.5 Legislation

A statute, also called an Act of Parliament, is the quickest and clearest method of creating new law or amending existing law to meet current requirements. An Act of Parliament

15 Schedule 9 Constitutional Reform Act 2005.

16 Practice Statement (Judicial Precedent) [1966] 1 WLR 1234, which emphasised that, while the Law Lords would regard their earlier decisions as 'normally binding', they would depart from them 'when it appears right to do so'.

17 *Murphy v Brentwood DC* [1991] 1 AC 398.

Table 1.2 Advantages and disadvantages to the doctrine of precedent.

	Advantages		Disadvantages
Certainty:	Precedent gives a degree of certainty and consistency to the law, which enables the likely outcome of a case to be predicted.	Rigidity:	The process gives little scope for manoeuvre and change only occurs once a case is brought and travels through the appeal courts. Parliament can, however, bring in legislation to change an unsatisfactory feature of the common law.
Detail:	Case law has many detailed rules which provide full information relating to decided cases, and a written code of law does not enable the same level of detail and precision.	Technicalities:	The methods used by the courts to avoid a precedent can confuse the law and produce a degree of uncertainty.
Practicality:	It is more convenient to have precedent than to argue a case on each occasion when a legal issue arises.	Bulk:	Owing to the volume of cases, it can be difficult to refer to every appropriate authority. In addition, many cases are unreported, but they remain as precedents.
Flexibility:	If necessary and appropriate, using the doctrine of precedent, a court can still avoid an unsatisfactory precedent by distinguishing or overruling a decision.	Time:	Associated with the disadvantage of rigidity, with the need to wait until a case arises that has the capacity to overrule another or for Parliament to legislate, the doctrine of precedent can enable a decision to remain good law despite criticism.

overrules any existing custom, case law or earlier Act of Parliament with which it conflicts. The supremacy of legislation over other sources of law is termed the Sovereignty of Parliament. The effect of this Sovereignty is that Parliament, comprising the House of Commons and the House of Lords, together with the reigning monarch, is sovereign and the legality of Parliament to make a specific law cannot be challenged. The courts must apply an Act once it becomes law, although it is a matter for the judges to interpret the contents of the Act (termed 'Statutory Interpretation', discussed at Section 1.3.5.3).

1.3.5.1 The Making of a Statute

In the UK, Parliament consists of two different legislative institutions: the House of Commons and the House of Lords. Ideas for new laws can be brought by both the government in power and by private members of Parliament (although the vast majority are brought by the government). Prior to coming into force, whilst in the drafting stage, the law is constructed into a bill, which is prepared by parliamentary draftspersons. Bills can be introduced by the government in either of the two Houses of Parliament; however, the majority are introduced in the House of Commons. A bill has to pass through several stages in both the Commons and the Lords before it receives the Royal Assent (the King's approval) and becomes an Act. Once a bill becomes an Act, it will remain law unless it is repealed. It is presumed not to be retrospective (back-dated) in effect, having application only following its entry into force. In the main, a statute does not expire or become obsolete simply by the passing of time, meaning there are many Acts which are antiquated and of no practical use. To prevent this, the Statute Law (Repeals) Acts repeals obsolete enactments on a regular basis. Occasionally an Act is only operative for a limited period, but as a general rule a statute ceases to have effect only once it is repealed by another statute.

1.3.5.2 Types of Legislation

1.3.5.2.1 Public Acts

Public Acts are the most common types of Acts of Parliament. They affect society as a whole.

1.3.5.2.2 Private Acts

These do not alter the general law but confer special or local powers.

1.3.5.2.3 Consolidating Acts

A statute which gathers together several Acts on one area of the law and re-enacts them so that all the statute law on a particular topic can be found in the same Act. This is periodically done with, for example, tax legislation and town planning.

1.3.5.2.4 Codifying Acts

Codification takes place when all of the law on a particular topic is enacted in one statute. It includes all previous case law, customs and legislation. The law in the majority of continental European countries is codified (for example, Code Pénal in France) but in common law countries, there is little codification. The classic example of codification in English law is the Sale of Goods Act 1893 (now 1979), which reduced all the law on the subject into a single Act.

1.3.5.2.5 Delegated Legislation

Parliament frequently passes the responsibility of enacting legislation to others. The framework of an Act is laid down by Parliament (through enabling legislation), while the delegated body can fill in the detail required (through subordinate legislation). This subordinate legislation appears in the form of rules, regulations and orders, while the legislators range from the government (the King in Council) to local authorities. Much of the law relating to building matters and the transfer of land is to be found in this form. Examples include building regulations, and many aspects of planning law and health and safety legislation. Delegated legislation is made by ministerial orders known as statutory instruments, which since 1946 have had to be published or 'laid' before Parliament before they become effective. A statutory instrument can be recognised by instead of having the word Act at the end of the name of the instrument (document), the order, rules or regulations will be cited (recorded) by reference to year and number with the letters SI indicating its status. For example, Higher-Risk Buildings (Descriptions and Supplementary Provisions) Regulations SI 2023, which was enabled by the Building Act 1984 and the Building Safety Act 2022. Two other forms of delegated legislation are by-laws and the regulations of professional bodies and trade unions. By-laws are local laws which regulate aspects of life. So-called autonomic legislation regulates the conduct of the members of professional associations such as the Royal Institution of Chartered Surveyors and The Royal Institute of British Architects and provides for sanctions where appropriate. Control over delegated legislation is exercised by Parliament and the courts.

Parliament: Committees of the House of Commons review statutory instruments and decide which of them should be brought to the attention of Parliament. The enabling Act (the individual Act which grants power to make particular regulations) sometimes itself requires that the instrument be brought to the notice of Parliament. Appropriate government ministers are answerable to Parliament in respect of regulations made by their own departments, while by-laws must be confirmed by a government department before they become law. Parliament also has the overall safeguard in that it may withdraw the delegated power if it so wishes.

The Courts: Although the courts cannot challenge the validity of an Act of Parliament, they can challenge delegated legislation on the basis that the sub-legislator has exceeded the powers which Parliament has conferred upon them. In this case, the statutory instrument will be held to be ultra vires (beyond the power) and the rules rendered void. Many statutes, those dealing with compulsory purchase of land and planning law, for example, contain provisions whereby delegated legislation can be challenged on the basis that it is ultra vires. Before certain types of delegated legislation are affected, a public enquiry is held so that the views of the public may be made known on the particular issues (see Table 1.3).

1.3.5.3 Statutory Interpretation

Although Parliamentary Sovereignty denies the courts the opportunity of challenging the supremacy of Parliament, it is for the courts to determine the meaning of a particular section of an Act or statutory instrument. In doing so, courts are attempting to discover Parliament's intentions (also termed the will of Parliament) from the language used in the provision. It is the responsibility of the courts to 'interpret the will of Parliament' as expressed in the statute. Judges must not imply words into a statute, instead they must interpret the provision from what the enactment says. Many Acts contain an interpretation section dealing with the words and phrases used within it. A good example of this is section 205 of the Law of Property Act 1925:

> 205 General definitions.
>
> In this Act unless the context otherwise requires, the following expressions have the meanings hereby assigned to them respectively, that is to say –
>
> **i.** 'Bankruptcy' includes liquidation by arrangement; also in relation to a corporation means the winding up thereof;

Table 1.3 Advantages and disadvantages of delegated legislation.

Advantages		Disadvantages	
Efficiency:	Delegation enables delegated legislation to be passed quicker by the relevant body as opposed to sole reliance on Parliament.	Bulk:	A result of the increase in efficiency and speed is that approximately 3,500 SI's come into force each year.[18]
Technicality:	Experts in a field are able to construct delegated legislation using their expertise.	Drafting:	In moving responsibility from Parliament to delegated bodies, the process of law-making is moved from elected representatives (MPs) to unelected civil servants.
Volume:	Delegation reduces the volume of work for Parliament by requiring Parliament to deal with general aspects of policy and delegating the detail to the sub-legislators.	Publicity and Consultation:	Out of the approximately 3,500 SI's which come into force, only around 1,000 need to be considered by Parliament.[19] Delegated legislation is therefore not created by elected persons and is not subject to the same publicity and consultation as Acts of Parliament.
Flexibility:	The rules can be quickly altered and amended as necessary.	—	—

ii. 'Conveyance' includes a mortgage, charge, lease, assent, vesting declaration, vesting instrument, disclaimer, release and every other assurance of property or of an interest therein by any instrument, except a will; 'convey' has a corresponding meaning; and 'disposition' includes a conveyance and also a devise, bequest, or an appointment of property contained in a will; and 'dispose of' has a corresponding meaning;

iii. 'Building purposes' include the erecting and improving of, and the adding to, and the repairing of buildings; and a 'building lease' is a lease for building purposes or purposes connected therewith; (...)

Parliament has also sought to assist the courts by passing the Interpretation Act 1978, which defines many expressions used in legislation unless a contrary intention is apparent. Schedule 1 defines words and expressions, and includes, for example:

> 'Land' includes building and other structures, land covered with water, and any estate, interest, easement, servitude or right in or over land. [1st January 1979].

18 UK Parliament, 2023.
19 Ibid.

'Writing' includes typing, printing, lithography, photography and other modes of representing or reproducing words in a visible form, and expressions referring to writing are construed accordingly.

'Month' means calendar month. [1850]

'Building regulations', in relation to England and Wales, has the meaning given by section 122 Building Act 1984.

To further assist judges in interpreting the will of Parliament, the courts have developed a number of rules. It is for the judge in each case to determine which is the appropriate rule to apply.

1.3.5.3.1 The Literal Rule

Where the words of the statute are clear and unambiguous, they are to be applied as they stand.

1.3.5.3.2 The Golden Rule

Where application of the literal rule results in an absurdity or inconsistency, the meaning to be given is that which expresses best the intention of Parliament from reading the Act in full.

1.3.5.3.3 The Mischief Rule

Here the court attempts to find out the mischief that the Act is attempting to remedy and interprets the Act accordingly.

In civil law systems (as opposed to common law) the overall intention or purpose of the legislation is paramount, and the background to the legislation is considered an essential part of the process. Legislation must be interpreted purposively (by looking at its purpose) to give effect to the broad intentions of Parliament.

1.3.6 Law Reform and the Law Commission

Reviewing and updating are vital aspects of a legal system, ensuring that law and its principles do not become out-dated and remain relevant. Whilst the vehicle for change is Parliament through the enactment of statute, there are numerous groups and individuals who inquire into the current presentation of the law and make proposals for amendment. One such example is campaigner, Gina Martin, who lobbied the Government for 2 years to criminalise 'upskirting', the result of which was the Voyeurism (Offences) Act 2019. Professional bodies such as the Law Society and the Bar Council, and external associations such as the National Council for Civil Liberties and lawyers' political groups (for instance, the Society of Labour Lawyers and its Conservative equivalent) seek to influence the present state of the legal system. There are also a number of standing committees of lawyers who advise on matters of law reform. At times (although fairly infrequently) the government appoints a Royal Commission to research a particular topic. The House of Lords Reform Commission is one example, which took place in 1999 and was the catalyst for the House of Lords Act 1999. The Act brought about many changes to the House of Lords, including the removal of hereditary peers and a significant reduction in the number of Lords. From research conducted in 2020, 33 Royal Commissions have been appointed since 1945.[20]

An important organisation which influences law reform is the Law Commission, established by the Law Commission Act 1965. It is a permanent organisation consisting of full time Commissioners, who are lawyers appointed by the Lord Chancellor and the Secretary of State for Justice. Their role is to recommend changes which should be made to the law, acting as an advisory body with the task of modernising the legal system. Its recommendations only become law if they are adopted by Parliament. In 2020–2021, the Law Commission published eight reports, covering, amongst others, leasehold reform, consumer sales contracts and modernisation of the communications. With regard to leasehold reform, reports covered leasehold enfranchisement, commonhold and the right to manage.

1.3.7 European Union Law

The UK officially left the European Union on 31 January 2020, although the Brexit transition period continued until 11 p.m. 31 December 2020. The withdrawal from the European Union came following a referendum held in 2016, which asked 'Should the UK remain a member of the European Union or leave the European Union?' The responses available were: 1) Remain a member of the European Union; 2) Leave the European Union. The UK population voted by 52–48% in favour of leaving the European Union.

Following the result of the referendum, from 31 December 2020, EU law ceased to apply in the UK. However, as EU law had a significant effect on the development of law in the UK since 1973, it was impractical for all to be repealed at the end of the transition period, the result of which would have been significant gaps in the legal framework of the UK.

To avoid such gaps, a statute was created which enabled withdrawal from the EU with certain safeguards in place. The European Union (Withdrawal) Act 2018 repealed the European Communities Act 1972 (S1) but retained the effect of EU-derived domestic legislation (S2 (1)) and EU regulations (S3). The Act determined that a court or tribunal in the UK would no longer be bound by any principles laid or decisions made by the European Court, nor could courts or tribunals refer any matters to the European Court (S6 (1)), and the Supreme Court would no longer be bound by any retained EU case authorities (S6 (4)). With regard to precedent, the Act determined that judgments of the European Court made on or before 11 p.m. on 31 December 2020 (the end of the transition period) would continue to be binding on UK courts, and those made after would not. However, UK courts are free to have regard to them where they are relevant to a matter before the courts (S6). Initially, the UK government envisaged that only the Supreme Court would be able to depart from pre-31 December 2020 judgments, however, in October 2020, it decided to extend the power to include the Court of Appeal and its equivalents in Scotland and

---

20 See https://researchbriefings.files.parliament.uk/documents/LLN-2020-0094/Royal-commissions-appointed-since-1945.pdf.

Northern Ireland. The test for departure from EU judgments is 'where it appears right to do so', which gives the courts a wide level of discretion. A UK-wide network of academics and researchers, coordinated from King's College London, publish a quarterly UK-EU regulatory divergence tracker. In the first quarter of 2024, January–March, the following developments were reported:

- 5 cases of active divergence (where the UK, or some part of it, changes its rules);
- 15 cases of passive divergence (where the EU changes its rules and the UK, or some part of it, does not follow);
- 1 case of 'NI divergence' (a new category covering cases where action is taken on the potential application of new or updated EU legislation in Northern Ireland);
- 1 case of procedural divergence (where new processes are introduced to change how pre-existing divergence is managed); and
- 3 cases of active alignment (where the UK takes steps to align more closely with EU rules, systems or programmes).[21]

1.4 The Court System in England and Wales

1.4.1 History

The operation of justice in England and Wales can be traced back to Anglo-Saxon times, when a combination of local courts and the King's court were used. Trial by ordeal was used until the twelfth century (when innocence or guilt was determined by reaction to an ordeal) and trial by combat until 1818. A version of the current day jury was introduced by Henry II in the twelfth century, using 12 local knights to settle disputes over land. The KB developed during this time; a term which continues to be used today. The first Magistrates' courts came into being in 1285, which saw 'good and lawful men' commissioned to keep the King's peace.[22] The fifteenth and sixteenth centuries saw the gradual introduction of a separation between the judiciary and government, with judges' salaries paid out of public funds and their removal from office only by 'due cause of law', as opposed to unfavourable judgments. This was codified in the Act of Settlement 1701. County Courts, holding responsibility for civil cases, were created under the County Courts Act 1846, and the Judicature Acts 1873–1875 (which merged common law and equity) laid the foundations for the operation of the courts today.

1.4.2 The Criminal Court Structure

1.4.2.1 Magistrates' Courts

The vast majority of criminal cases start off in Magistrates' courts and over 90% finish there.[23] Most towns have at least one Magistrates' court, and there are over 150 in England and Wales. The bench, the composition of judges, is either two or three magistrates, or a

21 J Reland, UK-EU Divergence Tracker Q1 2024 (London: UK in a Changing Europe, 2024).
22 See Courts and Tribunals Judiciary, Overview of the Judiciary.
23 See https://www.magistrates-association.org.uk/about-magistrates/jurisdictions/adult-court.

district judge. Where the bench has two or three magistrates, all have equal decision-making power. Magistrates are all volunteers (the role is unpaid), and they are lay persons, meaning they are not formally trained in the law. In court, they are supported by a legal adviser who sits in front of their bench. There is no jury in a Magistrates court.

The majority of criminal offences are categorised as either summary offences or indictable offences. For summary offences, Magistrates (or district judges in the Magistrates court) determine the verdict and the sentence. These are typically considered less serious offences, and include low-level motoring offences, disorderly behaviour and common assault. Indictable offences may only be tried on indictment, which means by the Crown Court before a judge and jury (see the following text). These are typically more serious offences, including murder, rape and grievous bodily harm.

On occasions, the Magistrates court will determine the case and pass it up to the Crown Court for sentencing. There are also a number of offences which are triable either way, meaning they can be heard either summarily or on indictment. Offences are categorised as such because they can vary significantly in their seriousness (the Sentencing Guidelines website examples theft, which could be of a chocolate bar, or could be of a priceless antique). For such offences, Magistrates can determine whether the case should be heard in the Crown Court and pass it up, or whether it should stay in the Magistrates court. If they decide it should stay in the Magistrates court, final decision sits with the defendant, who can either support remaining in the Magistrates, or choose the Crown Court instead.

1.4.2.2 Appeals from the Magistrates' Court

Appeals can be made against conviction or against the sentence passed, and can be heard by the Crown Court or the Divisional Court of the Kings Bench Division (KB).

1.4.2.3 The Crown Court

The Crown Court deals with the most serious criminal offences (indictable offences), alongside those triable either way passed up to them and appeals from the Magistrates court. There are around 70 Crown Courts located in towns and cities across England and Wales. The most famous of these is the Central Criminal Court, the Crown Court for the City of London (commonly known as the Old Bailey). Cases in the Crown Court may be overseen by Circuit judges, Recorders or High Court judges, alongside a 12-person jury comprised of members of the public. The jury determines whether a defendant is guilty or not guilty, whilst the judge is responsible for ensuring the trial is fair, providing the jury with legal directions, determining any legal issues which arise and imposing sentence.

1.4.2.4 Appeals from the Crown Court

A defendant may appeal against a sentence or conviction passed in the Crown Court to the Court of Appeal (Criminal Division) or the Divisional Court of the KB Division.

1.4.3 The Civil Courts

1.4.3.1 Magistrates' Courts

In addition to its function within the criminal justice system, the Magistrates court also holds civil jurisdiction, in particular with regard to proceedings in family law and civic financial liabilities. Family proceedings include applications for custody of children, maintenance orders and separation and adoption matters. The public is excluded from the proceedings; there are rules as to the composition of the 'bench' and strict limitations are imposed on press reporting. Other civil proceedings include council tax and appeals against the decisions of other bodies, such as licensing decisions against a local council.

1.4.3.2 Appeals from the Magistrates' Court

In certain cases, such as licencing and debt collection matters, appeals may be made from the Magistrates court to the Crown Court. As with their criminal jurisdiction, the Divisional Court of the KB Division can also hear appeals from the Magistrates, and for cases concerning family law proceedings, the Divisional Court of the Family Division hears appeals.

1.4.3.3 County Courts

The jurisdiction of the County Court is exclusively civil, meaning it can deal with matters including law of torts, contract law and recovery of land. Some can also deal with bankruptcy, insolvency and wills and trusts. A number of different judges sit in the County Court, including Circuit judges, District judges, Deputy District judges, Deputy Circuit judges and Recorders. The majority of civil cases do not have a jury (libel and slander trials being the primary exception), and it is the role of the judge to hear a case and make a determination based on the finding of facts and application of law. Judgment is passed and may include an entitlement of one party to damages (a financial amount), an injunction (preventing acts or actions, or requiring acts or actions) or a declaration (declaring a situation to be, such as determining a disputed boundary).

1.4.3.3.1 Appeals from the County Courts

Appeals from the County Court can be made be made in a number of ways:

- There is a right of appeal against the finding of a District Judge to a Circuit Judge;
- Either party can appeal against a County Court decision directly to the Court of Appeal;
- Where the County Court has bankruptcy jurisdiction, appeal can be made to a High Court judge in the Divisional Court of the Chancery Division.

1.4.3.4 The High Court of Justice

The work of the High Court is divided into three divisions, each of which has separate jurisdiction. The High Court deals with all high value and/or high importance civil law cases, as well as having supervisory jurisdiction over lower courts and tribunals (although there are a few statutory exceptions). The court is staffed by High Court Judges; its jurisdiction is principally civil in nature and is virtually unlimited.

1.4.3.4.1 The King's Bench Division

The KB Division is the largest of the three divisions and has the most varied jurisdiction, owing to its responsibility for dealing with all matters not covered by the other divisions. It is presided over by a President and staffed by High Court Judges. The KB Division deals with civil claims, including contract and tort cases, which, by reason of cost and/or complexity, are unsuitable for the County Court. Within the KB Division there are also a number of specialist courts, including:

- Admiralty Court: The oldest specialist court concerned with the consequences of maritime civil wrongs, including those in contracts and torts
- Commercial Court: Concerned primarily with banking and trade
- Planning Court: Deals with all challenges and reviews concerning planning matters
- Technology and Construction Court (TCC): Disputes arising from construction, engineering and technology disputes
- Administrative Court: Oversight of decisions of lower courts and tribunals and includes the Planning Court

One increasingly important aspect of the jurisdiction of the KB Division is its supervisory jurisdiction through the Administrative Court. This is a process whereby the court has the power to declare unlawful the decision of an inferior court, tribunal or other public body such as a local authority (if it is acting in a judicial manner). Where an individual, company or organisation challenges the lawfulness of the decision of a person or public body under public law, this is called judicial review. Judicial review concerning planning decisions is heard in the Planning Court.

Planning Court: Urban planning is integral to the built environment, and by association, its regulation through law. The primary responsibility for urban planning lies with local planning authorities (LPAs), who are local government bodies responsible for administering the majority of the planning system. The Planning Court deals with all judicial reviews and challenges involving planning matters, including (but not limited to):

- planning permission, other development consents, the enforcement of planning control and the enforcement of other statutory schemes;
- highways and other rights of way;
- compulsory purchase orders;
- village greens.[24]

To ensure planning matters are dealt with in a timely manner, cases concerning planning have strict limits to be applied (for example, determination of judicial review applications within 3 weeks) and those deemed 'substantial or difficult' are allocated to a judge with expertise in the issue at hand.[25] The Planning Court can sit in London, or one of five regional courts outside of London.[26]

1.4.3.4.2 Chancery Division

The Chancery division holds jurisdiction over seven specialist areas, divided into lists:

- The Business List
- The Financial List

---

24 See Court and Tribunals Judiciary for a full list, and Civil Procedure Rules 54.21 to 54.24.

25 Ibid.

26 Birmingham, Cardiff, Manchester, Leeds or Bristol.

- The Competition List
- The Insolvency and Companies List
- The Intellectual Property List
- The Property Trusts and Probate List
- The Revenue List

Their workload is varied and cases which reach the Chancery division are often complex and/or concern substantial amounts of money.

1.4.3.4.3 Family Division

The Family Division of the High Court hears predominantly complex cases, such as those concerning international child abduction, female genital mutilation and forced marriage. The Family Division also has an 'inherent jurisdiction', which is where a child who is the subject of legal proceedings must be protected (the most common example is where a child is made a ward of the court).

1.4.3.5 Appeals from the High Court

Either party may appeal against a High Court decision to the Court of Appeal (Civil Division). In exceptional cases, civil matters may be appealed directly to the Supreme Court from the High Court or one of the Divisional Courts. These appeals are called leapfrog appeals and are only permissible if a number of conditions are fulfilled, which include a certificate from the High Court, permission from the Supreme Court, satisfaction of 'relevant conditions'[27] and consent given by all parties.

1.4.3.6 The Court of Appeal

The Court of Appeal hears appeals from the Crown Court, the High Court and the County Court on questions of law or fact. The court is divided into a criminal and a civil division and is staffed by Lords Justices and Lady Justices of Appeal. The President of the civil division is the Master of the Rolls, and the President of the criminal division is the Lord Chief Justice. Most appeals are heard by three judges. The Court of Appeal can sit anywhere in England and Wales, but primarily it sits in London.

1.4.3.7 Appeals from the Court of Appeal

Either party to a case may appeal to the Supreme Court on a point of law of general public importance. This must be certified by the Court of Appeal and the Supreme Court must grant leave to appeal.

---

27 The 'relevant conditions' set out in section 12(3) Administration of Justice Act 1969 are that a point of general public importance is involved and that it either: '(a) relates wholly or mainly to the construction of an enactment or of a statutory instrument, and has been fully argued in the proceedings and fully considered in the judgment of the judge in the proceedings, or (b) is one in respect of which the judge is bound by a decision of the Court of Appeal or of The Supreme Court in previous proceedings, and was fully considered in the judgments given by the Court of Appeal or The Supreme Court (as the case may be) in those previous proceedings'.

1.4.3.8 The Supreme Court

In 2009, the Supreme Court became the highest court in the UK, replacing the House of Lords (in its role as final appeal court). Its focus is on appeals deemed to be of public and constitutional importance. The Supreme Court is a UK body, which means it is legally separate from the courts of England and Wales. It is the final appeal court for all cases in England and Wales and Northern Ireland and for civil cases in Scotland. The Court has 12 judges, called Justices of the Supreme Court, and it is headed by a President and a Deputy President. The Supreme Court sits in panels of an uneven number with a minimum of three judges, although cases are ordinarily heard by five judges. It is located in London, in the former Middlesex Guildhall on Parliament Square, separating judicial power from the Houses of Parliament, where the House of Lords historically sat.

As well as its appellate jurisdiction, the Supreme Court has devolution jurisdiction enabling it to hear cases on devolution matters under the Scotland Act 1998, the Northern Ireland Act 1998 and the Government of Wales Act 2006. This devolution jurisdiction was transferred to the Supreme Court from the Judicial Committee of the Privy Council. For an appeal to be heard by the Supreme Court, leave (permission) must be given by either the Court of Appeal or the Supreme Court itself.

The Supreme Court hears appeals from a limited number of courts:

- England and Wales: Court of Appeal (civil and criminal division) and, in limited cases, the High Court (leapfrog appeals)
- Scotland: The Court of Session
- Northern Ireland: The Court of Appeal in Northern Ireland and, in limited cases, the High Court (leapfrog appeals)

1.4.3.9 The Technology and Construction Court

The Technology and Construction Court (TCC) is a specialist group of courts, which includes both the High Court and the County Court. The TCC is led by a High Court judge and staffed by Circuit judges. The TCC deals predominantly with cases concerning buildings, engineering and surveying, service provision by professionals in the sector (such as surveyors and architects), local authority conduct with regard to land and buildings, environmental claims, including pollution and challenging the decisions of arbitrators. As a general rule, the claim value needs to be or exceed £250,000 to be considered by the TCC. Exceptions to this are permitted for 'good reason', which has in the past included international cases, a new point of law or a complex case.

1.4.3.10 The Judicial Committee of the Privy Council

The Judicial Committee of the Privy Council, (JCPC or Privy Council), originated as the highest court of appeal for both civil and criminal matters for the British Empire. Its jurisdiction was founded in the notion that 'the King is the fountain of all justice throughout his Dominions, and exercises jurisdiction in his Council, which act in an advisory capacity to the Crown'.[28] Its current presentation was established through the Judicial Committee Act 1833. In 1900, the Privy Council exercised jurisdiction as the final court of appeal over

28 F. Safford and G. Wheeler, *The Practice of the Privy Council in Judicial Matters* (1901), 699–707.

one-fifth of the globe and one-quarter of the world's population.[29] It remains the final court of appeal for a number of Commonwealth countries, UK overseas territories, Crown dependencies and military sovereign base areas:

- Crown dependencies including Jersey, Guernsey and the Isle of Man
- Commonwealth countries including The Bahamas, Antigua and Barbuda, Cook Islands and Tuvalu
- Overseas territories including Bermuda, Montserrat, Gibraltar and Falkland Islands
- Sovereign base areas in Akrotiri and Dhekelia in Cyprus

It comprises 'members' of the Privy Council, who are senior members of the judiciary in either the UK or certain Commonwealth countries. The Judicial Committee moved away from its base in Downing Street in 2009 and now shares a building with the Supreme Court in the former Middlesex Guildhall on Parliament Square. The bench is ordinarily composed of five judges to hear Commonwealth appeals and three judges for all other matters. As well as its overseas appellate jurisdiction, the Privy Council also hears appeals from the Disciplinary Committee of the Royal College of Veterinary Surgeons and certain schemes of the Church Commissioners. Instead of delivering a judgment, it tenders advice to the Sovereign.

The 2016 Supreme Court case *Willers v Joyce*[30] confirmed the status of decisions of the Privy Council in England and Wales. The case concerned two competing precedents: one from the House of Lords which when applied to the facts would lead to one conclusion, and another more recent Privy Council decision which would lead to a different conclusion. The question was whether a first instance judge was bound to follow the House of Lords decision or the newer Privy Council decision. The Supreme Court held:

> There is no doubt that, unless there is a decision of a superior court to the contrary effect, a court in England and Wales can normally be expected to follow a decision of the JCPC, but there is no question of it being bound to do so as a matter of precedent. There is also no doubt that a court should not, at least normally, follow a decision of the JCPC, if it is inconsistent with the decision of a court which is binding[31]

1.4.3.11 The European Court of Human Rights (ECHR), the Human Rights Act and the UK Courts

The ECHR is an international court which was established in 1959. Its jurisdiction is centred in hearing cases brought by individuals or states alleging violations of the European Convention on Human Rights. It is not an institution of the European Union, and therefore was not directly included in the 2016 referendum held in the UK. The European Convention on Human Rights is an international treaty which guarantees fundamental civil and political rights, such as right to life, protection of property and right to a fair hearing. The Human Rights Act 1998 is the domestic legislation which incorporated the European Convention on Human Rights into UK law, converting it from an international treaty to one with effect

29 Q.C. Clayton, *UK Constitutional Law Association*, 2021.
30 *Willers v Joyce* [2016] UKSC 44.
31 Para 16.

domestically. The Human Rights Act enabled all UK courts to determine whether public bodies have acted in a way compatible with the European Convention on Human Rights. It imposed on UK courts a duty to interpret legislation, as far as possible, in a way compatible with the European Convention on Human Rights and required all UK courts to take into account decisions of the ECHR (though they are not bound by them).

Despite political rhetoric in the UK discussing repeal of the Human Rights Act, as of 2024, this has not occurred. The Political Declaration accompanying the 2018 Withdrawal Agreement committed the UK to remaining a party to the European Convention on Human Rights, and in the EU-UK Trade Agreement, article 524 expressly commits parties to an 'obligation to respect fundamental rights and legal principles as reflected, in particular, in the European Convention on Human Rights'. Therefore, the relationship between UK courts, the European Convention on Human Rights and the ECHR has not changed following the UK's exit from the European Union.

1.4.3.12 Tribunals

Tribunals are judicial bodies which enable experts to deal with specialist areas of law. They are tasked with determining disputes in their particular area of law, and mostly see individuals bringing actions against government departments or agencies. The exception to this is the Employment Tribunal, which determines disputes between employees and employers. From April 2020 to March 2021, over 300,000 disputes were heard by tribunals.

Some tribunals are UK-wide, others are jurisdiction specific. A unified tribunals system was established by the Tribunals, Courts and Enforcement Act 2007, which has jurisdiction across the UK. These operate under a two-tier system, where the first-tier tribunal hears cases at first instance and the upper tribunal hears appeals from the first. The upper tribunal is equivalent to the High Court in the court hierarchy.

The first tier has seven chambers, each dealing with their own area of speciality:

- Property Chamber
- Tax Chamber
- Immigration and Asylum Chamber
- Social Entitlement Chamber
- War Pensions and Armed Forces Compensation Chamber
- General Regulatory Chamber
- Health, Education and Social Care Chamber

In the upper tier, the number of chambers is reduced to four:

- Administrative Appeals Chamber
- Immigration and Asylum Chamber
- Lands Chamber
- Tax and Chancery Chamber

1.4.3.13 Focus: First Tier Property Chamber

The Property Chamber is responsible for hearing disputes over property and land. The disputes are broadly divided into three categories:

- Residential property
- Land registration; and
- Agricultural land and drainage

Example residential property disputes include leasehold disputes, refusal of right to buy a council home and rent increases. Example land registration disputes include those concerning the land registry and registered land documentation, and agricultural and drainage include disputes between agricultural landlord and tenants and neighbours.

1.4.3.14 Focus: Lands Chamber

The Lands Chamber is one of four chambers in the upper tier. It hears appeals against decisions of the Property Chamber, along with the Welsh Residential Property Tribunal and Welsh Leasehold Valuation Tribunal. Alongside appeals, the Lands Chamber also hears cases on certain subjects at first instance, including disputes concerning compulsory purchase compensation, valuation disputes regarding business rates and disputes over valuations for capital gains tax or inheritance tax.

Tribunals ordinarily sit as a panel, with a judge and panel members holding specific subject-matter expertise. The judge is legally qualified, whereas the members are subject-specialist non-legal members of the panel. The type of tribunal will determine the powers held by the panel, for example leave or refusal to remain in the UK, provision of special educational assistance or compensation and costs.

Both tiers of the tribunal system can review and set aside their own decisions. The majority of the first tier tribunal can be appealed to the upper tribunal, and appeals from the upper tier tribunal may be made to the relevant Court of Appeal for each jurisdiction (England and Wales, Scotland or Northern Ireland).

1.5 Alternative Dispute Resolution

Alternative dispute resolution, commonly referred to as ADR, is a blanket term for dispute settlement outside of the court structure. Its use in England is documented from as early as 1066, where citizens held their own informal court sessions to resolve disputes, often presided over by respected (male) members of the community.[32] The most common forms of dispute resolution, which typically fall under the term ADR are: Negotiation, Mediation and Arbitration.

The current day use of ADR in civil disputes stems from the Woolf Reforms, which were a series of recommendations made by Lord Woolf in 1996, the aims of which were to rectify a system deemed 'too expensive, slow, adversarial, fragmented and uncertain'.[33] These recommendations culminated in the Civil Procedure Rules (see Section 1.7.1.1), which introduced a duty to consider ADR, cost implications for failing to do so and the active

32 M. McManus and B. Silverstein, 'Brief History of Alternative Dispute Resolution in the USA,' *Cadmus: Promoting Leadership in Thought That Leads to Action* (2011): 1 (3) 100–105.

33 D. De Girolamo and D. Spenser Underhill, 'Alternative Dispute Resolution and the Civil Courts: A Very British Type of Justice—The Legacy of the Woolf Reforms in 2022,' *Amicus Curiae* (2022): 4 (1) 129–154 (131).

encouragement of disputes being settled without litigation where possible.[34] Case authorities have repeatedly acknowledged the benefits of ADR, in particular mediation.[35]

An important distinction between the three forms of ADR is whether they are binding or non-binding. Negotiation and mediation alone are non-binding, which means either party to the dispute can pursue litigation through traditional legal channels should they be unhappy with the decision reached. Instead of relying on the formalised enforceability of decisions, non-binding ADR relies on the parties, having been active in the decision-making process, to respect the determination and enforce it themselves. In contrast, for binding ADR, which includes arbitration, the outcome is final and enforceable, with limited recourse to appeal.

In the case of *Cable & Wireless Plc v IBM United Kingdom Ltd*,[36] it was held that an agreement to use ADR is binding and enforceable by the courts. The claimant argued that an agreement to refer disputes to ADR was simply an agreement to negotiate. The court rejected this argument and recognised no distinction between an agreement to refer disputes to ADR and an agreement to arbitrate.

1.5.1 Negotiation

Negotiation is the most informal type of ADR, with parties seeking to reach an agreement without the involvement of a third party. They ordinarily proceed on a 'without-prejudice' basis, which means that statements made in an attempt to reach agreement are prevented from being used as evidence in future court proceedings. This is designed to encourage the parties to settle their dispute out of court, speaking openly without fear of that said being included later down the line should the negotiations fail. The informal nature of negotiation allows it to take place at any time and continue throughout a dispute, including during court preparations.

1.5.2 Mediation

Mediation involves the parties attempting to reach an agreement with the assistance of an independent third party. There are various forms of mediation, including:

---

34 Pre-action Protocol: 8. Litigation should be a last resort. As part of a relevant pre-action protocol or this Practice Direction, the parties should consider whether negotiation or some other form of ADR might enable them to settle their dispute without commencing proceedings; 10: 10. Parties may negotiate to settle a dispute or may use a form of ADR including – (a) mediation, a third party facilitating a resolution; (b) arbitration, a third party deciding the dispute; (c) early neutral evaluation, a third party giving an informed opinion on the dispute; and (d) Ombudsmen schemes; 11: If proceedings are issued, the parties may be required by the court to provide evidence that ADR has been considered. A party's silence in response to an invitation to participate or a refusal to participate in ADR might be considered unreasonable by the court and could lead to the court ordering that party to pay additional court costs.

35 See *Hurst v Leeming* [2002] EWCH 1051 (Ch); *Halsey v Milton Keynes General NHS Trust* [2004] 1 WLR 3002; *Jarrom v Sellars* [2007] EWHC 1366 (Ch); *Rolf v de Guerin* [2011] E In the case of Cable & Wireless Plc v IBM United Kingdom Ltd, it was held that an agreement to use ADR is binding and enforceable by the courts. The claimant argued that an agreement to refer disputes to ADR was simply an agreement to negotiate. The court, however, rejected this argument and recognized no distinction between an agreement to refer to ADR and an agreement to arbitrate. WCA Civ 78; *Northrop Grumman v BAE Systems (Al Diriyah C41)* [2014] EWCH 3148 (TCC); *DSN v Blackpool Football Club* [2020] EWHC 670 (QB).

36 All ER (Comm) 1041.

- Facilitative: The mediator facilitates the parties reaching an agreement as opposed to making a determination
- Evaluative: The mediator evaluates the strengths and weaknesses of a case
- Transformative: The mediator focuses on parties recognising each other's needs and interests to resolve their conflict[37]
- E-mediation: E-mediation takes place online, enabling those who are geographically distanced, or owing to circumstances of the conflict cannot/do not wish to be in the same physical space. It can be entirely automated, partly automated or facilitated by an independent third-party utilising video conferencing platforms.

The potential benefits of mediation have been explicitly discussed by the courts. In *Dunnett v Riltrack plc*[38] the Court of Appeal stated:

> Skilled mediators are now able to achieve results satisfactory to both parties in many cases which are quite beyond the power of lawyers and courts to achieve (...) when the parties are brought together on neutral soil with a skilled mediator to help them resolve their differences, it may very well be that the mediator is able to achieve a result by which the parties shake hands at the end and feel that they have gone away having settled the dispute on terms with which they are happy to live. A mediator may be able to provide solutions that are beyond the powers of the court to provide.[39]

1.5.3 Arbitration

In contrast to mediation and negotiation, arbitration is a more formal mode of ADR, regulated by the Arbitration Act 1996. All parties must consent to its use, ordinarily via a contractual agreement. An independent arbitrator with relevant expertise in the contested area will consider both facts and law before making an award. Their award is final and binding on the parties. The steps for arbitration commonly include:

- Agreeing to arbitrate
- Selecting an arbitrator
- Preparing for the hearing
- Parties presenting their cases
- Arbitrator making an award
- Enforcement of the award

There are advantages and disadvantages to each form of ADR, which are summarised in Table 1.4.

Which type of ADR is appropriate for a dispute will depend on the parties, their dispute, their relationship and their preferences.

---

37 See R. Bush, *The Promise of Mediation* (1994, Jossey-Bass).
38 *Dunnett v Riltrack plc* [2002] EWCA Civ 303.
39 Para 14.

Table 1.4 Advantages and disadvantages of types of ADR.

Form	Advantages	Disadvantages
Negotiation	Informal, saving time and costs, continue throughout, without prejudice to encourage openness	Potentially less effective in complex/high value cases, lack of third-party involvement if relationship degraded
Mediation	Various forms dependent on circumstances, third-party assistance	Non-binding, cannot compel evidence or documents
Arbitration	Flexibility, proceedings in private and expertise in arbitrator	Costs, limited scope for appeal, lack of binding precedent

1.6 Legal Professionals

It is likely that those involved in property and construction will, during the course of their professional careers, have to work with members of the legal profession. A legal professional is someone with a recognised level of legal knowledge, obtained through experience, qualifications or a combination of both.

1.6.1 Solicitors

For many, a solicitor is their first port of call when legal advice or services are needed. This can range from a duty solicitor provided when an individual is arrested, a family law specialist for a contentious (or non-contentious) divorce, a firm advising multinational corporations on competition law or guiding private equity firms on mergers and acquisitions to a solicitor facilitating commercial land procurement or a residential house purchase. Solicitors provide a range of services, including advice, drafting of documents, negotiating, regulatory compliance work and conducting litigation on behalf of their clients.

From September 2021, the Solicitors Qualifying Exam (SQE) became the centralised assessment required for qualification as a solicitor, replacing the Legal Practice Course. Qualification now consists of four stages:

- A degree (or equivalent) in any subject
- Passing SQE1 and SQE2 assessments
- A minimum of 2 years qualifying work experience
- Satisfactory character and suitability

Solicitors are traditionally salaried and work within a firm. There are various structures and sizes of firms available – they can range in size from multinational firms with over 600 solicitors to a sole practitioner working on their own. Regarding structure, some are LLPs (limited liability partnerships), others traditional partnerships and some limited liability companies listed on the stock market (although this is rare). There are five solicitors' firms head-quartered in London known as Magic Circle firms. They consist of Allen & Overy, Clifford Chance, Freshfields Bruckhaus Deringer, Linklaters and Slaughter and May. All are multinational firms, renowned for their expertise and involvement in high-profile and complex cases, with each broadly specialising in banking, capital market and corporate work.

Solicitors have the right to represent their clients in court, termed 'rights of audience', in courts to which they are admitted or registered. However, they are required to complete additional assessments in order to exercise such rights in higher courts.

Solicitors are regulated by the Solicitors Regulation Authority (SRA), with which all solicitors must register. Once admitted to the Roll of Solicitors, they become members of the Law Society, an independent professional body for solicitors. The SRA sets standards for behaviour and professional performance, which are contained in a Code of Practice. It has the authority to investigate and intervene in cases of professional misconduct and has certain disciplinary powers. The SRA can also refer cases of professional misconduct to the Solicitors Disciplinary Tribunal. Where appropriate, a solicitor's name may be struck off the Roll of Solicitors, and they can be liable to their clients if they act negligently in the conduct of a case.

1.6.2 Barristers

Barristers (also called counsel) act as both legal advisers and courtroom advocates. They draft the pleadings, which indicate the manner in which a case is to be brought and give their legal opinion when so required. Their knowledge is specialist, and their areas of practice are often more streamlined than that of solicitors.

Historically, the only route to instructing a barrister was through a solicitor, who would then instruct counsel on their client's behalf. In July 2004, public access rules were introduced which allowed clients to instruct a direct/public access barrister (one which has undertaken mandatory training) without the need for a solicitor. Despite this change, most instructions received by counsel arrive via solicitors.

To practise as a barrister, a person must have been called to the Bar by one of the Inns of Court (Lincoln's Inn, Gray's Inn, The Middle Temple or The Inner Temple). After satisfying the educational requirements, a newly called barrister who wishes to practise must undergo a period of pupillage for 12 months. During this time, an experienced barrister (known as a pupil master) supervises the pupil's work. Once qualified, barristers work on one of six circuits in England and Wales and, unless working primarily in London, will appear in cases across their circuit area.

All barristers are subject to the cab rank rule. The rule dictates that barristers receiving instructions through a solicitor, provided they are appropriate to their expertise and experience, must accept them, regardless of:

- the identity of the client,
- nature of the case,
- source of funding (public or private) or
- opinions regarding character, innocence or guilt, etc.

The rule has been traced back to the eighteenth century (potentially earlier),[40] and is designed to ensure access to justice, irrespective of counsel bias, thought or opinion.

40 A. Watson, 'The Origins and Development of the Cab Rank Rule for Barristers in England and Wales,' *Journal on European History of Law* (2022): 13 (1) 12–20.

Barristers are self-employed, however, for convenience, they often share offices, commonly called chambers, with each counsel contributing towards overheads. Most chambers are administered by a clerk, who is responsible for providing administrative and business support to the barristers.

Following a successful period of practice, barristers who have demonstrated 'excellence in advocacy in difficult cases in higher courts of England and Wales'[41] may apply to receive 'silk', becoming King's Counsel (KC). If successful, they are entitled to wear a silk gown in court, use KC post nominally (e.g. Juniper Jones KC) and their work becomes limited to serious and/or complex cases.

Barristers are individually regulated by the Bar Standards Board, which sets and enforces the standards of behaviour and conduct required.

1.6.3 CILEX Practitioner/Chartered Legal Executive/Chartered Lawyer

Chartered legal executives, also called CILEX Lawyers, conduct very similar work to solicitors, including taking direct instruction from clients, providing legal advice and negotiating on behalf of their clients. They are regulated by CILEX, the Chartered Institute for Legal Executives (this may change to the SRA) and their route to qualification differs from solicitors. CILEX Lawyers currently have two routes to choose from for qualification, either the CILEX professional qualifications (CPQ) or Level 6 Chartered Legal Executive apprenticeship. In contrast to solicitors, CILEX Lawyers train in and specialise in one area of law, ordinarily in one of the following:

- Family law
- Civil litigation
- Conveyancing
- Probate
- Commercial
- Employment
- Criminal litigation
- Public law

CILEX Lawyers have parity with solicitors in their area of specialism.[42] Once qualified, additional training is available for CILEX Lawyers to become a CILEX advocate, and/or a CILEX coroner and/or a CILEX judge.

1.6.4 Licensed Conveyancers (CLC Lawyers)

The Administration of Justice Act 1985 created licensed conveyancers, extending those entitled to offer conveyancing services beyond solicitors. The Act defines conveyancing services as 'the preparation of transfers, conveyances, contracts and other documents in

41 KC appointments https://kcappointments.org.
42 'CILEX Lawyers are able to undertake one or more of the reserved/regulated legal activities without supervision as a result of holding independent practice rights in their specialist area. It is this authorisation that establishes CILEX Lawyers as having parity with solicitors' CILEX, FAQs.

connection with, and other services ancillary to, the disposition or acquisition of estates or interests in land'.[43] Their work is restricted by statute to conveyancing services, within which they have the authority to do the same as a solicitor.

Licensed Conveyancers do not need a law degree; to qualify they must complete two conveyancing law and practice specific diplomas, combined with 1,200 hours practical experience. Upon successful completion, they receive a licence to practise. Once qualified, they can offer conveyancing services in a variety of settings. The Council for Licenced Conveyancers (CLC) examples solicitors' firms, housing associations, Local Authorities, banks and building societies, property development companies, railways and airports.[44] Licensed conveyancers are regulated by the CLC, hence their alternative title as CLC Lawyers. Established alongside licensed conveyancers in the Administration of Justice Act 1985, their regulatory responsibilities include, amongst others:

- Maintaining a register of all licensed conveyancers,
- Investigating alleged misconduct and taking disciplinary action, and
- Setting educational and training standards for those wishing to qualify as licensed conveyancers.

1.7 Court Procedure

The procedure to be followed once a case reaches court depends on whether the dispute is criminal or civil (see Table 1.5).

As a common law jurisdiction, both the criminal and civil court systems in England and Wales follow an adversarial system. This places primary responsibility for establishing the

Table 1.5 Comparison of civil and criminal courts.

	Criminal Court	**Civil Court**
Type of court	Dependant on whether the offence is summary, indictable or triable either way	Dependant on value and complexity of case
Burden of proof	Prosecution Appellant (in appeals)	Claimant Appellant (in appeals)
Parties	Crown (*R*) (Prosecution – on behalf of the State) Defendant Director of Public Prosecutions	Claimant Defendant
Standard of proof	Beyond reasonable doubt	Balance of probabilities
Jury	Crown Court	None

43 S11 (3) (a) Administration of Justice Act 1985.

44 See https://www.clc-uk.org/trainees/become-a-clc-lawyer/licensed-conveyancer.

facts as alleged be presented through evidence by those bringing the case (claimant in civil or prosecution in criminal) and disputing such evidence with the defendant. The judge is not responsible for investigating the facts as presented; instead, they are responsible for overseeing the case and ensuring legal rules and procedures are adhered to and directing a jury where necessary. This is contrasted with an inquisitorial system, as found in civil law jurisdictions (common across the continent of Europe). In an inquisitorial system, the judge searches for facts, listens to witnesses, examines documents and orders that evidence be taken, after which they make further investigations as/where necessary.

1.7.1 Procedure for Civil Cases

In 1998, following widespread criticism of the costs and delays encountered in civil justice, Lord Woolf produced a report recommending wide-spread changes. Lord Woolf's final report[45] proposed a new landscape for civil justice with the following features:

- Avoidance of litigation wherever possible.
- Less adversarial and more co-operative litigation.
- Less complex litigation.
- Shorter and more certain timescales for litigation.
- More affordable litigation.
- Equality between disputants.
- A court structure which meets the needs of litigants.
- Case management by judges rather than by the litigants' legal advisors.

The interim report[46] foresaw a formal role for ADR as an integral part of the new civil justice system. In this respect, it recommended:

- that courts should encourage the use of ADR.
- that parties should acknowledge at case management conferences and pre-trial reviews whether or not the parties had discussed the issue of ADR.
- that judges should consider a litigant's unreasonable refusal to attempt ADR when considering the future conduct of a case.

1.7.1.1 The Civil Procedure Rules (CPR)

The proposals included in Lord Woolf's report were incorporated in the government's 1998 white paper on the future of the legal system.[47] The first stage of the reforms was implemented with the introduction of the new CPR 1998, which came into force in 1999, and regulate the procedures of the High Court and County Courts in England and Wales. The CPR is also colloquially known as 'the White Book'.

---

45 Access to Justice: Final Report to the Lord Chancellor on the civil justice system in England and Wales, Lord Chancellor's Department, July 1996.

46 Access to Justice: Interim Report to the Lord Chancellor on the civil justice system in England and Wales, Lord Chancellor's Department, July 1995.

47 Modernising Justice: The Government's plans for reforming legal services and the courts (1998) Cm 4155.

The CPR and associated practice directions serve to 'govern the procedure for the initiation and progress of civil claims before the County Court, High Court and Court of Appeal (Civil Division) in England and Wales'.[48] They provide a structure under which civil claims must adhere, with defined rules and practice directions to be followed. This includes guidelines on behaviour prior to proceedings being issued, called pre-action protocols.

1.7.1.1.1 Overriding Objective

Part 1 CPR provides an overriding objective, the overall aim of the rules: To enable 'the court to deal with cases justly and at proportionate cost'.

Justly and proportionate includes (so far as is practicable):

- **a.** ensuring that the parties are on an equal footing and can participate fully in proceedings, and that parties and witnesses can give their best evidence;
- **b.** saving expense;
- **c.** dealing with the case in ways which are proportionate –
  - **i.** to the amount of money involved;
  - **ii.** to the importance of the case;
  - **iii.** to the complexity of the issues; and
  - **iv.** to the financial position of each party;
- **d.** ensuring that it is dealt with expeditiously and fairly;
- **e.** allotting to it an appropriate share of the court's resources, while taking into account the need to allot resources to other cases; and
- **f.** enforcing compliance with rules, practice directions and orders.[49]

The court must seek to give effect to the overriding objective, and the parties are required to assist the court in doing so.[50]

1.7.1.1.2 Alternative Dispute Resolution and the Civil Procedure Rules

Courts are required to further the overriding objective by 'actively managing cases'. This includes a number of practical activities affecting the ongoing progress of the case through the courts, and in the context of ADR it specifically includes:[51]

- encouraging the parties to co-operate with each other in the conduct of the proceedings.
- encouraging the parties to use ADR, and facilitating the use of such procedure, if the court considers it appropriate.
- helping the parties to settle the whole or part of their case.

Ordinarily, in civil matters (although at the discretion of the judge) an unsuccessful party will be ordered to pay the costs incurred by the successful party. However, such is the importance placed on the use of ADR, that the court may refuse a successful party costs if

---

48 As described by the Government Judiciary website: https://www.judiciary.uk/courts-and-tribunals/court-of-appeal-home/procedure-rules-for-the-court-of-appeal.

49 CPR 1.1.

50 CPR 1.2; 1.3.

51 CPR 1.4.

they have unreasonably refused to engage with ADR. The case of *Dunnett v Railtrack Plc*[52] provides the first example of costs penalties being imposed on a successful litigant because of their unreasonable refusal to mediate. The case concerned horses wandering onto a railway line and being hit by a train. Dunnett (the horse owner) failed in their claim for the value of the horses and nervous shock (post-traumatic stress disorder) in the first instance and applied for leave to appeal to the Court of Appeal. Leave was granted but the court recommended that the parties explore the possibilities of resolving the dispute through ADR. Dunnett contacted Railtrack suggesting that the matter be referred to ADR. Railtrack refused and instead made an offer in full and final settlement of the claim. The case proceeded to the Court of Appeal and Dunnett's appeal was dismissed. Dunnett, the unsuccessful party, would ordinarily be required to pay Railtrack's costs. However, the Court of Appeal noted the duty of the parties under the CPR to fully consider ADR, especially, as in the present case, where the court had suggested it. It was held that costs would not be awarded to Railtrack, given their refusal to contemplate ADR, leaving each party responsible for their own costs. Subsequent case law has explored what is and is not reasonable in this context and laid down guidance.[53]

1.7.2 Civil Proceedings: A Brief Overview

1.7.2.1 Pre-action

The CPR govern behaviour both during and prior to a claim being initiated. Pre-action protocols provide a framework for behaviour expected prior to the commencement of a claim, which includes parties providing the other with as much information as possible in relation to their claims and defences. Separate pre-action protocols exist for specific types of disputes, including construction and engineering and professional negligence claims. As with failure to engage with ADR, courts have the discretion to order costs against a party who has failed to comply with the relevant pre-action protocol, and/or has acted unreasonably prior to the commencement of proceedings.

1.7.2.2 Commencing Proceedings

Proceedings are commenced when the claimant issues a Claim Form. The Claim Form details the nature of the claim and is served on the defendant, with a copy held by the court. Service is ordinarily by post if the defendant is in England and Wales. The Claim Form may contain within it, or be served 14 days after, a Particulars of Claim. The Particulars of Claim set out the claimant's case, including specific facts relied upon. The defendant then has 14 days to respond with one of the following options:

1. Defend: If they wish to defend themselves against the claim, the defendant must do so within 14 days of receiving the Claim Form and Particulars of Claim (Part 15, CPR).
2. Admit: The defendant may admit all or part of the claim. If accepted, the claimant then requests judgment from the court (Part 14, CPR).

---

52 *Dunnett v Railtrack Plc* [2002] EWCA Civ 303.

53 *Halsey v Milton Keynes NHS Trust; Steel v Joy and Halliday* [2004] EWCA Civ 576.

3. No response: Defendant may fail to respond to the claim, either intentionally or accidentally. In most cases of a failure to respond, the claimant can apply to the court for a default judgment (judgment passed by the court without a trial) (Part 12, CPR).
4. Contest jurisdiction: The defendant may reply to the court acknowledging receipt of the Claim Form and associated documents and give notice of an intention to either dispute the jurisdiction of the court or argue that the court should not exercise its jurisdiction (Part 11, CPR).

In addition to the above responses, the defendant may feel that they have a claim against the claimant and make a counterclaim. They are able to do so without the court's permission if they file it with their defence but require permission if it is made at any other time (Part 20, CPR).

1.7.2.3 Case Management

As noted at Section 1.7.1, the court is under a duty to actively manage the case. This promotes a greater level of judicial control over the progression of the case, enabling the court to manage cost implications, encourage ADR and hopefully reduce potential delays.

An important element of this active management is the allocation of the case to the relevant track. There are three tracks which a case can be allocated: small claims track, fast track and multi-track. Each has its own rules and timetables. To which track a case is allocated will depend primarily (although not exclusively) on its financial value.

Small claims track: Ordinarily reserved for claims with a financial value of less than £10,000, with cases heard by a District judge in the County Court.

Fast track: Ordinarily reserved for claims with a financial value exceeding £10,000 but less than £25,000, where the trial is expected to last no more than one day. Cases are ordinarily heard in the County Court.

Multi-track: Reserved for cases of a particular level of complexity, and/or claims over £25,000, with cases generally heard in the High Court.

The court will set a timetable for various tasks to be completed, called 'giving directions'. It includes dates for providing witness statements, documentary evidence and, if necessary, the scheduling of any expert witnesses. The courts adopt a strict stance with regard to adhering to timetables. In the case of *Rollinson v Kimberley Clark Ltd*,[54] the defendant sought to alter the timetabled trial date due to the unavailability of one of their expert witnesses. The application was dismissed, and the court held:

> ... if it ever was acceptable ... it is certainly no longer acceptable when a trial date is bound to be fairly imminent, for a solicitor to seek to instruct an expert witness without checking and discovering his availability, or proceed to instruct him when there is no reasonable prospect of his being available for another year. The check having been made and the experts' availability in the near future being in doubt, then a different expert should be instructed.

54 *Rollinson v Kimberley Clark Ltd* [1999] Times Law Reports 22 June, CA; CP Rep 85.

In the case of *Matthews v Tarmac Bricks and Tiles Ltd*,[55] the defendant provided a date bracket during which their expert witnesses were unavailable without providing reasoning. Here is an excerpt of the conversation between judge and counsel:

JUDGE: 'Right, 15 July'.
COUNSEL: 'Neither Dr Calin nor Mr Dunkerley have availability on those dates. We consulted my learned friend earlier, the week not 5th July but the 6th, 7th, 8th and 9th July are available for all the medical experts. I do not know if those are the dates available to the court'.
JUDGE: 'No'.
'Why can't Dr Calin turn up on 15th July?'
COUNSEL: 'He has listed those dates as unavailable between 12th and 16th July'.
JUDGE: 'Why is he unavailable on 15th July?'
COUNSEL: 'I have no instructions as to why, it is simply a list of unavailable dates'.
JUDGE: 'How am I supposed to deal with the matter then? Is he subpoenaed somewhere else? Does he have to be somewhere else all the time? Is he able to give evidence by video link?'

Counsel replied that they had no idea.[56]

Owing to the lack of reasoning, the court set a date for trial within the expert's unavailable date bracket and the defendant appealed. The appeal was dismissed, with Lord Woolf MR stating:

> (...) it is essential that if parties want cases to be fixed for hearing in accordance with the dates which meet their convenience, those dates should be fixed as early as possible. The parties cannot always expect the courts to meet their convenience (...) If there is no agreement as to the dates which are acceptable to the court, the lawyers for the parties must be in a position to give the reasons why certain dates are not convenient to doctors. These cases emphasise the point that the professional expert witness owes an overriding duty to the court and not merely to his/her client and thus experts should be prepared to arrange or rearrange their affairs to meet the court's requirements.[57]

1.7.2.4 Expert Witnesses

The CPR restricts the use of expert evidence to 'that which is reasonably required to resolve the proceedings'.[58] Parties must apply for the court's permission should they wish to call an expert witness, and their request must include an estimate of costs.[59]

The duty of an expert witness, although instructed by a party to a claim, is to the court. Their role is to assist the court on matters within their expertise. This overrides 'any

55 *Matthews v Tarmac Bricks and Tiles Ltd* [1999] CPLR 463.
56 Ibid.
57 Ibid.
58 Part 35.1 Civil Procedure Rules.
59 Part 35.4 Civil Procedure Rules.

obligation to the person from whom experts have received instructions or by whom they are paid'.[60]

The court has the power to direct that expert evidence be given by a single joint expert rather than each party appointing an expert. The single expert is instructed jointly by the parties or appointed by the court if they are unable to agree. The amount of the single expert's fee can be limited by the court and the parties can be ordered to pay this amount into court. Each party may give instructions to the single joint expert, sending a copy to the other party at the same time.[61]

1.7.2.5 Offers to Settle

Part 36 CPR (as with the provisions regarding ADR) is designed to encourage parties to settle disputes without the need for a trial. Under this section of the CPR, both claimants and defendants can inform the other side what they will offer, or what they will accept, in order to resolve the dispute. A Part 36 offer can be made at any point until judgment is given, providing the parties with maximum time during which to make and consider an offer to settle. Offers are made 'without prejudice save as to costs', which means that the court will not be aware of any offers made or rejected until judgment has been passed and they are considering costs. 'Without prejudice' ensures offers made in an attempt to settle cannot then be used as evidence against the party which made them.

Parties are not bound to accept any offers made under Part 36, however, it may have cost implications if the judgment of the court, in favour of the claimant, is either less than that offered (if offer is made by the defendant) or equal to (if made by the claimant).[62]

- If the claimant fails to obtain a more advantageous judgment than a defendant's Part 36 offer (unless it considers it unjust to do so) the court can order the claimant pay both the defendant's costs and interest on costs.
- If the claimant obtains a judgment that is at least as advantageous if not better than the terms of the Part 36 offer, the court may order (unless it considers it unjust to do so) the defendant pay interest on the sum of money awarded, costs, interest on costs and an additional percentage of the sum awarded.

The cost implications can be significant, designed to encourage both parties to think carefully when making or rejecting a Part 36 offer. However, the offer needs to be a 'genuine offer to settle'[63] and if it is not, the court may conclude it unjust to grant any of the cost penalties/benefits provided in the CPR. In *Yieldpoint Stable Value Fund, LP v Kimura Commodity Trade Finance Fund Limited*,[64] the court held that the claimant's offer to accept 99% of the claim value constituted a very high offer, and not a genuine offer to settle. The judge concluded that their decision:

60 Part 35.3 Civil Procedure Rules.
61 Part 35.7 Civil Procedure Rules.
62 See Part 36.17 (1) (a) and (b).
63 *Yieldpoint Stable Value Fund, LP v Kimura Commodity Trade Finance Fund Limited* [2023] EWHC 1512 (Comm) para 27.
64 Ibid.

> should not be taken as any kind of discouragement to claimants making Part 36 offers. It is, if anything, an encouragement to make offers at a level not so perilously close to the full value of the claim in a case of such adversarial intensity.[65]

1.7.2.6 The Trial

The procedure laid down in the CPR has served to limit the number of cases which reach trial stage – the majority are do not end up in court, and those that do often don't progress to trial stage. Instead, they are resolved through ADR or settlements made through Part 36 offers. Those that do reach trial stage are almost all held in open court, which the public is able to attend.

The majority of civil cases do not have a jury, rendering the judge responsible for deciding the case based on fact-finding, evidence presented and application of law to facts. Once the judge has heard all submissions, they deliver their judgment. Judgment may be passed immediately (in more straightforward cases) or (in those more complicated) parties will receive judgment at a later date. Civil judgments, aside for successful allegations of contempt of court, do not involve punishment. Instead, there are a range of financial and non-financial remedies available where a judge finds in favour of a claimant. These include:

- Damages – a sum of money compensating the claimant
- An injunction – prohibiting someone from doing something or requiring someone to do something
- The determination of an issue, for example, defining a boundary

1.7.2.7 Costs

Once judgment has been delivered, the judge must address the question of costs. Costs may include legal professional fees, court fees, lost earnings and expert witness fees. The general rule is that the unsuccessful party will be responsible for the costs of the successful party. However, judges have a wide discretion and can depart from this rule as they deem necessary. Arguments will be made by the parties as to whether the general rule should apply or be departed from, and judges may determine that parties are responsible for their own costs (no costs order), or that the unsuccessful party is only responsible for a portion of the successful parties cost as opposed to all.

1.7.2.8 Enforcing Judgment

Whilst a judgment may award damages and/or costs and set a date by which payment must be made, it does not include enforcement mechanisms to secure the money. When the party fails to make payment, an application must be made to the court to enforce the judgment. This is not automatic – the person owed the money must take enforcement steps. The following terms are used:

> 'judgment creditor' – a person who has obtained or is entitled to enforce a judgment or order;
> 'judgment debtor' – a person against whom a judgment or order was given or made;[66]

---

65 Ibid para 29.
66 Part 70.1 (2) (a) and (b) Civil Procedure Rules.

Before doing so, it is important to ascertain whether the judgment debtor has sufficient funds and/or assets to fulfil the judgment, as time and money spent pursuing enforcement against one who cannot make payment is futile.

Enforcement mechanisms available include:

Warrant of control: Requesting the court to instruct agents (bailiffs) to collect money owed and identify goods that may be sold to raise funds.

Third party debt order: Freezing the amount owed which is held by a third party, such as a bank, preventing the judgment debtor from accessing the funds. Once an order is obtained, the third party is obliged to make payment to the judgment creditor.

Attachment of earnings order: The judgment debtor is to provide details of their employment to the court. Their employer is then ordered by the court to make deductions from their earnings and pay them to the court.

Charging orders: The judgment debt is secured through a charge placed on any interest held in property (including houses, land, shares, etc.). When the property is sold (assuming there is enough equity left after payment of any prioritised creditors, such as a mortgage provider) payment is made to the judgment creditor.

Insolvency proceedings: A bankruptcy order may be made against an individual or if the debtor is a company, an application made to have it wound up.

Each mechanism has its pros and cons, and determination of the most appropriate will be affected by the value of the judgment, the assets held by the judgment debtor and the costs and time involved in pursing each method of enforcement.

The Debt Respite Scheme (Breathing Space Moratorium and Mental Health Crisis Moratorium) (England and Wales) Regulations 2020 came into force in May 2021. It provides legal protection to debtors (including judgment debt) from the actions of creditors during what the legislation terms a moratorium period.[67] The regulations provide for two types of moratoria: a breathing space moratorium and a mental health crisis moratorium. Breathing space provides legal protections from creditor action for up to 60 days and includes pausing contact and enforcement from creditors and freezing interest and charges. A mental health crisis breathing space also provides legal protections from creditor action and is available to those receiving mental health crisis treatment. It lasts as long as the mental health crisis treatment, plus 30 days (regardless of the length of treatment).[68]

1.7.2.9 UK Government Online Platforms

The UK Government, through HM Courts and Tribunals Service, has developed a number of online platforms through which claimants can make claims and defendants can respond. The service available depends on the value of the claim – for example, Money Claim Online is available for claims where:

- The value is less than £100,000;
- There is one claimant and no more than two defendants; and
- The defendant (s) has an address in England and Wales.

---

67 S7 The Debt Respite Scheme (Breathing Space Moratorium and Mental Health Crisis Moratorium) (England and Wales) Regulations 2020 (SI 2020/1311).

68 The Insolvency Service, UK Government, Debt Respite Scheme (Breathing Space) Guidance for Creditors (June 2023).

A new money claim platform is currently being trialled for claims where:

- The value is less than £10,000;
- There is one claimant and one defendant; and
- The defendant has an address in England and Wales.

1.7.3 Role of National and Local Government

The framework of laws, both primary through Acts of Parliament and secondary through delegated legislation, involve both national and local government. For the built environment, local authorities, the administrative body in local government, play a key role in planning, developing and managing the built environment within their administrative boundaries.[69] Their role includes:

- Developing a local plan with planning policies and the allocation of sites for varying types of development
- Development management, including processing planning applications[70]

The work of local government takes place within a framework of national planning policy and guidance (issued by the Secretary of State for Communities and Local Government) and government identified national infrastructure needs. There are also several national government agencies, such as Historic England, Highways England and the Environment Agency, which hold responsibility for their respective areas.[71]

69 There are 317 local authorities in England and 22 in Wales.
70 Select Committee on National Policy for the Built Environment, Building better places, Chapter 2, The built environment: recent trends and emerging challenges.
71 Ibid.

2

Law of Contract

CONTENTS

2.1 Introduction

As citizens, we actively engage with the law of contract every day of our lives. Browsing in a shop, buying a train ticket, returning unwanted items, taking out or cancelling a mobile phone contract, ordering lunch in a restaurant, renewing insurance, paying a utility bill, working for an employer, renting a property, enquiring about a holiday – all of these acts are either preparing to enter a contract, entering a contract or terminating a contract. The law of contract arises daily in business and commercial life. The contract is the most important stage in the process when land or buildings are transferred and when building projects are undertaken. The 'golden age' of the law of contract was in the nineteenth century when its major principles evolved under free market ideologies. Many of the cases referred to in this chapter date from this period.

Contract law has developed predominantly through case authorities as opposed to statute. There are a number of relevant statutory provisions, such as the Misrepresentation Act 1967 and the Law Reform (Frustrated Contracts) Act 1943 which will be discussed in this chapter; however, the majority of the legal framework in this area has been created by the courts. This includes the Sale of Goods Act 1979, which, although now a statute, codified the existing common law as opposed to solely creating new legal principles.

A contract is a legally binding agreement. Each side is called a 'party to the contract', and they must contribute something to it for it to be valid. Not every agreement is a contract, nor is it intended to be so. A legally binding element must be present before a valid contract can emerge, and the parties must be able to demonstrate their intention to adhere to the agreement made. This intention is essential, as a contract is said to be the result of a *meeting of minds*,[1] in Latin, *consensus ad idem*. The protection afforded by entering into a contract is that if it is broken by one party to it, the other party is able to seek a remedy. A contract may be bilateral, where the parties exchange mutual promises, or unilateral, where one party promises to do something in return for the other party carrying out a task (a reward for information, or finding a missing pet, is a good example of a unilateral contract). With a unilateral contract, when the task is completed the promise becomes enforceable (I found your missing cat, you pay me £10).

In addition to traditional contracts, this chapter will introduce smart legal contracts (SLCs). An SLC has been defined by the Law Commission as 'a legally binding contract in which some or all of the contractual obligations are defined in and/or performed automatically by a computer programme'.[2]

2.1.1 Forms of Contract

A contract may be made in any form the parties wish. This is the case regardless of the sums of money involved or the complexity of the agreement. There are advantages to having a contract in writing, formally drafted, particularly where a large sum of money is involved or the matter is complicated. As will be discussed later in this chapter, a number of standard form contracts have been created – templates which can be used for varying types of contractual arrangements, removing the need to draft and negotiate individual agreements. Under English and Welsh law, a contract is not required to be in writing, and (within reason) the parties may insert whatever provisions they wish into the agreement. Historically, parties could contract as and how they wished; however, as the nineteenth century progressed, it became clear that complete freedom to contract could lead to problems. The courts recognised that there were situations in which a 'hands off' approach to allow the parties to do as they wish could lead to injustice. However, it is only relatively recently that the law has placed restrictions in statute. One example is the limits placed on the extent to which contracting parties may exclude responsibility for their liabilities (see the Unfair Contract Terms Act 1977).

There are a number of forms which a contract may take.

2.1.1.1 Simple Contract

These are contracts made orally, in writing or a combination of both. No particular form is required.

2.1.1.2 Deed

A contract made by deed is also known as a specialty contract. Until 1990, certain contracts had to be made 'under seal' and delivered 'as a deed'. The sealing of a contract referred to a more elaborate execution of a written contract than a mere signature. Typically it could involve an impression made by a signature ring or company motif set in wax dripped onto the document. A seal is no longer necessary but, to be valid, a deed must comply with the

1 P. Hamburger, 'The Development of the Nineteenth-Century Consensus Theory of Contract,' *Law and History Review* (1989): 7 241–330.

2 Law Commission 'Smart legal contracts: Advice to Government' Law Com No 401 2021.

requirements set out in section 1 Law of Property (Miscellaneous Provisions) Act 1989 in that it must:

- be in writing
- make clear on its face that it is intended to be a deed by the person making it or the parties to it. This can be done by the document describing itself as a deed or expressing itself to be executed as a deed 'or otherwise'
- be validly executed as a deed by the person making it or one or more of the parties to it (signed in the presence of a witness or witnesses).

A contract made by deed is further distinguished from a simple contract as no consideration is necessary (consideration is discussed at Section 2.2.1.2), and the limitation period is 12 years, as opposed to 6 years in the case of a simple contract.

2.1.1.3 Contract Which Must be Made in Writing or Evidenced in Writing

Certain types of contract must be in writing, although they do not have to be made by deed. This applies to consumer credit and hire agreements governed by the Consumer Credit Act 1974 (as amended by the Consumer Credit Act 2006). These Acts state that the relevant agreements are 'not properly executed' unless in the form prescribed. Failing to comply with the requirement renders the contract unenforceable. The requirement that a contract be in writing also applies to the sale or other disposition of an interest in land,[3] whilst contracts of guarantee need to be evidenced in writing pursuant to the Statute of Frauds 1677.

2.1.1.4 Standard Form Contract

A standard form contract (SFC) is a contract between two parties where the terms have been set. Such contracts are also called 'take-it-or-leave-it' contracts, as the content is pre-determined, leaving the parties with little scope to negotiate or amend any of the terms. SFCs are commonplace in construction and land transactions. Standard clauses have been settled over the years by negotiation between the various stakeholders in the relevant industries, and contract templates have been created. The purpose of these forms is to facilitate the conduct of trade and a fair allocation of risk between the parties, reducing drafting costs and time spent negotiating. Such contracts are often used in large scale construction works. The Joint Contracts Tribunal (JCT) and the New Engineering Contract (NEC) are the most common providers of SFCs for construction works. SFCs are discussed in detail in Chapter 3.

2.1.1.5 Smart Legal Contracts

As introduced earlier, a smart legal contract (SLC) is a legally binding contract in which some or all of the contractual obligations are defined in and/or performed automatically by a computer programme.[4] The use of SLCs is expected to expand and in doing so 'revolutionise the way we do business, particularly by increasing efficiency and transparency in transactions'.[5] In 2021, the Law Commission was tasked with evaluating whether the

3 S2 The Law of Property (Miscellaneous Provisions) Act 1989.
4 Law Commission (2021).
5 Ibid., 1.

existing contract law legal framework in England and Wales was applicable to SLCs. It concluded:

> the current legal framework is clearly able to facilitate and support the use of smart legal contracts. Current legal principles can apply to smart legal contracts in much the same way as they do to traditional contracts, albeit with an incremental and principled development of the common law in specific contexts.[6]

This view echoed that of Sir Geoffrey Vos, who in 2019 concluded that contract law is in a 'good position' to facilitate SLCs, recommending that statutory regimes be avoided, and reliance placed on the 'dependable and predictable' advantages of the common law.[7]

2.2 Contract Construction

2.2.1 Making a Valid Contract

For a promise or agreement between two or more parties to be initially enforceable as a contract, there are three essential elements:

- Agreement (with offer and acceptance)
- Consideration
- An intention to create legal relations.

All three elements must be present, and if any/all are missing, neither party will be bound by their respective promises.

2.2.1.1 Agreement

At its most basic, an agreement needs an offer and acceptance. Whilst in certain circumstances, it may be very easy to ascertain whether a valid agreement has come into being (for example, where a standard form of contract is used), in others, it may be harder to ascertain whether or not offer and acceptance have been made. For example, it may be in dispute whether a contract (and respective obligations) has come into being where parties have used a combination of statements made orally alongside documents in writing. The real test is whether the parties have *accepted* obligations to one another. If that can be established then a valid agreement may be inferred from the conduct of the parties.

In the case of *Trentham (G Percy) Ltd v Archital Luxfer Ltd*[8] a building subcontract was held to have come into existence even though the parties had not reached full agreement when the sub-contractor began the work. As the work progressed, outstanding matters were resolved by further negotiations. The judge was satisfied there was sufficient evidence

6 Ibid., 1.26, 5.

7 Sir Geoffrey Vos, 'Cryptoassets as property: how can English law boost the confidence of would-be parties to smart legal contracts?' (2 May 2019) Joint Northern Chancery Bar Association and University of Liverpool Lecture.

8 *Trentham (G Percy) Ltd v Archital Luxfer Ltd* [1993] 1 Lloyd's Rep 25.

to conclude that there was a binding contract; the parties had clearly intended to create a legal relationship between each other.

2.2.1.1.1 Offer

When considering offers, the party making the offer is called the offeror and the party accepting is called the offeree. To constitute an offer, there must be an intention that it will become binding if accepted. Two cases involving Manchester City Council and the sale of properties they owned to existing tenants demonstrate this point:

In *Storer v Manchester City Council*[9] the Council sent the claimant communication indicating all required was their signature for sale of the property to take place. The claimant signed the communication; however, the Council changed their mind with regard to the sale. The Court of Appeal held that the communication by the Council to the claimant was an offer, which the tenant accepted, and therefore there was a binding contract.

In contrast, in *Gibson v Manchester City Council*[10] the Council sent a document asking the tenant to make an offer to buy the property, explaining that the Council *may* be prepared to sell the property. Here, the House of Lords held that the Council had not made an offer, and therefore no binding contract existed. Distinctions between the two cases were the wording in *Gibson,* which stated '*may* be prepared to sell' and in *Storer*, a price had been agreed, whereas in *Gibson*, it had not.

The question of whether parties intended to make an offer was addressed in *RTS Flexible Systems Ltd v Molkerei Alois Muller GmbH & Co KG*:[11]

> Whether there is a binding contract between the parties, and if so, upon what terms depends not on their subjective state of mind, but upon a consideration of what was communicated between them by words and conduct, and whether that leads objectively to a conclusion that they ... had agreed upon all the terms which they regarded ... as essential.

Offer or Negotiations? As the case law demonstrates, not all communications regarding a potential agreement constitute an offer.

Statement of Intention: There is a difference between a party informing another that they *intend* to do something, and them stating that they *will* do something. Stating that they will do something is an offer, stating that they intend to do something is not an offer, and instead is a part of negotiations. In *Harris v Nickerson*[12] an advertisement listing items at an auction was held to be an intention to sell, not an offer that they would be sold.

Supply of Information: Where one party provides further information, this does not constitute an offer. In *Harvey v Facey*[13] a response to the question of what the lowest

9 *Storer v Manchester City Council* [1974] 3 All ER 824.
10 *Gibson v Manchester City Council* [1979] 1 All ER 972.
11 *RTS Flexible Systems Ltd v Molkerei Alois Muller Gmbh & Co KG* [2010] UKSC 14, 45.
12 *Harris v Nickerson* [1873] 37 JP 536.
13 *Harvey v Facey* (1893) AC 552.

acceptable price would be *if* they were to sell was not an offer, merely a supply of additional information.

An Invitation to Treat: An invitation to treat is not an offer, instead it is an invitation to a party or parties to make an offer, or to commence negotiations. Example of invitations to treat include:

Displaying Goods: The general rule is that the display of goods does not constitute an offer and is an invitation to treat. In *Pharmaceutical Society of Great Britain v Boots*[14] prescription drugs were displayed on a shelf in Boots chemist shop. The display of the goods was challenged as being in contravention of the Pharmacy and Poisons Act 1933, which required pharmaceuticals to be sold only in the presence of a qualified pharmacist. The claimants alleged that the sale occurred when the customer selected the pharmaceutical goods from the shelf prior to payment, rendering the display in contravention of the Act. The court held that the display of pharmaceutical goods in such a way did not constitute an offer. The offer for sale was not made when the customer selected the goods from the shelf, but when the goods were presented to the cashier. The court was satisfied that the cashier was supervised as required by the Act and that no contravention of the law had actually taken place. In *Fisher v Bell*,[15] a flick-knife was displayed in a shop window with a price tag attached. The seller was prosecuted under the (now repealed) Restriction of Offensive Weapons Act 1961, which made it an offence to offer to sell such items. The seller was acquitted on the basis that under the ordinary law of contract the display of the article in the shop window was merely an invitation to treat.

Advertisement Anticipating a Bilateral Contract: In *Partridge v Crittenden*,[16] the appellant listed a number of birds with their price under a heading 'Classified Advertisements' in a periodical called 'Cage and Aviary Birds'. The defendant received one of the birds, discovered that it was a wild bird and brought an action against the appellant arguing that its sale was contrary to the Protection of Birds Act 1954. At first instance, the court agreed. However, on appeal, the court held, citing the decision in *Fisher v Bell*:[17]

> (i)n my judgment the law of the country is equally plain as it was in regard to articles in a shop window, namely that the insertion of an advertisement in the form adopted here under the title "Classified Advertisements" is simply an invitation to treat.

In *Carlill v Carbolic Smoke Ball Company*,[18] Ms Carlill contracted influenza (a common cold or flu) after using the defendant's smokeball. A smokeball was, at the time, a popular preventative medicine, administered by inhaling fumes. The defendant had placed an advert in a national newspaper stating their confidence in the product, offering a reward for anyone who contracted influenza after using the smokeball and that the reward had been deposited in a bank. Ms Carlill requested the reward, which they refused to do, claiming the advertisement was an invitation to treat not an offer. Finding for Ms Carlill, the court held that the defendants had made an offer. The judge referred

14 *Pharmaceutical Society of Great Britain v Boots* [1953] 1 QB 401.
15 *Fisher v Bell* [1961] 1 QB 394.
16 *Partridge v Crittenden* [1968] 2 All ER 421.
17 *Fisher v Bell* [1961] 1 QB 394.
18 *Carlill v Carbolic Smoke Ball Company* [1893] 1 QB 256.

to their statement in the advertisement alleging they had deposited money and held that this demonstrated their intention to be bound by their offer and their willingness to enter into a unilateral contract upon the purchase of the product.

This is the advertisement:[19]

Request for Tenders: A request for tenders is an invitation to treat, whilst the making of a tender is the offer. In *Harvela Investments Limited v Royal Trust Company of Canada Ltd. and others*[20] the defendant invited two parties to submit, by a specified date, the amount they were willing to pay for a parcel of shares. The defendant had stated 'we bind ourselves to accept [the highest] offer' which complied with the terms of invitation.[21] One of the two parties (party 1) submitted a fix bid ('I offer £10, for example'), whereas the other (party 2) provided the option of a fixed bid alongside a referential bid ('I will offer £2 in excess of any other made'). The defendant accepted the referential bid from party 2,

---

19 Source: Alamy ID 2RNN609 https://www.alamy.com/victorian-advert-for-the-carbolic-smoke-ball-a-victorian-flu-remedy-which-claimed-to-be-a-cure-for-influenza-and-a-number-of-other-diseases-1890s-image564105257.html

20 *Harvela Investments Limited v Royal Trust Company of Canada Ltd. and others* [1985] 2 All ER 966.

21 Ibid., 973.

and party 1 appealed. The House of Lords found in favour of party 1, with the following reasoning:

1. Fixed bids, not referential bids, were the choice of defendants, ascertained by considering their *presumed intention*, established by looking at the terms of the invitation.[22]
2. The defendants choosing to sell the shares by fixed bids rendered the referential bid agreement between the defendant and party 2 invalid.
3. As the contract between the defendant and party 2 was invalid, their common intention to enter into an invalid contract was not transferrable to a valid contract: 'That each had misconstrued that unilateral contract cannot transform their common intention to perform an existing contract into an intention to make a fresh and different one'.[23]

Where the presumed intention is to enter into a contract through a tender process, the courts have found that an enforceable contract exists. In *Blackpool and Fylde Aero Club Ltd v Blackpool Borough Council*[24] the Council failed to consider the claimant's correctly submitted tender for services, thereby removing their possibility of being successful. This failure was found to have invalidated the tender as a whole, entitling the disgruntled parties to claim for damages. Similarly, in the case of *J & A Developments Ltd v Edina Manufacturing, Armoura Ltd*,[25] the three lowest tenderers were invited to take part in a further lowest bid reverse auction to win the work. The claimant, one of the three lowest original tenderers, successfully challenged the further round of bidding and was awarded damages compensating the business for the costs of preparing the tender.

Communicating an Offer It is essential that an offer is communicated to give the offeree the opportunity to accept or reject it. As a contract is the meeting of minds, there can be no agreement without knowledge. In the Australian case (persuasive, as opposed to binding) of *R v Clarke*,[26] the court held:

> there cannot be assent without knowledge of the offer; and ignorance of the offer is the same thing whether it is due to never hearing of it or forgetting it after hearing.

Only the offeree can accept the offer, as illustrated in *Boulton v Jones*,[27] which involved an unincorporated business whose ownership changed hands between the offer being made and being accepted. The agreement failed as the offer had not been made to the offeree seeking to accept it. However, if the offer is made to the world at large, exampled in *Carlill v Carbolic Smokeball Co* (see "Advertisement Anticipating a Bilateral Contract"), or with cases concerning a reward, then any person with notice of the offer may accept it.

Revoking an Offer An offer may be revoked at any time before acceptance; however, once valid acceptance has been made, the offeror is bound by the terms of the offer. In an auction sale, each individual bid is an offer which can be accepted or rejected at any time

---

22 Ibid., para 973 & 974.
23 Ibid., para 971.
24 *Blackpool and Fylde Aero Club Ltd v Blackpool Borough Council* [1990] 3 All ER 25.
25 *J & A Developments Ltd v Edina Manufacturing, Armoura Ltd* [2006] NIQB 85.
26 *R v Clarke* [1927] 4 CLR 227.
27 *Boulton v Jones* (1857) 6 WR 107.

before the auctioneer signals (usually by bringing down their hammer or gavel) acceptance of the offer they want. Auctions have introduced some interesting developments in the law of offer and acceptance. In the case of *Barry v Heathcote Ball & Co (Commercial Auctions) Limited*[28] the auctioneer failed to accept the claimant's bid for machinery even though it was the highest during the auction and no reserve had been set for the items. The auctioneer was liable to the claimant for the market value of the machinery involved, less the value of the claimant's bid. Similar rules apply to arrangements known as options to purchase. An offeror can be obliged to keep an offer open for a specific period provided the offeree has given consideration to have the offer kept open. In such circumstances there will be a breach of contract if there is an attempt to revoke the offer within that period.

Revocation of an offer only becomes effective when it is communicated to the offeree. In the case of *Byrne v Van Tienhoven*[29] the defendant attempted to withdraw their offer made by letter by sending a second letter revoking the first. The first offer had already been accepted (as evidenced by a telegram from the claimant) and the second letter was therefore not a revocation.

Revocation must be communicated to the offeree, but may take place indirectly if from a 'reliable source' such as a mutual friend. This communication need not necessarily be made by the offeror but must involve a reliable third party as opposed to a rumour or suggestion that the offer has been withdrawn. In *Dickinson v Dodds*[30] a third party successfully communicated the revocation of the offer to the offeree on the offeror's behalf.

Difficulty arises where an offer requires an act to be carried out, and the offer is revoked after the act has started but before it has been completed. Reward cases are a good example. In *Errington v Errington and Woods*[31] it was decided that the offer could not be revoked once the appropriate party had begun performance as required by the offer. In this case a father bought a house for his son and daughter-in-law. He told the daughter-in-law that if she paid off the mortgage, the house would be hers. He later changed his mind but the court held that the offer was sufficient to create a unilateral contract once the couple started making mortgage payments.

Duration of an Offer An offer may lapse and become incapable of being accepted with the passing of time. This occurs where there is a specified time limit within which acceptance may be made and that time has passed, or where no time limit is specified but there has been no acceptance within a reasonable period. The length of time deemed reasonable is dependent upon the circumstances of the case and the question of reasonableness can vary depending upon the nature of the contract. For example, an offer to sell perishable goods, such as fruit and meat, would lapse after a relatively short time.

2.2.1.1.2 Acceptance

Once it has been established that an offer has been made, the court must be satisfied that valid acceptance of the offer has taken place. It can be difficult to ascertain the exact moment when a contract was formed, in particular where contracts arise as the result of

---

28 *Barry v Heathcote Ball & Co (Commercial Auctions) Limited* (2000) *The Times*, 31 August (CA).

29 *Byrne v Van Tinenhoven* (1880) C P D 344.

30 *Dickinson v Dodds* (1876) 2 Ch D 463.

31 *Errington v Errington and Woods* [1952] 1 All ER 149.

long and complicated negotiations. In such cases, the conduct of the parties along with all their actions and statements will be considered to see whether or not they intended to contract and whether or not they were successful. Many of these rules are centred in the notion that the acceptance must be clear and comply with the terms of the offer.

Responding to the Terms of an Offer Acceptance of an offer must be in response to an offer and must correspond with the terms of the offer. In *Peter Lind Ltd v Mersey Docks and Harbour Board*[32] alternative tenders were submitted for the construction of a freight terminal. The offeree stated that they had accepted 'your tender' without specifying which one. The court held there was no contract between the two parties. In *Pickfords Ltd v Celestica Ltd*[33] the defendant argued that a contract had been formed where the claimant's offer was accepted subject to a proviso that their costs for moving should not exceed £100,000. It was held that this limitation on the claimant's offer was not an acceptance and instead was a counter offer.

Counter Offers Where one party adds new terms into a proposed agreement, this is not acceptance of an offer, and instead amounts to a counter offer. In *Hyde v Wrench*[34] an offer was made to sell a farm for £1,000. A counter offer of £950 was made and refused, after which the buyer tried to accept the original offer of £1,000. It was decided that the original offer had been 'killed' by the counter offer, rendering it no longer capable of being accepted. In these circumstances it is possible for the original offeror to accept the counter offer and the terms of that offer become the terms of the contract. In this situation the parties have 'changed hats' – the offeror becomes the offeree and vice versa. The parties may change hats several times during the course of negotiation before arriving at mutually agreeable terms of contract.

It might be the case that no final agreement is reached as to which offer should be accepted. Both parties may have their own preferred terms of business and seek to impose their terms on the other using the back and forth, offer and counter offer approach as above. This situation is known as the 'battle of the forms' a term which first came to light in the case of *Butler Machine Tool Co Ltd v Ex-Cell-O Corporation (England) Ltd.*[35] It has been established that the winner of 'the battle of the forms' is the person who submits the last counter offer which is accepted by the other party. In *TRW Ltd v Panasonic Industry Europe GmbH*[36] the High Court provided the following summary of the doctrine:

> Disputes where each party is seeking to rely on its own terms and conditions, to the exclusion of the other side's terms and conditions, have long been known as the 'battle of the forms'. In such cases the courts have endeavoured to apply the traditional concepts of offer and acceptance. This has led to what is sometimes called the 'last shot' doctrine: in other words, the party whose terms and conditions are in play and unanswered at the time that the work is done or the goods delivered is often said to

---

32 *Peter Lind Ltd v Mersey Docks and Harbour Board* [1972] 2 Lloyd's Rep 234.
33 *Pickfords Ltd v Celestica Ltd* [2003] EWCA Civ 1741.
34 *Hyde v Wrench* (1840) 3 Beav 334.
35 *Butler Machine Tool Co Ltd v ExCell-O Corporation (England) Ltd* [1979] 1 All ER 965.
36 *TRW Ltd v Panasonic Industry Europe Gmbh* [2021] EWHC 19 (TCC).

have fired the last shot, with its terms and conditions found to have been accepted by the fulfilment of the substantive contract.[37]

A counter offer must be distinguished from an inquiry or a request for information, which will not vary the terms of the original offer. The offer survives an inquiry or request for information, compared with a counter offer which 'kills' it. In the case of *Stevenson v McLean*[38] the offeree enquired whether a delivery of iron could be staggered over a 2 month period. The answer was no, but the offeree still wanted to go ahead with the contract, and the offeror was obliged to do so.

Time and Nature of Acceptance A contract takes effect once acceptance is communicated to the offeror. Where an offeror insists on a particular form of acceptance, that form must be adopted and the offeror can refuse to recognise acceptance made in any other way. In *Manchester Diocesan Council for Education v Commercial and General Investments Ltd*,[39] the court held that the defendant was entitled to specify a written notice to a specified address as the only method of acceptance. For a unilateral contract, the offeror may remove the need to communicate acceptance because of the terms of the offer (for example, as in *Carlill v Carbolic Smokeball Co* – see "Advertisement Anticipating a Bilateral Contract"). In such circumstances the performance by the offeree will be sufficient acceptance.

An offer can be accepted by conduct if the conduct unequivocally relates to the offer. In *Brogden v Metropolitan Railway Co*[40] the parties had acted in accordance with a draft agreement for the supply of coal. The draft agreement was held to be binding even though it was never formally executed.

A contract can come into existence during performance even if it cannot be precisely analysed in terms of offer and acceptance (*Trentham (G Percy) Ltd v Archital Luxfer Ltd* – see Section 2.2.1.1). An acceptance via post is effective when posted even if it is late or is never actually delivered, as long as there is proof of posting (the postal rule). The rationale for this is that the postal service is the agent of both the parties and has authority to act on their behalf in the contract formulation. An offeror can exclude acceptance by post, but they must specify and communicate that acceptance that posting is not enough for the postal rule to cease to apply. The post rule does not apply if it would give rise to 'manifest inconvenience or absurdity' as contemplated in the case of *Hollwell Securities v Hughes*[41] where a letter seeking to exercise an option to purchase was lost in the post. However, the situation is different where letters are delayed in the post, particularly, as in the case of *Adams v Lindsell*,[42] where the offer letter was wrongly addressed. In this case the acceptance was binding notwithstanding the sale of the goods in question to a third party in the meantime. The result was that the defendant was liable for breach of the contract formed upon the posting of the acceptance.

---

37 Ibid., para 29.

38 *Stevenson v McClean* (1880) 5 QB 346.

39 *Manchester Diocesan Council for Education v Commercial and General Investments Ltd* [1969] 3 All ER 1593.

40 *Brogden v Metropolitan Railway Co* [1877] 2 App Cas 666.

41 *Hollwell Securities v Hughes* [1973] 2 All ER 476.

42 *Adams v Lindsell* (1818) 1 B & Ald 681.

Instantaneous Communication As acceptance needs to be communicated to the offeror, the same rule applies to emails. These forms of communication are treated as instantaneous and take effect, in terms of acceptance, when received. The issue of where the contract was made arose in the case of *Entores v Miles Far East Corporation*.[43] The offeree was based in the Netherlands and the offeror in London. The acceptance was sent back by fax[44] from the Netherlands and was received in the London office. The issue of *where* the contract was made was important as this would dictate which country's laws would govern the contract. It was held that the contract was subject to English law – the key event being the receipt of the fax, not its sending.

The case of *Mondial Shipping and Chartering BV v Astarte Shipping Ltd*[45] considered a related topic concerning the status of transmissions made outside of normal working hours. Here a message was sent at 23.41. The issue was whether this was 'sent' on the actual day or deemed to be sent on the next day. The court found that the effective communication had happened on the next working day and decided the issues in the case accordingly.

Emails, mobile telephone text messages and WhatsApp messages (plus equivalent messaging services) are widely used as a means of communicating offers and counter offers, acceptances and rejections. On the face of it, the approach in the *Entores* case seems to apply equally well in relation to email – the acceptance is binding from the time the email is received by the recipient's server and is available to be read. One difference is that the sender might not know of the failure of the message to arrive until sometime after the message has been sent. Further, the message may not be read by the recipient until the account is checked at some future time. However, similar shortcomings can be experienced with other means of communication and the basic rules of offer and acceptance can be said to apply.

Acceptance by Emoji A recent Canadian case, *South West Terminal v Achter Land & Cattle*[46] considered whether a 'thumbs up' emoji constituted acceptance of an offer. The case concerned a supply contract, a photo of which was sent to the buyer (Chris) by the seller (Kent) with the message 'please confirm the contract'. Chris responded to the message with a thumbs up emoji ('👍'). When a dispute arose, Chris alleged that there was no valid contract, arguing that the thumbs up emoji had been used to indicate receipt of the message as opposed to acceptance of the contract. The Kings Bench Division for Saskatchewan disagreed, and held that the thumbs up emoji did constitute acceptance of the contract. In reaching their decision, the court considered previous communications between the parties, during which contracts had been entered into by Kent texting contracts and wording akin to 'please confirm the contract' and Chris replying via text with language including 'looks good', 'ok' or 'yup'.[47] The court therefore held:

43 *Entores v Miles Far East Corporation* [1955] 2 All ER 493.

44 Define fax for younger generation?! E.g. 'telephonic transmission of scanned-in printed material, including text or images. Faxes are usually sent to a telephone number associated with a printer, fax machine or other output device' (https://www.techtarget.com/searchnetworking/definition/fax#:~:text=A%20fax%20%2D%2D%20short%20for,machine%20or%20other%20output%20device).

45 *Mondial Shipping and Chartering BV v Astarte Shipping Ltd* [1995] CLC 1011.

46 *South West Terminal v Achter Land & Cattle* [2023] SKKB 116.

47 Ibid., para 21.

> In my view a reasonable bystander knowing all of the background would come to the objective understanding that the parties had reached *consensus ad item* – a meeting of the minds – just like they had done on numerous other occasions.[48]

As Canadian jurisprudence, this case is not binding; however, it will be persuasive should similar facts arise in the courts in England and Wales.

Letters of Intent and Pre-contractual Work Letters of intent are indications by a potential party to a contract of an intention to contract at a future date. The status of these letters depends on their wording but where appropriate they can constitute a valid acceptance of an offer. Such letters may make provision for goods to be delivered or rendered before the actual formation of the contract. When the contract is eventually signed it will 'relate back' so as to apply to what was done previously. In *Trollope & Colls Ltd v Atomic Powers Constructions Ltd*,[49] a particularly complicated tendering and quotation arrangement concerning civil engineering works in the building of a nuclear power station rendered work starting before the contract had been entered into. The contract was eventually agreed and entered into 10 months after the work began. The court held that the contract was intended by the parties to be retrospective, to govern their relationship from the inception of the work.[50]

In *British Steel Corp v Cleveland Bridge and Engineering Co Ltd*[51] claimants were approached by the defendants to produce steelwork nodes for a bank development in Saudi Arabia. Extensive negotiations took place in an attempt to reach mutually agreeable contractual terms, during which time the claimant produced and supplied nodes (which were not used, and delivered outside of the sequence requested by the defendant) and the defendant refused to make final payment. The claimant brought an action for the value of the goods, but argued no contract have been entered into. The defendant brought a counter-claim for breach of contract, arguing that the claimant's conduct in manufacturing the nodes assisted in creating a binding contract. The court held that no contract existed:

> the parties had confidently expected a formal contract to be concluded and the letter of intent had requested the plaintiffs to commence work, which they had done in order to expedite performance under the anticipated contract. Since the parties had ultimately been unable to reach final agreement on the price or other essential terms, the contract was eventually not entered into and therefore the work performed in anticipation of it was not referable to any contractual terms as to payment or performance. In those circumstances, the defendants were obliged to pay a reasonable sum for the work done pursuant to their request.[52]

The entitlement was on a *quantum meruit* basis. Quantum meruit is where a judge determines that a claimant is entitled to be compensated by the defendant by receiving

---

48 Ibid., para 36.
49 *Trollope & Colls Ltd v Atomic Powers Constructions Ltd* [1963] 1 WLR 119.
50 Ibid., para 342.
51 *British Steel Corp v Cleveland Bridge and Engineering Co Ltd* [1984] 1 All ER 504.
52 Ibid., 505.

a reasonable price or remuneration. This entitlement can be found notwithstanding any deficiency in the parties contractual arrangements as in the present case.

The final question to consider in this section is whether a course of dealings between two businesses can amount to a binding agreement that future work will be awarded on similar terms? This is relevant to the construction industry where partnering and framework agreements are popular.[53] In *Baird Textiles Holdings Ltd v Marks and Spencer plc*,[54] the claimant had supplied garments to the defendants for a period of 30 years on a series of individual orders. In October 1999 the defendant terminated all supply arrangements without warning. Although there wasn't an existing contract between the parties, the claimant sought damages based on the previous dealings, entitlement to a notice period and further orders. The court held that the relationship between the parties was only as good as the last order and the defendant had, by its actions, clearly not intended for there to be any commitment beyond this flexible arrangement.

2.2.1.2 Consideration

The party who wishes to enforce a contract must show that consideration has been provided for the obligation they are seeking to be enforced. The classic definition of consideration comes from the case of *Currie v Misa*:[55]

> a valuable consideration, in the sense of the law, may consist either in some right, interest, profit or benefit accruing to one party, or some forbearance, detriment, loss or responsibility given, suffered or undertaken by the other.

Consideration has been described as 'contractual glue'; something that binds the offer and acceptance together, where its absence means that the agreement falls apart. A contract is essentially a promise requiring reciprocal obligations between the parties, and this mutuality, where something is given by each side, is consideration. Examples of consideration include the payment of money, the provision of goods, the performance of services or the transfer of land. A distinction is made between executed consideration, where the price is paid for the other party's act, and executory consideration, where the parties exchange promises to carry out obligations in the future. Unless a contract is made by deed, it must be supported by consideration, otherwise it will be unenforceable.

2.2.1.2.1 Consideration Must Have Some Value but Need Not Be Adequate

This means that the consideration must have some worth but the courts will not interfere with an agreement made between the parties, provided it is in the absence of fraud or other underhand dealings. In *Mountford v Scott*[56] a token payment of £1 securing an option to purchase a house for £10,000 was held to be adequate consideration, while in *Chappell Co*

---

53 Partnering is where multiple organisations and participants work together in long-term alliances, see Procure Partnerships Framework 'The relevance of construction partnering in 2024', April 2024. Framework agreements are designed to be used by those who procure work on a regular basis and want the benefit of long-term relationships, see JCT Framework Agreement, edition 2016.

54 *Baird Textiles Holdings Ltd v Marks and Spencer plc* [2001] EWCA Civ 274.

55 *Currie v Misa* (1875) LR 10 Ex 153.

56 *Mountford v Scott* [1975] 1 All ER 198.

Ltd v Nestle Co Ltd [57] the wrappers from bars of chocolate were held to constitute good consideration when capable of being exchanged in part payment for goods. Token consideration of this nature is quite common on land transactions, where the land is in effect gifted. It also appears in such agreements as collateral warranties.[58] Forbearance to sue (agreeing not to pursue a claim in return for a promise by the other party) may be adequate consideration. In *Carlill v Carbolic Smokeball*[59] (see "Advertisement Anticipating a Bilateral Contract") paying for and using the smokeball was deemed to be adequate consideration.

2.2.1.2.2 Performance of an Existing Contractual Duty Is Not Good Consideration

It will not amount to consideration where a party performs an act which is simply a discharge of an existing obligation owed by contract. A similar rule applies where the existing duty is owed by law. In *Collins v Godefroy*[60] the defendant agreed to pay the claimant money if he gave evidence at a criminal trial. A claim for money promised failed because the claimant was obliged by law to give evidence. It will amount to good consideration if the obligation is a contractual one only if a party does more than they were bound to do under the terms of the contract. In *Stilk v Myrick*[61] a sailor (claimant) was on a return voyage from London to the Baltic. Two sailors in their crew deserted the ship, and the master (defendant) promised to divide the wages of the deserters between the remaining crew on their return. Upon their arrival back to the UK, the master refused. The court held that the claimant was not entitled to the additional money. Their original contract operated for the entirety of the voyage, which was to 'do all required' – the crew were contractually bound to carry out any extra work by the terms of their contracts. In contrast, in *Hartley v Ponsonby*,[62] the original crew number was stated in the agreement. When a number deserted, the voyage, from Australia to India, became unsafe and the vessel unseaworthy. The master agreed to pay the sailors additional money to make the voyage, however refused to pay the additional amount upon completion. The court held that any extra work undertaken for the voyage was an addition to the crew's contractual obligations, and a successful claim could be made in respect of the additional work which had been carried out:

> the ship was unseaworthy; and that, owing to the excessive labour which would be imposed, it was not reasonable to require the mariners to go to sea. If they were not bound to go, they were free to make a new contract: and the master was justified in hiring them on the best terms he could make.[63]

In *Williams v Roffey Bros Ltd*[64] the defendants were contractors responsible for the refurbishment of a block of flats for the benefit of the employer. Mr Williams, a joiner, contracted to carry out joinery work on the flats for £20,000. The contract included a provision

---

57 *Chappell Co Ltd v Nestle Ltd Co* [1987] AC 87.
58 See Section 2.2.2.2.3 for an explanation of warranties.
59 *Carlill v Carbolic Smokeball* [1893] 1 QB 256.
60 *Collins v Godefroy* (1831) 1 Dowl 326.
61 *Stilk v Myrick* (1809) 2 Camp. 317.
62 *Hartley v Ponsonby* (1857) 7 El. & Bl. 872.
63 Ibid., 1473.
64 *Williams v Roffey Bros Ltd* [1990] 1 All ER 512.

that if the work was not completed by a specific date then damages would be payable by the defendants as liquidated damages to the employer. The claimant had contracted at an unprofitable amount and was therefore in no hurry to complete the contract. Somewhat concerned that the contract might not be finalised on time, the defendant promised to pay the claimant, by word of mouth, an extra £10,300 in respect of the flats so long as the work was completed according to schedule. The joiner carried out the work and claimed the extra sums. The Court of Appeal held that the additional amount was payable, notwithstanding the terms of the original agreement. Consideration had been given for the contractor's promise to make the additional payment. The contract had been completed, the damages payable to the employer in respect of late completion had been avoided and it had not been necessary to employ others to finish off the joinery work.

2.2.1.2.3 Consideration Must Not Be Past

An act is regarded as past consideration if one party performs an act before any promise of reward is made by the other. The practical effect of this rule is that it is not possible to develop a social arrangement into a contract by making a promise of consideration after the arrangement has been carried out. In *Re McArdle*[65] alterations and improvements to a house were carried out and paid for before the other parties to the contract agreed to reimburse the costs. The Court of Appeal held that the works had been completed before the execution of the document, rendering the consideration for the agreement a 'wholly past consideration', and therefore the agreement unenforceable.[66]

Exceptions

- Consideration is not past where there is an implied promise to pay. It is common practice to pay for certain transactions after completion of the event, such as a taxi journey or a meal in a restaurant.
- Cheques were frequently paid in connection with goods and services received in the past, and S27 Bills of Exchange Act 1882 established that the cheques are to be honoured in respect of past debts.

2.2.1.2.4 Part Payment of a Debt

A debtor is not discharged from the obligation to pay the total balance, even where under agreement, they pay a lesser sum than that due. As held in *Foakes v Beer*,[67] a creditor can go back on an agreement and bring an action for the balance. The House of Lords held that Ms Beer's promise to forgo the interest on a debt, provided that Dr Foakes paid off the main debt by instalments was unenforceable. However, where something extra is done (paying early, or providing goods rather than money), then the whole debt is discharged, as held in *Pinnel's Case*.[68] In the case of *D & C Builders Ltd v Rees*,[69] builders felt they had no choice

65 *Re McArdle* [1951] 1 All ER 905.
66 Ibid., at 910.
67 *Foakes v Beer* [1881–85] All ER Rep 106.
68 *Pinnel's Case* (1602) 5 Co Rep 117a.
69 *D & C Builders Ltd v Rees* [1966] 2 QB 617.

but to accept a lower sum from their client. It was held that there was no reason in law or equity why the claimant should not enforce the full amount of the debt.

The judgment in *Collier v Wright*[70] has effectively nullified the rule that part payment can never be sufficient by expanding the doctrine of promissory estoppel to come to the aid of the debtor in all such cases. In this case the creditor voluntarily accepted part payment of a debt. The debtor relied on this acceptance and paid the amount agreed. The creditor then sought the remainder of the original debt. Applying *Foakes v Beer*[71] the Court of Appeal held that this was not a binding agreement due to a lack of consideration. However, using the doctrine of promissory estoppel, the creditor was estopped (see Section 2.2.1.2.6) from going back on their promise to accept less despite the lack of consideration for such an agreement.

2.2.1.2.5 Consideration Must Move from the Promisee

Only a party who gives consideration under a contract (or their agent) can bring an action in the event of a breach of contract. This rule is similar to, but must be distinguished from the privity rule (see Section 2.2.4).

2.2.1.2.6 Promissory Estoppel

Promissory estoppel is an equitable remedy which may be available where one party has forfeited rights under a contract and the other party has relied upon the promise not to enforce those rights. The promisor (who made the promise) is estopped (prevented) from going back on the promise even though no consideration has been given for the waiver, provided certain conditions are fulfilled. The doctrine has its roots in the nineteenth century and in particular the case of *Hughes v The Metropolitan Railway Company.*[72] The case concerned a request by a landlord to the tenant to carry out repairs on a rented property. The request was followed by a negotiation between the parties on a new lease, during which time the tenant delayed the repairs. The negotiations did not come to anything and the landlord cited the tenant's failure to carry out repairs as grounds for terminating the lease. The Court of Appeal held that the landlord was estopped from terminating the lease because the tenant had relied on the landlord's implied waiver of the requirement to repair during the course of the negotiations:

> Equity will relieve a lessee against forfeiture for breach of a covenant to repair when the landlord has by his conduct misled the lessee into supposing that the covenant would not be insisted on.[73]

The current development of the doctrine dates from what is known as the 'High Trees' case, – *Central London Property Trust Ltd v High Trees House Ltd.*[74] This case concerns the lease of a block of flats in London during the Second World War. The threat of harm from enemy bombing meant only a few of the flats in the block were let to tenants and it became apparent that the defendants would be unable to pay the rent required by the landlord. The

70 *Collier v Wright* [2007] EWCA Civ 1329.
71 *Foakes v Beer* [1881–85] All ER Rep 106.
72 *Hughes v The Metropolitan Railway Company* (1876) 1 CPD 120.
73 Ibid., 132.
74 *Central London Property Trust Ltd v High Trees House Ltd* [1947] KB 130, 131.

landlord made a written promise to reduce the rent. However, by the beginning of 1945 all the flats were let but the defendants continued to pay the reduced rent. In September 1945, the landlord started to charge the full rent, and claimed arrears. The court held:

> where parties enter into an arrangement which is intended to create legal relations between them and in pursuance of such arrangement one party makes a promise to the other which he knows will be acted on and which is in fact acted on by the promisee, the court will treat the promise as binding on the promisor to the extent that it will not allow him to act inconsistently with it even although the promise may not be supported by consideration in the strict sense and the effect of the arrangement made is to vary the terms of a contract under seal by one of less value[75]

Before the doctrine can come into being there must be an agreement between the parties, an unequivocal promise by one party to the other and, at least for the time being, an indication that those rights will be waived. The defendant must have given no consideration for the promise but acted upon it by relying on it. The promisor is then estopped from altering their position under the contract if to do so would cause harm to the other party.

Estoppel can only be used as a defence to a claim, not as a cause of action as of itself. Whether or not promissory estoppel suspends an obligation or discharges it completely is the subject of debate (see *Tool Metal Manufacturing Co Ltd v Tungsten Electric Co Ltd*).[76]

2.2.1.3 Intention to Create Legal Relations

As a contract is a legally binding agreement, the parties must intend that their agreement should be regulated and have the protection of the law for it to become a contract. Where no such intention can be shown there is no contract. Many agreements are never intended to be legally binding whilst for others the presumption will exist that the parties intended to be bound. The test for determining whether the parties intended to enter into a legal binding agreement is objective, and depends heavily on context (see *President of the Methodist Conference v Preston*).[77] The courts will ask whether a reasonable person in such an agreement would have intended to create legal relations (see *Edmonds v Lawson*).[78]

2.2.1.3.1 Business Agreements

In business and commercial agreements, it is presumed that the parties intend to create legal relations. This includes an agreement to build or to transfer land or buildings. This presumption can be challenged (rebutted) if there is evidence to the contrary, or as in the case of *Milner & Son v Percy Bilton Ltd*[79] the words used were too vague to amount to a definite commitment to sell land. To rebut the presumption, there must be strong evidence from the agreement that the parties do not intend to create legal relations. The parties are not bound where the agreement is expressed to be 'binding in honour only' or similar.

---

75 Ibid., 131.

76 *Tool Metal Manufacturing Co Ltd v Tungsten Electric Co Ltd* [1955] 2 All ER 657.

77 *President of the Methodist Conference v Preston* [2013] UKSC 29.

78 *Edmonds v Lawson* [2000] EWCA Civ 69.

79 *Milner & Son v Percy Bilton Ltd* [1966] 1 WLR 1985.

This area is akin to the historic 'gentlemen's agreement'; the problem being that if one or other of the parties no longer wishes to behave how a gentleman should, they can consider themselves no longer bound. A common occurrence in conveyancing transactions and correspondence is the use of the phrase 'subject to contract'. The phrase is often seen on letters sent to the parties to a conveyance by estate agents. The purpose of the letter is often to record the agreement made on price and to signal that both parties must now complete the other formalities of agreement required to bring about the transaction with the assistance of their legal advisors. The use of this phrase is sufficient to prevent any agreement being reached even if the words in the letter itself create the opposite impression.

2.2.1.3.2 Social and Domestic Agreements

For social and domestic agreements, it is presumed that the parties do not intend legal relations to arise. This was the finding in the case of *Balfour v Balfour*[80] where an agreement to pay maintenance before divorce proceedings had started was found not to be binding as 'the parties did not intend that they should be attended by legal consequences'.[81] The same was found with regards an agreement between a mother and their adult child in *Jones v Padavatton*.[82]

Rebutting the Presumption The presumption that social and domestic agreements do not create legal relations is a rebuttable presumption. This means that is a presumption made by the courts which can be deviated from if the contrary is proved – there is an assumption that legal relations were not intended; however, facts may demonstrate that indeed, legal relations were intended. This happened in the case of *Simpkins v Pays*[83] which involved an agreement between three cohabitees to share the winnings from a lottery syndicate. The agreement was binding notwithstanding the domestic setting. Rebutting the presumption that legal relations were not intended can occur through the formality of the agreement, whether consideration has passed between the parties and the language used. In *Spelling v John Spelling Ltd*,[84] mutual promises between codirectors, who were brothers, that they would not withdraw money from a family business were deemed to be binding. In *Darke v Strout*[85] the court held that an agreement for child maintenance rebutted the presumption owing to both the formality of the agreement and the foregoing of statutory rights to child maintenance. In *Soulsbury v Soulsbury*[86] an agreement which saw one party forgoing spousal maintenance in exchange for a bequest in the will of the other did rebut the presumption, and legal relations were held to have been intended.

80 *Balfour v Balfour* [1919] 2 All ER Rep 860.
81 Ibid., 864.
82 *Jones v Padavatton* [1969] 2 All ER 616.
83 *Simpkins v Pays* [1955] 1 WLR 975.
84 *Spelling v John Spelling Ltd* [1973] QB 87.
85 *Darke v Strout* [2003] EWCA Civ 176.
86 *Soulsbury v Soulsbury* [2007] EWCA Civ 969.

2.2.2 Representations and Terms of a Contract

Representations are statements made *prior* to a contract being entered into, whereas terms are the *contents* of a contract. It is important to distinguish between them.

2.2.2.1 Representations

A representation is a statement of fact, made during contract negotiations, which acts to induce the other party to enter into the contract or to take some action with regards it. The representation must be true on the date that it is made. A false representation may give a potential claimant a right to claim on the basis of misrepresentation. If the misrepresentation is actionable, the remedies are governed by the Misrepresentation Act 1967 and not by the rules relating to remedies for breach of contract. The intentions of the parties and what they understood the representation to mean are relevant when deciding whether a misrepresentation has taken place (see Section 2.2.3.3). If these enquiries are inconclusive, the judge will consider what an intelligent bystander would infer from the words and behaviour of the parties at the time the representation was made.

2.2.2.2 Terms

Terms are the contents of the contract which define the rights and responsibilities of the parties. They may be expressed or implied, written or verbal. Implied terms arise in other ways.

2.2.2.2.1 Express Terms

Express terms can be oral or in writing – in either form, the parties are said to have 'expressed themselves' on a particular subject which is included in their contract. Where a contract has been made on a solely oral basis, the meaning of terms is a question of fact. The court must decide the issue from evidence which is given to it. Where a contract has been made in writing, the 'parol evidence' rule applies which prevents oral or other extrinsic evidence from being admitted which vary or contradict the terms of the written agreement. There are some exceptions to this rule, among the most important being:

- to prove a trade custom or usage;
- to indicate the existence of a vitiating factor (see Section 2.2.3);
- where the written contract is not the whole contract.

2.2.2.2.2 Implied Terms

A contract may contain terms which are not expressly included but are implied, either by custom, the courts or statute.

Custom A term can be implied by the custom of a particular geographical area. In *Hutton v Warren*[87] the claimant, a tenant of a farm was given notice by the landlord to quit before the crops (which the claimant had planted) were harvested. Local custom dictated that the tenant was allowed to recover a fair allowance for seeds and labour involved in the planting of a crop where a tenant was prevented from harvesting the crop. A term

87 *Hutton v Warren* (1836) 1 M&W 466.

was therefore implied into the lease to this effect. A term will not be implied by custom if the express wording of the contract shows that the parties had a contrary intention.

The Courts The courts will imply a term in the following sets of circumstances.

a. Where it is a necessary incident of the type of contract in question
The reasonableness of the term and the nature of the subject matter are important in this context. In contracts to build, where a builder constructs a house, there is a term implied that the dwelling will be reasonably fit for habitation when completed. Similar terms are implied in respect of the quality of work and the time in which the contract will be completed. Likewise, on the employer's part, it is implied that the contractor will be given possession of the site on which the building works are to take place and that a reasonable sum shall be payable for the work. These terms may be rebutted where there are express terms to the contrary.
b. To give the contract 'business efficacy'
Business efficacy involves the notion of making a contract into a workable agreement in such a manner as the parties would clearly have done if they had applied their minds to the matter arising. From this the court creates the *common implied intention* of the parties. It may be necessary to fill a gap in the contract and the term(s) must be formulated with a sufficient degree of precision. There must be no express term dealing with the same matter, while the stipulations to be implied must be so obvious that they go without saying. The principle comes from *The Moorcock*,[88] where a vessel was damaged when unloading cargo owing to the unevenness of the riverbed which had not been maintained properly. It was decided that there was an implied term in the contract that the owners of the wharf had impliedly contracted to take reasonable care to see that ships unloading their cargos were safe and would not be damaged on the riverbed. The case of *Liverpool City Council v Irwin*[89] demonstrates the application of the procedure within a built environment context. The Council let flats in a tower block to the tenants. The lease didn't contain any obligations on the Council as to the maintenance of the building. The flats were poorly maintained by the Council, with broken lifts and rubbish left in walkways. The defendant withheld their rent in protest at the condition of the premises, arguing that the Council were in breach of an implied term of the lease that they should adequately maintain the buildings. The House of Lords agreed and implied a term into the lease using the common implied intention rule.
c. Where a term is implied by the previous course of dealings between the parties
Terms will be implied into a contract of a similar kind where the parties have previously entered into contracts of the same particular variety containing express terms. This will only occur in the absence of express stipulation to the contrary.

Statute In some instances, statute will imply terms into a contract. Examples are the Sale of Goods Acts 1979 and the Supply of Goods and Services Act 1982 (as amended by the Sale and Supply of Goods to Consumer Regulations 2002).

---

88 *The Moorcock* (1889) 14 PD 164.
89 *Liverpool City Council v Irwin* [1976] 2 All ER 39.

The Sale of Goods Act 1979: The Sale of Goods Act 1979 implies terms into contracts for the sale of goods as follows:

Title (section 12): In every such contract, there is an implied condition on the part of the seller that they have the right to sell the goods or that he will have the right at the time when the property is to pass. If this condition is broken, the buyer may treat the contract as at an end even though they have done some act which would otherwise have amounted to acceptance. Section 12 also provides that there is an implied warranty that the goods are free and will remain free from any encumbrances not known to the buyer before the contract is made.

Description (section 13): The vast majority of sales are by description (i.e. the goods are not physically examined by the buyer before purchase) and in such a case there is an implied condition that the goods will correspond with that description. This provision also applies to private sales. It extends to matters such as measurements, quantity and methods of packing as in the case of *Moore & Co v Landaur & Co.*[90] The claimants were entitled to reject imported goods merely because they were packed in boxes of 24 rather than 30 as agreed.

Satisfactory quality (section 14): The following provisions only apply where the goods are sold in the course of a business. By section 14(2) there is an implied condition of satisfactory quality except as regards defects specifically drawn to the buyer's attention before the contract is made or where the buyer examines the goods before the contract as regards defects which the examination ought to reveal. 'Satisfactory quality' means that the goods meet the standard that a reasonable person would regard as satisfactory having regard, inter alia, to their description and price. The Sale and Supply of Goods to Consumers Regulations 2002 have improved the position of the consumer further by adjusting the burden of proof. Goods returned by the consumer within the first 6 months from the date of sale requesting a repair are assumed to have been faulty at the date of purchase unless the retailer can establish otherwise.

Section 14(3) relates to fitness. The implied condition is that the goods are reasonably fit for any purpose which the buyer makes known to the seller. This purpose will normally be implied but if goods have a number of purposes, the buyer must indicate the one required.

Sample (section 15): Certain items such as tiles, carpets and wallpaper are bought on the basis of a sample inspected before the sale takes place. In such circumstances the following conditions are implied:

- that the bulk will correspond with the sample in quality;
- that the buyer will have a reasonable opportunity of comparing the bulk with the sample;
- that the goods shall be free from any defects rendering them unsatisfactory which would not be apparent on reasonable examination of the sample.

The Supply of Goods and Services Act 1982: A contract for the sale of goods must be distinguished from a contract for the supply of services where goods are also being sold under the contract. A contract for work done and materials supplied comes into this category. The sale aspect of the contract is governed by sections 2–5 of the 1982 Act which contains implied

---

90 *Moore & Co v Landaur & Co* [1921] 2 KB 519.

terms similar to the Sale of Goods Act 1979 (sections 12–15). The work aspects are governed by Part 2 of the Act which imply terms relating to reasonable skill and care, reasonable time for completion, and reasonable charges for services where no price has been fixed at the outset. The supplier must be acting in the course of a business for the terms to apply.

Consumer Rights Act 2015: The Consumer Rights Act 2015 came into force in October 2015, setting minimum standards for the sale of goods and services. The contracts covered by the Act are divided into contracts for goods, contracts for services and digital content contracts. Under the Act, goods and digital content must be of satisfactory quality (S9; S34), fit for particular purpose (S10; S35) and as described (S11; S36). Services must be performed with reasonable care and skill (S49), a reasonable price paid for the service (S51), and it be performed within a reasonable period of time (S52).

The Late Payment of Commercial Debts (Interest) Act 1998: This Act was introduced to improve the position of small businesses being kept out of money owing to them by larger businesses. The Act implies terms into contracts between qualifying businesses that simple interest calculated at the appropriate rate can be claimed in the event of late payment.

2.2.2.2.3 Conditions and Warranties

Conditions and warranties are two different types of contractual term, and the rules governing them apply equally whether the term is express or implied. This distinction is important because there are different remedies if there is a breach of contract and things go wrong. There is no special test to determine into which category a term falls. Each situation has to be decided on its own merits.

Conditions Conditions are the more important terms of contract. These are terms of the contract *but for which* the injured party would not have entered the contract. A breach of condition (known as a repudiatory breach) allows the injured party to treat the contract as finished whereupon they will be discharged from their obligations under the contract. In addition, the other party can be sued for damages. The contract is rendered voidable, which means the innocent party has a choice between treating the contract as having been irreparably damaged by the breach of condition (this is known as rescission), or continuing with the contract notwithstanding the breach. The choice is based around the fact that the innocent party should be entitled to keep the benefit of the contract if they wish. In either case it is open to the innocent party to pursue a claim for damages.

Warranties These are terms which are secondary or ancillary to the main purpose of the contract. A breach of warranty allows the injured party to claim damages but not to repudiate the contract. The contract is not voidable. The contract survives the breach of a minor term whilst preserving the right to damages for the innocent party. It is for a court, not the parties, to determine the category of term.

The difference between conditions and warranties and the practical consequences of the difference can be seen through a comparison of the cases of *Poussard v Spiers*[91] and *Pond*

---

91 *Poussard v Spiers* (1876) 1 QBD 410.

and Bettini v Gye.[92] Both cases involved singers who were late for their performances at theatres, and were told that the agreements to hire them had been fundamentally breached by their lateness and their contracts terminated. In *Poussard's* case the court agreed. The singer had missed the all-important opening night and their absence amounted to a breach of a condition. Bettini, however, had only missed rehearsals, and the court determined that this was a breach of a warranty as opposed to a condition, rendering the producers able to sue in damages, but not terminate the contract.

An aspect of a contract may be classified as a term, but is neither a condition nor a warranty. The difficulty which arises is then to determine whether or not the injured party can rescind (avoid) the contract. Such provisions have become known as intermediate or innominate terms. The consequences of the breach are important here. Unless the contract makes it clear that the parties intended that no breach of the contract should entitle them to terminate the contract, the term will be classified as an intermediate term. The question is whether or not the nature and effect of the breach are to deprive the injured party of substantially the benefit which it is intended they should obtain under the contract. If so, the injured party is entitled to terminate the contract as well as claiming damages. This was considered in the case of *The Hansa Nord*.[93] The question here was whether an innominate term of the contract that 'shipment be made in good condition' should be treated as a condition or a warranty. The claimant sought to reject the contract based on a small percentage of the goods being sub-standard. The defendant suspected that the real reason for the rejection was a reduction in the market value which rendered the cargo much less profitable. The court did not view the partial unsoundness of the cargo to be a ground for total rejection and treated the breach as a warranty, entitling the claimant to damages only.

2.2.3 Vitiating Factors

A vitiating factor is something which affects the validity of the contract. The contract may appear to have the essential requirements for a valid contract – offer, acceptance, consideration and intention to create legal relations; however. something has occurred or become apparent, which renders the contract no longer enforceable.

The impact of successfully establishing a vitiating factor will make the contract either:

- Void (no contract)
- Voidable (the contract exists but can be avoided at the choice of the innocent party).
- Binding (an enforceable contract exists)

2.2.3.1 Capacity of the Parties

The first challenge to an agreement is based around the question of capacity. The central premise is that a person may lack capacity to enter into a contract. Historically, there was a binary distinction between natural persons and artificial persons, with natural persons being human beings, and artificial being corporations, companies and local authorities.

92 *Pond and Bettini v Gye* (1876) 1 QBD 183.
93 *The Hansa Nord* [1975] 3 All ER 739.

With the increase in computer systems based on artificial intelligence forming contracts,[94] this area of law and its associated binary distinctions will inevitably develop very quickly. However, at present, natural persons are those presumed to have capacity to contract. There are exceptions to this rule, including with regard to capacity of minors, those with mental illness and those incapacitated through intoxication.

2.2.3.1.1 Minors

As a general rule, contracts are not binding on minors.[95] A practical exception to this rule is to be found in respect of contracts of employment which are beneficial to the minor (a contract with a newsagent to deliver newspapers to the local neighbourhood for example). Another exception involves contracts for necessaries. The idea here is that minors are obliged to pay for goods or services they need. The rather bizarre corollary is that minors do not need to pay for goods or services they do not need. This was demonstrated in the case of *Nash v Inman*.[96] A Saville Row tailor attempted to recover £122 16s 6d for items including 11 fancy waistcoats supplied to an undergraduate. The action failed as the minor could demonstrate that they were already adequately supplied with clothes and those supplied by the tailor did not amount to necessaries.

2.2.3.2 Mistake

A mistake arises where the parties make an error as to a term of the contract which prevents there being *consensus ad idem* (or meeting of the minds). Mistake does not affect the validity of a contract unless it is fundamental mistake, known as an operative mistake, which will render the contract void. As discussed above, mistakes and contracts entered into through the use of artificial intelligence is gaining the attention of the courts, recently in the Singaporean case of *Quoine Pte Ltd v B2C2 Ltd*.[97] Trading was carried out by Quoine's algorithms and when a mistake was made, Quoine reversed the transactions on the ground that they were clearly a mistake. B2C2 Ltd argued that the transactions were binding contracts. The court held that the programmes, the algorithms which made the mistake, were 'mere machines'[98] and the knowledge was held by the programmer of the machine, as opposed to the machine itself. As the programmer was not aware of the mistake, the contract was held to be enforceable.

In a limited set of circumstances, the contract will be voidable (this may be the position where there is a mistake as to the identity of the person contracted with). Special rules apply to documents. The contract is binding where a person signs a document and by so doing enters a contract. This is so even if the signatory has not read the document nor

---

94 'AI system users may task their AI virtual assistants to purchase an object on the internet. Or, systems may be programmed with the purpose of autonomously forming contracts of a specific type, as is sometimes done in the context of high-frequency stock transactions' M Herbosch, 'Contracting with Artificial Intelligence: A Comparative Analysis of the Intent to Contract' The Rabel Journal of Comparative and International Private Law, Bd. 87, H. 4 (November 2023) 672–706, 673.

95 A minor is defined as someone under the age of 18 years (S1 Family Law Reform Act 1969; Chitty on Contract (2008)).

96 *Nash v Inman* [1908] 2 KB 1.

97 *Quoine Pte Ltd v B2C2 Ltd* [2020] SGHC(I) 02.

98 Ibid., 89.

understands it. The principle of *caveat emptor* – let the buyer beware- applies here. There is a very limited defence based on *non est factum* (it is not my deed), where a person is induced by a fraud or a trick to sign a document. In practice, the defence is difficult to rely on because the signatory must show:

- That all reasonable precautions were taken when signing the document, and;
- The document signed was radically different from the one the person thought they were signing, or;
- The person signing the document was under some legal disability, such as being illiterate, blind or senile.

An example of the third point above occurred in *Lloyds Bank v Waterhouse*[99] where a person failed to inform the bank that they could not read before signing a bank guarantee, relying on the bank's misrepresentation as to its nature. They were able to avoid a claim based on the guarantee by reason of the operative mistake.

There are some circumstances where the equitable jurisdiction of the English legal system will intervene where the mistake is a non-operative one. This includes rescission of the contract and possible rectification of a contract if it does not accurately express the agreement reached between the parties. In such circumstances, equity will rectify the agreement so as to make it conform to the original agreement. In *Craddock Bros v Hunt*[100] there was an oral agreement to sell land. This was put into writing but, by mistake, the document missed out any reference to part of the land which had been already been paid for. It was held that the agreement would be rectified. The rule does not apply if there is simply a mistake by one of the parties in expressing intention. In *W Higgins Ltd v Northampton Corporation*[101] the claimant stated an incorrect price for work in connection with a tender relating to the building of houses. The error was due to incorrect estimating on the claimant's part. The tender was accepted by the local authority without realising a mistake had been made but the contract could not be rectified. In this instance the principle was *caveat venditor* – let the seller beware. The claimant found itself in the position that it could not now avoid a contract where they had legitimately (but erroneously) offered to carry out the work for the price stated.

2.2.3.3 Misrepresentation

Misrepresentation is concerned with the effect of statements which are made before a contract is formed, representations. A representation is a statement of fact, as opposed to a statement of opinion which is made by one person to another with the object of persuading or inducing the other party to enter into a contract. Where the other party relies on the statement made, a contract is formed and the statement turns out to be incorrect, a remedy may be provided through the law of misrepresentation. In *SK Shipping Europe Ltd v Capital VLCC Corp and another*[102] the Court of Appeal held that a party seeking to rescind a contract for misrepresentation must show 'the representation played a real and substantial part'[103] in inducing it to enter into the contract. The court continued:

99 *Lloyds Bank v Waterhouse* [1991] 10 Trading LR 161.
100 *Craddock Bros v Hunt* [1923] All ER 394.
101 *W Higgins Ltd v Northampton Corporation* [1927] 1 Ch 128.
102 *SK Shipping Europe Ltd v Capital VLCC Corp and another* [2022] 2 All ER (Comm) 784.
103 Ibid., 805.

(t)he misrepresentation need not be the only reason for the party's decision to enter into the contract, but the representee will have no grounds for complaint if it would have entered into the contract on the same terms even if the representation had not been made. The relevant enquiry is whether the claimant would have entered into the contract if the representation had not been made at all, not whether it would have done so if it had been told the true position.

An example of an opinion rather than a fact comes from the case of *Bisset v Wilkinson*[104] where the vendor of a farm in New Zealand expressed the opinion that the farm would support 2,000 sheep. In fact, the farm had never held any sheep. The claimant's sheep farming business failed but they were unable to sue for misrepresentation based on what was an honestly given opinion. A misrepresentation can be fraudulent, innocent or negligent. Fraudulent misrepresentation was discussed at length in the case of *Partakis-Stevens & Anor v Sihan & Ors*,[105] noting 'fraud is proved when it is shown that a false representation has been made: (1) knowingly; or (2) without belief in its truth; or (3) recklessly, careless whether it be true or false'.[106]

Remedies are governed by the Misrepresentation Act 1967 and the tort of deceit. A claimant in such circumstances will be able to claim damages and/or rescind the contract. The court has power to refuse rescission and to award damages instead in the case of a non-fraudulent misrepresentation. A delay in applying for rescission may also be fatal to such a claim. This occurred in the case of *Zanzibar v British Aerospace (Lancaster House) Ltd*[107] where problems experienced with a private jet aeroplane were not reported until several years after the alleged problems first arose.

2.2.3.4 Duress, Undue Influence and Inequality of Bargaining Power

As a contract is a 'meeting of minds', a contract may be challenged on the basis that it was not freely entered into. Coercion, actual threats or undue pressure can all serve to vitiate a contract. However mere inequality of bargaining power is, as a general rule, insufficient in seeking to set aside agreements. Statutory interventions such as the Unfair Contract Terms Act 1977 and Unfair Terms in Consumer Contracts Regulations 1999 go towards protecting consumers in commercially vulnerable positions. The Consumer Credit Act 2006 allows the court to adjust a credit agreement if the court decides that the relationship between lender and borrower is unfair.

2.2.3.5 Illegality

A contract containing an illegal element is void. The illegal aspect may be in breach of a statute provision, or it may be against public policy to allow certain types of contract to be enforced. Examples include defrauding the Inland Revenue or contracts involving the commission of a crime. The contract price will not be recoverable where a building contractor enters a contract knowingly in contravention of a law. In *Stevens v Gourley*[108]

---

104 *Bisset v Wilkinson* [1927] AC 177.
105 *Partakis-Stevens & Anor v Sihan & Ors* [2022] EWHC 3249 (TCC).
106 Ibid., 187.
107 *Zanzibar v British Aerospace (Lancaster House) Ltd* (2000) The Times, 23 March.
108 *Stevens v Gourley* (1859) 7 CB NS 99.

statutory provisions required buildings to be made of incombustible materials. The contract was found to be illegal when the builder erected a wooden building upon wooden foundations. A distinction occurs when the contract appears be perfectly valid at the outset and becomes illegal while in the process of performance. The contractor may be able to recover the price for the work depending upon the circumstances. In *Townsend Builders Ltd v Cinema News*[109] specifications for temporary work to be undertaken were in breach of a statutory provision but the completed work was not in breach. Payment could be claimed, as the contract was not fundamentally illegal and the builder was unaware of the contravention until the work was well advanced.

2.2.4 Privity of Contract

A fundamental principle of the common law is that no person can sue or be sued on a contract unless they are a party to it. To sue or be sued under a contract, there must be privity of contract. This can cause particular problems in the construction industry where there are many parties involved in a building project. Some of the participants will have privity of contract between themselves while others will not. The rule means that a stranger (or third party) cannot bring an action under a contract to which they are not a party, even if the terms of the contract express that the third party should benefit. The principle is illustrated by *Tweddle v Atkinson*[110] where a couple were about to marry. The parents of each agreed between themselves that they would make payments to the couple. The husband sought to enforce the contract when the bride's parents refused to pay. It was held that there was no privity of contract between the parties, between the groom and their father-in-law, and therefore the claim could not be enforced.

There are, however, a number of exceptions to the rule. Examples include third party insurance policies and the agency relationship, where a principal can sue and be sued in respect of a contract made by an agent. Tripartite arrangements, known as trusts, are similar exceptions. The privity rule has been criticised by the higher courts. A successful attack was made on the rule with the enactment of the Landlord and Tenant (Covenants) Act 1995 which abolished the rule between a landlord and the assignee of an original tenant in a leasehold transaction.

It has become standard practice in large scale construction projects for those who finance the transactions to insist that all the parties involved enter into contracts (collateral warranties) with each other. The reason for this is because of the difficulties which claimants have able to successfully bring an action against a defendant in the tort of negligence for financial losses. The collateral warranty is a way of ensuring that in the event of default an injured party will have a potential defendant to bring an action and claim damages.

This tendency to insist on the use of additional contracts (warranties) has so far continued notwithstanding the change in the law brought about by the Contracts (Rights of Third Parties) Act 1999. This non-mandatory Act allows a third party to bring an action on

109 *Townsend Builders Ltd v Cinema News* [1959] 1 WLR 119.
110 *Tweddle v Atkinson* (1861) 1 Best & Smith 393.

a contract to which they are not a party but which purports to transfer a benefit on them. The effect of these provisions, when used, is to circumvent the privity of contract rule.

2.2.5 Exemption and Limitation Clauses

It is common practice in contract formation for a party to insert a clause which, in the event of their breach, will either exclude liability completely under the contract or limit liability to a specific amount of money. The former type of clause (absolute exclusion) is an exemption clause whilst the latter (financial limitation) is known as a limitation clause. Such clauses are used by suppliers of goods and services in respect of potential problems such as defective materials and unsatisfactory work. The courts have always disliked exemption and limitation clauses, tending to decide against them if there is any ambiguity in what the clause may mean or whether it has been incorporated properly in any given situation.

2.2.5.1 Common Law

An exemption or limitation clause is valid at common law when certain basic requirements are satisfied. In *L'Estrange v Graucob*[111] such a clause was upheld notwithstanding that it was written in 'legible but regrettably small print' in a sales agreement. The claimant failed to read the document before signing it but had the opportunity of doing so. A person seeking to rely on such a clause must show that it is a term of the contract and that as a matter of construction it covers the damage in question. In *Chappleton v Barry UDC*[112] a claimant was injured by a hired deckchair when it collapsed on them. At the time of hiring the deckchair no notice was given of the exclusion clause on which the Council sought to rely. The clause was contained in a receipt given to the claimant at which they only glanced. The judge held it was unreasonable to communicate conditions by means of a mere receipt. Such a clause is therefore not effective if the clause or the notice is contained in a document which the average person would not assume to contain contractual terms.

The clause will only be a contractual term if adequate notice is given of it, or such a term is implied by a clause having been incorporated into documents where there has been a previous course of dealings between the parties. A common practice is to print such clauses on order forms or on a notice. Notice of the clause must be given before or at the time of the contract. Belated notice of an exclusion clause was given in the case of *Olley v Marlborough Court.*[113] A contract for the hire of a hotel room was made over the telephone. A fur coat was stolen from the hotel room during their absence. The hotel sought to rely on a notice avoiding liability from theft displayed in the hotel's lobby. The judge deemed that this notice was not adequate as the contract for the hire of the room had been made over the telephone and this unilateral attempt to introduce new terms once the contract had been completed would not be successful. Where such clauses are properly incorporated, the position is that liability can only be limited or excluded by clear words. The purpose of the exemption clause is another factor for the court to consider in deciding whether

111 *L'Estrange v Graucob* [1934] 2 KB 394.
112 *Chappleton v Barry UDC* [1949] 1 KB 532.
113 *Olley v Marlborough Court* [1949]1 All ER 127.

or not it is reasonable as demonstrated by the case of *O'Brien v Mirror Group Newspaper Limited*.[114] This case involved scratch cards distributed with a British newspaper. Due to an error on the cards, 1,472 people were told they had won £50,000 each. The claimant attempted to hold the defendant to their promise to pay. The defendant relied on its terms and conditions in seeking to avoid liability. The judge allowed the defendant to rely on the clause, even though the terms and conditions were not printed in the edition of the paper the claimant purchased. The effect of the exclusion clause here was not to exclude liability altogether but to prevent a windfall for the claimant.

2.2.5.2 Statute

The primary statutory provisions regulating unfair reliance on exemption clauses is the Unfair Contract Terms Act 1977 (UCTA) and the Consumer Rights Act 2015.

2.2.5.2.1 Unfair Contract Terms Act 1977 (UCTA)

UCTA covers liability in respect of a breach of contract and in respect of the tort of negligence. The Act applies to contracts made between businesses, between businesses and consumers, employment contracts and even, to some extent, 'private contracts' where neither party is a business; however, insurance contracts and land contracts are not covered under UCTA.[115] Any provision in a contract excluding or restricting liability for death or personal injury is void. In other cases based on negligence, liability can only be excluded or limited if it is fair and reasonable to do so. The reasonableness provision also applies in contractual cases. The fair and reasonable provision will also apply where a party to a contract deals as a consumer or contracts on the other party's standard business terms. In *Smith v Eric S Bush*,[116] a firm of general practice surveyors inserted an exemption clause into a valuation report for mortgage purposes which had been prepared for a building society. The report was shown to the purchasers. The House of Lords concluded that it would not be fair and reasonable in the circumstances to rely on the disclaimer. The factors to be considered when deciding whether a purported exclusion is fair and reasonable include:

- The practical consequences of exclusion – in particular, the cost and availability of insurance cover.
- Equality of bargaining power between the parties.
- Whether it is practicable for the relevant party (or parties) to seek advice from an alternative source.
- An exclusion could well be reasonable if the task is unusual or dangerous.

A seller may exclude liability under sections 13–15 in a non-consumer sale which is made in the course of business if it can be shown that it is fair and reasonable to do so. The majority of sales in a construction context will be non-consumer in nature. UCTA lays

---

114 *O'Brien v Mirror Group Newspaper Limited* [2001] EWCA Civ 1279.

115 See Schedule 1, para 1 (a) and (b), see The Law Commission and The Scottish Law Commission 'Unfair Terms In Consumer Contracts: Advice to the Department for Business, Innovation and Skills' March 2013.

116 *Smith v Eric S Bush* [1990] 1 AC 831.

down guidelines as to the factors to be taken into account when applying the reasonableness test. The principal ones are as follows:

- The relative strength of the bargaining position of the parties taking into account the availability of suitable alternative products and sources of supply.
- Whether the buyer received an inducement to agree to the term.
- Whether the buyer knew or ought reasonably to have known of the existence and extent of the term.
- The extent to which the goods were manufactured, processed or adapted to the special order of the buyer (S11 UCTA 1977 s11).

In the case of *Rees-Haugh Limited v Redland Reinforced Plastics Limited*[117] the judge decided it was not fair and reasonable for the defendant to rely on an exclusion clause in their terms and conditions of sale. They sold pipes to the claimant which were not fit for purpose for which the defendant knew they were required. Following this case, it is difficult to see how a party can escape liability for supplying defective goods. Similarly, in the case of *Feldaroll Foundry plc v Hermes Leasing (London) Ltd*[118] liability for a Lamborghini Diablo motor car bought for £64,995 but sold with a serious and dangerous steering defect could not be avoided by the defendants.

An auction sale or a sale by tender is not a consumer sale. An exemption clause may be valid subject to the reasonableness test if a private buyer buys at auction. It is presumed that a sale is a consumer sale, but once the seller has proved it is a non-consumer sale it is for the buyer to show that it would not be fair and reasonable to rely on the term.

2.2.5.2.2 Consumer Rights Act 2015

The Consumer Rights Act 2015 governs contracts between trader and consumer. It includes a requirement for consumer contracts to be fair (S62), defining a term as unfair if:

> (c)ontrary to the requirement of good faith, it causes a significant imbalance in the parties' rights and obligations under the contract to the detriment of the consumer (S62 (4)).

Part 1, schedule 2 Consumer Rights Act 2015, contains an 'indicative and non-exhaustive list' of terms within a consumer contract which may be regarded as unfair. The list includes:

- Terms seeking to exclude or limit liability of traders for death or serious injury as a result of their act or omission
- Terms requiring consumers who fail to fulfil their obligations pay disproportionately high compensation
- Terms enabling a trader to indefinitely terminate a contract without reasonable notice (unless there are serious grounds for doing so)
- Terms enabling a trader to unilaterally alter a contract without valid reason specified in the contract

---

117 *Rees-Haugh Limited v Redland Reinforced Plastics Limited* [1984] Cons.I.L.L. 84.
118 *Feldaroll Foundry plc v Hermes Leasing (London) Ltd* [2004] EWCA Civ 747.

In the Scottish case of *King v Black Horse & Park's Ayr Ltd*[119] the claimant had bought a vehicle from Parks Ayr, financed through Black Horse. They sought to return the car, claiming a full refund after discovering it had a defect. However, in the period between discovery of the defect and the attempted return, they continued to both use the vehicle and make payments under the finance agreement. Counsel for the claimant successfully argued that the Consumer Rights Act 2015 had 'created a more powerful remedy for consumers than they had previously enjoyed under the previous common law right'.[120]

2.3 Contract Conclusion

2.3.1 Discharge of a Contract

When a contract ends, it is said to be discharged. The rule is that on discharge, the parties are freed from their obligations. Contracts do not end automatically, and discharge must come about by an act of the parties.

Discharge can come about in one of four ways:

- Performance;
- Agreement;
- Frustration; or
- Breach of an appropriate term of the contract.

2.3.1.1 Performance

To discharge by performance, each party must do what they have promised to do. A person who claims to be discharged from obligations on the basis of performance must show that whatever was agreed has taken place, for example, work has been completed, goods supplied or land transferred. A building or engineering contract will be discharged by performance when the contractor has completed the work, and the employer has paid sums due. The contract has not been performed if there are hidden defects. This common law rule is enshrined in *Cutter v Powell*,[121] where the defendant agreed to pay Cutter a sum of money for performing duties as a seaman on a ship during a 10-week voyage; however, Cutter died 7 weeks after the commencement of the voyage. His widow attempted to recover wages under the contract, but their claim was unsuccessful because the 10-week contract had not been performed. Similarly in *Sumpter v Hedges*[122] the claimant builder contracted to construct two buildings on the defendant's land for an agreed price. The buildings were half finished when the project was abandoned due to lack of funds. The claimant was unable to recover any money in respect of the work carried out.

---

119 *King v Black Horse & Park's Ayr Ltd* [2024] CSIH 3.
120 Judgment report, Tanfield Chambers, 9 February 2024 (https://www.tanfieldchambers.co.uk/2024/02/09/iain-mitchell-kc-succeeds-in-important-consumer-rights-act-2015-case)
121 *Cutter v Powell* (1795) 6 Term 320.
122 *Sumpter v Hedges* [1895] 1 QB 673.

The courts have recognised certain exceptions to the requirement of full performance, where a claim may be made for a reasonable amount for work carried out on the basis of a *quantum meruit* application. This is to avoid possible injustice and prevent unfair manipulation of the common law rule of full performance. *Quantum meruit* means, 'as much as it is worth', and can be used either for part performance of a contract, or where no contract exists.

2.3.1.2 Exceptions

2.3.1.2.1 Severable Contracts

Payment can be claimed for work done on completion of each stage where a contract is severable, also sometimes described as divisible. However, if the contract is an entire one, the work must be completed in full before the party becomes liable to pay. The terms of the contract are important in this context and much will depend on the intention of the parties. The courts tend to lean against finding a contract entire. A severable contract will arise where payments are due from time to time (such as interim or stage payments in construction contracts) and the other party's obligations are rendered in return.

2.3.1.2.2 Substantial Performance

This arises where performance under a contract, although not complete, is very close to being so. In such a case a claim may be made for the work completed subject to any counterclaim in respect of work remaining unperformed. The contract price can be claimed subject to a deduction equal to the cost of remedying any omissions or defects. In essence, the defects must be of a trifling nature before the exception can be claimed. In *Hoening v Isaacs*[123] the doctrine was applied where the cost of remedying the defects amounted to £56 on a contract worth £750. In *Dakin v Lee Ltd*[124] the court stated that if a builder has done work under an entire contract, but the work has not been completed in accordance with the contract, a claim can be made on a *quantum meruit* unless the customer received no benefit from the work, the work was entirely different from that which was contracted for, or the contractor had abandoned the work. The exception will not apply if the contract has not been substantially completed. The actual cost of remedying the defects in relation to the contract price is a relevant factor. In *Bolton v Mahadeva*[125] a contract was entered into to install a central heating system for £560. The system performed very poorly, and the remedial work would have involved a further cost of £174. The judge held that there had not been any substantial performance and that the claimant was entitled to nothing for the work done.

2.3.1.2.3 Prevention of Performance

A claim for damages can be made on a quantum meruit for work carried out if a party to a contract is prevented by the other party from performing what they have agreed to do. In *Roberts v Bury Improvement Commissioners*[126] a contractor was not in default where an architect neglected

---

123 *Hoening v Isaacs* [1952] 2 All ER 176.
124 *Dakin v Lee Ltd* [1916] 1 KB 566.
125 *Bolton v Mahadeva* [1972] 2 All ER 1322.
126 *Roberts v Bury Improvement Commissioners* (1870) LR 5 CP 10.

to supply them with necessary plans which prevented the contractor from completing the work by the contract date. The contractor was entitled to be paid for the work performed.

2.3.1.2.4 Without a Contract

In *Moorgate Capital (Corporate Finance) v H.I.G. European Capital Partners LLP*,[127] the court discussed quantum meruit claims at length, providing clarity on when it may be possible for a claimant to rely on it where no contract exists between the parties. The claimant had been involved in the introduction to, and acquisition by the defendant of a target company (Bezier). The defendant offered £80,000 to the claimant by way of thanks (*ex gratia* payment) for the introduction; however, the claimant argued there was an oral contract, made at a social occasion, promising £1 million if the acquisition was successful. The claimants claimed breach of the oral contract, and as an alternative (if the court found that there was no contract), a claim on the basis of quantum meruit. The court held that no contract existed, and that Moorgate was a 'disappointed risk-taker'.[128] In order for a quantum meruit to succeed, the claimant had to establish:

- The defendant has been enriched (benefited);
- The enrichment was at the claimant's expense;
- The enrichment was unjust;
- The possibility of any other legal remedies must have already been exhausted.[129]

In *British Steel Corp v Cleveland Bridge and Engineering Co Ltd*[130] (facts at Section 2.2.1.1.2, 'Letters of Intent and Pre-contractual Work') the court held:

> If (...) no contract was entered into, then the performance of the work is not referable to any contract the terms of which can be ascertained, and the law simply imposes an obligation on the party who made the request to pay a reasonable sum for such work as has been done pursuant to that request, such an obligation sounding in quasi contract or, as we now say, in restitution.[131]

2.3.1.3 Agreement

As contracts are created by agreement, so it follows they may be discharged by agreement too. Another contract must be entered into if the parties agree to waive their obligations under an existing contract. This will be appropriate where neither of the parties has completed their obligations under the contract. Where one of the parties has completed obligations under the contract but the other party has not, the party to whom the obligation is owed may agree with the other party to accept something different in place of the former obligation. This is known as the doctrine of accord and satisfaction. The subsequent agreement represents the accord, and the new consideration which has been

---

127 *Moorgate Capital (Corporate Finance) v H.I.G. European Capital Partners LLP* [2019] EWHC 1421 (Comm).
128 Ibid., 102.
129 Para 85, 86 citing *Benedetti v Sawiris* [2013] UKSC 50, [2014] AC 938, 10.
130 *British Steel Corp v Cleveland Bridge and Engineering Co Ltd* [1984] 1 All ER 504.
131 Ibid., 511.

given being termed the satisfaction. Alternatively, an obligation under a contract may be discharged by the operation of one of the terms of the contract itself. Contracts of employment often contain provisions whereby the contract can be determined by either party giving a period of notice to the other. In building and engineering contracts it is common to find provisions whereby the contract can be determined before completion on the happening of specific events. The serious default or insolvency of the other party is a common example.

2.3.1.4 Frustration

As a rule, contractual obligations are absolute, and a contract is not discharged simply because it is more difficult or expensive than expected to carry it out. However, a contract can be discharged if it can be established that it has been frustrated. 'Frustration' in this context means impossibility. In *Davis Contractors Ltd v Fareham UDC*[132] Lord Radcliffe provided the following:

> (f)rustration occurs whenever the law recognizes that without default of either party a contractual obligation has become incapable of being performed because the circumstances in which performance is called for would render it a thing radically different from that which was undertaken by the contract. *Non haec in foedera veni.* It was not this that I promised to do[133]

To succeed, the claimant must show that the circumstances have changed to such an extent that the performance of the contractual obligation has become fundamentally different. In *J. Lauritzen AS v Wijsmuller BV (The Super Servant Two)*[134] Lord Bingham detailed the fundamental aspects of frustration as:

1. to give effect to the demands of justice, to achieve a just and reasonable result, to do what is reasonable and fair, as an expedient to escape from injustice where such would result from enforcement of a contract in its literal terms after a significant change in circumstances
2. Its operation is to 'kill the contract and discharge the parties from further liability under it', it cannot be 'lightly invoked', and it must be kept within 'very narrow limits and ought not to be extended'
3. Its impact is to bring an end to a contract 'forthwith, without more and automatically'
4. 'It should not be due to the act or election of the party seeking to rely on it', it must instead be due to 'outside event or extraneous change of situation'
5. The event must be 'without blame or fault on the side of the party seeking to rely on it'.[135]

Although historically rarely invoked in the law of contract, the COVID-19 pandemic led to a number of cases seeking to use the doctrine of frustration as Governments mandated populations stay at home.

---

132 *Davis Contractors Ltd v Fareham UDC* [1956] AC 696.
133 Ibid., 729.
134 *J. Lauritzen AS v Wijsmuller BV (The Super Servant Two)* [1990] 1 Lloyd's Rep. 1.
135 Ibid.

2.3.1.4.1 Examples of Frustration

Destruction of the Subject Matter If the subject matter is destroyed and its existence is crucial to the performance of the contract, then the contract will be frustrated. In *Taylor v Caldwell*,[136] a building which was to be used for a series of concerts was destroyed by fire. The court held that the contract was discharged as 'from the nature of the contract, it appears that the parties must ... have known that it could not be fulfilled unless ... some particular specified thing continued to exist'.[137]

Changes in the Law The doctrine of frustration will apply if a change in the law makes the contract impossible to carry out. The case of *Denny Mott and Dickson Ltd v James B Fraser & Co Ltd*[138] provides an example. War-time regulations banned the sale of timber so a contract attempting to sell timber between the parties was deemed to have been frustrated. During the coronavirus pandemic, lockdown laws, alongside public policy considerations of ensuring those laws were observed, rendered contracts frustrated. However, a grey area emerged where government guidance was provided as opposed to legislation.

Inability to Achieve the Main Object of the Contract The contract will be frustrated if the basis upon which both parties entered the contract is destroyed. To succeed on this basis there has to be a complete non-occurrence. Comparing the cases of *Krell v Henry*[139] and *Herne Bay Steam Boat Co v Hutton*[140] illustrates how this point of law operates in practice. Both cases involve the coronation of Edward VII. The first contract was for the hire of a hotel room with a view of the coronation procession route. The second case involved a contract for the hire of a boat to watch/take part in a royal regatta. The King cancelled his appearance at both events due to ill health. Both claimants alleged that their contracts had been frustrated by this occurrence as the main object of the contract –seeing the King – would not now be possible to achieve. The cases were decided differently. In the first case, concerning the hotel room, it was held that the contract had been frustrated whilst in the second, concerning the regatta, no frustration was found. The key was that in the second case, the regatta went ahead as planned and the King's appearance was only of minor importance to the enjoyment of the day itself.

Death, Personal Incapacity or Illness Death or permanent incapacity will frustrate a contract for personal services. There is a similar effect where a party is likely to be ill or incapacitated for a considerable period of time. These events are sufficient to make the contract fundamentally different from that originally envisaged and it will be discharged. This occurred in the case of *Morgan v Manser*[141] where a comedian, working under the name Charlie Chester, was called up to serve in the armed forces during the duration of the Second World War. The disruption caused by the 6-year war to a 10-year management contract was sufficient for the parties to treat the contract as having been frustrated. Cancellation of one

---

136 *Taylor v Caldwell* (1863) 3 Best & Smith 826.

137 Ibid., 833.

138 *Denny Mott and Dickson Ltd v James B Fraser & Co Ltd* [1944]AC 265.

139 *Krell v Henry* [1903] 2 KB 740.

140 *Herne Bay Steam Boat Co v Hutton* [1903] 2 KB 683.

141 *Morgan v Manser* [1948] 1 KB 184.

or a number of performances by a person who later provides the service required will not amount to a frustrating event.

2.3.1.4.2 Examples Where Frustration Will Not Apply

The Contract Becoming More Onerous to Perform or Less Financially Rewarding The fact that a contract proves more difficult or more expensive to perform will not frustrate the contract unless the difficulty arises from some fundamental change of circumstances. In *Tsakiroglou v Noblee Thorl GmbH*[142] a contract to ship ground nuts from the Mediterranean to India was not frustrated by the temporary closure of the Suez Canal. The cargo would have to be sent around the Cape of Good Hope instead, which was at least twice as far as the standard route. The resulting increased time and expense did not amount to frustration. In *Davis Contractors Ltd v Fareham UDC*[143] builders agreed to erect 78 houses in 6 months. The period extended to 22 months owing mainly to a lack of skilled labour and a shortage of materials. Building costs in that period rose considerably and the builders contended that they should be entitled to claim on a quantum meruit. The House of Lords decided that the contract was not frustrated, it was simply more difficult to carry out. In the case of *Amalgamated Investment and Property Co v John Walker*[144] the claimants alleged frustration of a contract when, after exchange of contracts, but before completion of the purchase of industrial premises, the Department of the Environment listed the property which was the subject of the sale. The Court of Appeal held, rejecting the appeal, that listing was an inherent risk in all property transactions relating to buildings of historical and architectural interest and the transaction after listing was not radically different than it was previously.

Self-induced Frustration A frustrating event must not have been one which the parties could have contemplated when making the contract. The courts will give effect to the intention of the parties where express provision has been made in the contract for the contingency in question. The event causing the frustration must not have been due to the conduct of the parties.

The courts were reluctant to allow claims of frustration to succeed during the COVID-19 pandemic. Two cases, *Salam Air SAOC v Latam Airlines Groups SA*[145] and *Wilmington Trust SP Services (Dublin) Ltd v Spicejet Ltd*[146] concerned aircraft leases during the pandemic. In *Salam*, the claimants sought an injunction to prevent the defendant calling for payment under the lease owing to the air travel restrictions imposed. The court acknowledged that the travel industry had become 'challenging' but argued it was an insufficient basis for frustration. In *Wilmington* the defendant had a 10-year lease with the claimant over three aircrafts. They stopped making payment during the COVID-19 pandemic, arguing that national Governments grounding the aircrafts had frustrated the lease. The court held that the lease had not been frustrated, as the defendant had agreed all the risks of the aircrafts during the 10-year lease period. Similarly, in *Bank of New York Mellon (International) Ltd v Cine-UK*

142 *Tsakiroglou v Noblee Thorl GmbH* [1961] 2 All ER 179.
143 *Davis Contractors Ltd v Fareham UDC* [1956] AC 696.
144 *Amalgamated Investment and Property Co v John Walker* [1977] 1 WLR 164.
145 *Salam Air SAOC v Latam Airlines Groups SA* [2020] EWHC 2414.
146 *Wilmington Trust SP Services (Dublin) Ltd v Spicejet Ltd* [2021] EWHC 1117.

Ltd,[147] tenants of a commercial building argued their lease had been frustrated due to an 18-month forced closure. The court held that an 18-month closure in the context of a 15-year lease did not make the contract impossible or radically different from that originally agreed.

2.3.1.4.3 Effect of Frustration

A frustrating event discharges the contract from the time of the frustrating event. It does not frustrate it from the outset (*ab initio*). All contracts (other than insurance and shipping primarily) are governed by the Law Reform (Frustrated Contracts) Act 1943 which allows:

- Money that has been transferred before the frustrating event to be recovered, and money due is no longer due.
- Expenses incurred prior to the frustrating event may be deducted from money due to be returned.
- A party who has carried out work or services prior to the frustrating event may claim compensation on a *quantum meruit* basis.

Where the common law rules still apply (primarily insurance and shipping contracts), it is not possible to recover money which has been paid before the frustrating event takes place unless there has been a total failure of consideration (the other party failing to perform their part of the contract).

2.3.1.5 Breach of an Appropriate Term of the Contract

Any failure by a party to a contract to fulfil obligations under it amounts to a breach. A breach gives rise to an obligation on their part to pay damages to the person who has suffered loss (subject to a valid exemption clause to the contrary). The obligations of the parties to perform the contract remain unchanged unless the breach can be classified as a repudiatory breach. In each case, the issue as to whether the breach is to be taken as a repudiation depends upon the importance of the breach in relation to the contract as a whole. Repudiation will assert itself in a building contract where execution of the works is so unsatisfactory as to affect the very basis of the contract. The injured party has the option either to terminate the contract or to affirm it in the case of a repudiatory breach. The appropriate test to ascertain whether or not a party has repudiated the contract is whether or not a reasonable person would believe that the other party did not intend to be bound by the contract. If the test is satisfied the injured party may treat the contract as at an end and is released from further performance. The claimant may rescind the contract but must act without delay to do so. Unjustified rescission of a contract does not always amount to a repudiation.

The injured party need not wait for the date set for performance where they know that a breach will take place. A right of action exists immediately as if there were a breach, and the claimant may sue for breach of contract. In the case of *Lovelock v Franklyn*[148] the defendant committed the breach when they sold an item they had contracted to sell to the claimant to a third party instead. The claimant knew of the sale to the third party and was

147 *Bank of New York Mellon (International) Ltd v Cine-UK Ltd* [2021] EWHC 1013.
148 *Lovelock v Franklyn* (1846) 8 KB 371.

able to seek damages before the envisaged sale between the defendant and the third party took place.

2.4 Remedies

2.4.1 Damages

Damages are a common law remedy, awarded to an injured party for loss suffered as a result of a breach of contract. The overall aim of damages is to put the party in the position they would have been in had the contract been performed as expected.

2.4.1.1 Liquidated and Unliquidated Damages

Liquidated damages are a fixed amount, agreed by the parties in advance and included within their contract, prior to any breach occurring. They predict possible breaches, such as delays, and specify the damages owed should they occur. Contrastingly, unliquidated damages are determined by the court after a breach has occurred, where parties did not include possible breaches and resulting damages in their contract. Any loss suffered as a consequence of a breach, whether physical or financial in nature, can be claimed by a successful claimant. The potential financial liability of a defendant with regard to unliquidated damages could be unlimited, whereas with liquidated damages, the amounts owed for breaches are specified.

2.4.1.1.1 Liquidated Damages

In *Triple Point Technology Inc v PTT Public Company Limited*,[149] the Supreme Court recognised the commercial benefits of liquidated damage clauses through the certainty provided, with Lord Leggatt explaining:

> Liquidated damages clauses are a standard feature of major construction and engineering contracts and commonly provide for damages to be payable at a specified rate for each week or day of delay in the completion of work by the contractor after the contractual completion date has passed. Such a clause serves two useful purposes. First, establishing what financial loss delay has caused the employer would often be an intractable task capable of giving rise to costly disputes. Fixing in advance the damages payable for such delay avoids such difficulty and cost. Second, such a clause limits the contractor's exposure to liability of an otherwise unknown and open-ended kind, while at the same time giving the employer certainty about the amount that it will be entitled to recover as compensation. Each party is therefore better able to manage the risk of delay in the completion of the project.[150]

149 *Triple Point Technology Inc v PTT Public Company Limited* [2021] UKSC 29.
150 Ibid., para 74.

For a contract provision for liquidated damages to be valid, it must be a *genuine* attempt to pre-estimate the likely loss suffered as a consequence of the breach. They are therefore ordinarily respected regardless of the actual loss suffered.

As explained by Lord Leggatt, it is common practice for construction and engineering contracts to contain a liquidated damages clause for delay alongside an extension of time clause, giving the contractor the right to extra time if they are delayed by matters outside the control of either party or due to the default of the employer and/or their agents. Relevant matters would include industrial action, bad weather, or the employer delaying the execution of the works by failing to supply necessary plans or give possession of the site. Any claim to liquidated damages will be lost if any delay in the performance of the contract is caused by the employer.

Liquidated damages clauses must be distinguished from penalty clauses. A penalty clause is intended to deter parties from breach, imposing an often-disproportionate amount of money should a breach occur. Because of this, they are often deemed invalid, owing to their aim of penalising as opposed to compensating. The leading case is *Dunlop Pneumatic Tyre Co Ltd v New Garage Ltd.*[151] The contract between the parties provided that the defendant would have to pay £5 for every tyre it sold under the price provided by the claimant. In this instance the courts were satisfied that this was an attempt to quantify the effects of a breach of the contract, as opposed to a penalty, and it was therefore upheld. Lord Dunedin listed the following principles to assist when determining whether a provision is a liquidated damages clause or a penalty:

- The name which the parties give to the clause is not conclusive and it is the task of the court to decide the category.[152]
- The essence of liquidated damages is that the sum stated is a genuine pre-estimate of the probable loss, while the essence of a penalty is that it is a threat to carry out the contract.[153]
- 'It will be held to be penalty if the sum stipulated for is extravagant and unconscionable in amount in comparison with the greatest loss that could conceivably be proved to have followed from the breach (...)
- It will be held to be a penalty if the breach consists only in not paying a sum of money, and the sum stipulated is a sum greater than the sum which ought to have been paid'[154]

There is a presumption that where a single sum is made payable on the happening of one or more events, some of which are serious and some of which are of little consequence, the sum is likely to be a penalty. However, in *Holding BV v Talal El Makdessi and ParkingEye Ltd v Beavis,*[155] the Supreme Court took the opportunity to review the law on penalties for the first time since *Dunlop.* Parking Eye charged £85 to those overstaying in their car parks, and Mr Beavis argued this was not a genuine pre-estimate of loss suffered by his over stay, and instead constituted a penalty. The court considered what made a clause extravagant or unconscionable,

151 *Dunlop Pneumatic Tyre Co Ltd v New Garage Ltd* [1915] AC 79.
152 Ibid., 86.
153 Ibid.
154 Ibid.
155 *Holding BV v Talal El Makdessi and ParkingEye Ltd v Beavis* [2015] UKSC 67.

and held: 'a damages clause may properly be justified by some other consideration than the desire to recover compensation for a breach'.[156] The court considered commercial justification and deterrence, and held that neither resulted in a clause being a penalty.[157]

There is a likelihood of greater losses emanating from a major breach than from a minor one. In *Law v Redditch Local Board*[158] the sum stated in the relevant clause was to be paid on the happening of a single event only. Therefore, it was deemed to be a valid pre-estimate of likely loss and was considered to be a liquidated damages clause.

2.4.1.1.2 Unliquidated Damages

As unliquidated damages are to be determined by the court, as opposed to specified in contract, and a number of legal rules are applicable to their determination. There must be an actual loss, and a claimant needs to demonstrate:

1. The breach *caused* the amount claimed
2. The loss was not too *remote*
3. Reasonable steps were taken to *mitigate* (reduce) loss.

Unliquidated Damages: Remoteness and Causation The rule in *Hadley v Baxendale*[159] states that the only losses recoverable are those which may fairly and reasonably be considered as arising naturally from the breach of the contract, or losses which may reasonably be supposed to have been in the contemplation of both parties at the time they made the contract in the event of a breach. The facts in *Hadley* involve the repair of a shaft used in a mill. An example of the rules as to the recoverability of damages under what became known as the *Hadley v Baxendale* tests came from the decision in *Victoria Laundry Ltd v Newman Industries Ltd*.[160] The claimants ordered a new boiler for their business which arrived late. The claimants sought lost profits for the time they were without the boiler, and future loss from being unable to fulfil a profitable contract with the Government. They were entitled to recover damages for normal loss of profits by applying the first part of the *Hadley v Baxendale* test. The boiler supplier should have anticipated the lost profits. The contentious item was whether the claimant was entitled to recover further losses due to the loss of the government contract. The defendants were unaware of the existence of the government contract, and it could not therefore be said to be within the parties' reasonable contemplation as envisaged in the second part of the *Hadley v Baxendale* test.

This narrow approach to the remoteness of contractual damages was upheld by the House of Lords in the case of *Transfield Shipping Inc v Mercator Shipping Inc* (*The Achilleas*).[161] The claimant chartered a ship from the defendants for a 7-month period. The claimant was late

---

156 Ibid., para 28.
157 Ibid. 'deterrence is not penal if there is a legitimate interest in influencing the conduct of the contracting party which is not satisfied by the mere right to recover damages for breach of contract' (para 99) and 'In short, commercial interests may justify the imposition upon a breach of contract of a financial burden which cannot either be related directly to loss caused by the breach or justified by reference to the impossibility of assessing such loss' (para 145).
158 *Law v Redditch Local Board* (1892) 1 QB 127.
159 *Hadley v Baxendale* (1854) 9 Ex 341.
160 *Victoria Laundry Ltd v Newman Industries Ltd* [1949] 1 All ER 997.
161 *Transfield Shipping Inc v Mercator Shipping Inc* (*The Achilleas*) [2008] 2 Lloyd's Rep. 275.

in returning the ship, causing losses to the defendant who had arranged for a third party to re-charter the ship on its return. The claimant was content to pay damages based on the normal market rate of charter rates but the defendant insisted on additional damages caused by the volatility in the market being experienced at that time. Their lordships decided that only the damages based on a normal market rather than an exceptionally high market rate could be claimed from the defaulting party. Another case involving chartered ships is *Golden Strait Corporation v Nippon Yusen Kabushiki Kaisha*.[162] This case raised the issue of the effect upon a repudiated contract of an event which would have cancelled the contract in the normal chain of events. In this case the outbreak of the Iraq war in 2003 would have triggered rescission had the contract still been live. The House of Lords decided that the actual outbreak of the war limited the scope for damages to be recovered under the contract from the defaulting party.

In *Quinn v Burch Bros Ltd*[163] the defendants, in breach of contract, failed to supply the claimant plasterer with a step ladder. As an alternative he used a trestle table which slipped, causing injury to the claimant. The Court of Appeal took the view that the injury was the claimant's fault and that the defendant's breach of contract did not cause the injury. The breach of contract had merely given the claimant the opportunity to injure themself – it was impossible to say the defendant had caused the injury in law.

Mitigation of Loss The injured party has a duty to mitigate any losses suffered. This means that reasonable steps must be taken to minimise damage. An employee who is wrongly dismissed must attempt to find alternative employment while a buyer of goods which are not delivered must try to buy replacements as cheaply elsewhere. Failure to do so is taken into account when the court is assessing damages. Only reasonable steps to mitigate need be taken – the claimant is not expected to incur great expenditure or undertake significant risks.

Unliquidated Damages: Classification of Damages

General Damages: The measure of damages awarded is usually the actual monetary loss. The cost of reinstatement will constitute general damages in cases of defective building work. This occurred in the case of *East Ham Corporation v Bernard Sunley & Sons*.[164] If this formula is incapable of representing the actual loss to the claimant then the damages will amount to the decrease in the value of the property.

Consequential Loss Damage: These are additional losses suffered as a consequence of the defendant's breach of contract and can be awarded as a further 'head' of damages.

Damages for Mental Distress: The traditional rule was that damages for breach of contract should not take account of any mental distress and inconvenience suffered by the claimant. This rule is illustrated in the case of *Addis v Gramophone Co Ltd*,[165] where a company wrongfully dismissed its manager in a way that was 'harsh and humiliating'. The claimant received damages for loss of salary and commission, but nothing for their injured feelings. Deviation was made from that position in *Jarvis v Swan Tours Ltd*,[166]

162 *Golden Strait Corporation v Nippon Yusen Kabushiki Kaisha* [2007] 2 WLR 691.
163 *Quinn v Burch Bros Ltd* [1966] 2 QB 370.
164 *East Ham Corporation v Bernard Sunley & Sons* [1966] AC 406.
165 *Addis v Gramophone Co Ltd* [1909] AC 488.
166 *Jarvis v Swan Tours Ltd* [1973] 1 All ER 71.

where the Court of Appeal decided that in an appropriate case such damages could be an additional element in the sum awarded. This case involved a holiday to which the claimant was looking forward to immensely. They had a thoroughly miserable time due mainly to events advertised in the holiday brochure either not occurring at all or being sub-standard. The claimant was awarded damages for loss of enjoyment on the holiday. The damages awarded amounted to twice the original price of the holiday itself.

From *Jarvis* the principle emerged that damages may be awarded where the object of the contract is to give pleasure, relaxation, peace of mind or freedom from molestation. The case of *Farley v Skinner*[167] extended this principle further to apply to contracts which were not solely for pleasure, relaxation and peace of mind. The claimant had asked their surveyor to consider in their report the issue of aircraft noise above a property they were considering buying near Gatwick Airport in London. The surveyor reported that the property was unlikely to suffer greatly from such noise. Unbeknown to the surveyor the property was close to a navigation beacon over which the aircraft 'stacked up' in busy periods. The claimant was entitled to recover damages from the surveyor for loss of enjoyment due to regular noise pollution suffered.

Damages for loss of enjoyment are not usually permitted on commercial contracts. However, they were awarded in the case of *Watts v Morrow*[168] where physical discomfort and mental distress resulted from repairs necessitated to remedy defects a surveyor had failed to notice during their work.

2.4.1.2 Limitation of Actions

Limitation periods are the time periods within which a claimant must start an action for damages. As a general rule, a claimant must pursue a claim with due diligence while potential defendants should not have the threat of litigation pending indefinitely. Specific time periods are laid down by statute within which actions for damages must be brought. This is in part due to the reliability of evidence, which diminishes over time as memories fade.

2.4.1.2.1 Limitation in Contract

S5 Limitation Act 1980 states that if a claim for breach of contract is based on a simple contract, it must be brought before the expiration of 6 years from the date on which the alleged breach occurred. S8 deals with a deed, where the action must be brought within 12 years from the date the alleged breach. The claim is statute-barred (barred by statute) and cannot be brought if it is not started within these time limits. If the breach is a continuing one, a claimant can choose the last date that the defendant was in breach before the time period begins to run.

2.4.1.2.2 Fraud or Concealment

Limitation periods have to provide for the possibility of a defendant acting fraudulently or concealing the true state of affairs from a potential claimant. The current provisions are to be found in sections 31 and 32 Limitation Act. S32 covers where the claimant is unaware of the true state of affairs because of the defendant's fraud or deliberate concealment

---

167 *Farley v Skinner* [2001] 4 All ER 801.
168 *Watts v Morrow* [1991] 4 All ER 937.

of a breach of contract. The limitation period does not begin to run until the claimant has discovered the fraud or concealment, or could, with reasonable diligence have discovered it. An example of the rule is *Clark v Woor*,[169] where the claimant commissioned the defendant (a builder) to construct a bungalow. The claimant specified the materials to be used and gave detailed instructions. The defendant knowingly used inferior facing bricks from those specified and concealed the true state of affairs from the claimant. No supervising architect or surveyor was involved in the contract. The claimant became aware of the defects 8 years after construction of the bungalow. The claim was held, by the Court of Appeal, not to be statute-barred. In *Applegate v Moss*[170] the defendant builders agreed in 1957 to build houses on a raft foundation supported by specified steel network. Cracks appeared beneath the houses 8 years after their completion. On inspection it was revealed that there was no raft and the reinforcement was inferior to that specified. The claimants succeeded in their action by taking advantage of the concealment provisions. A similar result was reached in *King v Victor Parsons and Co*,[171] where the defendants concealed the fact that a house had been built on a rubbish dump that had been filled in and did not have any proper foundations. The claimant's claim was not deemed to be statute-barred when cracks appeared outside the limitation period Lord Denning M.R stated:

> The word fraud here is not used in the common law sense. It is used in the equitable sense to denote conduct by the defendant or his agent such that it would be against conscience for him to avail himself of the lapse of time. The cases show that, if a man knowingly commits a wrong (such as digging underground another man's coal); or a breach of contract (such as putting in bad foundations to a house), in such circumstances that it is unlikely to be found out for many a long day, he cannot rely on the Statute of Limitations as a bar to the claim.[172]

2.4.2 Equitable Remedies

Equitable remedies may be available where the common law remedy of damages is inadequate or inappropriate. Such remedies are discretionary, meaning they are not automatically available in the event of succeeding in a case. Certain general principles apply to the grant of equitable remedies while others apply to individual remedies. In all cases:

- The conduct of the parties is taken into account.
- No equitable remedy will be available if damages are considered to be an adequate remedy in the circumstances of the case.
- Limitation periods are not relevant to equitable remedies.
- Time is of the essence in such circumstances and each equitable remedy must be sought with reasonable promptness.

169 *Clark v Woor* [1965] 2 All ER 353.
170 *Applegate v Moss* [1971] 1 QB 406.
171 *King v Victor Parsons and Co* [1973] 1 WLR 29.
172 Ibid., 209, 210

2.4.2.1 Specific Performance

Specific performance is a court order requiring the defendant to carry out a promise according to the terms of the contract. It is appropriate where the subject matter of the contract is not freely available, for example, land, or a rare painting or antique. In such cases the payment of a sum of money would not be adequate compensation in the event of a breach of contract. It is primarily used as a threatened remedy where contracts for the sale or lettings of land are broken. Specific performance will not be awarded to enforce a contract for personal services or where the contract requires supervision to ensure that it is being enforced properly. This was the case in *Wolverhampton Corporation v Emmons*[173] where the defendant owned the land on which the claimant sought an order compelling specific performance of a building contract. The court refused to grant the order in these circumstances, and held that a claim for damages was more appropriate in the circumstances. Specific performance of a building contract may be awarded where:

- The building work to be carried out is clearly specified in the contract.
- The claimant has a special interest in having the work done which cannot be satisfied by an award of damages.
- The builder is in possession of the land, so it is not practicable to employ another builder.

2.4.2.2 Injunction

This equitable remedy can be used to prevent a person from continuing a wrong or alternatively can be used to compel a party to do something to remedy a breach of contract. Unlike specific performance, it can apply to contracts containing a personal services element. The usual rules as to equitable remedies apply and an injunction will not be granted if damages are an adequate remedy. In *Bath and NE Somerset District Council v Mowlem plc*[174] it was decided that contractual provision for liquidated and ascertained damages would not prevent the council from obtaining an injunction to restrain the contractor's refusal of access to the site to replacement contractors. Failure to obey an injunction is a contempt of court and may result in the imposition of a fine or imprisonment.

2.5 Agency

The agency relationship is of vital importance in commercial and business life. An agent is a person who acts on behalf of another (the principal). An agent may conduct the principal's affairs in many ways, but their primary function is to create contractual relationships between the principal and a third party. Where the agent contracts with such a party they do so on behalf of the principal. The effect of this is to create an enforceable contract between principal and third party with the agent dropping out of the transaction. This relationship is a familiar characteristic of business life. Companies will often contract through their directors and managers, while partners will act on behalf of their firms. Self-employed and

---

173 *Wolverhampton Corpn v Emmons* [1901] KB 515.

174 *Bath and NE Somerset District Council v Mowlem plc* [2004] BLR 153 and 100 Con LR 1 CA.

employees can act in this capacity, and auctioneers, estate agents, architects and engineers are all examples of agents.

2.5.1 Creation

2.5.1.1 Express Authority

An agent may be expressly appointed – orally or in writing. Typical agent/principal relationships include estate agents to find prospective purchasers for properties, an engineer to administer a contract on behalf of an employer, site agents acting as an employer's agent on site, and a salesperson selling goods on behalf of a company. No particular form of appointment is required unless the agent is empowered to execute deeds, in which case the authority must be given by power of attorney.

2.5.1.2 Implied Authority

The relationship of principal and agent will be inferred if, by their conduct, the parties have acted in such a manner so that it may be deemed to exist. This may occur where one party receives a commission, accepts goods, or pays for items ordered by another person. In *Ryan v Pilkington*[175] an estate agent was instructed to find a buyer. They found a buyer and accepted a deposit from them, though deposit acceptance had not been authorised. The court held that despite having not been expressly authorised to accept deposits, they were acting as agent when they did so. The owner was therefore liable for the deposit when it was misappropriated by the estate agent.

2.5.1.3 Necessity

An agency of necessity arises in an emergency where a carrier of goods needs to take immediate action to protect them. This may occur when the carrier cannot obtain instructions from the person on behalf of whom the goods are being carried. The carrier may deal with the goods as is considered appropriate either by sale or by storage in order to preserve them. The agent must act in good faith and in the interests of the parties concerned. The implication of an agency of necessity will result in the carrier being able to claim payment in respect of their efforts to preserve the goods.

2.5.2 Ratification

The principal is not bound if an agent either has no authority to act on their principal's behalf or exceeds their authority. As an exception to this rule the principal has the option of confirming transactions which were made without their authority. If this option is exercised the agent's acts are legitimised from the outset. The principal can adopt the transaction so as to obtain the benefit and undertake the obligations agreed. The agent, however, is personally liable if the principal does not ratify the transaction. Certain conditions apply:

- The principal must have existed, and the third party must have been informed by the agent that the agent was acting on behalf of the principal.

---

175 *Ryan v Pilkington* [1959] 1 WLR 402.

- The principal must have had capacity to contract when the agent acted.
- Ratification must take place within a reasonable time.
- The contract must be capable of ratification.

2.5.3 Estoppel

If a principal, by conduct or acquiescence, allows third parties to believe that somebody is acting as their authorised agent, the principal will be estopped from denying the existence of the agency where the third party relies on such conduct or representation to their detriment. This is the case where the principal had no intention of creating the principal/agent relationship or the agent has no authority. Where a principal becomes aware of the likelihood of this problem arising, they should inform appropriate third parties with whom the agent has been dealing. If this occurs the principal will not be bound by the agent's acts. Such an agency will only apply if the person dealing with the alleged agent has no notice of the lack of authority.

2.5.4 The Scope of an Agent's Authority

To a large extent the agent's authority will depend on what has been agreed between the principal and agent. The actual authority that has been specifically granted to an agent can be implied by the nature of the job, task or particular business. In some cases, an agent obtains status from the authority and powers which third parties assume they possess. This is known as the 'ostensible' or 'apparent' authority of an agent. A principal will be liable in respect of those acts which are usually undertaken by an agent in respect of a particular job. An engineer, architect or site agent will bind the principal when carrying out the normal tasks associated with these professions under a contract even though the specific individuals do not have express authority to act in a particular way. Any agent signing a cheque or a contract on behalf of a principal should make it abundantly clear that the transaction is being carried out on behalf of the principal and should qualify any signature as such. Failure to do so will make the agent personally liable on the cheque or contract. A person who is not an agent but holds themselves out to be so is personally liable on a contract. A problem which can arise is that of the undisclosed principal. It may be that an agent, when dealing with a third party, fails to disclose the nature of their position and the third party takes the agent to be a principal. In such circumstances the third party may elect to bring a claim against the agent or the principal on the contract (provided the principal can be identified). The agent will not be liable on the contract where the agent discloses their position but refuses to identify the principal. Another factor is the extent of the agent's implied authority to the third party so far as their power to contract is concerned. An auctioneer has implied authority to make statements relevant to individual properties, however an estate agent has no implied authority to give a warranty that premises can be used for a specific purpose. In *Hill v Harris*,[176] an estate agent was deemed to have no authority to warrant that premises used for boot and shoe making could be occupied for a confectionery and tobacco business and was held personally liable. A similar finding was made in the

---

176 *Hill v Harris* [1965] 2 QB 601.

case of *Nimmo v Habton Farms*[177] where an agent went beyond their authority in agreeing terms for the purchase of a racehorse which subsequently had to be destroyed.

2.5.5 The Agency Relationship

The relationship of principal and agent imposes certain duties and obligations on both parties. The concept is primarily based in contract, although agency is a major exception to the privity rule (as a principal may bring an action under a contract made by an agent). In addition to the contractual aspects, there is also a fiduciary element of trust underlying the obligations between the parties.

2.5.5.1 Duties of an Agent

Skill and Care: An agent must exercise skill and care in the performance of their duties. The standard expected is that of a reasonably experienced member of whichever profession the agent belongs. Where an agent holds themselves out as having special skills, they must be able to apply them. There is a duty to obtain the best price possible if an agent is employed to sell. In *Keppel v Webster*,[178] estate agents were liable when they failed to inform their client that they had received a higher offer for their property.

Accounts: An agent must account to their principal in respect of all transactions connected with the agency. Accounts should be provided to the principal when requested. All sums received on the principal's behalf should be handed over, even if the agreement under which the money was received was illegal. The agent must not combine the principal's property with their own.

Delegation: An agent cannot further delegate duties to another, except in the usual course of business (by employing assistants and administrative staff) unless it is standard practice in a particular type of agency to delegate duties. Some delegation may be required for the proper performance of work. It is not normal in the construction industry for delegation to be allowed unless there is express authority.

Obedience: The agent is under a duty to obey the instructions of the principal unless they are illegal. If they fail to do so, an agent may be in breach of contract.

Good Faith: This is the very essence of the agency relationship – an agent must disclose anything which might affect the principal's position under the contract, and an agent must not act for both sides in a transaction. In *Fullwood v Hurley*[179] an agent acted for both sides in the purchase of a hotel without the knowledge of the respective parties. The court held that they were only entitled to commission from the seller who initially instructed them. The agent must not take a secret profit from their position, nor must they take bribes. Instead, the agent is entitled to commission or other agreed remuneration. In *Mahesan v Malaysia Officers Housing Association*,[180] both the amount of the bribe and the secret profit were recovered by the principal where the agent had accepted

177 *Nimmo v Habton Farms* [2004] QB 1.
178 *Keppel v Webster* [1927] 1 KB 527.
179 *Fullwood v Hurley* [1928] 1 KB 498.
180 *Mahesan v Malaysia Officers Housing Association* [1970] 1 WLR 241.

money allowing a third party to make a secret profit. The agent is accountable to their principal in respect of any benefit received from the unauthorised use of their position. If the obligation is broken, the principal may dismiss the agent without notice, recover the secret profit and withhold any commission payable. In the event of bribery, both the agent and the person paying the bribe may be guilty of a criminal offence.

2.5.5.2 Duties of the Principal

Payment: Any agreed amount of commission may be claimed by the agent, however payment can only be effectively claimed if there is an express or implied provision to that effect. The amount depends upon the contract or the custom in a particular trade or business.

Indemnity: The agent must be reimbursed for expenses properly incurred whilst carrying out their duties. Entitlement may be lost if the agent acts beyond the authority given to them or if they perform such duties negligently.

Lien: Any agent has a right to retain possession of goods where the principal has not paid their proper remuneration or reimbursed them.

2.5.6 Principal, Agent and AI

Conflicting theories exist on the role of agents and AI. Questions have centred in computer scientists as principal and AI as agent[181] and AI as integral to the role of agents (for example, a finance portfolio manager where the portfolio is AI-designed)[182] considering whether principal–agent relationships extend to include non-humans. In 2009, Chopra and White noted:

> Of relevance here is the concept of authority found in agency law, which circumscribes the authority the agent has to make decisions on behalf of the principal. Implicit in the existence of that authority is the discretion to take decisions the principal herself would not have taken. Thus, prima facie, artificial agents, concluding contracts on behalf of the corporations or users that deploy them, function like legal agents.[183]

This theory is centred in capacity and comparison – a legal agent does not need capacity to bind a principal, and by comparison, ships and companies recognition as artificial legal persons. In 2022, Aksoy stated:

---

181 E.S. Kim, 'Deep Learning and Principal-Agent Problems of Algorithmic Governance: The New Materialism Perspective,' *Technology in Society* (2020): 63 101378.

182 L. Fortin-Tyson, 'AI and Decision-Making: A Principal-Agent Perspective' 1CRED, Université Panthéon-As (2024).

183 S. Chopra and L.F. White, 'Artificial Agents and the Contracting Problem,' *Journal of Law, Technology, and Policy* (2009): 363–364.

> The AI agent does not have legal personality. It cannot be sued in court and it has no patrimony. Therefore, applying the law of agency seems to depend on granting intelligent agents a legal personality. Without legal personality, no declaration of intent would exist; without a declaration of intent, the law of agency is not applicable. Applying agency law principles to the problems that arise as a result of transactions generated by AI agents creates more problems than solutions. Therefore, applying the law of agency seems to depend on granting intelligent agents a legal personality.[184]

As the use of AI expands, so questions surrounding its role in agency-principal relationships, either as supplementary to or as an integral aspect of will continue to arise.

2.5.7 Termination of Agency

The agency relationship may be concluded by an act of the parties or by operation of law. A professional person will cease, in the ordinary course of events, to act as an agent on completion of the contract which they were engaged. Appointment as an agent may be limited to one or various stages of the work in construction projects. If the contract is for a fixed term, the relationship may terminate by expiration of time. A principal may revoke an agency appointment for good reason but will be subject to a claim for damages by the agent if the revocation was not justified. Death or insanity of either of the parties will terminate the relationship. Bankruptcy of either party will also bring the agency to an end.

2.5.7.1 The Commercial Agents (Council Directive) Regulations 1993

These regulations came into force on 1 January 1994 and extend the common law rights of commercial agents against their principals. Where the Regulations apply they include provisions for the remuneration of the agent where the agreement is silent on the issue. The Regulations provide for the agent's entitlement to commission both during and after the agency agreement has been terminated. Compensation following termination of the agency agreement is also included.

2.6 Construction Industry Contracts

As mentioned at the beginning of this chapter it is a widespread practice in commercial life to use standard forms of contract (SFCs). Contracts involving the sale of land and buildings are notable examples. In the construction and engineering industry, there are a many standard forms. In 1964, the Banwell Committee recommended the use of one single standard form of contract in the construction industry. This call for a single standard form has been repeated on several occasions through the decades. However, the reality has been an upsurge in the varying types of forms used. Although not essential, it is more convenient and safer to use a standard form where the contract is complex and expensive, and in many

---

184 P.C. Aksoy, 'AI as Agents,' in *The Cambridge Book of Artificial Intelligence, Global Perspectives on Law and Ethics*, ed. L.A. DiMatteo, C. Poncibo, and M. Cannarsa (Cambridge University Press, 2022), 146–160.

cases, a contracting party has little option other than to be a party to such an arrangement, although it is open to the parties to agree to modify the forms where appropriate. Using SFCs provides the parties to a contract with a degree of certainty as to their likely obligations under the contract, and their constant use in practice means that its users should be well versed in the form's application and how it distributes risk among those contracting.

Simply because a standard form of contract is used does not mean that the ordinary rules of contract law can be avoided. All of the standard forms of contract discussed here and used in the UK have been amended to ensure compliance with the Housing Grants, Construction and Regeneration Act 1996.

The Royal Institute of British Architects (RBIA) conduct a quadrennial (four yearly) survey into construction contracts.[185] Highlighting the relevance of SFCs, the 2022 survey asked 950 participants[186] *Which contracts have you/your organisation used most often?* and reported:

> When it comes to the contracts that people use most often, the most popular is the JCT contract suite (59%), followed by the RIBA building contracts (15%), then the NEC contracts (13%) and bespoke contracts (7%).[187]

Participants were also asked '*Which of the following contracts have you/your organisation used during the past 12 months*?' to which, summarised, the responses were:

- JCT contracts: 71%
- NEC contracts: 31%
- RIBA building contracts: 28%
- Bespoke contracts: 23%[188]

Replicating data obtained in previous RIBA reports,[189] SFCs in the design and construction industry are by far the most common form of contract.

2.6.1 JCT Standard Forms of Contract, 2024

In 1931 the JCT was set up, consisting of representatives from the construction industry and the professions involved in major building works. The JCT 2024 is the latest edition of the JCT standard forms of contract, within which there are 12 standard form contracts available for use. These include:

2.6.1.1 Construction Management Contract

For use on construction projects, where separate trade contracts are used for the work, and a construction manager oversees the work.

---

185 RIBA Construction Contracts and Law Report.

186 Comprised of 'clients, contractors and consultants/advisers, such as architects' RIBA Construction Contracts and Law Report, 2022, 5.

187 Ibid., 16.

188 Ibid., 17.

189 NBS, National Construction Contracts and Law Report, 2018, https://www.thenbs.com/knowledge/nbs-national-construction-contracts-and-law-survey

2.6.1.2 Design and Build Contract
For use where a contractor carries out both the design and the construction work.

2.6.1.3 Major Project Construction Contract
For use with large scale construction projects, where the contractor is responsible for the design and completing major work.

2.6.1.4 Measured Term Contract
For use by employers who have regular maintenance, minor works and improvements projects to be carried out by a single contractor over a specified period of time.

2.6.1.5 Standard Building Contract
For use in large or complex construction projects, normally administered by an architect, quantity surveyor or contract administrator.

2.6.2 Institute of Civil Engineers (ICE) Infrastructure Conditions of Contract

The first edition of the ICE contract was published in 1945, with the seventh and final edition published in 2001. The focus of the contract is on civil engineering, and the engineer has extensive powers of supervision and control. The engineer is not, as such, a party to the contract. The contract is made between the promoter/employer and the contractor. The engineer acts as an agent of the employer and in accordance with normal agency rules must act in the best interests of the employer. The engineer will have a contract with the employer based on the appropriate conditions of engagement.

2.6.3 Other Forms of Main Contract

2.6.3.1 FIDIC International Conditions
Since 1956, civil engineering contracts containing an international element have been able to take advantage of this form which is based on ICE conditions. The national law governing the contract must be stated in part 2. The engineer is appointed to act as representative and agent for the client. The contract contains the normal provisions to be found in standard forms relating to building works and provides for resolution of disputes by arbitration under the International Chamber of Commerce rules ICC.

2.6.3.2 GC/Works/1
These are encountered on government-based projects. A major characteristic of this form is the extensive powers of the employer, who is referred to as 'the authority'. The form provides for the appointment of a project manager who has similar powers to those of the engineer under the ICE conditions. This contract has some interesting provisions including the authority being able to order the contractor to accelerate their work and to make payment by reference to a cash flow 'S' curve rather than by reference to the measured work performed.

2.6.3.3 Sub-contracts

Sub-contracting is a major feature of the UK construction industry, with a considerable proportion of the work undertaken being carried out by specialists responsible for certain aspects of the contract. The practice of the employer making individual agreements with sub-contractors is not common in England and Wales and the standard procedure is for the work to be contracted to the main contractor who then sub-lets aspects of it but remains responsible for the overall work completed.

2.6.3.4 Management Contracts

The essence of a management contract is that the main contractor does not physically undertake any of the building work involved. Instead, the actual physical work is carried out by 'works contractors' (sub-contractors) and the main contractor manages the operations. The advantage to the management contractor is that contractual liability is diminished because, as a general course, the management contractor is only liable if the sub-contractor can also be held responsible.

2.6.3.5 NHBC Schemes

The National Housebuilding Council (NHBC) has been in existence since 1936 and now operates under the trademark of 'Buildmark'. This body was established by leading builders on a voluntary basis to encourage consistent high standards in house building. The system operates by the maintenance of a register of builders and developers whose work adheres to the standards prescribed by the Council. Those builders on the register enter into a standard form agreement with the first purchaser and with the NHBC. After stating that they are a party to the scheme, the builder warrants that the property has been built properly and that it complies with the Council's requirements. By registration on the scheme, the builder authorises the building council to issue the appropriate Buildmark documents. An insurance system operates to cover any defects arising in dwellings covered by the scheme.

In order to be covered by the scheme the defects must become apparent and be notified to the council within the first 10 years of construction. It is only in the 'initial guarantee period' of 2 years that full cover is given to the purchaser by the builder. During the remaining 8 years 'structural guarantee period', the NHBC (rather than the builder themselves) agrees to cover defects but is limited to major damage covered by structural defects or settlement/subsidence problems. Subsequent purchasers may also obtain the benefit of the scheme for the remaining unexpired term of the guarantee. The Council employs officers to inspect work completed and in the event of non-compliance a builder may be removed from the register. The contract specifies the obligations of the Council to satisfy any judgment obtained by the purchaser against the builder relating to defects in the construction of a dwelling. In practice, disputes are dealt with by conciliation and arbitration. The NHBC is one of the few regular users of the 'approved inspector' system in the building regulation process (see Chapter 5, paragraph 5.6).

2.6.3.6 NEC 4 Engineering and Construction Contract

The original version of this form, the NEC was published in 1993 by the Institution of Civil Engineers. The NEC was praised in the Latham Report as being a means of responding to growing discontent within the industry to long winded contractual procedures and adversarial attitudes. The NEC sought, and has succeeded, in being applicable to both building and engineering projects. A further objective for the NEC was to accommodate all varieties of design responsibilities. This is achieved by the flexibility of using core clauses which can be adapted to various types of projects. Secondary option clauses can also be 'bolted on' to the contract to suit the client's requirements. All the clauses are written in plain English using only common words and written in the present tense.

2.7 Housing Grants, Construction and Regeneration Act 1996 (HGCRA)

Commonly referred to as the Construction Act, the HGCRA, specifically Part 2 which deals with Construction Contracts, sought to empower those within the construction industry who had found themselves at the mercy of their contractual partners when a dispute arose. Under the Act, a party may now know why they have not been paid and, if they do not approve of the reasons given, have the power to do something about it through the dispute resolution procedure of adjudication. Adjudication has replaced litigation and arbitration as the industry's preferred form of dispute resolution. The Act also requires that Construction Contracts include certain payment mechanisms.

The use of standard contracts and the HGCRA are considered in detail in Chapter 3.

2.7.1 Background

This Act was the result of a number of the recommendations made in the Latham Report and subsequent Department of the Environment Consultation papers. It is also consistent with the overall desire of the Woolf reforms (see Chapter 1) to promote alternative dispute resolution as a means of resolving disputes. It received the Royal Assent in July 1996 and applied to all construction contracts entered into after 1 May 1998. Several small amendments have been made to the Act following a long consultation with construction industry stakeholders. Twelve years after the Construction Act came into force, it was amended by Part 8 Local Democracy, Economic Development and Construction Act 2009. The amended Act applies to construction contracts entered into on or after 1 October 2011 (England and Wales).

2.7.2 Definitions and Scope

The Act applies to 'Construction Contracts' which are defined as agreements with any person for the carrying out of construction operations. It extends to subcontracts and management contracts. It also covers agreements for the provision of architectural design or surveying work, and advice on building, engineering, interior work and exterior decoration or landscaping work in relation to construction operations.

2.7.3 Adjudication

Section 108 Act provides that a Construction Contract must contain certain provisions relating to adjudication otherwise the provisions of the 'Scheme' will apply. This was confirmed in *Yuanda (UK) Co Ltd v WW Gear Construction Ltd*[190] wherein the court held:

> if the contract does not comply – in any respect – with the requirements of subsections (1) to (4), the adjudication provisions of the Scheme apply. As we have already seen, the adjudication provisions in the Scheme are those contained in Part I. If there is any non-compliance, the adjudication provisions in Part I of the Scheme are brought in – lock, stock and barrel.

The 'Scheme' is therefore the default position with which contracts drafts people must comply. The right to adjudication arises in respect of any dispute occurring between the parties to a construction contract, and where Construction Contract content is inadequate, the Scheme will apply 'lock, stock and barrel'.

Construction contracts must contain (or, without which, will be implied into the contract) the following provisions:

- The right of any party to give notice of intention to submit a dispute to adjudication at any time.
- A timetable which provides for an adjudicator to be appointed and the dispute referred within 7 days of notice.
- The adjudicator shall reach a decision within 28 days of the matter being referred to them, this period to be extended by mutual consent of the parties.
- The 28-day period may be extended by another 14 days with the consent of the party who originally referred the matter.
- The adjudicator has a duty to act impartially.
- The adjudicator must take the initiative in ascertaining the facts and the law.
- The adjudicator's decision will be binding until the dispute is finally determined by arbitration or by a court of law.
- The adjudicator is not liable for acts or omissions in carrying out their functions unless they acted in bad faith.
- The adjudicator's decision may be regarded by the parties as a final determination of the matter despite the interim nature of their decision.

2.7.4 Payment Mechanism

Sections 109–112 Act covers payment under construction contracts, including for a system of stage payments and the prohibition of payments under construction contracts being dependent on payment from a third party. It also includes:

190 *Yuanda (UK) Co Ltd v WW Gear Construction Ltd* [2010] EWHC 720 (TCC).

- The entitlement to payment by instalments, stage payments or otherwise by periodic payments (s109);
- an adequate mechanism for determining what payments become due under the contract, and when, along with a final date for payment for any sums which become due (s110);
- payment notices (s110A and s110B);
- payment of the notified sum (s111); and
- a right to suspend for non-payment (s112).

In contrast to the adjudication approach, where inadequacies render the Scheme applying in its entirety, for payment mechanisms, the statutory regime is applicable only where necessary to rectify non-compliance. This position was confirmed in *Bennett (Construction) Limited v CIMC MBS Limited*[191] within which the Court of Appeal held:

> (t)he purpose of the Act was to provide for certain minimum, mandatory standards so as to achieve certainty and regular cash flow. Save in perhaps exceptional circumstances, it was not designed to delete a workable payment regime which the parties had agreed, and replace it with an entirely different payment regime based on a radically changed set of parameters. It seems to me that that could only happen where the regime which had been agreed was so deficient that wholesale replacement was the only viable option.

---

191 *Bennett (Construction) Limited v CIMC MBS Limited* [2019] EWCA Civ 1515.

3

Construction Contract Law

CONTENTS

3.1 What Is Construction Law?

There is no specific body of law called 'construction law' but it is a term used to describe all law which relates specifically, or generally to the construction industry and more particularly to the operation of construction contracts. Much of the law of contract and tort will apply in all industries in the same way as they do to construction, however, there are also some specific laws and regulations which were (are) enacted to alleviate perceived problems with the industry's operation, such as the construction part of the Housing Grants Construction and Regeneration Act 1996 (as amended) (HGCRA).

3.1.1 What Is a Construction Contract?

At the most basic level, a construction contract is a legally enforceable agreement, between two parties, for work and materials. In practice, it is more complex than that as there are usually several contracts for each construction project each with differing parties, all with different responsibilities. There is a wide statutory definition of what is a construction contract provided in Section 104 of the HGCRA, as follows:

104 Construction contracts.

1. [...] "construction contract" means an agreement with a person for any of the following—
   a. the carrying out of construction operations;

b. arranging for the carrying out of construction operations by others, whether under sub-contract to him or otherwise;
c. providing his own labour, or the labour of others, for the carrying out of construction operations.

Section 105 provides a very wide definition of 'construction operations' and covers most things in the industry including all stages of construction and renovation projects and Section 106 explains that the HGCRA does not apply to contracts with residential occupiers; that is individuals having construction work undertaken to their primary dwelling.

3.1.2 Key Parties to/in Construction Contracts

Most contracts will only have two parties, the employer and the contractor. The employer is the party paying for the work and the contractor is the party doing the work. However, most construction projects will have considerably more parties involved and each one of those parties will be either an employer or contractor in one or more contracts which all relate to the same project. Try not to confuse the terms employer and contractor for client and main contractor. For example, in a contract between the main contractor and a sub-contractor the main contractor will be called the employer, and the sub-contractor will be called the contractor.

The client on a project will be the party for which the project is being completed. That is the party paying the whole of the project's costs and to which the finished project will belong. Frequently the client will employ other parties to give instructions on the contract(s), such as architects, quantity surveyors or contract administrators.

The architect or design team are those who design the building to the client's needs and wants. The architect is often empowered to give instructions on behalf of the client, for things such as changes to materials or design, subject to what the contract allows. The architect is traditionally employed as the contract administrator.

The contract administrator is the party tasked with ensuring that the requirements of the contract are administered. For example, that payment notices are prepared and sent and that correct payments are made per the contract sum. In other words, any administrative tasks required by the contract are the responsibility of the contract administrator. They also act as an interface between the client and the contractor and oversee work on site. The contract administrator is not always a party to the contract but is often a role undertaken by one of the architect, quantity surveyor or construction manager.

The quantity surveyor is responsible for valuing the works and materials for the project and the production of the bill of quantities (BoQ). The BoQ, is a document appended to the contract which details the specifics of the materials and labour and the costs of them. They may also be given the role of contract administrator.

Structural engineers are part of the design team and may be employed directly by the client or subcontracted to the architects or contractors. They are responsible for the structural integrity of the building.

A management contractor is employed by the client if the client would prefer a design and build project. The management contractor will manage the whole project. The works contractor is the party which physically undertakes the building works.

3.1.3 Types of Contracting Structures

There are different methods of contracting in common use. General contracting, which is often called the traditional method, is where a client employs all parties under separate contracts. It is called the traditional method because it is how it was always done; however, it is becoming less common. Other procurement methods include design and build, management contracting and partnering/collaborative contracting.

As can be seen in Figure 3.1, denoted by the solid lines, the client employs the designers, engineers, quantity surveyors and main contractor under separate contracts. The main contractor will employ several sub-contractors for distinct parts of the project, also denoted by solid lines.

When the client employs a contractor and an architect, the architect, with input from engineers, designs the build, and manages it in the role of contract administrator. The contractor works for the client but takes instruction from the architect, although there is no direct link between the client unless collateral contracts are in place. There is no contractual link between the architect and contractor.

There is no contractual responsibility between the designers, which may cause problems if one is reliant upon another to complete their job before them.

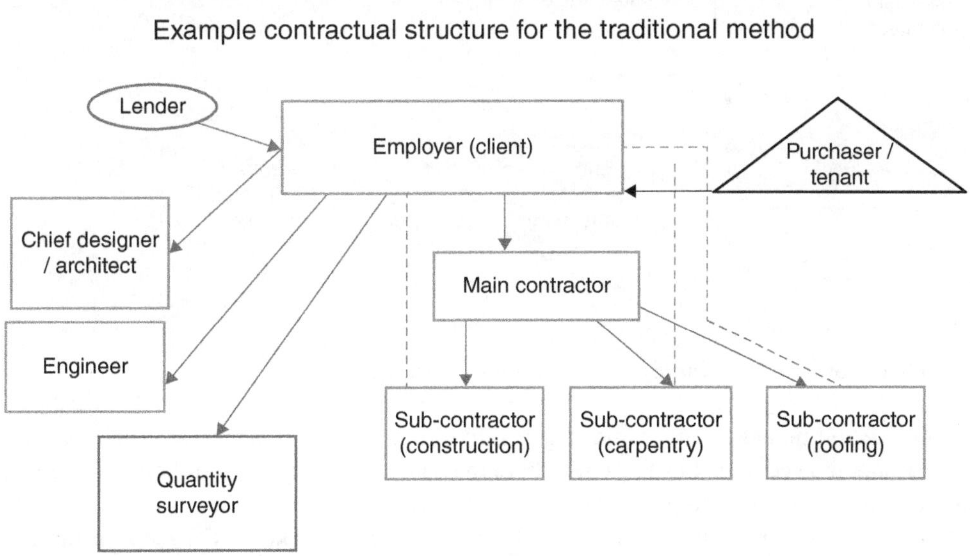

Figure 3.1 Contractual structure of general contracting.

The sub-contractors are linked to the client by collateral contracts/warranties (denoted by broken lines), but the sub-contractor cannot sue the client if they do not get paid and nor does the client have any control over how the sub-contractor undertakes the work.

The traditional method is used less often than its name suggests and is now used for projects such as landmark buildings, complicated buildings, where the client wants to participate considerably in the designing of the building, in the case of the refurbishment of an existing building, and civil engineering works.

Figure 3.2 is an example of the contracting structure when the client employs a main contractor/managing contractor only and that party employs all other parties. This is a much simpler structure, for the client.

Design and Build has become much more popular than the traditional method. It is a simpler contractual structure and risk lies with just one party; the main contractor which has all contractual responsibility. The main reason that design and build was not more frequently used is a social one: until recently it was unheard of for firms of designers to be subcontractors of builders.

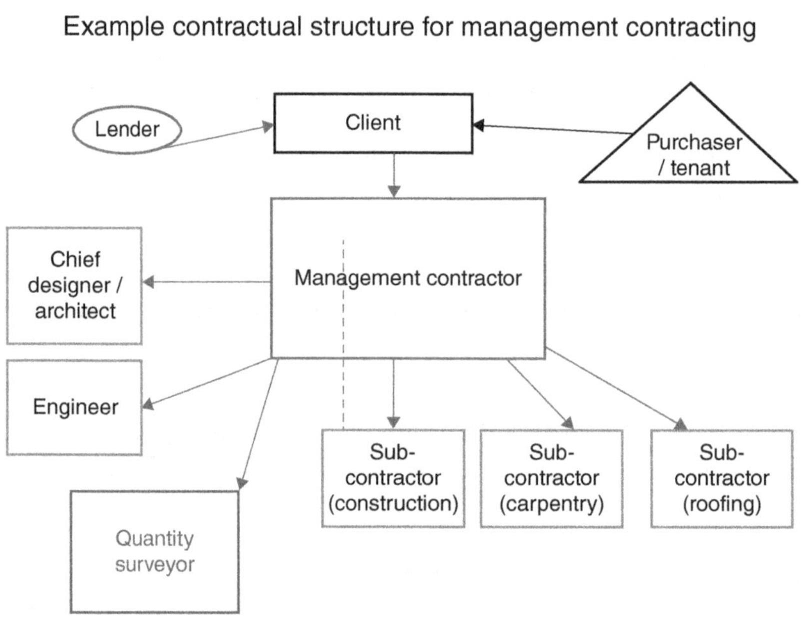

Figure 3.2 Contractual structure of management contracting.

Construction management contracts are used in the context of extensive developments such as shopping centres, in situations where the contractor needs to start before design is complete and/or the building is needed in a hurry, by a set date.

In the above circumstances, the contractor is not placed to take on the risks ordinarily taken on by a contractor because such projects are subject to constant changes, but like design and build, the project is managed entirely by 'one pair of hands'.

Collaborative contracting (sometimes called partnering) is an initiative for all parties to work together with mutual trust and respect. The contractor carries less risk and parties learn from each other about how projects may be completed more efficiently. Difficulties or differences should be addressed as they arise, involving all the parties, with the hope that projects may be completed at a lower cost.

A Government initiative from 2011 made collaborative contracting a requirement for public sector contracts. Initially parties would use standard form contracts with a partnering agreement on the side, encouraging parties to abide by a partnering charter, until institutions started to develop contracts for the purpose.

3.1.4 Standard Form Contracts

Standard form contracts are contracts which have already been partially drafted. The 'standard' terms which are used for most projects have already been written and should, therefore, not need to be renegotiated. In theory one need only input the specific details of the project and the parties, and the rest is already taken care of. Unfortunately, it is seldom that simple with parties frequently requesting amendments to what were designed as standard terms. In general, there are two types of standard form contracts; the first type is those written by one party which are written in such a way as to protect that party. They will often contain pre-requisites to enter and are offered on a 'take it or leave it' basis. These are usually put forward by exceptionally large undertakings which are large enough to make such a demand and still find contractors to undertake the work. For example, a large supermarket or shopping centre chain.

The second type are those written by various bodies which seek to spread the risk fairly between employer and contractor. These are contracts such as the Joint Contracts Tribunal (JCT) suite of contracts or the New Engineering Contract (NEC) suite of contracts.

There are various standard form contracts in common use within the industry, drafted by companies and/or professional institutions for use by their members or anyone willing to pay for the drafted standard form contract. The most common ones tend to be the JCT suite of contracts, written by the Joint Contracts Tribunal and the NEC suite of contracts written by the New Engineering Contracts. Other contract suites include FIDIC (International Federation of Consulting Engineers), ICE (Institution of Civil Engineers) and ACA (Association of Consulting Architects) standard form of contract for project partnering.

Both JCT and FIDIC's contract conditions concentrate on the obligations of the parties, like most contracts in most businesses. The NEC and ACA, however, place the emphasis in the contract conditions on how the project is to be managed and are collaborative in their approach. The idea for these types of contracts is to reduce the number of disputes that may arise.

A standard form contract may be amended. Parties are free to agree on all terms of their contract between them, which includes using a standard form contract, such as the NEC, and making their own bespoke changes. This should always be done with great care. Contracts are complex documents with clauses which often cross reference other contract clauses – sometimes several other clauses – and frequently several other documents, such as drawings or specifications. If the amendment is not carefully considered, it could invalidate other parts of the contract by making them a nonsense or simply changes other clauses inadvertently. What is worse is that where there is a contradiction in terms i.e. one part of the contract says one thing and a different part says something else, the *contra proferentem* rule comes into play, which means that the meaning will be construed (interpreted) against the person who proffered (proposed) the term. In short, a term that was designed to protect you will no longer protect and may even go against you.

It is clearly especially important that all contract documents be crosschecked carefully to ensure that each document matches its counterparts and that there are no conflicting or confusing terms within the contract and all its associated documents. This becomes even more important if you have subcontracts which should have the same terms as the main contract.

3.2 Formation of Construction Contracts

Construction contracts are formed in the same way as any contract. They must contain agreement (offer and acceptance), consideration and an intention of the parties to create legal relations (to be legally bound) Please see Chapter 2 in this book for details of what makes a contract legally binding.

3.2.1 Tendering Considerations

A call for tender, in legal terms, is an invitation to treat and nothing more. The winning tender is an offer which then, theoretically, could be accepted. In the construction industry, it is exceedingly rare, for anything other than a contract for a small and straightforward job, for the tender to be accepted without further negotiation.

Whilst a call for tender does not usually form a contract, there are some occasions when a contract is formed by implication based on the requirements for the tender process. Responding to tender requests is a speculative endeavour with the tenderer accepting the risk that their bid may not win. However, a call for tenders may become a contract to consider the tender where the party seeking tenders has indicated that complying tenders will be considered,[1] and/or that all tenderers will be treated fairly.[2]

Despite that preparing a tender is not normally paid for, and continuing with the idea of fairness, a tenderer asked to undertake more than is necessary is entitled to be paid for that work. For example, in *William Lacey (Hounslow) Ltd v Davis* [1957],[3] the claimant had tendered to reconstruct war damaged property. The defendant required a grant from the War Damage Commission and asked the claimant to prepare estimates and schedules for the grant application on the understanding that the claimant would be given the contract for the work. Instead, the defendant sold the property with the benefit of the grant. The court, whilst acknowledging that tendering is prospective, implied that on this occasion there was a term that the defendant would pay a reasonable sum for the work which had been over and above the usual tendering requirements.

---

1 *Blackpool and Fylde Aero Club Ltd v Blackpool Borough Council* [1990] 3 All ER 25.
2 *Harmon CFEM Facades (UK) Ltd v The Corporate Officer of the House of Commons* (2000) 67 Con LR 1.
3 2 All ER 712.

The most common response to a tender in the construction industry is a letter of intent. A letter which suggests that the tender is accepted subject to contract i.e. further negotiations on the specific details of the works and the contractual terms.

3.2.2 Use of Letters of Intent

It has been said that in 85% of cases, work is started based on a letter of intent.[4] Letters of intent come in many forms, and it is the content of the letter which will determine whether any contract is formed using it. It is for this reason that when drafting a letter acknowledging an intent to enter a contract, one must understand the exact nature of the intention and be very precise with the drafting to ensure that the letter does as the sender intends. For example, is the letter, merely responding to previous negotiations and asking for further negotiations before agreement, or is it suggesting that work take place prior to finalisation of the full contract? And, if so, is it clear exactly what work is to be undertaken and how much will be paid for that work? A poorly considered or written letter of intent could result in there being no contractual obligation when one was required or a contractual obligation where one was not intended. This is only a problem if one party (or both) has undertaken any work/fulfilled any obligations in relation to the project which is still in negotiation. Whilst, at first thought, only the contractor will suffer from not being paid, the employer should be aware that without a binding contract, there will be no guarantees of the workmanship or materials and no recourse for losses or delays from what would have been breach of contract, had a legally binding contract existed.

3.2.2.1 Do We Have a Contract?

When considering a dispute between parties relating to whether payment is due, or an obligation to repair or correct something referenced in the letter or associated negotiations, the courts will look at all the correspondence and actions of the parties as a whole[5] to ascertain whether an agreement (legally binding contract) exists between the parties and what was agreed. This will include any email or written communications, any draft drawings, specifications, or bill of quantities as well as the wording of the letter of intent. It can also include oral communications (although these are much more difficult to prove).

We now know what the court is looking at, but what is it specifically that it is looking for? The court is trying to ascertain if a contract came into being and, if so, if any of the agreed terms have been breached. It is highly unusual for a court to find that a contract for the whole of the originally planned works has been made, although this can happen.[6] It is more likely that an ancillary contract has been formed based on the work requested in the letter and nothing more. An ancillary contract requires the same essential elements of any contract; agreement, consideration, and an intention to create legal relations (see Chapter 2).

4 *Jarvis Interiors v Gilliard Homes* [2000] BLR 33.
5 *Gibson v Manchester City Council* [1979] 1 All ER 972.
6 *RTS Flexible Systems Ltd v Molkerei Alois Muller GmbH* [2010] UKSC 14.

Let's start with agreement: When parties haven't finalised a written contract, it is often difficult to see where offer and acceptance occurred, but despite this a contract can nevertheless for formed, as in the case of *Trentham (G Percy) Ltd v Archital Luxfer*[7] where a contract was accepted by performance, despite that all the terms of the contract had not been agreed. The court will therefore look to see if, at any time, an agreement came into being through the actions of the parties. To form a contract, only the essential terms need to be agreed. *British Steel Corporation v Cleveland Bridge & Engineering Co Ltd* [1984] 1 All ER 504 outlined what the court considers as essential as being those terms that are required to make the contract work i.e. can both parties perform their obligations without any additional information. The essential terms are thought to be:

- the scope of the work or services to be undertaken. That is what, when, where, and how;
- the price or rates for the work. It could, however, be implied that a fair price would be paid (*Drake & Scull Engineering Ltd v Higgs and Hill Northern Ltd*)[8];
- the time within which the work or services are to be performed; and
- the method by and time within which payment is to be made. This, too, may be a little redundant since payment clauses are implied into all construction contracts by the Housing Grants Construction and Regeneration Act 1996 (Section 3.4 in this chapter).

Consideration is generally easier in the cases of letters of intent, as there is almost always a price in the response to tender. Consideration is the exchange of promises.[9] Each party must provide something to the other. This is sometimes described as a benefit and burden. Each party has a burden to discharge in exchange for a benefit. In construction contracts, this is generally very clear. The contractor agrees to do work (the burden) in exchange for payment (the benefit) and the employer agrees to make payment (the burden) in exchange for the completed work (the benefit). It is the exchange of these promises that creates the consideration, not the execution of them. *Re Casey's Patents*[10] advises us that where one party has requested work of another, in a business context then it is assumed that it will be paid for, so the price may be calculated at a later date. Furthermore, failure to do the work or pay the price does not mean that the contract lacks consideration, it merely means that one party has breached the contract.

Finally, we come to the intention to create legal relations. Here, the courts may look at the agreement and consideration, if one of those is missing, then they may conclude that that is because the parties did not intend to create legal relations (to be legally bound). A lack of clarity can also denote a lack of intention as well as a lack of agreement. If there is clarity, then in business situations it is assumed that the parties wish to be legally bound by their agreement, unless they include an express statement to the contrary.[11] Most commonly, that express statement is the phrase 'subject to contract'. Where a party states that

---

7 [1993] 1 Lloyed's Rep 25.
8 (1995) CLJ 214-226(7).
9 Dunlop v Selfridge Ltd [1915] AC 847.
10 [1892] 1 Ch 104.
11 *Rose and Frank Co v Crompton Bros Ltd* [1925] AC 445.

their agreement is subject to contract, what that party means is that either party may walk away at anytime[12] up until a formal contract is agreed.

There are, however, instances where the courts have said that there is a contract, despite the use of the words 'subject to contract' or similar. Firstly, where an ancillary contract is said to have been agreed, the courts may deem the words 'subject to contract' to refer to the main contract and not the ancillary work requested at an earlier stage. In *Turriff Construction & Turriff Ltd v Regalia Knitting Mills* (1971) 9 BLR 20, a sub-contractor had begun work on a letter of intent, which had been marked 'the whole to be subject to agreement on an acceptable contract'. As the sub-contractor had requested the letter as comfort that they would be paid, the court found that an ancillary contract had been formed and that the statement regarding subject to agreement, referred to the 'whole' contract and did not apply to the requested work which created an ancillary contract.

In *Trentham (G Percy) Ltd v Archital Luxfer Ltd* [1993] 1 Lloyd's Rep 25, work had been started by the sub-contractor at the request of a letter of intent and monthly payments had been made as the work progressed. Lord Justice Steyn stated that, where work had been done and paid for, no reasonable businessman would conclude that no contract existed and that, therefore, where work had been done and paid for, the court will always try to imply that a contract had been formed. This cannot always be the case though. In *J Jarvis & Sons Plc v Gilliard Homes Ltd* [1999] ABC.L.R. 11/12 work started, and payments were made, but the letter of intent contained a condition precedent using the words 'If we do not enter into a formal contract with you...' and went on to set out what would happen in that situation. In other words, we do not have a contract until... The court held that *Trentham* did not apply in this situation, because the parties had agreed that no contract would exist and, whilst the price had been agreed, the other main terms had not (i.e. the essential terms were missing). The court went on to say that it was loath to find that no agreement existed between two experienced businessmen, but all had been agreed 'subject to contract'. In other words, experienced businesspeople should know what they are doing when using the words 'subject to contract'.

The final example is where parties have agreed 'subject to contract' but then proceeded by acting as if the contract was in place. In *RTS Flexible Systems Ltd v Molkerei Alois Muller GmbH* [2010] UKSC 14, the court held that the parties' conduct was such that they had waived their right to claim that the earlier stipulation of 'subject to contract' still stood. The court referred to the reasonable honest businessman test and asked, 'would a reasonable honest man assume that there was an intention to be legally bound?' The court found that on this occasion, the reasonable, honest person would believe the parties to be legally bound. The parties had agreed that no contract would exist between them until such time as the document had been signed and delivered in triplicate. Whilst the signing never took place, all other aspects of the contract were adhered to. The court held that the parties' conduct clearly indicated that they had decided to waive their right to that particular term. This would indicate that failure to physically sign the documentation will not prevent the agreement becoming binding, if there is other evidence of the parties' intentions.

12 *Regalian Properties v London Docklands Development Corp* (1995) 11 Const LJ 127.

3.3 Workmanship and Materials

The quality of workmanship and the quality and type of materials are key in all builds. The contract, therefore, should be clear as to what is to be used and the standard of workmanship required. Where parties have made no stipulations, then the following terms will automatically be implied as if they were part of the contract agreed between the parties.

3.3.1 Implied Terms Re Workmanship

The common law clause in most contracts regarding workmanship stems from the seventeenth century case of *Duncan v Blundell*.[13] This case applies to all contracts where work will be done in a workmanlike manner, with the skill and care of an ordinary competent contractor. This common law is supplemented by statutory law in the Supply of Goods and Services Act 1982. Section 13[14] states '... where the supplier is acting in the course of a business, there is an implied term that the supplier will carry out the service with reasonable care and skill'.

3.3.2 Duty to Warn of Danger in Carrying Out the Work

Part of the duty to use skill and care is a duty to warn an employer if the contract requires work to be undertaken that may be dangerous.[15] It is no defence to claim that you were unaware, if a competent contractor would have been aware. In *Lindenberg v Canning & ors*[16] the contractor, following design drawings, removed a wall which was a supporting wall. The employer sued the contractor and the designer. Removing the wall caused a partial collapse of the building. The contractor claimed that he only needed to warn of danger of which he was aware and that as he had not known that the wall was a supporting wall he was unaware of the danger. The wall was some nine inches thick, which led the court to find that the contractor was incompetent, because a competent builder would have realised that it was very likely to be a supporting wall. The case confirmed that the duty is to warn of design defects of which the contractor is or ought to be aware. Actual awareness is not required, provided that an ordinary competent contractor should have been aware. Whilst the designer who had provided the drawings was found primarily responsible for the costs of reinstatement, the contractor had to pay 25%.

A similar situation occurred in the case of *GCA Brown Ltd v Carr*[17] where there was an error in the drawings. On this occasion, the contractor didn't blindly follow plans, but instead, chose to alter the work requested. Sadly, the change did not make the problem safer and there was still a collapse. As the contractor had amended the works, rather than warn and seek further instruction, they had effectively accepted design responsibility for the changes which they had made to the design and were, therefore, fully responsible for the collapse

13 (1820) 171 ER 749.
14 The Supply of Goods and Services Act 1982.
15 *SM Goldstein & Co (PTY) Ltd v Catkin Park Hotel* [2004] BLR 369.
16 (1992) 62 BLR 147.
17 [2006] EWCA Civ 785.

A contractor is not under a duty to warn of a danger of which they are unaware (unless, of course, they should have known, see *Lindenberg v Joe Canning* above), particularly if they are not the contractor undertaking the work which carries the danger. *Aurum Investments Ltd v Avonforce Ltd (in Liquidation) and others*[18] involved a project to excavate and build a basement and garage under a property in North London. The structural engineer for the main contractor recommended underpinning of the neighbour's wall, prior to excavation. This was done under sub-contract by a specialist underpinning firm. Despite this, the wall collapsed during the excavation due to a lack of lateral support. The main contractor, defending the claim against them from the employer, added the underpinning sub-contractor to the claim, claiming that the underpinning sub-contractor should have warned of the possibility of collapse during excavation. The court held that the underpinning sub-contractor had no duty to warn as it could not have anticipated that the excavation work would be carried out in such a way as to compromise the safety of the underpinning, and, as the court was aware that the main contractor was advised by structural engineers, who were better qualified to advise than the underpinning sub-contractor. Furthermore, the excavation work (which caused the danger) was not undertaken by the underpinning sub-contractor, nor were the methods of excavation known to them.

Finally, warning alone may not be enough. The Court of Appeal made it clear in *Plant Construction Plc v Clive Adams Associates and JMH Construction Services Ltd*[19] that dangerous work should not be undertaken, when it held that the contractor should have warned 'in more vigorous terms'. JMH were subcontracted, on a 'design and build' basis, to Plant Construction which had been employed by Ford Motor Company to carry out works at one of their plants. The subcontracted work involved excavating pits to be used for engine mounting. JMH were to undertake the sub-structure work, whilst Clive Adams and Associates were subcontracted as consultant structural engineers to design and monitor the sub-structure works. One of the pits was to be very close to a pillar which was part of the roof support structure. The excavation needed to go under part of the pillar for a temporary period. JMH and Clive Adams designed a temporary structure, but Ford's engineer insisted that their method wasn't necessary, and that Acrow props could be used to take the weight of the pillar which was to be partially excavated. JMH and Clive Adams expressed concern but were asked by Plant Construction to undertake the work using Ford Motor Company's engineer's method of support. During the period when the temporary roof support was in place, there was heavy snow. The extra weight caused the roof structure to collapse. Ford successfully sued Plant for just over £1.3 million. Plant sought to recoup this loss together with £615,000 of costs and repair work from Clive Adams and JMH. Clive Adams settled for £250,000, the maximum value of their liability insurance policy, but JMH proceeded with its defence of the claim and lost. As contractors on a design and build basis, they were responsible for the design of the support structure, despite warning that the ultimate client's request may not be strong enough. This leaves contractors in a tricky position. Do as the client requests to maintain a good working relationship or refuse to undertake potentially dangerous work. The law has made it clear that doing potentially

---

18 [2000] 2 All ER 385.
19 [2000] BLR 137.

dangerous work is not an option, but commercial pressures from clients are not always easy to navigate. Whilst, from a contractual perspective, an indemnity could be sought to confirm no liability for proceeding with the work, it cannot indemnify a company from potential criminal responsibility under legislation such as the Corporate Manslaughter and Corporate Homicide Act 2007[20] for causing the death of a person. An alternative way of dealing with the issue of danger might be to use a form of dispute resolution; a second opinion on the safety of the aspect would strengthen the argument for proceeding, or not, as the case may be.

3.3.3 Implied Terms Regarding Materials

As with workmanship, the law has also implied terms into contracts both through legislation and common law regarding quality and fitness for purpose of materials. Responsibility depends on who purchases the goods and who chooses them for the purpose of use. The Sale of Goods Act 1979 and the Supply of Goods and Services Act 1982 both imply terms regarding materials for commercial contracts. The Consumer Rights Act 2015 covers liability to consumers for domestic contracts relating to the standard of workmanship and materials. These are what are referred to as your 'statutory rights'. The statutory terms from the 1979[21] and 1982[22] Acts concern title of the goods, description of the goods and fitness for purposes of the goods:

- Title – that the seller has the right to sell and that the goods are free from encumbrances. That is that they are owned by the seller and there are no debts secured against them;
- Description – where goods have been described or compared with a sample, those goods will match the description or sample; and
- Fitness for Purpose and Satisfactory Quality – that goods sold (materials used) '[...] will be reasonably fit for the purpose for which they are required and [...] of satisfactory quality'.[23]

Additionally, case law implies warranties into contracts that the materials will be of good quality, and will be fit for their purpose, except where the employer places no reliance on the contractor's skill and judgement in selection of the materials.

The key aspect here is 'use of skill and judgement' when choosing the materials. Where a contractor must merely accept goods delivered or is told to purchase a particular material from a particular supplier, the contractor is not said to warrant the material as of good quality or fit for purpose.[24] However if a contractor is told to buy a particular material, but not from where to buy it, they do warrant that the material purchased will be of merchantable quality even if they do not warrant that it will be fit for purpose. In *Young & Marten*

20 Corporate Manslaughter and Corporate Homicide Act 2007.
21 Sale of Goods Act 1977.
22 Supply of Goods and Services Act 1982.
23 S. 4 Supply of Goods and Services Act 1982.
24 *Gloucestershire County Council v Richardson* [1968] 1 AC 480.

Ltd v McManus Child Ltd[25] the Court of Appeal held the contractor liable for the material purchased, when it subsequently turned out to be faulty. The contract specified a particular roof tile from a particular manufacturer, but the contractor was responsible for sourcing the material and, therefore would use their own 'skill and judgement' in so doing. On this occasion, the 'skill and judgement' of the contractor wasn't at issue because the materials had latent defects that no other contractor would have spotted and which were not noticed until after completion of the building. Nevertheless, the Court said the warranty as to the quality of materials was still breached. It came to that conclusion for policy reasons and because not to do so would leave the employer inadequately compensated for the faulty materials. By making the contractor liable, the contractor could claim under the Sale of Goods Act 1979[26] against the seller for breach of contract. This would create a chain of liability in that the seller could similarly claim against the company from which they purchased and so on, all the way back to the manufacturer, which would ultimately have to pay for the faulty material. If the contractor had not been found liable, the employer would have still been able to claim from the manufacturer but under the law of the tort of negligence rather than under contract law. Under negligence the employer would only have been compensated for any consequential losses as a result of the poor quality, but would not have been able to claim for the re-building of the roof itself. For more information on the difference between claims in torts and claims in contract, see Chapters 2 and 4, respectively.

Fitness for purpose of a material has two aspects. Firstly, if the material is not of merchantable quality, as in the case of Young & Marten, the material is also not fit for purpose. Secondly, and more usually, fitness for purpose refers to the suitability of the material for its use. Where a contractor is told what to use, they do not use their 'skill and judgement' in choosing the material for its purpose and therefore do not warrant that the material will be fit for that purpose (notwithstanding that it must still be of good quality).

Ultimately, the choice of material is a matter of design. In a design and build contract, the contractor will always be responsible for material and workmanship, but where the contract is merely to build to the employer's specifications, then the employer (or whoever the employer contracted to do the design work) will be responsible for the fitness for purpose of the material for a particular use. In *Rotherham Metropolitan Borough Council v Frank Haslam Milan and M G Gleeson*[27] the contractor was provided with a choice of materials to use for backfilling. The question was whether that choice meant that the contractor used its skill and judgment or whether the contract meant that all the materials listed were considered fit for use.

The contract was the JCT Standard Form of Building Contract, 1963 edition:

Clause 1(1) required the Contractor to:

> carry out and complete the Works shown upon the Contract Drawings and described by or referred to in the Contract Bills....in compliance therewith, using materials...of the quality therein specified...

25 [1969]1 AC 454.
26 Section 14, Sale of Goods Act 1979.
27 [1996] 78 BLR 1.

Clause 6(1) stated:

> all material, goods and workmanship shall so far as procurable be of the respective kind and standards described in the Contract Bills

The Contract Bills read:

> Granular hardcore shall be well graded or uncrushed gravel, stone, rock fill, crushed concrete or slag or natural sand or a combination of any of these. It shall not contain organic material, material susceptible to spontaneous combustion, material in a frozen condition, clays or more than 0.2% of sulphate ions as determined by BS 1377.

The contractor chose to use 'slag'. Slag is a common waste product from mining and steel production. In this case steel slag was used. The building was constructed over the top of a number of cellars and after completion cracks appeared in the ground floor slab as a result of the unsuitable nature of the fill used around the foundations. At trial the issue was whether the type of fill material used was dependent on the skill and discretion of Haslam. This Appeal case held Haslam not to be responsible for the material's unsuitability because it had been chosen from a list of material deemed suitable by the employer (employer's designer). The material chosen and used was of merchantable quality (unlike the material in *Young & Marten*). Furthermore, the architect approved the chosen material for backfill. At the time of the work, in the late 1970s, it was not generally known that steel slag had expansive properties and should not be used as backfill. Had it been generally known, the contractor would have had a duty to warn the employer of the dangers of its use for that purpose (see section 3.3.2 above).

3.3.4 Design Liability

At its simplest, liability for design lies with the party which carried out the design. In traditional contract structures, where the employer employs both a contractor and a designer under separate contracts, then the designer (architect or engineer) is responsible. Unless, as has been explained above, the contractor does not warn the client of any design errors that may be dangerous and just merely carries them out (see section 3.3.2 above). In which case the contractor will bear some of the responsibility for losses caused.[28]

The designer is not able to delegate its responsibility to the client for any part of the design. If the client is requesting something beyond the designer's expertise, then, according to *Moresk Cleaners Ltd v Hicks*,[29] the designer has three options:

- Refuse the commission (not agree to do the design for the client);
- Explain to the client about the lack of specific expertise and suggest that the employer hire's a specialist for that particular part of the design; or

---

28 *Lindenberg v Canning & ors* (1992) 62 BLR 147.
29 (1996) 4 BLR 50.

- Employ a specialist themselves in the knowledge that they will still have liability for defective design, but that they can, in turn, pass that liability down the contractual chain i.e. the designer is still responsible to the client, but the designer's contract with the specialist will enable them to claim against the specialist.

The designer may seek approval from the client to delegate responsibility, and this option is often included in the various standard form contracts. For particularly complex builds delegation of responsibility may be implied from the circumstances. In *Merton London Borough Council v Lowe*,[30] the court held that the architect was entitled to employ a specialist contractor who specialised in the use of a particular proprietary ceiling.

Where a client is persuaded to employ a specialist directly, then care should be taken when recommending a party for the work. A party must use reasonable care and professional skill in recommending a specialist. Under the law of tort for negligence (see Chapter 4), if their recommendation is negligent, then they may become liable for the client's losses. In *Pratt v George J Hill Associates*,[31] the architect recommended a builder as 'very reliable' but they were actually incompetent. The client was in arbitration with the builder over the work when the builder became insolvent. The client subsequently sued the architect for its losses and was found liable for the amount which the client had overpaid to the builder and for the costs of the arbitration against the builder.

The architect (designer) is under a continuing obligation to oversee the construction of their design, including any part of the design which they have subcontracted to a specialist. Notwithstanding that the architect subcontracted the work due to a lack in their own expertise, responsibility is retained for directing the work. If a danger or problem occurs, or may occur, they must warn the client.

In *Investors in Industry Commercial Properties Ltd v South Bedfordshire DC*, 1986 WL 408142, where the architect employed structural engineers to design foundations for a property to be built over a filled in swimming pool, Lord Justice Slade explained: 'Whilst they are not expected to be experts, they are still to warn of anything which would be considered to be in the knowledge of an ordinary competent architect. In relation to the work allotted to the expert, the architect's legal responsibility will normally be confined to directing and co-ordinating the expert's work in the whole. However, this is subject to one important qualification. If any danger or problem arises in connection with the work allotted to the expert, of which an architect of ordinary competence reasonably ought to be aware and reasonably could be expected to warn the client, despite the employment of the expert, and despite what the expert says or does about it, it is in our judgment, the duty of the architect to warn the client. In such a contingency he is not entitled to rely blindly on the expert, with no mind of his own, on matters which must or should have been apparent to him'.[32]

Where a contractor is employed merely to build to the specification provided in the contract documents, then they have no responsibility for design, unless they actively participate in that design for specific parts, often called contractor's design portion, or by accepting responsibility in another way, such as changing the design without consultation.

---

30 (1981) 18 BLR 130.
31 (1987) 38 BLR 25.
32 *Investors in Industry Commercial Properties Ltd v South Bedfordshire DC*, 1986 WL 408142.

3.3.5 Standard of Design Liability – Fitness for Purpose

The standard for liability for design depends on whether the design is undertaken by the contractor or by an independent designer. In traditional procurement methods, where the design team is employed directly by the client, the designer does not warrant that the finished building will be fit for purpose, however if the same party designs and builds then they may be held liable if the property is not fit for purpose, unless they make it clear in the contract that they make no such representation.

For pure design only, the designer's (eg architect) liability will only arise where there is professional negligence (*Hawkins v Chrysler (UK) Ltd and Burne Associates*).[33] Hawkins was employed by Chrysler which had installed showers in its factory for its workers. Hawkins slipped and was injured on the wet tiles. Burne was the engineer who had designed, specified and supervised the installation of the showers. Hawkins sued Chrysler for his injuries and Chrysler sought an indemnity from Burne, contending that Burne owed them a duty not only to exercise reasonable skill and care but also to design the showers and the floor so that they were fit for their purpose. The trial judge held that there was no breach of the duty to exercise reasonable skill and care but that there was a breach of a duty to provide as safe a floor as was practicable. The Court of Appeal agreed that there was no breach of the duty to use reasonable skill and care, but that there was also no implied warranty to provide as safe a floor as possible or that it would be fit for purpose.

For design and build packages, the contractor is implied to warrant that the finished building will be fit for purpose (i.e. that there will be strict liability for error in the design). With a design and build, the design responsibility can be passed down the contractual chain to sub-contractors, as in *Greaves & Co (Contractors) Ltd v Baynham Meikle and Partners*.[34] Greaves was contracted to design and build a warehouse. The first floor was to be used for storing oil drums which would be moved around by forklift trucks. Consulting engineers were subcontracted to undertake the design and were told precisely what the building's purpose was to be. A design defect meant that the vibration from the forklifts made the floor break up. Greaves as the design and build contractor were found liable to their client, so they sued the subcontracted designer. The Court of Appeal found that there was negligence on behalf of the subcontractor and that even had there been no negligence, they would still have been liable for the failure of the design because it was not fit for purpose.

To avoid potential liability for fitness for purpose of design, the contract can make it clear that the main contractor's liability goes no further than it would for an architect (or other professional) holding themselves out to be competent to take on the design. An example of this may be found at clause 2.17.1 of the Joint Contract Tribunal's Design and Build 2016 contract. Such a clause would reduce the design duty to exercising reasonable care and skill only and remove the fitness for purpose aspect.

---

33 (1986) 38 BLR 36.
34 [1957] 3 All ER 99.

3.3.6 Duration of Design Liability

The architect's job isn't just to design, but also to oversee the implementation of the design. The architect remains under a continuing obligation to see that the design will work (*Brickfield Properties Ltd v Newton* [1971] 3 All ER 328).

Liability to oversee lasts until practical completion, through the defects liability period and probably until the issue of the final certificate (*Merton LBC v Lowe & Another* (1981) 18 BLR 130).

3.3.7 Compliance with Building Regulations

In a contract for the design only, the architect undertakes to use professional skill and reasonable care but does not warrant that the design will not contravene any legal principle, which includes complying with the Building Regulations (*BL Holding Ltd v Robert J Wood & Partners* [1979] 12 BLR 1). It is the contractor who undertakes the building works that is responsible for compliance with Building Regulations.

For design and build contracts there is strict liability to the contractor for any breach of the Building Regulations (*Newham BC v Taylor Woodrow (Anglian) Ltd* [1981] 19 BLR 99). This is because the builder is responsible for complying with the regulations and with design and build the builder is the same company as the designer.

3.3.8 Compliance with Statutory Requirements

Under a standard building contract, there is usually a clause in the contract which states that the contractor is not usually liable for breach of any statutory requirements where they carry out the works in accordance with the contract requirements. The designer is responsible where law is breached as a result of their design.

Example Clause: 2.17.3 of the JCT Standard Building Contract with Quantities 2024:

> ...the Contractor shall not be liable under this Contract if the Works [...] do not comply with the Statutory Requirements to the extent that the non-compliance results from the Contractor having carried out work in accordance with the documents referred to...

It will come as no surprise that where a contract is for both design and build that the contract will make it clear that the contractor is responsible for ensuring that the works comply with the law. This is because, with design and build, the contractor is both designer and builder and therefore takes on the responsibilities of both roles.

3.3.9 Dealing with Defective Work

The approach to dealing with defective work will depend on the contract's requirements. In general, however, the approach will be different depending on when the error(s) or concerns are discovered. There are three different times when an error may be discovered: during the construction period; during the rectification period and after the final certificate.

The contract will outline the standard of workmanship and materials, and where none is listed for a particular aspect, then it will be subject to implied terms, as discussed above at paragraphs 3.3.1 and 3.3.3. Where something is found not to meet the requirements of the contract, during the construction period, it is usual for the contract administrator, on behalf of the employer, to send a notice of non-compliance stating what the issue is and what the employer would like the contractor to do about it. Most contracts will allow for three options. The first option is to ask for the fault to be removed, the second option would be to ask for a change to be made to the work to make it acceptable and the third is to agree that, whilst the work isn't what was required, it may stay in place, subject to a deduction in the contract sum to compensate for the difference.

Where the work is removed, there is no need to send instructions for it to be rebuilt correctly, because the contract already requires the contractor to undertake the work. There will be no extension of time given to the contractor (see Section 3.5 below), nor will there be any payment for loss and or expense. Similarly, where a change to the work is required, a variation will be issued, but there will be no extension of time or payment of loss and or expense.

The rectification period is the period of time after the building has been completed and possession handed to the employer after the issue of a practical completion certificate. This period has various names, such as defects liability period or snagging period.

In *P & M Kaye v Hosier & Dickinson*[35] it was said that 'By issuing his certificate of practical completion [the certifier] signifies his satisfaction with the works at the end of the construction period; but this is subject to any latent defects which become apparent to him during the defects liability period'.

The effect of the practical completion certificate is that the defects liability period starts, the contractor's liability to pay liquidated damages ends (see Section 3.5 below), the employer's right to issue instructions to the contractor ends, the contractor's responsibility to insure the building ends, half of the retention money is repaid to the contractor and, for all practical purposes, the limitation period starts (see below).

The period for discovering defects will be stated in the contract and is often between 6 and 12 months. During the period the employer's agents will compile a list, often referred to as a snagging list, but also called a list for rectification or a schedule of defects. The list given to the contractor at the end of the period. However, if something dangerous is found, the employers may issue instructions to make the building safe, before the end of the period. Following this, there is a period of time allowed for the contractor to rectify (or make good) the issues. There is rarely a timeframe stated in the contract for this, because it depends on how much work needs to be undertaken. It is, therefore, to be undertaken in a reasonable time scale.

Once defects have been attended to, any certificates of making good have been issued, all extensions of time and financial matters have been finalised, the next and final stage is the issue of the final certificate.

The final certificate has the effect of providing conclusive evidence in any proceedings (including litigation, arbitration and adjudication) that:

35 [1972] 1 All ER 146, at 165.

All work expressly left to the contract administrator's satisfaction meets that requirement; deductions/additions to the Contract Sum have been completed correctly; all extensions of time are correct; and all money claims for loss and or expense have been accounted for.

After this certificate, any claim for anything included in the certificate made by adjudication, arbitration or other proceedings must be commenced within 28 days of the issuance of the Final Certificate. *London Borough of Barking and Dagenham v Terrapin* Construction Ltd (2000) BLR 479 asked the question whether the architect's satisfaction expressed in the certificate applies to patent and latent defects? The answer was that yes, both patent and latent defects were included.

Furthermore, in *Crown Estates Commissioners v John Mowlem & Co* (1995) 70 BLR 1 it was held that there are three ways to deal with materials and workmanship in contracts: as per the specifications in the contract; as per the terms implied into the contract (see paragraph 3.3.1 and 3.3.3 above); and as per the Architect's/contract administrator's satisfaction and that all three of these were expressed as being satisfactory in the final certificate. A claim for anything which is not satisfactory must be brought within 28 days, unless the certificate has been issued incorrectly.

The final certificate is an evidential bar to later claims in litigation or arbitration (even if the limitation period has not yet expired), unless claims are started within 28 days. Furthermore, where a contract gives power to an arbitrator to open up, review and revise a certificate, the power only exists for 28 days following the Final Certificate. However, this does not bar a claim in litigation, unless the contract expressly or implicitly says so. In other words, a court may open up or overturn a certificate even after the 28 days limit.[36]

Even where a certificate is conclusive evidence there may still be grounds to have it set aside, if it wasn't issued in the correct form, at the correct time or by the correct person; where the contract administrator has certified on something which the contract gave them no power to certify; where there is fraud and collusion between the certifier and one of the parties; and where the employer has improperly pressurized the certifier.[37]

This does not mean that no claims may be made, at all against the contractor, 28 days after the final certificate. The contract doesn't just simply cover what is to be built, but it will also contain warranties for matters such as life span. For example, a warranty that the building will not require maintenance or repair for a period of 20 years.

Where the final certificate does not bar claims, the Limitations Act will still limit the amount of time that a claimant can make their claim in litigation. The Limitations Act 1980 provides that an action for breach of simple contract must be made before the end of 6 years from the cause of action accruing.[38] The cause of action would be the breach of contract (breach of warranty, occurrence of professional negligence etc.). For construction contracts, the limitation period starts at the issue of the practical completion certificate. Most contracts will be simple contracts which will have a limitation period of 6 years. On occasion the contract may be made by deed and if so, the limitation period is 12 years.[39]

---

36 *Beaufort Developments (NI) Ltd v Gilbert-Ash NI Ltd* (1998) 88 BLR 1.

37 *Cantrell v Wright & Fuller Ltd* [2003] BLR 412.

38 Section 5, Limitation Act 1980.

39 Section 8, Limitation Act 1980.

In cases of fraud or concealment, a claimant may commence a claim within 6 years (or 12 years if under deed) of having become (or ought reasonably to have become) aware of the fraud or concealment.[40]

Section 14 of the Latent Damage Act 1980 allows the owner of the property to make a negligence claim against the party responsible for the damage (the defendant) within 3 years of having had knowledge of, or from when they ought reasonably to have had knowledge of, material facts which enable the claimant to bring a claim for negligence.

3.4 Payment

Prior to the enactment of the Housing Grants Construction and Regeneration Act 1996 (HGCRA), there was a significant number of disputes relating to payment within the construction industry which led to many smaller companies going into liquidation due to poor cashflow often caused or at least exacerbated by lengthy disputes. This was confirmed by a joint government and industry commissioned report produced by Lord Latham in 1994 entitled 'Constructing the Team',[41] but more commonly referred to as The Latham Report. The enactment of the HGCRA was a direct result of the report.

Amongst other recommendations, such as a quicker means of dispute resolution (see Chapter 8), the report recommended a more stringent payment regime which would outlaw 'pay when paid' clauses, allow an unpaid contractor to suspend work when not paid, and provide clarity when an employer deducted sums from the payments due to the contractor. Part II of the Act concerns the construction industry and provides a broad definition of the 'construction contract' to which it applies. The Act does not apply to residential occupiers[42] or to employment contracts[43] (S. 104 (3)).

3.4.1 Housing Grants Construction and Regeneration Act 1996

The Housing Grants Construction and Regeneration Act 1996 (as amended by the Local Democracy Economic Development and Construction Act 2009) defines a construction contract as follows:

> **104 Construction contracts.**
>
> **1.** In this Part a "construction contract" means an agreement with a person for any of the following—
>   **a.** the carrying out of construction operations;
>   **b.** arranging for the carrying out of construction operations by others, whether under sub-contract to him or otherwise;

40 Sections 2 and 32, Limitation Act 1980.

41 D. Cahill and M.C. Puybaraud. 'Constructing the Team: The Latham Report (1994),' in *Construction Reports 1944–98*, ed. M. Murray and D. Langford (John Wiley & Sons, Inc., 2008), https://doi.org/10.1002/9780470758526.ch11.

42 Section 106 Housing Grants Construction and Regeneration Act 1996.

43 Section 104 (3) Housing Grants Construction and Regeneration Act 1996.

   c. providing his own labour, or the labour of others, for the carrying out of construction operations.
2. References in this Part to a construction contract include an agreement—
   a. to do architectural, design, or surveying work, or
   b. to provide advice on building, engineering, interior or exterior decoration or on the laying-out of landscape, in relation to construction operations.
3. References in this Part to a construction contract do not include a contract of employment (within the meaning of the Employment Rights Act 1996).[44]

All contracts which fall within this definition, and which are not with an owner occupier, must adhere to this Act with respect to the payment terms of the contract.

Firstly, all contracts, where the expected duration of the works will exceed 45 days, must make payment by instalment (s.109 HGCRA). The parties are free to agree the time and amounts of interim payments, but if they fail to do so, then the regime set out in Part II of the Scheme for Construction Contracts Regulations[45] (the Scheme) will apply to the contract, which states that payment will be on the basis of work done and materials supplied during each successive period of 30 days.

Section 110(1)(a) states that every construction contract must have an adequate mechanism for determining what payments become due and when, and S 110 (1)(b) that every construction contract shall provide for a final date for payment in relation to any sum which becomes due. The Act only requires parties to agree on a final date and does not specify when this should be. The worry is that strong parties, such as employers and main contractors, may impose unreasonable dates far in the future for payment, which goes against the spirit of the Act which supports speedy payment. The final date for payment under the Scheme is 17 days.

Section 110(3) states that 'if or to the extent that a contract does not contain' adequate mechanisms for payment, 'the relevant provisions of the Scheme for Construction Contracts apply' ('the Scheme'). Section 114 provides that the provisions from the Scheme operate by way of implied terms (see Chapter 2).

Where parties fail to agree an adequate mechanism, as required by the Act, the Scheme may be used, in part or in whole, depending on the adequacy of the mechanism proposed and the relevance and certainty of the parties' own agreement.

Where parties have attempted to agree a payment mechanism, but only part of if falls foul of the Act, then there is only the requirement to use such part(s) of the Scheme as is necessary to make the agreement compliant. There is no need to reject all that the parties have agreed in favour of the mechanism from the Scheme. As Lord Justice Coulson stated at paragraph 67 of *Bennet v Verbus*[46] '*the purpose of the Act was to provide for certain minimum, mandatory standards so as to achieve certainty and regular cash flow*'. Therefore, an entirely different payment regime from the one agreed '*could only happen where the*

44 Section 104 Housing Grants Construction and Regeneration Act 1996 (as amended).
45 The Scheme for Construction Contract Regulations (England and Wales) 1998.
46 *Bennett (Construction) Limited v CIMC MBS Limited (formerly Verbus Systems Ltd)* [2019] EWCA Civ 1515.

regime which had been agreed was so deficient that wholesale replacement was the only viable option'. In that case, the payment mechanism was deemed compliant, but the Court of Appeal still answered the question as to how much of the Scheme would be implied into the parties' contract.

The importance of the parties' original agreement was also stressed by the Court of Appeal in *Balfour Beatty v Grove Developments*.[47] The parties had agreed on a payment schedule with 23 valuation dates from September 2013 to July 2015, but the works overran, and work had not been completed by the last date in the schedule. The dispute concerned whether Section 109 would require continued interim payments or if, per the original schedule, the next payment would be at completion. According to Jeremy Glover of Fenwick Elliot, the Court of Appeal (CA) noted 'that the express words used made it clear that the parties were only agreeing a regime of interim payments up to the contractual date for practical completion. There was no provision for interim payments after July 2015. The CA considered that this was a classic case of one party making a bad bargain and the CA would not (and could not) use the canons of construction to rescue one party from the consequences of what that party had clearly agreed'.[48]

Both these cases serve as a reminder of precision when drafting contracts or amending commonly used terms in standard form contracts. In both instances, the parties had amended the standard JCT contract payment terms.

The Act also requires parties to issue payment notices and payless notices. Payment notices are documents which detail how much should be paid at the due dates for payment, based on the amount of work undertaken up to that date. A payless notice is required when an employer has the right to withhold any payment due from the notice.

Section 110A: Provides that a construction contract will require that either (1) the payer gives notice to the payee, not later than 5 days after payment is due, or (2) require the payee to give notice; and section 110B says if notice is to be given by the payer and is not received in time, the payee may give notice to the payer. What that means is that if, for example, the parties have agreed that payment will become due 2 months after possession and each 1 calendar month thereafter (e.g. on the 15th), then the due date for payment will be the 15th. If the employer is to provide the payment notice, it must be given on or before 20th of each month (within 5 days of the due date). The parties' contract should say which party is to provide the notice. If the employer is designated as the party to provide the notice and fails... to do so, then the contractor may provide the notice. If the contractor is to provide the notice, there is no limit of days beyond the due date, presumably because the contractor is the party requiring payment.

Section 111 allows the paying party upon receiving a payment notice to advise of any sums which they are withholding from payment, by providing a Pay Less Notice. The Notice must state the amount to be paid and the basis of its calculation and must be given within the 'prescribed period' designated by the parties. If no such period is recorded,

---

47 [2016] EWCA Civ 990.

48 J. Glover, *Balfour Beatty Regional Construction Ltd v Grove Developments Ltd*. Fenwick Elliot, 2016. https://www.fenwickelliott.com/research-insight/newsletters/dispatch/archive/balfour-beatty-grove (accessed 20 June 2024).

then the Scheme applies which says it must be given no later than 5 days before the final date for payment.

According to *Melville Dundas v Wimpey*,[49] the House of Lords (predecessor to the Supreme Court) has pointed out on two occasions that the purpose of the notices is to formalise payment process so that a contractor knows immediately and with sufficient clarity the payment that should be made and why any of it is being withheld, so that the contractor can seek early resolution through adjudication if necessary.[50]

3.4.2 Common Law Rights to Deduct from Certified Sums

Whilst the terms of the contract will detail what deductions may be made from the certified sums, there may also be common law rights of set off and abatement. Abatement is a form of a right of set off which allows deduction of sums from money due in respect of poor workmanship, whereas set off more usually is a right to deduct sums relating to money owed by the payor to the payee for other matters, not related to the project for which payment is requested. Set-off could be used against sums owed on other contracts, although this is not usually the case in construction contracts unless sums owed are clearly due. *B Hargreaves Ltd v Action* 2000 Ltd[51] provides an example of this when several contracts were signed between the same parties at the same time, when payment was claimed on one contract the main contractors were not allowed to set-off for poor work on some of the other contracts. The defence of set-off at common law was not available because the sums sought to be set off were not money demands which could be ascertained readily and without difficulty. The sums relied on could not be ascertained without arbitration or litigation.

The debate as to whether sums could be deducted from sums which have been certified as due by the architect began with the case of *Dawnays Ltd v FG Milner Ltd*[52] in the early 70s, when the Court of Appeal held that a main contractor could not set off a claim for the subcontractor's delay against a certified sum. The Court held that it could not and was keen to show that cashflow was of utmost importance with Lord Denning MR saying, 'An interim certificate is to be regarded virtually as cash [...] Payment may not be withheld on account of cross-claims, whether good or bad, except so far as the contract specifically provides'. In this case the damages due for delay had yet to be proven, so in actual fact weren't yet due. However, the case provided precedence and was followed until it was criticised by the House of Lords in *Gilbert-Ash (Northern) Ltd v Modern Engineering (Bristol) Ltd.*[53] The House of Lords did not overrule *Dawnays* but it has not been followed since.

In *Gilbert-Ash* it was held that the payer is entitled to raise any set-off available to them under the general law unless the contract expressly removes that right and that there is no need for the contract to mention a right to the defence of abatement or to any common law remedy. If a defendant can prove that defects exist and that they have caused a reduction in the value of the thing constructed, the defendant will only be liable to pay an amount that

49 *Melville Dundas Ltd (in Receivership) v George Wimpey UK Ltd* [2007] BLR 257.
50 Ibid., 257.
51 [1993] BCLC 1111, 36 ConLR 74, 62 BLR 72, [1992] CILL 720, (1992) Times, 29 December.
52 [1971] 2 All ER 1389.
53 [1974] AC 689.

accounts for this reduction in value. This became known as the Gilbert-Ash principle. The wording of the contract was different from that in *Dawnays* in that the *Gilbert-Ash* contract expressly stated that the contractor could set-off from certified sums any '*bona fide* contra account and/or other claims'. Deductions were allowed for poor workmanship and delay.

The *Gilbert-Ash* principle was applied in *Acsim (Southern) Ltd v Danish Contracting Ltd*[54] where the main contractor tried to withhold a payment under a sub-contract. The sub-contract expressly stated that: 'rights to set-off are fully set out in these conditions and no other rights whatsoever shall be implied as terms of this sub-contract relating to set-off'. However, the Court of Appeal said this statement did not exclude the defence of abatement at common law and so the deduction for poor workmanship was allowed.

In summary, it would appear that the common law right to set off is not allowed for construction contracts but that the defence of abatement for work for that specific contract will always be available. Unlike set-off, the right to the defence of abatement cannot be excluded in the contract wording. In *Stewart Dill Ltd v Horatio Myer & Co Ltd*[55] the Court of Appeal found that such a term would be unreasonable under the Unfair Contract Terms Act 1977. Of course, as we are talking about construction contracts, a pay less notice will always be required which should include details of the defence of abatement.

The wording of the contract will be key in the decision of the courts when it comes to set-off as the courts will wish to ascertain the intentions of the parties (see Chapter 2), deleted terms in the agreement process may be used to indicate the intentions of the parties. In *Mottram Consultants Ltd v Bernard Sunley & Sons Ltd*,[56] the House of Lords held that the parties did not intend to have a right of set-off after the parties had deleted the contractual clause relating to it.

A further question in relation to deductions from certified sums is what happens if a pay less notice is validly issued with respect to liquidated damages for delay (see Section 3.5) but a claim for an extension of time is being processed before the final date for payment? This was answered by the House of Lords in *Reinwood Ltd v Brown & Sons Ltd*.[57] A notice of non-completion was issued on 14 December 2005 and the interim certificate for payment on 11 January 2006, with a final date for payment of 25 January 2006. On 17 January a withholding notice (pay less notice) was issued to deduct liquidated damages of £61,629. Before payment, but after the issuance of the withholding notice, the contract administrator granted an extension of time, which would reduce damages to £12,326. The contract administrator deducted the full amount from the certified sum, in line with the withholding notice. The contractor ended his employment due to non-payment. Upholding the decision of the Court of Appeal, the House of Lords held that the employer's right to deduct liquidated damages was not lost by the grant of the extension of time even if its effect was to cancel the certificate of non-completion. The cancellation of the non-completion certificate did not have retrospective effect, and the employer was therefore entitled to rely on that notice and deduct the amount until the next payment certificate.

54 1989 WL 1720281.
55 [1992] 2 All ER 257.
56 (1974) 2 BLR 28.
57 [2008] UKHL 12.

3.4.3 Retention Clauses and Performance Bonds

Retention clauses are common throughout the industry. The clause will entitle the employer to automatically deduct a percentage from the certified sum and retain it in case of the development of any defects. At practical completion 50% of the retention fund is paid to the contractor. The remaining 50% is generally kept until completion of the snagging list or the issuance of the final certificate. The retention fund should be held in trust by the employer for the contractor. The trust will ring fence the money for the contractor in the event of bankruptcy of the employer. Under Trust law, the trustees are usually required to invest the money, however construction contracts usually remove this requirement. Should the employer fail to create a trust for the fund, and subsequently become insolvent, then the fund will be used to pay all the creditors and not go directly to the contractor. It is, therefore, wise for the contractor to seek confirmation of the formation of the trust's creation.

There has been criticism of the system of retention clauses over recent years. With the importance of cashflow to the industry it seems at odds to have large amounts of cash merely being held by main contractors and employers and research undertaken as part of a government consultation by the Department for Business Energy and industrial Strategy found that in 2017 between £3.2 and £5.9 million pounds[58] were being held in retention in UK construction industry. A Private Member's Bill was proposed by the House of Lords, with the first reading 25 October 2021 but failed to proceed further. The Bill proposed that any clause in a construction contract (as defined by the Housing Grants, Construction and Regeneration Act) which enables a payer to withhold retention monies will be of no effect from 25 January 2025 and that any retentions withheld at that date must be repaid in full within 7 days. The Bill was considered to be needed because the cash would be better for the UK economy if it were in circulation; there were problems with companies entering liquidation whilst holding retentions and some companies retain the money for very minor issues. Those against the legislation were reluctant to interfere with the parties' right to freely contract.

An alternative is a performance or retention bond. The bonds serve as a financial guarantee that defects or issues arising during or after construction will be rectified by the contractor, guaranteeing that all work will be completed at the end of the project. The bond is given by the bank (or other financier), insurance company or parent company of the contractor. The employer would be entitled to payment of the bond in the event that the contractor did not complete the work. There is, therefore, no money deducted from payments due to the contractor.

3.5 Liquidated Ascertained Damages

Liquidated damages, or more correctly termed, liquidated ascertained damages (LADs) are widely used in the construction industry, but seldom used in other commercial contracts. In simple terms they are a pre-agreed sum for breach of contract and are used as an alternative to unliquidated damages for breach of contract which not only need to be proved

58 BEIS Research Paper no.17 – Retentions in the Construction Industry.

and calculated after the breach but are also subject to mitigation (see Chapter 2). In the construction industry, LAD clauses are more commonly used for breaching the agreed date for completion, however, that is not their only use in contract law, and if they are not formulated properly they can be challenged as illegal clauses (see 3.5.3 below).

Delays in the production or renovation of buildings can be very expensive for the employer who is wanting to sell or let that building from a particular time and is more than likely paying a lender for the work incurring daily interest. The employer cannot take all the risk relating to delays, so passes some of the risk to the contractor by way of an LAD clause. Effectively, the clause means that delays caused by the contractor (which are not made up before the agreed completion date) are paid for using liquidated damages, by debiting the LAD figure from the payments due to the contractor (see 3.4.2 above).

With usual damages, the innocent party must prove the losses incurred (see Chapter 2) but for LADs, the sum is due at breach even if no loss has occurred[59] which makes the process of claiming LADs less time consuming. However, the same principle applies if the loss exceeds the LAD figure, no more can be claimed.[60] This creates certainty for the parties each knowing what will be due in the event of delay. Certainty is particularly useful to the contractor which will be able to plan whether to take the hit of the LAD sum, or to provide additional resources to the project to ensure on-time completion. The courts have made it clear that certainty is something that they are keen to uphold and that the LAD figure, once agreed, should not be changed, even in the contractor's favour. In *Stanner Electric v R Mansel*[61] there was a LAD clause relating to late completion for electrical work on two houses of £5,000 per week for delay. One of the houses was completed on time, but the other was delayed. Mansel sought LADs from Stanner for the delay but claimed only £2,500 per week. The court held that if the sum could be changed then it hadn't been 'pre-calculated' and was, therefore, unenforceable as it constituted a penalty (see 3.5.2 below).

3.5.1 Prevention Principle and Extension of Time

There is a legal principle in contract law, known as the prevention principle, which says that a person cannot benefit from a claim for breach of contract if the reason for non-performance is because that party prevented the other from performing its obligation. In other words, a party cannot benefit from their own wrongdoing. This principle is why construction contracts wishing to have LADs for delay must also have clauses outlining what will happen if the employer or employer's agents cause delay. The principle has been discussed on many occasions with respect to LADs and dates for completion of the work advising that if the employer causes a delay and there is no clause in the contract to extend the amount of time for completion, then they will not be able to claim LADs and time will be 'set at large'. If time is set at large then no matter what other delays may occur (even those caused by the contractor) no LADs will be payable and the contractor will have a reasonable time to complete the work.

59 *Clydebank Engineering & Shipbuilding Co v Casteneda* [1905] AC 6.

60 *Bath & North East Somerset District Council v Mowlem Plc* [2004] EWCA Civ 115.

61 (1988) CILL 399.

In the Court of Appeal case of *Trollope & Colls Ltd v North West Metropolitan Regional Hospital Board*,[62] Lord Denning MR explained that 'It is well settled that in building contracts – and in other contracts too – when there is a stipulation for work to be done in a limited time, if one party by his conduct – it may be quite legitimate conduct, such as ordering extra work – renders it impossible or impracticable for the other party to do his work within the stipulated time, then the one whose conduct caused the trouble can no longer insist upon strict adherence to the time stated. He cannot claim any penalties or liquidated damages for non-completion in that time'.

Jackson J in *Multiplex Ltd v Honeywell Ltd (No 2)*[63] added to the jurisprudence by providing three principles of the application of the prevention principle in construction contracts:

1. actions by the employer, which are perfectly legitimate under a construction contract, may still be characterised as prevention if those actions cause delay beyond the contractual completion date;
2. acts of prevention by an employer do not set time at large if the contract provides for extension of time in respect of those events;
3. in so far as the extension of time clause is ambiguous, it should be construed in favour of the contractor.

More recently, in 2018, *North Midland Building Ltd v Cyden Homes Ltd*,[64] Coulson LJ explained that the principle operated as an implied term and that only a term to the contrary would defeat it and, more importantly, said 'If the parties do not stipulate that a particular act of prevention triggers an entitlement to an extension of time, then there will be no implied term to assist the employer and the application of the prevention principle would mean that, on the happening of that event, time was set at large'.

3.5.2 Managing Delay to Preserve LADs

In order to ensure that the prevention principle doesn't compromise the agreed LADs for late completion, the contract must allow for, what is commonly referred to as, an 'extension of time' for completion of the works if delay is caused by the employer, their agent or neutral events such as flood, fire, and force majeure (serious disruption beyond anyone's control). Force majeure was used significantly during the COVID-19 pandemic when workforces were asked to stay at home and later adjust ways of working to prevent the spread of illness. The 2024 suite of JCT contracts has now added 'epidemic' to its list of reasons for an extension of time, or Adjustment of the Completion Date as the JCT refer to it.

In such clauses delays are usually classified as being caused by the employer, caused by the contractor, or caused by neutral events. Where a delay is caused by the employer, or a party working on behalf of the employer (e.g. an engineer, contract administrator or supplier of the employer), the contractor will be granted additional time to allow for the delay. It is usual that they will also be paid any additional costs as a result of the delay. If the delay

---

62 [1973] 1 W.L.R. 601 at 607.
63 [2007] Bus LR Digest.
64 [2018] EWCA Civ 1744.

is caused by the contractor, of course, no adjustment is made and unless the contractor can make up the time by the completion date LADs will be payable. Finally, where a delay is caused by a neutral event the risk is apportioned between the two. An extension of time will be granted but no loss or expenses will be paid to the contractor.

Matters are not always as straightforward as they seem, because sometimes delay has more than one cause. For example, if access to site is delayed but the contractor couldn't have started work because its materials hadn't arrived. When two or more events are said to have caused the same delay, it is referred to as concurrent delay.

When it comes to concurrent delay, the English courts treat the matter differently from the Scottish courts. In England and Wales, where one cause would allow a contractor an extension, but the other cause was of its own making which wouldn't allow an extension, the contractor is nevertheless entitled to an extension of time for the full delay.[65] This seems to be aligned with the prevention principle in that whenever the employer causes delay they cannot benefit from LADs. However, the Scottish courts apportion the losses between the concurrent causes of the delay so that the contractor only receives a proportional extension to the completion date.[66] Of course, the maxim that parties are able to agree their own terms in contract means that a term can be included which makes it clear what will happen in the case of concurrent delay. In *North Midland Building Ltd v Cyden Homes Ltd*[67] the contract stated that no extension would be granted to the contractor in the event of the contractor being responsible for any part of concurrent delay.

3.5.3 Liquidated Damages Clause or Penalty Clause?

In civil law in the UK, a contract breaker is not punished, they must merely compensate the loss they have caused to the other party. Contract law prohibits a contract term which punishes a party for breach of contract, so penalty clauses are not allowed. However, it is not unusual (although it is becoming less so) for industry professionals to refer to LAD clauses as penalty clauses. It doesn't matter what the parties call the clause, it is the way that it operates that may make the clause illegal and therefore unenforceable.[68]

More than 100 years ago, the Court of Appeal provided us with propositions to determine whether a clause is a liquidated damages clause or a penalty clause in *Dunlop Pneumatic Tyre Co Ltd v New Garage Ltd*[69]:

- The name given to the clause by the parties is not conclusive and what must be examined is the effect of the clause
- Liquidated damages are a genuine pre-estimate of the probable loss that will occur as a result of the breach
- Should be decided upon the terms and inherent circumstances of each particular contract, judged as at the time of the making of the contract, not as at the time of the breach

65 *Walter Lilly & Co Ltd v McKay* [2012] EWHC 1773 (TCC).
66 *City Inn Limited v Shepherd Construction Ltd* [2010] BLR 473.
67 [2018] EWCA Civ 1744.
68 *Dunlop Pneumatic Tyre Co Ltd v New Garage Ltd* [1915] AC 79.
69 Ibid.

- Where the sum is extravagant and unconscionable compared to the highest probable loss, then it will be presumed to be a penalty clause
- The clause must not apply to minor breaches in the same way as to major breaches
- It doesn't matter if there is no exact way to calculate the probable loss unless the loss occurs because that was the 'bargain' agreed between the parties.

Over the years various cases have clarified these propositions, but by far the majority have held that the clause under question was not a penalty, but a legitimate liquidated damages clause. In 2005, *Alfred McAlpine Capital Projects v Tilebox Ltd*[70] was heard in the High Court by Justice Jackson. The case was to decide whether £45,000 per week for liquidated damages where a delay exceeded two and a half years was extravagant and unconscionable. Jackson J said that 'an agreed pre-estimate of loss does not have to be right to be reasonable' and that there 'must be substantial discrepancy for it to amount to a penalty'. He went on to say that it is rare to find a penalty because 'the fact that two parties who are well capable of protecting their respective commercial interests agree the provision means that the method of calculating LADs is unlikely to be oppressive'.

It should be noted that it is possible to add a limitation clause to limit the amount to be paid.[71] For example, a longstop of 1 year or a maximum figure for LADs can be added to the clause.

The latest case law to clarify the law surrounding the legality of 'penalty clauses' concerned two different cases referred to the Supreme Court: *Cavendish Square Holdings BV v Talal El Makdessi; Parkingeye LTD v Beavis.*[72] Both cases looked at the words 'extravagant' and 'unconscionable' and at what could be included in a genuine estimate of loss. Whilst neither case concerned the construction industry, their ruling helps to clarify what may be included in a genuine estimate of loss to compensate the affected party. Both Makdessi and Beavis challenged their respective clauses as being unenforceable penalty clauses, claiming that calculations of the figures weren't merely to compensate but were also to punish. The Court found that neither term had been penal.

Lords Neuberger and Sumption delivered a joint judgment stating, at paragraph 32, that 'The true test is whether the impugned provision is a secondary obligation which imposes a detriment on the contract-breaker out of all proportion to any legitimate interest of the innocent party in the enforcement of the primary obligation'. In simpler terms, what they meant is that to establish whether a clause is legitimate or not, you first must look at what the term seeks to protect and then at what compensation they attribute to protecting themselves from that potential loss (the estimate of probable loss). They went on to say that 'compensation is not necessarily the only legitimate interest that the innocent party may have in the performance of the defaulter's primary obligation' meaning that there are often intangible interests which need protection such as reputation loss or, in the case of Makdessi, business goodwill.

---

70 [2005] EWHC 281.

71 *Tripple Point Technology Inc v PTT Public Company Ltd* [2019] EWCA Civ 230.

72 Cavendish Square Holdings BV v Talal El Makdessi; Parkingeye LTD v Beavis [2015] UKSC 67 at 32.

The Lords[73] were also keen to remind us of the legal principle of freedom of contract (that the parties are free to make their own agreement without interference from the law.) They cited Lord Woolf in *Privy Council in Philips Hong Kong Ltd v Attorney General of Hong Kong*[74] outlining that 'the court has to be careful not to set too stringent a standard and bear in mind that what the parties have agreed should normally be upheld', not least because '[a]ny other approach will lead to undesirable uncertainty especially in commercial contracts'.

Lord Mance agreed with Neuberger and Sumption adding: 'What is necessary in each case is to consider first whether any (and if so what) legitimate business interest is served and protected by the clause and second whether assuming such an interest to exist the provision made for the interest is nevertheless in the circumstances extravagant, exorbitant or unconscionable'.[75]

In summary, the case tells us that if the clause seeks to protect a genuine interest, then provided the sum attributed to that interest is not extravagant, exorbitant or unconscionable then the clause will be allowed. It also confirmed that legitimate interests can be intangible (e.g. good will or reputation) and that the Court will protect the right of the parties to freely agree contract terms. As Jackson J said in *McAlpine*[76] it is rare to find a penalty which has been agreed between the parties.

To summarise, the courts are trying to balance the rights of parties to make their own agreement against the rights of contracting parties not to be punished for breach of contract. It seems to be harder to have a clause set aside as being a penalty, unless the agreed penalty is diverted from or no effort has been made to calculate the likely cost of loss.

3.6 Variations of the Contract

A contract cannot be changed once it has been agreed by the parties, unless those parties have added provisions to their agreement to allow for those changes. These provisions are known as variation clauses or modification clauses, because they vary (modify) the existing agreement. Without an appropriate variation clause, the employer would not be able to change the agreed plans or materials, without asking the contractor to change their agreement. The contractor would not be legally obligated to accept any changes. With no legal obligation, the contractor could agree a new contract for the changes but be in a position to charge any price it wished, knowing that it already has the contract for the work. It would be impractical for the employer to engage a third party to undertake the changes because the contractor will be obliged to carry out the works as originally agreed and if the employer no longer wants that work done then they will have to negotiate out of the contract for that work before asking a third party to carry out the new request.

The most common variation clauses deal with changes to the works, but there are several others throughout most standard form contracts, such as clauses allowing for price

73 Ibid., at 33.
74 (1993) 61 BLR 41, 59.
75 Cavendish Square Holdings BV v Talal El Makdessi; Parkingeye LTD v Beavis [2015] UKSC 67 at 152.
76 Alfred McAlpine Capital Projects Ltd v Tilebox Ltd [2005] EWHC 281.

fluctuations and extensions of time for delay and changes to the contract sum with respect to additional funds for loss and expense as a result of the employer or employer's agent, particularly relating to extensions of time clauses (see paragraph 3.5.2 above).

As a contract can be formed orally, variations allowable under the contract terms may also be made orally. Some parties agree that they will all be in writing by agreeing a non-oral modification (NOM) clause. The parties in *Rock Advertising Limited* v *MWB Business Exchange Centres Limited* had agreed a NOM clause but then tried to amend their contract orally to allow clauses to be made orally going forward. Unsurprisingly they could not do that. Lord Sumption said 'Party autonomy operates up to the point when the contract is made but thereafter only to the extent that a contract allows. In other words, parties are free to bind their future relationship by agreement and, since the contract only permitted written amendments, the parties had already agreed an oral amendment would be invalid. This would include an amendment to the NOM clause itself'.[77]

3.6.1 Restriction to Large Scale Changes

Construction contracts generally allow for a very wide range of amendments to the contract works. Changes may be required simply because at the time of agreement the design team had not fully completed the design, or due to changes in the client requirements, loss of existing works due to fire or flood, changes to legislation or the need to seek alternative materials to complete the work to meet supply issues or changes to Building Regulations.

For example, the JCT describes variations to the contract as:

5.1.1 the alteration or modification of the design, quality or quantity of the Works including:
- 5.1.1.1 the addition, omission or substitution of any work;
- 5.1.1.2 the alteration of the kind or standard of any of the materials or goods to be used in the Works;
- 5.1.1.3 the removal from the site of any work executed or Site Materials other than work, materials or goods which are not in accordance with this Contract;[78]

Clauses in the NEC and FIDIC contracts are similarly wide to allow for the myriad of changes which may be required as the building progresses. It would be difficult for the contractor to plan if they were expected to take on any and all changes to the works and the law does not expect them to. Firstly, a contract may expressly restrict the scale of variation and, they are implicitly restricted from extreme changes to the nature of the work by the description of the works in the contract's recitals. Secondly, common law restricts variations to those that would have been in the contemplation of the parties at the time the contract was made. i.e. small changes to the work but not changes to the type or scope of the work.

The question of whether a change could be dealt with as a variation was heard in *Blue Circle Industries Plc*.[79] The contract was for the dredging of a lake. At the time of agreeing the contract the matter of what would happen to the dredged material had not been

---

77 *Rock Advertising Limited* v *MWB Business Exchange Centres Limited* [2018] UKSC 24 at para 11.
78 Clause 5.1.1 JCT Standard Building Contract With Quantities 2024.
79 *Blue Circle Industries Plc v Holland Dredging Company (UK) Ltd* (1987) 37 BLR 40.

discussed and it was to be dealt with under a variation clause. The client subsequently asked the dredging company to use the dredged material to build an island in the lake. The dredging company refused because it was not in the scope of the contract, had not been in their contemplation and was, in any event, beyond their expertise. The court agreed saying that the changes had not been in contemplation of the parties at the time that the contract was formed. The changes requested were said to go to the root of the contract, so the variation was not allowed.

However, the outcome was different when the sheer number of changes were claimed not to have been in the parties' contemplation. The contract in the Court of Appeal case of *McAlpine Humberoak Ltd*[80] related to a vast offshore installation in the North Sea off Shetland. The contract was for 7 pallets for a weather deck for a tension-leg platform. 22 drawings became 161 drawings. The court found that the changes could all be accommodated through variations because, despite that no one could not have imagined so many variations, the substantial changes did not destroy the identity of the contract.

To summarise, a contract can allow as many changes as necessary to affect the clients' wishes provided that they do not change the type of work being undertaken.

The ability to make changes is very important to the employer, to ensure that it is not restricted by its original plans for the building. Contractors may also welcome changes that allow for additional work, because that means additional income. What may be tricky for contractors is pricing. If a job has been poorly priced the additional work will be priced within the constraints of the original contract and will follow the bill of quantities prices. There could also be a problem with knowing how long they may be on a particular job which will impact their availability for the next client.

3.6.2 Valuing Changes to the Works

The contract's variation clauses should allow for the contractor to be paid for additional work and be given an extension of time to complete work (should they be subject to a specific completion date) as well as any necessary additional payment with respect to loss and expense (see paragraph 3.5.2).

There are three ways to agree the price for variations. By straightforward agreement, in reference to the bill of quantities or with a contractor's quotation. Agreement is exactly as it sounds; the parties agree a figure. Usually this will be for small changes. The traditional way is for the contract administrator to calculate the payment by reference to the bill of quantities (BoQ). Same work and same conditions are valued at BoQ rates, similar work in similar conditions is valued pro-rata to the BoQ, any work which cannot be accurately measured may be undertaken at a price for day works, and anything remaining would be worked out at fair rates and prices. Re-rating of existing work could be required if the new work will make other work on site more difficult or time consuming.

When calculating fair rates and prices allowances should be made for the profit of the contractor and for additional overheads incurred by the contractor. The question of whether, when calculating a fair valuation, allowance should be made for overheads and profits

80 *McAlpine Humberoak Ltd v McDermot International Inc* (1982) 58 BLR 1.

in its calculation was discussed in *Weldon Plant Ltd v The Commission of New* Towns.[81] The High Court held that a fair valuation will normally consist of costs plus a reasonable percentage for profit, but that overheads required separate consideration. Overheads for fixed or running costs of a business did not have to be proved as having been actually incurred for the purposes of a fair valuation and that proof that costs had been incurred was not required for a fair valuation, but that their approximate amount must be established. Time related overheads need to be proved.

Where a contractor is asked to provide a quotation, they would usually do so with reference to the BoQ and would be able to claim for the cost of preparing the quotation. The quote would be sent to the employer's quantity surveyor for consideration.

3.7 Protecting Third Parties

There are many parties involved in the construction of buildings. There will be several parties involved in design and construction and there will also be lenders to the employer and sometimes the contractor. There are usually several contracts between various different parties (see paragraph 3.1.2) for each build and there needs to be some way of protecting all the parties. In addition, it is rare that a completed building is occupied or remains in the ownership of the employer. These parties need protection and there are several ways in which protection can be provided.

3.7.1 Contract (Rights of Third Parties) Act 1999

As privity of contract prevents anyone from claiming damages under a contract who isn't a party to the contract (See Chapter 2). The government enacted the Contract (Rights of Third Parties) Act 1999 to bypass the privity rules, but the construction industry usually excludes the Act from contracts because it creates too much risk of exposure to claims from many different parties. The Act would confer rights to parties beyond those expected. For example, a sub-contractor's obligations regarding quality of work would be treated as conferring a benefit on the employer, so that it may claim directly against the sub-contractor, the employer's payment obligations may be treated as a directly enforceable right by the sub-contractor, and the obligations owed to the employer by the contractor/designer may be inferred directly on the purchaser or tenant of the completed building.

The industry prefers to use either collateral warranties or schedules of third-party rights. Both methods ensure that the contracting parties are aware of all those with potential claims against them and the nature of the claims are limited to those agreed.

Future owners of property may still be able to claim for negligence (see Chapter 4) but what may be claimed for will be limited. The building contractor is only liable in tort for injury to persons; and damage to other property caused by the damaged building. The defects caused to the building by the negligence are considered to be pure economic loss and cannot be recovered in Tort.[82]

---

81 [2000] EWHC Tech. 76.

82 *D&F Estates Ltd v Church Commissioners for England and Wales* [1989] AC 177.

3.7.2 Collateral Warranties

The industry hasn't adopted the Contracts (Rights of Third Parties) Act 1999 and still uses collateral warranties. A collateral warranty is a contract which runs alongside the main contract which ensures that an injured party will always have someone to sue for damages where the Act has been excluded and the loss is one for which they cannot claim in tort (i.e. is purely economic loss).

At tender it will be made clear that the contractor will have to enter collateral warranties with specified third parties. It will owe the third party (new owner/tenant/funding institution) the same duties as it owes the employer. It is also usual that the contract will contain a clause that a similar collateral warranty will be obtained from any sub-contractor and supplier, etc.

The warranties create a contractual link between the parties, allowing those parties to sue the contractor/designer/sub-contractor directly for breach of contract where necessary. They lessen the importance of suing in torts and can be assigned to new owners of the building.

Collateral warranties are not without their problems. Parties providing collateral warranties want to limit their liability to their contribution to the defect/deficiency and never agree to more liability than that imposed by the original contract. Beneficiaries want an indemnity against all losses (economic and consequential) and require warranties that the building will be fit for purpose. It is a matter of striking a balance between these two competing requirements.

3.7.3 Schedules of Third Party Rights

Traditionally the employer would sue the main contractor who in turn would sue the sub-contractor and so on through a chain of liability. As collateral warranties can become complex, many standard contracts identify certain persons (e.g. purchasers/tenants and funders) who may claim third party rights. These clauses often stipulate precisely what those rights will be. For example, the JCT provides third party schedules to its contracts relating to purchaser and tenants, and a funder. The definition in the contract of these will contain a list or description of who those parties are.

3.7.4 Statutes Protecting Occupiers of Dwellings

Approximately 45% of construction in the UK is home building. For newly built properties, the NHBC Scheme operates. The Scheme provides a certificate with new build homes which is effectively an insurance policy paid for by the contractor to cover any defects which may occur within the first 10 years of construction. An owner with a NHB Certificate may claim to have the issue(s) corrected under the Scheme.

Due to the vulnerability of those living in properties, there is more protection under the law, even for those who are not the owner. The Defective Premises Act 1972 (the DPA) requires that professional contractors, architects, engineers, etc., undertake work in a professional manner so that the finished property is fit for human habitation. The Act stipulates that the work of those building:

i. is done in a *workmanlike manner*
ii. with *proper materials and*
iii. the *dwelling will be fit for habitation* when completed

In *Uratemp Ventures Ltd v Collins*[83] the House of Lords advised that the word 'dwelling' was defined as the place 'where a person lives or resides' and makes one's home.'

The subject of what is unfit for habitation under the DPA was discussed in the Technology and Construction Court (TCC) of the High Court in the case of *Bole v Huntsbuild.*[84] HHJ Toulmin CMG QC said that Section 604 of the Housing Act 1985 provided a definition of unfitness for habitation and went on to provide a checklist of the considerations under the DPA.

The finding of unfitness for habitation:

a. is a matter of fact in each case
b. extends to defects of quality rendering the dwelling unsuitable, as well as to dangerous defects
c. A defect in one part may render a dwelling unfit even if the defect does not extend to other parts
d. The Act also applies to latent defects
e. Consideration must be given to the effect of the defects as a whole.

The TCC also discussed liability under the DPA in *Harrison & ors v Shepherd Homes Ltd & ors.*[85]

The court held that the defendant was liable to the house owner under the sales contract when homes developed defects in foundations, it was also liable under DPA 1972, even to subsequent purchasers, because homes were not fit for human habitation due to the defective foundations. Until this case, it was not clear whether the DPA applied where the contractor both (i) carried out the design (ii) then did the work.

In the wake of the Grenfell Tower fire many leaseholders were left with the prospect of replacing external cladding on their buildings following safety concerns relating to their homes. The cost was prohibitive to many, and the fairness of the situation was raised in Parliament. Why should an owner of a property pay for defects in the building, rather than those responsible for the defect? This led to the enactment of the Building Safety Act 2022. According to the Ministry of Housing, Communities and Local Government and Department for Levelling Up (2022), '[T]his Act makes ground-breaking reforms to give residents and homeowners more rights, powers, and protections – so homes across the country are safer.

It delivers far-reaching protections for qualifying leaseholders from the costs associated with remediating historical building safety defects, and an ambitious toolkit of measures that will allow those responsible for building safety defects to be held to account.

It overhauls existing regulations, creating lasting change and makes clear how residential buildings should be constructed, maintained and made safe.

83 [2001] UKHL 43.
84 *Bole v Huntsbuild Ltd* [2009] EWHC 483 (TCC).
85 [2011] EWHC 1811 (TCC).

The Act creates three new bodies to provide effective oversight of the new regime: the Building Safety Regulator, the National Regulator of Construction Products and the New Homes Ombudsman.

Together these changes mean owners will manage their buildings better, and the home-building industry has the clear, proportionate framework it needs to deliver more, and better, high-quality homes. which is designed to protect leaseholders from paying for defects in the building of or maintenance works to the property'.[86]

3.8 Insurance

Insurance is taken to protect the parties and third parties from losses which may be caused by the contractor during construction, by loss to the work or materials or by the negligence of the contractor which causes defects to the building.

Insurance policies are a contract where one party (the insurer) agrees to indemnify another party, or parties, (the insured) against any loss arising as a result of a certain occurrence.

Most construction contracts will normally provide for liability insurance policies with an indemnity undertaking; a material damage insurance policy; and a professional indemnity insurance policy.

3.8.1 Indemnity Undertakings and Public Liability Insurance

Indemnity is the principle whereby one person undertakes to put another in the same position after a loss as was the case immediately before the loss. In addition to the requirement for liability insurance the contract will require an indemnity undertaking from the contractor to the employer to protect the employer from claims against them from third parties due to the contractor's work. If damage occurs to a neighbouring property during construction, the neighbour may sue the property owner under the torts of nuisance or trespass (see Chapter 4), rather than sue the contractor, even though the employer/owner may not have done anything wrong. The indemnity clause is there to protect the employer from this type of situation.

In the indemnity clause, the contractor indemnifies the employer against loss that may be suffered by the employer due to claims made by third parties arising out of the work that the contractor is doing. The indemnity given is often (broadly) restricted to loss caused by negligence on the part of the contractor in the course of carrying out the works under the contract.

The indemnity undertaking is not worth much unless it is accompanied by a public liability insurance policy. The contract will, therefore, provide that the contractor takes out public liability insurance in order to ensure that funds are available for the eventuality of loss. Public liability insurance constitutes a contract in the form of an indemnity: It is a promise by an insurance company to the contractor. As this policy is taken out for the sole

---

86 Ministry of Housing, Communities and Local Government and Department for Levelling Up, Housing and Communities, *Guidance the Building Safety Act* 2022. The Building Safety Act - GOV.UK (www.gov.uk).

purpose of covering any losses which may be incurred by the contractor in respect of the indemnity undertaking, it is essential that the contract between the insurance company and contractor and the contract between the contractor and the employer are 'back-to-back'. That is, that each should be in the same terms and subject to the same exceptions. An indemnity undertaking given for something which is not insured will leave the contractor exposed to meeting the employer's losses and an insurance policy for something for which there has been no undertaking would be a waste of money.

The employer will be named as a joint policy holder, so it can make a claim against the policy rather than the contractor. However, as public liability policies cover losses by the 'public' i.e. third parties, the employer will need the policy to include a cross indemnity clause which will enable the employer to claim against the policy in respect of its own losses (without it, the employer would not be a third party so would not be able to claim).

In addition to public liability for negligence, the employer may also require the contractor to take out insurance in respect of the liability of the employer. This policy will cover third party losses which are not as a result of the contractor's negligence. The Contract Particulars will state if this additional policy is required. The contractor must be party to the policy, despite not being able to claim, but it needs to agree to the conditions of issue regarding methods for undertaking the works.

There are usually limitations to contractor's insurance of liability of the employer. They will usually only cover damage to buildings and will have lots of exceptions. They are also expensive, so if risk to third parties is low (e.g. work on a greenfield site), the employer may not require it.

3.8.2 Material Damage Insurance

Material damage insurance is the insurance required to safeguard the construction of the works themselves. Material damage insurance is limited to the restoration of bricks and mortar unlike indemnity insurance, which concerns liability. The policy will differ depending on whether the work is for a new building, or is to an existing building.

Policies for new buildings are usually on an 'all risks' basis. They are always in joint names of the contractor and the employer and cover loss and/or damage to work executed and to site materials. Under joint names policies the insurance sums would be split equally between the parties, the construction contract should include an agreement that the money will go to the employer and that the contractor will be employed to re-build/repair the damage.

Where work is to an existing building, the employer will usually source the policy, because there is usually an existing policy in regard to the existing building which will be amended to cover the period of refurbishment. The owner/employer will notify the insurance company that construction work will be taking place in the existing building, and also that the contractor is to be a joint name on the policy for the duration of that work. Again, there will be an agreement in the contract that the employer will receive the funds and the contractor will be given the work. The insurance of the works will be an 'all risks' basis (like for a new build), but insurance of the existing building is on a specified perils basis only. The policy will provide a list of what is covered.

3.8.3 Professional Indemnity Insurance

Professional indemnity insurance is required for all businesses. These policies are taken out by the contractor for all the works they undertake as part of the business. They are not usually project specific. The policies protect the contractor against claims that they have not used 'reasonable competence and skill' when undertaking their work. The construction contract is likely to state what the minimum liability for the policy is to be and a copy will need to be provided to the employer. The policy limit is usually at least the value of the contract and often higher. The larger the undertaking, the higher its coverage will be. Obviously the higher the insured figure, the higher the cost.

Due to the high cost of professional indemnity policies, a subcontractor involved in only a small part of the works will not be in a position to take out insurance covering the possibility that the sub-contractor might cause destruction to the whole of the works so far completed. Accordingly, contracts will provide for the insurance of the works (material damage) to include cover for subcontractors, to a limited extent. For an example see clause 6.9 of the Joint Contracts Tribunal Standard Building Contract with Quantities 2024. In the JCT contract suit, none of the cover for sub-contractors is on an all risks basis; the provision for sub-contractors in regard to the works insurance is for 'specified perils' only. In addition, where there is an existing building, the JCT does not include provision for sub-contractors to be insured in regard to damage they might cause to the existing building in the course of carrying out their work.

4

Law of Torts

CONTENTS

4.1 Introduction

A tort is a civil wrong. The law of torts is developed from common law principles, and (unlike the law of contract) there is no complete body of rules which apply to all torts (in the way that all contracts are governed by the same general principles which remain fairly static). Duties in tort are imposed automatically by the law, in contrast to the law of contract where parties enter into an agreement with one another. Although a number of torts were established by the end of the nineteenth century, the twentieth century saw major developments in this area of law, with the expansion influenced by the rise of capitalism and manufacturing, together with advancements in transport, technology and construction activities.

A claim in tort is concerned with remedying the losses claimed by parties, called the claimant(s) and the defendant(s). A person who commits a tort (defendant) is known as a tortfeasor. Where more than one person is responsible for the commission of the tort, they are known as 'joint' tortfeasors making either or both of the defendants liable for the full extent of the claimant's injuries. The main remedy sought is damages (money), acting as compensation for loss to property, reputation, money, physical injury or some other interest protected by law. The loss may have occurred owing to the defendants' act, omission, or provision of advice. There can be an overlap between liability in tort and other areas of law, for example road traffic accidents or accidents at work. In such circumstances, each set of proceedings is dealt with individually. Claims in the law of tort are subject to the civil burden of proof, where the claimant must prove the case on the balance of probabilities.

The law of torts covers a variety of civil wrongs, including defamation, negligence, trespass and nuisance. Each tort has its own, distinct set of legal rules. Torts vary in the mental culpability required to incur liability, with some requiring the defendant to have intended to do the act, others requiring negligence, and some no mental culpability at all (strict liability torts). Strict liability torts impose liability for the consequences of actions even though the defendant neither desired them nor ought necessarily to have avoided them. State of mind, mental culpability, in such circumstances, is disregarded. Examples of strict liability torts include product liability claims, based on the Consumer Protection Act 1987, and claims based on breach of statutory duty. Loss or damage, represented by an award of damages, is not always a prerequisite of a successful claim. In some circumstances, a defendant's conduct may be actionable as a tort even though the claimant has sustained no loss. These torts are said to be actionable *per se*. Where there are repeated trespasses over a person's land, even though the landowner has suffered no loss or damage, an action may be brought in tort to restrain the trespasser from passing over the property.

It is important to note that the vast majority of tortious claims never see the inside of a court, and are instead settled long before trial (only around 5% reach court).[1] For the majority of cases, where a claimant is successful, the damages will be paid by an insurance company. Without the existence of insurance, many claimants, probably a majority, would be left without compensation. In motor accident cases insurance is compulsory while many professions make it a condition of practice that their members are insured. Property owners take out insurance policies to cover damage to buildings and/or contents while if premises are let the lease will often contain provisions as to who has responsibility for insurance. Likewise, most of the established forms of building contract require insurance against public liability. In addition to private insurance schemes, another source of compensation is the social security system for those who qualify.

4.1.1 Introducing Torts

The main torts covered in this chapter are:

4.1.1.1 Negligence

Where a person's actions cause harm to another. Three elements must be present for a claim in negligence:

1. Defendant owed a claimant a duty of care
2. The defendant breached their duty of care
3. Reasonably foreseeable damage was caused by the breach of duty of care.

---

1 See Chapter 1, and Courts and Tribunals Judiciary, England and Wales. See also G Sturge, Court Statistics for England and Wales, House of Commons Library (September 2024).

4.1.1.2 Vicarious Liability

The liability of an employer for the acts or omissions of their employee when carried out during the course of their employment.

4.1.1.3 Nuisance

Private nuisance is where the actions of a landowner on their own land cause substantial interference to the use of enjoyments of land by another. Public nuisance is an act or omission that endangers public health, life, property, etc.

4.1.1.4 Trespass

The protection under law from the unlawful interference with one's land, person or property.

4.1.1.5 Defamation

Collective term for the law protecting a person's reputation from harm caused by the publication of false statements. Two separate harms are covered by the term defamation – libel and slander.

4.2 Negligence

Negligence is concerned with circumstances where one causes harm to another. It is wider than most other torts, and liability may arise in a variety of situations. Liability in negligence is concerned with a duty of care – was one owed, was it breached and was damaged caused by the breach? It is therefore dependent on the claimant being able to establish three elements:

1. The defendant owed the claimant a duty of care – duty owed
2. The duty of care was breached (broken) by the defendant – duty breached
3. The claimant suffered damage as a consequence of the breach of duty of care – causal link

These three requirements were established in the leading case of *Donoghue v Stevenson*.[2] Two friends visited a café, where the claimant was treated, by their companion, to a bottle of ginger beer manufactured by the defendants. Having sampled some of the contents, they realised that the bottle contained parts of a decomposed snail. The claimant suffered nervous shock and became ill with gastroenteritis. The claimant did not have a contract with the cafe owner, as the item had been sold to their friend, so they brought an action against the manufacturers of the ginger beer in tort. The House of Lords held that a manufacturer owes a duty of care to the ultimate consumer of goods, irrespective of whether a contract exists between the relevant parties.[3]

---

2 *Donoghue v Stevenson* [1932] AC 562.

3 *Grant v Australian Knitting Mills* [1936] AC 85.

4.2.1 Duty of Care Owed

The first question to be answered in a claim of negligence is whether a duty of care was owed from the defendant to the claimant. Before 1932, there were limited situations where the courts recognised the existence of a legal duty of care – examples included the relationship between doctor and patient and lawyer and client. The courts were reluctant to deal with the issue of where such a duty should arise. Claimants were required to show that their case came within an existing category of duty or that a new area of duty should be introduced. The issue became more problematic where contractual duties existed, with the courts tending to avoid holding liability in torts when someone was not a party to a contract. The evolution of the law in this area, in answering whether a duty of care is owed by defendant to claimant, has been developed through a number of key cases.

4.2.1.1 Donoghue v Stevenson

There were no firm principles relating to the duty of care until the decision in *Donoghue*,[4] cited above. In their judgment, Lord Atkin pronounced a general test, the neighbour principle, where a person owes a duty of care to their neighbour. They then defined a neighbour as someone who is 'so closely and directly affected by my acts that I ought reasonably to have them in contemplation as being so affected when I am directing my mind to the acts or omissions which are called in question'.[5]

4.2.1.2 Dutton v Bognor Regis Urban District Council and Anns v Merton London Borough Council

Courts were cautious in their development of duty of care in the years following *Donoghue v Stevenson*.[6] It was not until the 1970s and the early 1980s that the higher courts embarked on an expansionist role. In a number of leading cases, the courts found a duty of care to exist in situations where they had not previously done so. Examples include *Dutton v Bognor Regis UDC*[7] and *Anns v Merton LBC*.[8] This latter decision created a presumption of the existence of a duty of care which the defendant then had to rebut on policy grounds. The case had a significant effect on construction activities and, in particular, on local authorities when carrying out their inspection and approval activities of new buildings. Liability was imposed in negligence where previously no duty of care was owed. From the mid-1980s onwards the 'retreat from Anns' began. In a series of cases,[9] culminating in *Murphy v Brentwood DC*,[10] the Law Lords became highly critical of the decisions based on *Dutton* and *Anns*.

---

4 *Donoghue v Stevenson* [1932] AC 562.
5 [1932] AC 562 at Ibid., 577.
6 Ibid.
7 *Dutton v Bognor Regis Urban District Council* [1972] 1 All ER 462.
8 *Anns v Merton LBC* [1978] AC 728.
9 *Peabody Donation Fund [Governors] v Sir Lindsay Parkinson & Co Ltd* [1985] AC 210; *Yuen Kun Yeu v A-G of Hong Kong* 1988 [AC] 175; *D & F Estates Ltd v Church Commissioners for England* [1989] AC 177.
10 *Murphy v Brentwood DC* [1991] AC 398.

4.2.1.3 Caparo Industries Plc v Dickman

A key case in the development of the neighbour principle is the decision in *Caparo Industries v Dickman.*[11] Caparo, the claimants, bought shares in, and eventually took over, a company on the statutory audited accounts provided by Dickman. The accounts were inaccurate and showed a £1.3 million profit as opposed to a loss of £465,000. Caparo brought an action in negligence against Dickman. The House of Lords held that Dickman were not liable in negligence owing to the purpose of the audit, and Lord Bridge outlined a new three stage test for determining whether a duty of care was owed:

1. Foreseeability of damage (neighbour test).
2. Proximity of relationship.
3. Whether it is just and reasonable to impose a duty of care (policy).

This three pronged approach was confirmed in *Marc Rich & Co AG v Bishop Rock Marine Co Ltd and others, The Nicholas H.*[12] Each factor cannot operate independently of the other two. The courts have not closed the categories of negligence but a claimant seeking to establish a new duty situation will have to establish that such an imposition accords with previous analyses of justice and policy. The 'Caparo' approach was confirmed in *Mitchell [A P] v Glasgow City Council.*[13]

4.2.1.3.1 Foreseeability

This first requirement confirms that a duty of care is not owed to the world at large. This is the factual aspect of the duty of care and is really a refined version of the 'neighbour' test in Donoghue v Stevenson. It means that a claimant must show that, at the time of the defendant's negligent act, it was foreseeable that some damage to that particular claimant was foreseeable. If damage to someone else is foreseeable, but not to the claimant, the action will fail. In *Bourhill v Young,*[14] the action failed when the claimant alleged that she had suffered nervous shock after hearing the impact of a crash which resulted in her giving birth to a stillborn child. She was outside the area of foreseeable shock and the claim failed.

4.2.1.3.2 Proximity

Foreseeability of harm is an aspect of proximity while whether proximity exists, in a particular set of circumstances, is also influenced by policy considerations. Proximity is not easy to define as it can mean different things in different situations. It probably indicates a relationship between two parties where it is fair and reasonable that one should owe the other a duty of care. In road traffic accident cases the requirement is satisfied by the existence of foreseeability, while in negligent misstatement cases1 the parties will normally have to establish some prior relationship. In psychiatric damage cases, where the claimant is a secondary victim, the claimant is required to have 'close ties of love and affection' with the victim. In *Hill v Chief Constable of West Yorkshire,*[15] relatives of the victims of a serial

---

11 *Caparo Industries v Dickman* [1990] 2 AC 605.

12 *Marc Rich & Co AG v Bishop Rock Marine Co Ltd and others, The Nicholas H* [1996] AC 211.

13 *Mitchell [A P] v Glasgow City Council* [2009] UKHL 11.

14 *Bourhill v Young* [1943] AC 92.

15 *Hill v Chief Constable of West Yorkshire* [1992] 2 All ER 625.

killer had no claim against the police where it was alleged that they had failed to use reasonable care to apprehend the murderer. It was held that there was no proximity between specific individuals and the police in the exercise of their duties.

4.2.1.3.3 Just and Reasonable

The third element of *Caparo* confirms that no duty of care will be imposed unless it is just to do so in the circumstances. This is the policy factor where judges have to decide whether there should, or should not be, a duty in the particular circumstances. Numerous issues apply here: whether the parties have insurance cover, the overburdening of particular professions and the 'floodgates' argument where to impose liability would result in too many claims of a particular type being brought before the courts are a few examples. The House of Lords in *Hill* confirmed that the police enjoy immunity from actions in negligence but it appears that the courts are not prepared to give public bodies immunity in every situation. The issue has arisen in a human rights context.[16] The immunity enjoyed by public bodies has also been scrutinised in this way.[17] Those involved in the judicial process are immune from any civil proceedings against them during the course of a trial. This would include an action in negligence. Judges, magistrates, witnesses and arbitrators enjoy this privilege. There have been cases where persons appointed to perform some form of professional task have sought the immunity that an arbitrator has from claims in negligence against them. These have been unsuccessful. Examples include certifying that a building contract is progressing satisfactorily[18] and making a valuation of shares.[19] The immunity enjoyed by advocates, while arguing cases in court, appears to have been lost.[20]

4.2.1.4 Murphy v Brentwood District Council

The case of *Murphy v Brentwood District Council*[21] concerned a new semi-detached house which had been built on a concrete raft on a landfill site. The raft was not adequate for the purpose and 11 years after construction the claimant discovered cracks which appeared as the house subsided. The claimant sold the property to a purchaser for £35,000 less than its value in good condition. Plans had been submitted to the local authority seeking permission to build the house, and these had been approved. The claimant brought an action against the local authority for their negligence in approving them. The House of Lords dismissed the claim on the basis that the damage suffered was purely economic in nature. They did not follow their earlier decision in *Anns v Merton Borough Council.*[22] It was emphasised that a defect which does not render a building an immediate danger to the health and safety of its occupants is purely economic in nature and not foreseeable. Any remedy should be in contract and not in tort in such cases.

---

16 *Osman v United Kingdom* [1999] Crim LR 82.
17 X *v Bedfordshire County Council* [1995] 3 All ER 353.
18 *Sutcliffe v Thackrah* [1974] AC 727.
19 *Arenson v Casson, Beckman, Rutley & Co* [1977] AC 405.
20 *Hall [Arthur & Co] v Simons* [2000] 3 All ER 673.
21 *Murphy v Brentwood District Council* [1991] AC 398.
22 *Anns v Merton Borough Council* [1978] AC 728.

4.2.1.4.1 Pure Economic Losses

The courts have always been reluctant to allow liability for pure economic losses which arise from negligent acts even if they are foreseeable. Pure economic loss was recently defined by the Supreme Court as "'pure economic loss', meaning economic loss that is not consequent on damage to, or loss of, the claimant's property (or on personal injury to the claimant)".[23] This position has been adopted for a number of reasons: liability is potentially unlimited, such losses are not possible to insure against, are usually too remote and are essentially a concept more suited to the law of contract than the law of tort. The leading case is *Cattle v Stockton Water Works*.[24] In this case, the claimant was building a tunnel for a landowner when the defendant company's water main leaked into the area of the works. This delayed the project and reduced the claimant's profit. No cause of action was found to arise as no property had been damaged or personal injury sustained by the claimant. The loss of profit was a purely economic loss. In *Spartan Steel v Martin & Co*[25] the defendants negligently cut an electric power cable resulting in loss of power to the claimants who manufactured steel alloys. A consignment of steel in the claimant's furnace, at the time of the power cut, had to be destroyed to stop it from severely damaging the furnace. The claimants succeeded in their claim for physical damage and the loss of profit on the steel in the process of production. The claim for loss of profits on four more consignments of steel, which were planned but not carried out, failed as they were classified as being purely economic in nature. A similar approach was taken in *Weller & Co v Foot and Mouth Disease Research Institute*[26] where a virus escaped from the defendant's premises causing an outbreak of foot and mouth disease. The claimant auctioneers suffered losses when a ban was put on the movement of cattle preventing any sales of livestock taking place. An action for loss of profits failed as they were treated as being purely economic in nature. In *Greater Nottingham Co-operative Society Ltd v Cementation Piling & Foundations Ltd*[27] the claimants sustained purely economic losses due to the negligence of the defendants in carrying out piling work. The contract between the parties contained no provisions relating to this issue and no claim was allowed in the tort of negligence.

Pure economic loss under tort law can be of particular relevance to the construction industry, often owing to a lack of contractual relationship between claimant and defendant, preventing a claim under contract law and necessitating one in negligence. It can also arise as a claim running concurrent to one in contract, where the court considers both areas of law, as in *Beattie Passive Norse Ltd and another v Canham Consulting Ltd*.[28]

The rule from *Murphy v Brentwood District Council*[29] stated 'if the claimant discovers the defect before damage occurs he has a claim for economic loss if there is a special relationship'.[30] Two recent construction cases considered economic loss and negligence.

---

23 *Armstead v Royal & Sun Alliance Insurance Company Ltd* [2024] UKSC 6.

24 *Cattle v Stockton Water Works* (1875) LR 10 QB 453.

25 *Spartan Steel v Martin & Co* [1973] 1 QB 27.

26 *Weller & Co v Foot and Mouth Disease Research Institute* [1965] 3 All ER 560.

27 *Greater Nottingham Co-operative Society Ltd v Cementation Piling & Foundations Ltd* [1988] 2All ER 971.

28 *Beattie Passive Norse Ltd and another v Canham Consulting Ltd* [2021]196 ConLR 85.

29 *Murphy v Brentwood District Council* [1991] AC 398.

30 Ibid 15.

Vinci Construction UK Ltd v Eastwood and Partners (Consulting Engineers) Ltd and another[31] provided a useful summary of the law regarding economic loss in construction law cases:

1. A claim in tort based on negligence is incomplete without proof of damage. There are two kinds of loss which are recognised as actionable damage for the tort of negligence, namely, physical damage and economic loss: *Rothwell v Chemical & Insulating Co Limited*[32]
2. In a case where there is physical damage, the current state of the law is that the claimant's cause of action accrues when that physical damage occurs, regardless of the claimant's knowledge of the physical damage or its discoverability: *Cartledge v Joplin*[33]
3. In a case where there is economic loss, the claimant's cause of action accrues when the claimant relies on negligent advice or services to its detriment, including incurring a liability (unless such liability is purely contingent, in which case it is not actionable damage until there is measurable loss): *Law Society v Sephton; Axa Insurance Limited v Akther & Derby*[34]
4. In a case where the claimant relies on negligent advice or services and, as a result, the structure contains an inherent design defect which does not immediately cause physical damage, the claimant's cause of action accrues at the latest on completion of the structure, at which point the claimant has a defective asset and suffers economic loss, regardless of its knowledge of the latent damage.[35]

BDW Trading Ltd v URS Corporation Ltd[36] concerned a civil engineering company (URS) which provided structural drawings for a developer (BDW) for two residential developments. Significant structural defects were subsequently discovered; however, no physical damage had occurred. The Court of Appeal held:

> the law imposed (...) a duty to take care was the risk of economic loss that would be caused by a construction of a structure using a negligent design such that it was built containing structural deficiencies or defects. That was a standard duty imposed on a design professional which was co-existent with that professional's contractual obligations. The risk of harm was that, in breach of the professional's duty, the design of the buildings would contain structural defects which would have to be subsequently remedied.[37]

4.2.2 Duty of Care Breached

The second question to be answered is whether the duty of care owed by defendant to claimant was breached. This is answered by assessing the acts or omissions of the

31 *Vinci Construction UK Ltd v Eastwood and Partners (Consulting Engineers) Ltd and another* [2003] EWHC 1899 (TCC).
32 *Rothwell v Chemical & Insulating Co Limited* [2007] UKHL 39 per Lord Hoffmann at [7].
33 *Cartledge v Joplin* [1963] AC 758.
34 *Law Society v Sephton* [2006] UKHL 22; *Axa Insurance Limited v Akther & Derby* [2009] EWCA Civ 1166 per Arden L.J. at [30]–[33].
35 *New Islington and Hackney Housing Association Ltd v Pollard Thomas & Edwards Ltd* [2001] PNLR 20 per Dyson J. at [38]–[43].
36 *BDW Trading Ltd v URS Corporation Ltd* [2024] 2 All ER 118.
37 Ibid., 121.

defendant against the acts or omissions of a *reasonable person* in the same circumstances, has their act or omission fallen below the standard that could reasonably be expected? This is an objective test, adjudging the acts or omissions against that of a reasonable person as compared to a subjective test which focuses on what the defendant thought/believed at the time. The objective test was formulated in *Blyth v Birmingham Waterworks Co*[38]:

> Negligence is the omission to do something which a reasonable man, guided upon those considerations which ordinarily regulate the conduct of human affairs, would do, or doing something which a prudent and reasonable man would not do.[39]

It was further explained in *Bolam v Friern Hospital Management Committee*[40]:

> In the ordinary case which does not involve any special skill, negligence in law means this: Some failure to do some act which a reasonable man in the circumstances would do, or doing some act which a reasonable man in the circumstances would not do; and if that failure or doing of that act results in injury, then there is a cause of action. How do you test whether this act or failure is negligent? In an ordinary case it is generally said, that you judge that by the action of the man in the street. He is the ordinary man. In one case it has been said that you judge it by the conduct of the man on the top of a Clapham omnibus. He is the ordinary man.[41]

The courts take into account a variety of factors to help determine the appropriate standard of care. In any particular case a judge may be balancing a number of these factors to ascertain where it should lie, and the courts evaluate the concept in terms of risk. In *Bolton v Stone*[42] the claimant was hit by a cricket ball. As it was improbable that the ball would be hit out of the ground, or cause injury if it did, the defendant was not liable. A different conclusion was reached in *Hilder v Associated Portland Cement Manufacturers Ltd*[43] where the defendant allowed children to play football on waste ground, which they owned, next to a busy road. Balls frequently went onto the road and one caused the claimant motorist to crash resulting in their death. In *Paris v Stepney BC*[44] the claimant, who was blind in one eye, was blinded in the other eye during the course of their employment. The claimant contended that their employers were negligent because they had not provided goggles. The argument was upheld, and the House of Lords emphasised that a higher degree of care is always required when dealing with persons suffering from a mental or physical disability, children (especially young ones) and elderly people. In *Haley v London Electricity Board*[45]

---

38 *Blyth v Birmingham Waterworks Co* [1843–60] All ER Rep 478.
39 Ibid., 480.
40 *Bolam v Friern Hospital Management Committee* [1957] 2 All ER 118.
41 Ibid., at 121.
42 *Bolton v Stone* [1951] AC 850.
43 *Hilder v Associated Portland Cement Manufacturers Ltd* [1961] 3All ER 709.
44 *Paris v Stepney BC* [1950] UKHL 3.
45 *Haley v London Electricity Board* [1965] AC 778.

the defendants were placed under a higher duty of care in circumstances where they knew of the existence of blind people in the locality and did not take adequate steps when fencing off excavation works on the highway. In *Withers v Perry Chain Co Ltd*[46] the claimant was prone to suffer from dermatitis, and so was given the most grease-free job available by their employer. The claimant nevertheless contracted the ailment. As their employer had done everything possible to protect them, the company was not liable. The only other alternative would be to have dismissed them. The utility of the defendant's act is also of importance. The risk must be balanced against the end to be achieved. Sometimes, it is appropriate to consider what the cost and difficulty would be in avoiding an identifiable risk. As long as everything reasonable in the circumstances has been done, there will be no liability.

4.2.2.1 The Objective Test: Skills and Age

Negligence is based on fault so the claimant must establish that the defendant has fallen below the standard of care expected of them. However, what if the defendant is inexperienced or unskilled? In *Nettleship v Weston*[47] the claimant had agreed to teach the defendant how to drive. During one of their lessons, the defendant struck a lamppost, injuring the claimant. The court held that, despite being a learner driver, the defendant owed a duty of care to their passenger and whether that had been breached was to be assessed using the same objective standard as any other road user, not the standard of a learner/inexperienced driver. However, in *Orchard v Lee*,[48] the court did account for the age of the defendant when applying the objective test, and the objective standard was applied to someone of the same age. In *Orchard*, during the course of a game of 'tag' in a school playground, a 13-year-old collided with a lunchtime supervisor. The court held that the child had not breached their duty of care, as a reasonable-13 year-old would not have foreseen the risk of injury through playing tag. This decision affirmed the earlier decision regarding children in *Mullin v Richards*,[49] wherein the claimant and the defendant, who were 15 years old, were fighting with plastic rulers in a classroom. A fragment broke off the defendant's ruler and flew into the claimant's eye causing them to lose sight in that eye. The Court of Appeal decided that a 15-year-old child could not have foreseen the likelihood of harm as a consequence of their behaviour.

4.2.2.2 The Objective Test: Professionals

The standard of care expected by professionals is assessed against another similarly skilled person, as detailed in *Bolam*:

> The test is the standard of the ordinary skilled man exercising and professing to have that special skill. A man need not possess the highest expert skill at the risk of being found negligent. It is well established law that it is sufficient if he exercises the ordinary skill of an ordinary competent man exercising that particular art.

---

46 *Withers v Perry Chain Co Ltd.*

47 *Nettleship v Weston* [1971] 3 WLR 370.

48 *Orchard v Lee* [2009] EWCA 295.

49 *Mullin v Richards* [1998] 1 All ER 920.

Termed 'the *Bolam* test', this test is applied in all cases concerning the alleged negligence of those with specialist knowledge or skill,[50] although it most commonly arises in cases concerning clinical/medical negligence. In *Wells v Cooper*[51] the defendant had fixed a door handle onto a door. Evidence showed that they did the job as well as an ordinary carpenter. The handle came off in the claimant's hand and they were injured. As the defendant had exercised the skill of a reasonably competent carpenter and therefore was not liable.

The courts rely heavily on expert evidence from practitioners and codes of practice. Such experts are usually appointed by the relevant parties but can be appointed by the court. In *Abbey National Mortgages plc v Key Surveyors Nationwide Ltd*[52] appointment of a joint expert by the court, in addition to experts nominated by the relevant parties, was upheld by the Court of Appeal in a case involving negligent mortgage valuations relating to residential properties. In *Samson v Metcalfe Hambleton & Co*[53] it was emphasised that expert witnesses should be from the same profession as the defendant. In this case, which involved cracks in a wall, the Court of Appeal took the view that a structural engineer was not an appropriate expert witness in a case involving alleged negligence by a building surveyor.

Although a professional person must be skilful and careful, being incorrect is not necessarily negligent, for example, an inaccurate valuation of premises, or of the cost of carrying out building works, is not necessarily negligent. Where a valuation is carried out by unorthodox methods, but comes within a 'bracket' of figures that a competent practitioner would arrive at, it is unlikely that there will be a breach of duty following *Bolam*. In determining whether a valuer has exercised a reasonable degree of skill and care, various factors have to be considered. These include the scope of the instructions given, knowledge of the law and adherence to current procedures and practices. It is normally assumed that the inexperienced professional person will seek the advice of those who are more experienced in complicated situations. Where a surveyor is carrying out a valuation for mortgage purposes, a limited visual inspection will suffice, unless the circumstances warrant further investigation, in which case the surveyor must obtain the information which it is reasonable to have before making the valuation.

Application of the *Bolam* test requires the input of others also possessing specialist skills and knowledge to ascertain whether the defendant acted as a reasonable person. However, *Bolitho v City and Hackney Health Authority*[54] held that even where a body of professionals with skills and knowledge would have acted as the defendant did, this is not conclusive. Though rare, the House of Lords held:

> But if, in rare cases, it can be demonstrated that the professional opinion is not capable of withstanding logical analysis, the judge is entitled to hold that the body of opinion is not reasonable or responsible.[55]

---

50 See *Spellman v Portsmouth Hospitals University NHS Trust* [2024] All ER (D) 10 (August); *FXS (through his father and litigation friend JLM) v The Mulberry Bush Organisation Ltd* [2024] EWHC 1406 (KB), [2024] All ER (D) 29 (June).

51 *Wells v Cooper* [1958] 2 QB 265.

52 *Abbey National Mortgages plc v Key Surveyors Nationwide Ltd* [1996] 1 WLR 1534.

53 *Samson v Metcalfe Hambleton & Co* [1998] 2 EGLR 103, CA.

54 *Bolitho v City and Hackney Health Authority* [1997] UKHL 46.

55 Ibid., 243.

The objective test as applied to professionals with specific skills and knowledge can therefore be summarised through two questions:

1. Has the defendant acted in accordance with a practice accepted as proper by a respectable body of opinion?
2. If yes, is the practice itself reasonable and logical?[56]

4.2.3 Causal Link (Causation)

The third requirement in a negligence claim is causation. The claimant must prove a causal link between the defendant's breach of duty and the harm which occurred to the claimant.

There are two aspects to causation which need to be established by the claimant:

1. The breach of duty must be linked to the harm 'in fact' (factual causation) and
2. The breach of duty must be linked to the harm must 'in law' (legal causation).

The defendant's breach of duty of care must have *caused* the claimant's loss, and as in contract claims, the damage must not be too remote. Causation is 'a highly fact-sensitive arena'[57] as evidenced by the case authorities below.

4.2.3.1 Factual Causation

The question to be asked is – Did the defendant's breach in fact cause the claimant's harm?

This is also termed the 'but for' test, which asks, but for the defendant's actions, would the harm have occurred? If the answer is no, then factual causation is established. If the answer is yes, then factual causation is not established.

In *McWilliams v Sir William Arrol & Co Ltd*[58] the claimant was killed when they fell while not using a safety harness. Statute required that harnesses should be supplied but the defendants avoided liability because they could show that the claimant would not have worn a harness even if one had been supplied. The test can only be used where a definitive answer can be given. It may be there are a number of possible causes of the claimant's loss. In such cases, of concurrent multiple causes, the courts have tended to take the view that if the defendant's action or inaction has materially increased the risk of injury to the claimant, they will be liable. Sometimes, when the claimant is injured by the defendant's negligence, but before the case is heard, an unrelated consecutive event occurs that causes the claimant the same loss for which they are suing the defendant. Where two independent events cause the same harm the 'but for' test is applied so that the defendant will usually escape liability for harm caused by the second event. In *Performance Cars Ltd v Abraham*[59] the defendant collided with a Rolls Royce, which was subsequently struck by another car. The first defendant was liable for the cost of the respray to the car while the second defendant was not liable. Difficulty arises where a second independent event causes similar but increased harm. Policy issues often apply in these cases with the courts trying to achieve a balance of not over or under compensating claimants.

---

56 Horsey and Rackley *Tort Law* (6th ed.) (OUP, 2019).

57 *Beattie Passive Norse Ltd and another v Canham Consulting Ltd* [2021] EWHC 1116 (TCC) para 106.

58 *McWilliams v Sir William Arrol & Co Ltd* [1962] 1 WLR 295.

59 *Performance Cars Ltd v Abraham* [1962] 1 QB 33.

4.2.3.2 Legal Causation

The Court of Appeal provided the following guidance for establishing legal causation:

> conduct which contains no element of fault will not without more be treated as a cause in law ... It is often said that legal causation is a matter of fact and common sense. Causation involves taking account of recognised legal principles but, that having been done, it is a question of fact in each case.[60]

4.2.3.2.1 Remoteness of Damage

The consequences of a defendant's act can be so far reaching that as a matter of policy, a limit is put on their liability. As highlighted by the Supreme Court in 2024 'general principles (...) limit the recovery of damages in tort, including the limitation that loss is not recoverable if it is too remote a consequence of the wrong'.[61] Originally the rule was that a defendant would be liable for anything that was a direct consequence of their act; however, this was replaced by the *reasonable foreseeability* test which was formulated by the Privy Council in 1961. It seems that only the general and not the specific type of damage needs to be foreseen. If the type of damage suffered is foreseeable, it does not matter that it came about in an unforeseeable manner.

As articulated by the Supreme Court:

> The test for remoteness in the tort of negligence, as laid down in *Overseas Tankship (UK) Ltd v Morts Dock & Engineering Co, The Wagon Mound* [1961] AC 388, is that loss is too remote to be recoverable as damages if the type of loss suffered was not reasonably foreseeable at the time of the breach of duty. But if the type of loss was reasonably foreseeable, it does not matter that the precise manner in which it was incurred was not reasonably foreseeable: *Hughes v Lord Advocate* [1963] AC 837.[62]

In *Hughes v The Lord Advocate*[63] employees carrying out street works left a manhole uncovered inside a tent. A number of lit paraffin lamps were left at the corners of the tent at night. A boy entered the tent with one of the lamps. The lamp fell into the hole, causing an explosion, and the boy was badly burnt. The court held that although this was an unlikely sequence of events, some fire-related damage was a foreseeable consequence of leaving the site unattended. A similar approach was taken in *Jolley v London Borough of Sutton*[64] where a teenager was seriously injured by an abandoned boat which fell onto them. The House of Lords took the view that some harm was reasonably foreseeable in the circumstances and the local authority was liable as they should have removed the boat from the area.

4.2.3.2.2 The 'Thin Skull' Rule

The thin skull, or egg shell rule, is that one must take their victim as they find them. This means that a defendant will be liable for all the damage suffered by the claimant if it is

---

60 *County Ltd v Girozentrale Securities* [1996] 3 All ER 834, para 857, 858.
61 *Armstead v Royal & Sun Alliance Insurance Company Ltd* [2024] UKSC 6.
62 Ibid., para 47 (i).
63 *Hughes v The Lord Advocate* [1963] AC 837.
64 *Jolley v London Borough of Sutton* [2000] 1 WLR 1082.

foreseeable that the claimant will suffer the general type of harm that they do in fact suffer. This is so even if the claimant, due to some kind of sensitivity, suffers to a greater extent than would normally be foreseen. In *Smith v Leech, Brain & Co*[65] the defendant's employee was negligently splashed on the lip by molten metal. This caused a pre-malignant condition to develop. The claimant later died of cancer and their widow sued. The defendants were liable. Even though the death from cancer was not foreseeable, some harm resulting from the negligence was. The rule has been applied to a variety of 'sensitivities' even where the harm suffered is psychiatric injury. It does not apply where the claimant's initial loss is increased by their lack of financial resources to take steps to minimise their loss.

4.2.3.2.3 Intervening Acts

An intervening act (or '*novus actus interveniens*') breaks the chain of causation between the claimant and the defendant. The occurrence of such an act, after the defendant's breach of duty has taken place, has the effect of exonerating the defendant for losses suffered by the claimant which occur after the intervening act has taken place. The courts have been somewhat erratic in the application of this doctrine often obscuring legal principles with policy considerations when deciding who should bear the loss in any particular case.

The intervening act can arise in three ways. The cause may be that of a third party in which case a new defendant may be introduced into the scenario. In *Baxhall Securities Ltd v Sheard Walshaw Partnership*[66] the chain of causation was broken when a firm of surveyors, on inspecting a roof, failed to discover defects caused by the negligence of the architects who designed the structure. For the act of the third party to break the chain of causation the defendant must not have any duty to guard against the third party's act and the consequence of the third party's act must be foreseeable. In *Ward v Cannock Chase District Council*[67] the claimants lived next door to a house that the defendants had allowed to fall into a serious state of repair. While the defendants repaired the property next door the claimants were required to move out of their house. In the claimant's absence, vandals broke into the house and caused damage. The court decided that there was no break in the chain of causation as the council had failed to effect the repairs quickly enough. They were liable in negligence. The second way in which an intervening act may come about is where a natural act occurs. This will rarely break the chain of causation but in those situations where the defendant can show that the act is unforeseeable and is independent of their own negligence they may be relieved of liability. Finally, the chain of causation may be broken by an intervening act of the claimant. In this case there is an assertion that the claimant is responsible for their losses. If that is so the defendant is exonerated from any liability. To succeed it must be shown that the claimant's actions are unreasonable.

4.2.4 Proof in Negligence Cases

The normal burden of proof in civil actions applies here. The claimant must prove the facts relied upon on the balance of probabilities. Once the appropriate standard of care has been

65 *Smith v Leech, Brain & Co* [1962] 2 QB 405.
66 *Baxhall Securities Ltd v Sheard Walshaw Partnership* [2002] EWCA Civ 09.
67 *Ward v Cannock Chase District Council* [1986] 3 All ER 537.

established the claimant must prove that the defendant was negligent rather than the other way around. Evidence must be produced to demonstrate how the defendant behaved showing that this was below the required standard. There are two exceptions to this.

4.2.4.1 S11 Civil Evidence Act 1968

Often the facts on which a negligence case is based will result in a prosecution being brought against the defendant as well. This provision provides that a conviction on a criminal charge is admissible as evidence in a civil case based on the same facts. In a negligence case this has the effect of creating a rebuttable presumption of negligence. In other words, it is for the defendant to show that on the balance of probabilities they were not negligent.

4.2.4.2 Res Ipsa Loquitur

This means literally, 'the thing speaks for itself'. This assists a claimant where there is no known cause of the accident. Its effect is to raise a presumption of negligence on the defendant's part which the defendant must then rebut. The principle was raised in *Scott v London & St Katherine's Docks*[68] where bags of sugar fell on the claimant when they were standing near the door of the defendant's warehouse. At first instance the case failed, in the absence of evidence of negligence, but on appeal the claimant succeeded. Three requirements must be satisfied for the plea to succeed.

4.2.4.2.1 The Thing Causing the Damage Must Have Been Under the Defendant's Exclusive Control

In *Gee v Metropolitan Railway*[69] the claimant fell out of a train when they leaned on the door as it was moving out of a station. The door had been under the defendant's control just before leaving the station and this raised a rebuttable presumption of negligence. In *Easson v LNER*[70] a boy fell out of a train some seven miles after the last stopping place. The defendant did not have sufficient control over the manually operated door as anyone might have unsecured the door since the last stop.

4.2.4.2.2 Res Ipsa Loquitur Cannot Be Relied Upon Where the Cause of Action Is Known

In *Barkway v South Wales Transport Co*[71] a bus swerved and crashed injuring the claimant. The cause of the accident was a burst tyre. As all the facts were known the doctrine could not be relied upon.

4.2.4.2.3 The Accident Should Be of a Sort That Does Not Normally Happen in the Absence of Negligence

In *Chaproniere v Mason*[72] a stone was found inside an iced bun. It would not have been there but for the negligence of the defendant. The traditional view was that where the

---

68 *Scott v London & St Katherine's Docks* (1865) 3 H & C 596.
69 *Gee v Metropolitan Railway* (1873) LR 8 QB 161.
70 *Easson v LNER* [1944] 1 KB 421.
71 *Barkway v South Wales Transport Co* [1950] 1 All ER 392.
72 *Chaproniere v Mason* (1905) 21 TLR 633.

doctrine applies the burden of proof is shifted to the defendant who must prove that they were not negligent[73]. A different approach was taken in *Ng Chun Pui v Lee Chuen Tat*[74] where it was considered that all a defendant need do to avoid liability is to give an explanation for the accident which is consistent with negligence while there is an absence of negligence on their part. The claimant must then prove that the defendant was negligent.

4.2.5 Psychiatric Injury

It may be that when a claimant brings an action based on personal injury the loss suffered by the claimant may not be a physical injury but instead a 'recognised psychiatric illness or disorder'.[75] The courts were originally reluctant to allow claims in nervous shock cases, as they were originally called, because of the problem of fraudulent claims, the difficulty of calculating damages in respect of such actions and the fear that making such incidents actionable would give rise to too much litigation. Initially the courts would only allow such a claim when it was accompanied by physical injury. The law developed when the legal system began to compensate those persons who suffered from psychiatric injury where the claimant feared for their own safety.[76] The principle was taken a step further in *Hambrook v Stokes*[77] where the claimant's wife, fearing that her daughter had been hit by a lorry, suffered nervous shock leading to her death. The claim succeeded as the court considered that a claimant's action could succeed if nervous shock was caused by fear of harm to one's spouse or children. The law was extended to cover the situation where the claimant feared for the safety of their work colleagues[78] and also where the claimant was a rescuer.[79] This expansionist approach reached its peak in *McLoughlin v O'Brian*.[80] The claimant's husband and children were injured in a car crash. The claimant arrived at the hospital about an hour after the accident and was informed of the death of one of her children and saw the three other injured members of her family in a very poor condition of health. The claimant, who was a woman of reasonable fortitude, suffered nervous shock and a change of personality. The House of Lords held that since the claimant's relationship with the victims was sufficiently close and the woman was present at the 'immediate aftermath' of the accident she could claim successfully.

4.2.6 Negligent Advice

An issue which the law of negligence has had to address is whether an action should succeed where a claimant has relied on a negligently made statement and consequently suffered financial loss. A major problem is that such losses will often be purely economic

73 *Henderson v Henry E Jenkins & Sons* [1970] AC 282.
74 *Ng Chun Pui v Lee Chuen Tat* [1988] PIQR 170.
75 Per Lord Bridge in *Attia v British Gas* [1987] 3 All ER 455 at page 462.
76 *Dulieu v White & Sons* [1901] 2 KB 669.
77 *Hambrook v Stokes* [1925] 1 KB 141.
78 *Dooley v Cammell Laird* [1951] 1 Lloyds Rep 271; *Young v Charles Church* [1997] BMLR 146.
79 *Chadwick v British Railways Board* [1967] 1 WLR 912.
80 *McLoughlin v O'Brian* [1983] AC 410.

in nature and the law of negligence has shown reluctance towards such claims.[81] Where the parties are in a contractual position the claimant may be able to take advantage of the provisions laid down in the Misrepresentation Act 1967. The tort of deceit may be applicable to this situation but it only applies to fraudulently made statements.[82] A significant development took place with the decision in *Hedley Byrne v Heller & Partners Ltd.*[83] The claimant advertising agents acted on behalf of a client known as Easipower. As they had not previously worked for the client they asked Easipower's bank for a credit reference. The bank replied that the company was 'good for ordinary business arrangements'. Easipower went into liquidation owing the claimants a considerable sum of money. Although the defendants avoided liability by inserting a valid disclaimer with their advice, the Law Lords decided that an action could be brought in these circumstances. '*Hedley Byrne*' is an important decision as it recognised that a duty of care would arise in certain situations where a person gives negligent advice which results in financial loss. It also decided that the duty can be owed where there is no contractual liability and where the claim is in respect of purely economic losses. In such cases, there is an assumption of responsibility by the party who actually gives the advice.

4.2.6.1 The Pre-requisites of Liability

4.2.6.1.1 Special Relationship Between the Parties

This is where there is a relationship of trust between the parties and it will arise where the defendant knows, or ought reasonably to foresee, that the claimant will rely on their skill and judgement. As a general rule the advice must be formally given.[84] Many of the reported cases involve claims against accountants and valuers. In *Yianni v Edwin Evans*[85] such a relationship was considered to exist where a surveyor, instructed by a building society to value a house for mortgage purposes, owed a duty to the purchaser of the house where it was foreseeable that the valuation would be relied upon. Although this is a first instance decision, it was approved in *Smith v Eric S Bush*[86] on similar facts. If a valuer is appointed by a receiver, no duty of care is owed as the valuer is acting for the receiver and the advice may well have not been acted upon.[87] In *Caparo v Dickman*[88] it was held that where accountants are instructed to audit a company's accounts their duty is owed to the existing investors as a group but not to specific shareholders.

4.2.6.1.2 Specialist Skill of the Person Giving the Advice

A duty only arises where the defendant is in the business of giving such advice or represents competence to do so.[89] The minority view in '*Evatt*' was that a duty to take reasonable care is not the same as a duty to meet a professional standard of competence. In *Tai Hing*

81 See Paragraph 3.6.3.
82 *Derry v Peake* (1889) 14 App Cases 337.
83 *Hedley Byrne v Heller & Partners Ltd* [1964] AC 465.
84 However, see *Chaudhry v Prabhakar* [1988] 3 All ER 718.
85 *Yianni v Edwin Evans* [1988] 2 QB 438
86 *Smith v Eric S Bush* [1990] 1 AC 831.
87 *Raja v Austin Gray* [2003] 13 EG 117.
88 See Paragraph 3.6.4.
89 *Mutual Life & Citizens Assurance Co v Evatt* [1971] AC 793.

Cotton Mill Ltd v Liu Chong Hing Bank[90] the view was taken that silence or inaction could not amount to a misstatement unless there is a duty to disclose.[91]

4.2.6.1.3 Reliance

The claimant must reasonably rely on the defendant's advice and the reliance must be reasonably foreseeable to the defendant. There is a greater likelihood of liability arising where the claimant is a lay person seeking advice from a professional person than where both parties are engaged in professional activities. In *Welton v North Cornwall DC*,[92] the claimants undertook alterations to their premises in circumstances where an environmental health officer negligently required them to carry out works which were not required. It was clear that the officer knew that their instructions would be relied upon by the claimants and the officer inspected the alterations as they were being carried out. The test is whether the defendant ought reasonably to be expected to know of the advice given. In *Lambert v West Devon BC*,[93] the defendant breached the duty of care, which they owed to the claimant, where a planning officer told the claimant they could proceed with development where the officer did not have the powers to deal with the matter themselves.

4.2.7 Occupiers Liability

Liability for negligence may arise in respect of defective premises and this is governed primarily by statute. It is concerned with the extent of the liability of an occupier of premises when a person enters those premises and suffers physical loss. The issue of damage to personal property sometimes arises as well. The law is to be found in two statutes – the Occupiers Liability Act 1957 and the Occupiers Liability Act 1984. The principal Act is the Occupiers Liability Act 1957. This Act applies only to lawful visitors and provides that an occupier of premises owes a duty of care to see that such visitors will be reasonably safe when using the premises for the purpose(s) for which they are present. Trespassers are not governed by the 1957 Act; however the Occupiers Liability Act 1984 provides that in some circumstances an occupier may owe a duty of care to a trespasser.

Both Acts are concerned with defective premises. Premises include any fixed or moveable structure. In addition to land and buildings it has been held to include cranes, scaffolding, ladders, ships and aircraft. Liability rests with the occupier and not beyond in respect of both Acts. An occupier is one who has control over the premises and it is a question of fact in each case as to who has occupation. Premises may have more than one occupier.[94] Where large scale building works are in progress the site owner and the main contractor may be both in occupation.[95] Where a lease is entered into liability rests, in the majority of cases, with the tenant. An empty building may be occupied. In *Harris v Birkenhead*

---

90 *Tai Hing Cotton Mill Ltd v Liu Chong Hing Bank* [1980] AC 80.
91 Per Ibid., 87.
92 *Welton v North Cornwall DC* [1997] JPL 1.
93 *Lambert v West Devon BC* [1997] 98 LGR 45.
94 *Wheat v Lacon & Co Ltd* [1966] AC 552.
95 *AMF International v Magnet Bowling Ltd* [1968] 1 WLR 1028.

Corporation[96] a local authority failed to block up a derelict house which was subject to a compulsory purchase order. They were liable as occupiers when a 4-year-old child gained entry through an unsecured door and fell from a second floor window. Public rights of way [highways] are excluded from both Acts and are governed by the common law.

4.2.7.1 Lawful Visitors

Under S2(2) of the Occupiers Liability Act 1957, occupiers owe a duty of care to lawful visitors. The Act covers damage to persons and to property. A lawful person is a person who expressly, or by implication, has been given the right to enter premises. This would include those persons who have entry as of right, by authority imposed by law, such as Health and Safety officials, Customs and VAT officers. As far as express permission is concerned, this is a question of fact. The courts are reluctant to infer that an implied permission exists and the burden is on the person claiming the permission to prove it. The presence of a path or walkway up to a front door impliedly gives a person permission to enter premises and state their business to the occupier. This licence extends no further than the front door. An occupier may set restrictions or limitations on visitors entering the premises. A guest in an office, or in a hotel, would become a trespasser if they went through a door marked, 'Danger. Staff only' or 'Private'. In *Westwood v The Post Office*[97] an employee who disregarded a notice which said, 'Only the authorised attendant is permitted to enter' was held to be a trespasser when they were killed by falling through a defective trapdoor. An occupier may revoke the right of a lawful visitor to remain on the premises at any time. In such circumstances, the visitor must be given a reasonable time in which to leave after which they become a trespasser. A person who starts off as a lawful visitor may become a trespasser if they abuse the purpose for which they are present. Where a person enters premises under a contractual right the obligations under the 1957 Act will be implied into the contract. While the visitor is on the premises the occupier must take care to see that the visitor will be reasonably safe in using the premises for the purpose for which they are invited or permitted to be there. Whether the duty has been breached is a question of fact in each case based on the general law of negligence. It is the visitor and not the premises that has to be made reasonably safe. The duty only extends to the purpose for which the visitor was actually allowed entry. In *Ward v Tesco Stores Ltd*,[98] a customer slipped on yoghourt which had spilled onto the floor in the defendant's store. There was evidence to the effect that spillages were not cleaned up effectively after they occurred and the defendants were held to be negligent. In *Fryer v Pearson*,[99] there was no breach of duty when a family visitor was injured by a needle when kneeling on the floor. There was no evidence that the occupiers knew the needle was there or that is created any danger.

4.2.7.1.1 Some Problem Areas

The degree of care owed depends upon the status of the visitor. The occupier must be prepared for children not to be as careful as adults. In the case of a child, the test is a

96 *Harris v Birkenhead Corporation* [1976] 1 WLR 279.

97 *Westwood v The Post Office* [1973] 1QB 598.

98 *Ward v Tesco Stores Ltd* [1976] 1 All ER 219.

99 *Fryer v Pearson*

subjective one and the premises must be safe for a child of that age. Even if children are lawful visitors they may be attracted by some dangerous object to exceed the scope of their right to be on the premises. This is the concept of 'allurement' which might place a child visitor at risk of harm. In *Glasgow Corporation v Taylor*[100] the local authority was liable when a 7-years-old boy stole some attractive berries from a botanical gardens, open to the public, and died from poisoning. In *Jolley v London Borough of Sutton*[101] the attraction was an abandoned boat which fell on a 14-year-old boy who was trying to lift it off the ground. An occupier can expect very young children to be accompanied by an adult. In *Phipps v Rochester Corporation*[102] a 5-year-old boy fell into a trench when collecting blackberries. The defendants were held not to be liable as this was the kind of danger from which a reasonable parent ought to protect their child. Similarly, in *Simkiss v Rhondda BC*[103] a 7-year-old was injured when they fell down a steep hill where they were having a picnic opposite the block of flats where they lived. Evidence was submitted to the effect that their father regarded the site as safe so there was no reason for the defendant local authority to consider it to be dangerous.

When tradesmen enter premises to carry out work, the occupier can expect skilled visitors to take any necessary precautions as long as the occupier leaves them free to do so. In *Roles v Nathan*[104] the occupiers were not liable when chimney sweeps were killed by a leak of carbon monoxide gas when sealing a hole in a boiler. They should have been aware of the danger and ensured that the boiler was turned off. In *General Cleaning Contractors v Christmas*[105] the occupier was not liable when a window cleaner sustained injuries where a defective window caused them to fall from their ladder. The cleaner ought to have been aware of the risk. Where a person is injured or killed because of the faulty work of an independent contractor the occupier may be able to exclude liability if they can show that they took care in selecting the contractor and took reasonable steps to ensure that the work had been carried out properly. In *Haseldine v Daw*[106] the claimant was killed when a lift fell to the bottom of the shaft. The maintenance of the lift had been delegated to a reputable firm of specialist contractors and because of the technical nature of the process the occupiers could not be expected to check that the work had been carried out properly. There can be liability if the work is capable of being checked by the occupier with relative ease to ensure that it was satisfactory. There may also be situations where the occupier should check that the independent contractor is adequately insured. In *Kealey v Heard*[107] the owner of a number of houses, who was having them converted into flats, was held liable when a plasterer was injured because of faulty scaffolding erected by another (unknown) independent contractor. The court considered that the employer should have supervised the works as they had overall control of the building activities on the property and had not discharged their duty by delegating the works to an independent contractor. In large scale construction

---

100 *Glasgow Corporation v Taylor* [1922] 1 AC 44.
101 *Jolley v London Borough of Sutton* [2000] 3 All ER 409.
102 *Phipps v Rochester Corporation* [1955] 1 QB 450.
103 *Simkiss v Rhondda BC* [1982] 81 LGR 460.
104 *Roles v Nathan* [1963] 1 WLR 1117.
105 *General Cleaning Contractors v Christmas* [1953] AC 180.
106 *Haseldine v Daw* [1941] 2KB 343.
107 *Kealey v Heard* [1983] 1 WLR 573.

projects an occupier would be expected to have the contractor's work supervised by a surveyor, engineer or architect as appropriate.[108]

4.2.7.1.2 Warnings and Defences Under the 1957 Act

A warning may absolve the occupier from liability in which case it discharges any duty of care which might have been owed by the occupier to the visitor. The warning must come from the occupier and it must be adequate in that it specifies the danger clearly so that the visitor can avoid it. The occupier's duty is to render the visitor safe rather than the premises. In *Rae v Mars (UK)*,[109] where a surveyor was injured when inspecting a storehouse in a factory, it was suggested that if unusual dangers exist there should be additional warnings indicating the immediacy of the danger together with the possibility of additional safeguards such as barriers if they are appropriate. There is no duty on an occupier to warn of obvious dangers[110] but if the danger is not obvious the warning must be detailed enough for the occupier to put the visitor on guard for their own safety.

The following defences may have application to lawful visitors:

Volenti: Where a visitor voluntarily accepts the risk and choses to enter the premises the defence of consent may be applicable.

Contributory Negligence: Visitors who fail to use reasonable care for their own safety may find their damages reduced when an apportionment takes place between the occupier and the visitor.

Exclusion: An occupier may attempt to exclude liability by a notice communicated to a visitor or by a contractual term. Any limitation of liability by the occupier must be read subject to the Unfair Contract Terms Act 1977 in situations where there is 'business liability'. This includes professions and activities undertaken by central and local government. Any attempt to exclude liability for death or personal injury caused by negligence will not be upheld. In the case of property damage the stipulation will not be upheld unless it is reasonable in the circumstances. If lawful visitors have little option other than to enter the premises the occupier will find it difficult to exclude liability.

4.2.7.2 Trespassers

Trespassers are not governed by the Occupiers Liability Act 1957. Historically, an occupier of premises owed no duty of care to trespassers. A trespasser may be injured by the steps that the occupier has taken to keep them out, by the condition of the premises or by an activity which is taking place on the land. An occupier is entitled to place static deterrents on the property such as broken glass[111] or to place spikes on top of a wall but must not create hidden dangers such as traps or manholes. At common law apart from having a duty not to deliberately inflict damage on trespassers an occupier was not liable for a trespasser's injuries. In *Addie v Dumbreck*[112] the defendant colliery owner was held to owe no duty of

---

108 See *A M F International v Magnet Bowling* [1968] 1 WLR 1028 and Paragraph 3.13.
109 *Rae v Mars (UK)* [1990] 1 EGLR 161.
110 Cotton v Derbyshire Dales District Council [1994] EWCA Civ 17; *The Times* 20 June 1994.
111 *Clayton v Deane* (1817) Taunt 489.
112 *Addie v Dumbreck* [1929] AC 358.

care towards a child trespasser who was crushed by haulage gear at a colliery. A significant development took place when the House of Lords introduced the concept of a 'duty of common humanity'. In the case of *British Railways Board v Herrington*[113] a 6-year-old boy was electrocuted on a railway line after climbing through a fence which had not been properly maintained. Children regularly played near the line and railway staff were aware of their regular presence on the track. Local inhabitants also crossed the line as a short cut from one side of the railway embankment to the other. It was admitted that the boy was a trespasser but the House of Lords decided that the Board owed a duty to act with 'common humanity' towards child trespassers. They had not done so and were consequently liable. The Law Lords appeared anxious to lay down a standard higher than the common law position but not as high as the duty to take reasonable care owed under the Occupiers Liability Act 1957. Liability would arise if the occupier knew of the danger, and the likelihood of the trespass, in addition to having the ability and resources to prevent the accident. The case was subjected to critical reviews and comments and the problem of the relationship between trespassers and occupiers was referred to the Law Commission. The report of the Commission (No. 75) formed the basis of the Occupiers Liability Act 1984.

4.2.7.2.1 The Occupiers Liability Act 1984

The Act applies to all persons other than lawful visitors. In addition to trespassers it will include those using a private right of way. Those using a public highway are specifically excluded. It does not apply to claims in respect of lost or damaged property. The Act does not provide that an occupier automatically owes a duty of care to trespassers. An occupier will only owe a duty of care to a trespasser if S1 [3] 1984 Act is satisfied. For the section to apply the occupier must:

- Be aware of the danger or have reasonable grounds to know it exists.
- Know, or have reasonable grounds to believe, the trespasser is in the vicinity of the danger or is likely to come into the vicinity.
- The risk is one against which they may reasonably be expected to offer to the other person some protection.

The tests centre around the requirement for reasonable behaviour by the occupier and in the few cases that have been dealt with by the courts, S1 (3) has been interpreted in the context of 'common humanity'. The standard expected of the occupier will vary from case to case. Important factors are the character of the trespass, where it has taken place and the likelihood of injury. The greater the risk, the more precautions the occupier will have to take. Is the trespasser a stranger to the locality who has lost their way or a burglar inspecting a target property? Certain premises, such as railway lines and construction sites, require greater supervision than a private residence.

There are few examples of successful claims based on the Act. A number of cases concern swimming accidents.[114] In '*Tomlinson*', the defendant local authority owned a park which included a lake. Warning signs which prohibited swimming were erected by the

---

113 *British Railways Board v Herrington* [1972] AC 877.

114 *Tomlinson v Congleton Borough Council* [2003] 3 WLR 705; *Donoghue v Folkstone Properties* [2003] EWCA Civ 231; *Rhind v Astbury Water Park* [2004] EWCA Civ 756.

defendants because of the dangerous condition of the water. It was known that people did swim in the lake so the local authority decided to make the lake inaccessible to the public. The work was delayed due to lack of funds. The claimant, aged 18, jumped into the lake and was severely injured when they struck their head. The Law Lords took the view that the claimant had chosen to run the risk of their injuries and, in any case, a reasonable occupier ought not to be obliged to go to the financial cost of avoiding the danger. In *Higgs v Foster*[115] a police officer who trespassed on premises, while on surveillance of suspected criminals, fell into an inspection pit and was seriously injured. Their claim for personal injuries failed as the occupier could not have suspected their presence or that they would enter the area via the pit.

4.2.7.2.2 Warnings and Defences Under the 1984 Act

S1 (5) of the 1984 Act covers warnings. Any warning notice will discharge the duty as far as adults are concerned. In the case of children it depends on age as to whether or not they can read or understand it.

The following defences may have application to trespassers.

Volenti: S1 (6) of the 1984 Act preserves the defence of consent:

> No duty is owed by virtue of this section to any person in respect of risks willingly accepted as his by that person (the question whether a risk was so accepted to be decided on the same principles as in other cases in which one person owes a duty of care to another).

In *Ratcliffe v McConnell*[116] a trespasser dived into the shallow end of a swimming pool and was injured. They disregarded an appropriate warning notice and were taken to have accepted the risk.

Contributory Negligence: Although not specifically referred to in the Occupiers Liability Act 1984 the defence would apply.

4.2.8 The Defective Premises Act 1972 and the Building Safety Act 2022

Those who instruct construction professionals to carry out building works, relating to residential dwellings, may wish to consider whether this Act can assist them. Frequent problems, in a construction context, are latent defects and faulty workmanship. Where a builder is carrying out work they may incur negligence liability. If the builder is also the owner of the property and transfers the title to a new owner there is no liability. A series of cases from *Dutton v Bognor Regis UDC*[117] attempted to extend the liability of the builder in respect of damage to the building itself but the decision in *Murphy v Brentwood DC*[118] emphasised that such damage would be considered to be purely economic in nature and

---

115 *Higgs v Foster* [2004] EWCA Civ 843.
116 *Higgs v Foster* [1999] 1 WLR 670.
117 Paragraph 3.6.1.
118 Paragraph 3.6.1.

therefore not recoverable. A claimant may sue for personal injury, or damage to property on account of latent defects, but this is rarely the core issue. Consequently, the provision in S3 of the 1972 Act which made it possible to bring proceedings, even though the building had been disposed of, is not of great practical importance.

S1 Defective Premises Act imposes the principal obligation to build dwellings properly:

> A person taking on work for or in connection with the provision of a dwelling (whether the dwelling is provided by the erection or by the conversion or enlargement of a building) owes a duty—
>
> **a.** if the dwelling is provided to the order of any person, to that person; and
>
> **b.** without prejudice to paragraph (a) above, to every person who acquires an interest (whether legal or equitable) in the dwelling;
>
> to see that the work which he takes on is done in a workmanlike or, as the case may be, professional manner, with proper materials and so that as regards that work the dwelling will be fit for habitation when completed.

The Act applies to a wider range of individuals than the builder. Architects are included but those exercising simply inspection or valuation functions will not be. The enactment is narrow in operation. It only applies to 'dwellings'. Commercial premises are excluded. It excludes those dwellings which are subject to 'approved schemes' such as NHBC. The effect is that virtually all new domestic properties will be excluded.

The Building Safety Act 2022 significantly increased the limitation period during which claimants are able to bring a claim under the Defective Premises Act. Under the S135 of the 2022 Act, the limitation period was extended from 6 years to:

- 30 years from the date upon which the right of action occurred where the right of action occurred prior to 28 June 2022, and
- 15 years where the right of action occurred on or after that date.

In *URS Corporation Limited v BDW Trading Limited*,[119] the Court of Appeal considered whether the revised limitation periods applied to claims already under way before the 2022 Act was in force. They held that they did, noting 'the longer limitation periods are to be treated as always having been in force' and that, accordingly, 'there was never a time when those extended periods did not apply'.[120]

4.2.9 Limitation of Actions in Negligence

The Limitation Act 1980 governs claims in the law of tort. Unless altered by an alternative statute, a claim in negligence is statute-barred unless brought within 6 years from the date on which the cause of action accrued. Exceptions exist, as noted above, with defective buildings, and the 1980 Act itself provides exception for personal injury actions, which

119 *URS Corporation Limited v BDW Trading Limited* [2023] EWCA Civ 772.
120 Ibid., para 162.

must be brought within 3 years. One problem with limitation periods is that of hidden or latent damage, which only manifests itself after the limitation period has expired. The law on limitation, in negligence cases dates from *Cartledge v Jopling and Sons Ltd.*[121] This case affirmed the position that a cause of action accrued at the date when the damage or injury took place and not when it was discovered. Shortly after this decision the Limitation Act 1963 was enacted to allow claimants, in personal injury cases, additional time in which to bring actions. The issue arose in *Sparham-Souter v Town & Country Developments [Essex] Ltd.*[122] This was a defective foundations case which involved claims against the builders of houses and the local authority. The Court of Appeal took the view that the 'reasonable discovery' test was applicable. The cause of action accrued when the damage was discovered by the injured party, or ought to have been, if the claimant had acted with due diligence. These rules were developed in the now discredited decision in *Anns v Merton LBC.*[123] Some years later the decision in *Pirelli General Cable Works v Oscar Faber & Partners*[124] overruled the reasonable discovery test. The case concerned a chimney which developed cracks and had to be replaced. The chimney was built in 1969 and the claimant discovered the damage in 1977. The Law Lords decided that the cause of action accrued when damage occurred to the building regardless of whether it was discoverable at that time. The claim failed and was statute barred. In 1984 the Law Reform Committee published their report titled 'Latent Damage'.[125]

4.2.9.1 The Latent Damage Act 1986

The Act was a compromise between the '*Sparham-Souter*' and '*Pirelli*' positions. The primary limitation period is 6 years from the date when the cause of action accrued. This is the date when the damage occurred. A claimant who cannot satisfy that provision has an alternative time period in which to bring a claim. The period is 3 years from the date when the damage was discovered or ought to have been discovered. This secondary limitation period is subject to a longstop provision. It provides that an action for damages for negligence cannot be brought more than 15 years from the date on which any act or omission alleged to constitute negligence occurred. This provision does not apply to personal injury claims. These limitation rules only apply to claims in respect of damages. If an equitable remedy is sought, such as a claim for an injunction, the maxims of equity will apply and the remedy must be claimed as soon as is reasonably possible.

4.2.10 Defences to Negligence

In negligence actions, apart from showing that one of the essential elements of the tort is missing, the defendant may raise a defence.

---

121 *Cartledge v Jopling and Sons Ltd* [1963] AC 758.

122 *Sparham-Souter v Town & Country Developments [Essex] Ltd* [1976] QB 858.

123 *Anns v Merton LBC* [1978] AC 728; see Paragraph 3.6.1.

124 *Pirelli General Cable Works v Oscar Faber & Partners* [1983] 2 AC 1.

125 [Cmnd 9390 November 1984].

4.2.10.1 *'Volenti Non Fit Injuria'* (Consent)

This is a complete defence. It arises where the claimant knew of the risk involved, understood the nature and degree of it and freely accepted it. However, if the claimant had no option but to accept the risk it does not apply – there must be a genuine free choice. For example, a rescuer does not necessarily accept a risk voluntarily. In *Haynes v Harwood*[126] a police officer was injured when attempting to stop a runaway horse. The officer did not act voluntarily because they were under a duty to try and protect the public by stopping the animal, therefore *volenti* was not applicable. This case can be contrasted with *Cutler v United Dairies*[127] where a private individual attempted to calm a horse which was unlikely to harm anyone. The claimant was injured but it was held that they had freely consented to run the risk and the defence succeeded.

4.2.10.2 Contributory Negligence

The defence applies where a claimant suffers damage in part due to their own negligence as well as through the negligence of the defendant. Until 1945 it was a complete defence and no damages were payable if it succeeded. Now the effect of proving contributory negligence is to reduce the damages awarded to the claimant. In practice, the claimant's damages are reduced to the extent that the court considers them liable for the loss suffered. The defendant must show that the claimant failed to take reasonable care for their own safety and contributed to their own loss. Common practical examples are where passengers in vehicles fail to wear seatbelts[128] and motor cyclists fail to wear crash helmets.[129] In *Wheeler v Copas*[130] the claimant bricklayer's damages were reduced by 50% when they were injured by falling off a ladder which they had borrowed. The ladder was very 'flimsy' and not suitable for carrying heavy building materials.

4.3 Vicarious Liability

Vicarious liability attaches legal responsibility to a person for torts committed by others. Their liability arises because of the relationship between the parties and is known as vicarious liability. It provides a method of making a person, other than the actual tortfeasor, liable for the commission of the tort. In practice the only relationship which gives rise to this rule, to any degree in English law, is that between employer and employee. The principle is that an employer is liable for torts committed by employees during the course of their employment, and the act complained of by a claimant will normally be based on negligence. A more limited form of vicarious liability arises between principal and agent[131] and between partners in a firm.[132] It should be remembered that this principle does not

126 *Haynes v Harwood* [1935] 1 KB 146 Paragraph 3.3.
127 *Cutler v United Dairies* [1933] 2 KB 297 Paragraph 3.3.
128 *Froom v Butcher* [1976] QB 286.
129 *O'Connell v Jackson* [1972] 1 QB 72.
130 *Wheeler v Copas* [1981] 3 All ER 305; see Paragraph 3.3.
131 See Chapter 2.
132 See Chapter 2.

remove liability from the employee who committed the tort, and the tortfeasor and the employer may both be found liable. As the employer is obliged to take out public liability insurance any claimant may find that the employer is more likely to be able to pay out on a judgment than the employee who lacks sufficient funds. If the employer satisfies the judgment, they may be able to claim a contribution from the employee under the Civil Liability (Contribution) Act 1978.

4.3.1 Employees and Independent Contractors

There can be no liability imposed on the employer unless the person responsible for the tort is an employee. This was traditionally known as the master/ servant relationship and is dependent on there being a contract of service between the parties. This has been contrasted with the arrangement where an employer nominates a self-employed independent contractor to carry out work based on a contract for services. In the latter case there will be no vicarious liability incurred as a result of the contractor's acts. Difficulties have always existed in distinguishing between the relationships but in the last 20 years, because of the numerous varieties of working relationships which have developed, the problem is greater than ever. An important factor is the amount of control which the employer has over the worker together with payment of wages and rights of dismissal and suspension.[133] A commonplace arrangement, which has existed in the construction industry, is the use of labour-only subcontractors who are classified as independent contractors. They agree to work for a lump sum without any tax or insurance contributions being taken into account.

4.3.1.1 Liability for Independent Contractors

There are a limited number of situations where an employer may be liable for the acts of an independent contractor.

4.3.1.1.1 Selection of the Contractor

In *Kealey v Heard*[134] the owner of a number of houses, who was in the process of having them converted into flats, was held liable where a plasterer was injured because of faulty scaffolding erected by another (unknown) independent contractor. It was decided that the employer should have supervised the works as they had overall control of the contract.

4.3.1.1.2 Contractor Employed to Carry Out the Tort

In *Ellis v Sheffield Gas Consumers Co*[135] the defendants hired contractors to dig up a road without having any authority to do so. When the claimant was injured, because of a hole that had been dug, the defendants were liable as the defendants had sanctioned the tort.

4.3.1.1.3 Non-delegable Duties Imposed by Statute or Common Law

There are a number of instances (primarily statutory) where there is an obligation imposed on a person to act in a particular manner. In such circumstances, the obligations cannot

133 *Viasystems [Tyneside Ltd] v Thermal Transfer [Northern] Ltd* [2005] EWCA 1151.
134 *Kealey v Heard* [1983] 1 All ER 973.
135 *Ellis v Sheffield Gas Consumers Co* (1853) 2 E & B 767.

be delegated to another. Highway operations are a good example.[136] It can arise also on a common law basis.[137]

4.3.2 Course of Employment

Once it has been determined that the employer/employee relationship exists the courts must be satisfied that the employee was acting in the course of employment before the employer can be held liable in respect of their actions. This is a question of fact that can cover wrongful acts that have been authorised by the employer and acts which were authorised but were carried out in an unauthorised manner. The question is whether the employer has prohibited the act itself, in which case the employee cannot be in the course of employment when performing it, or whether the employer has prohibited a particular method of carrying out the act in which case the employee may be in the course of employment. An employer will not generally be liable where the employee's act is outside the scope of their employment. In *Kooragang Investments Pty Ltd v Richardson & Wrench Ltd*[138] an employed valuer was deemed to have acted outside the course of their employment when carrying out valuations for a client whom their employers had blacklisted. Where an employee is acting on their own account and is involved in an unauthorised escapade they are said to be on a 'frolic of their own' and the employer will not be liable. In *Hilton v Thomas Burton [Rhodes] Ltd*[139] employers were not liable when four employees left work to go to a café seven miles from the demolition site where they were working. Shortly before reaching the café, they decided to turn back and one of their party was killed due to the negligence of the driver.

4.4 Nuisance

Nuisance comes in two main forms: private and public. Private nuisance is an established tort while public nuisance is primarily a criminal offence which causes danger or inconvenience to the public at large. When a public nuisance occurs it may also give rise to a claim for civil remedies by a claimant who has suffered 'special damage'. Environmental legislation also gives local authorities powers to proceed quickly when a nuisance situation is likely to affect the health of people in a particular locality. This is known as a statutory nuisance. There is another tort which is concerned with the manner in which land is used which has tended to overlap with private nuisance. This is the rule in the case of *Rylands v Fletcher*.[140] The decision was traditionally seen as an attempt to impose strict liability on landowners who damage their neighbour's land; however, to be liable, the perpetrator of this tort must be able to foresee the likelihood of its occurrence. Liability for the consequences of allowing it to take place is strict.[141]

---

136 *Gray v Pullen* (1864) 5 B & S570.

137 *Honeywill & Stein v Larkin Bros Ltd* [1934] 1 KB 191.

138 *Kooragang Investments Pty Ltd v Richardson & Wrench Ltd* [1982] AC 462.

139 *Hilton v Thomas Burton [Rhodes] Ltd* [1961] 1 WLR 705.

140 *Rylands v Fletcher* (1868) LR 3 HL 330.

141 *See Cambridge Water v Eastern Counties Leather* [1994] 2 WLR 53; *Transco plc v Stockport Metropolitan Council* [2003] UKHL 61.

4.4.1 Private Nuisance

A private nuisance is wrongful interference with a person's use or enjoyment of land. It is a tort which protects a person from interference with the land which they occupy and hold rights in. The tort was developed in the nineteenth century in an attempt to give claimants a remedy where their land, or buildings, became affected by the problems which had been exacerbated by the industrial revolution and the growth of manufacturing industry. The law attempts to strike a balance between allowing persons to use their land as they wish and the rights of persons not to be affected by the actions of their neighbours.

In 2023, the Supreme Court summarised the three principles of nuisance:

> Since the nineteenth century, whether an activity is a nuisance turns on the application of the following three principles. First, malicious interference with a neighbour's enjoyment of land is automatically a nuisance. Secondly, 'those acts necessary for the common and ordinary use and occupation of land and houses may be done, if conveniently done, without subjecting those who do them to an action': (...) Thirdly, in all other cases, whether a landowner's activity is a nuisance turns simply on whether, having regard to the locality, the activity harms the amenity of his/her neighbour's land to a sufficient extent.[142]

4.4.1.1 Core Principles of Private Nuisance

4.4.1.1.1 Scope

The focus is on the claimant's enjoyment of their rights over land, as opposed to the personal discomfort of those occupying the land. In their article on the subject, Professor Francis Newark provided the following as a distinction:

> the interest of the plaintiff which is invaded is not the interest of bodily security but the interest of liberty to exercise rights over land in the amplest manner. A sulphurous chimney in a residential area is not a nuisance because it makes householders cough and splutter but because it prevents them taking their ease in their gardens.[143]

4.4.1.1.2 Cause

There are not finite categories or prescribed limitations on that capable of being a nuisance, meaning anything which interferes with the enjoyment of rights in land is capable of being a nuisance. As noted by the Supreme Court, a nuisance:

> (...) may be something tangible, as where—to take a recent example—an incursion of Japanese knotweed from neighbouring land gave rise to a claim: see *Williams v Network Rail*. Or it may be something intangible, such as fumes, noise, vibration or an unpleasant smell. In all such cases, however, the basis of the claim is not the physical invasion itself but the resulting interference with the utility or amenity value of the claimant's land. Moreover, there is no requirement that the interference

142 *Fearn and others v Board of Trustees of the Tate Gallery* [2024] AC 1.
143 Professor Francis Newark 'The Boundaries of Nuisance' (1949) 65 LQR 480, 488–489.

> must be caused by a physical invasion and, as commentators have pointed out, there are many cases which do not fit this model[144]

4.4.1.1.3 Substantial Interference with Ordinary Use

As the law in this area seeks to maintain a balance between the right of an occupier to use their land and the right of a neighbour not to be interfered with, the courts have utilised 'unreasonable', 'unduly' and 'unlawful' when assessing a defendant's use of land. However in *Fearn and others v Board of Trustees of the Tate Gallery*[145] the Supreme Court posed the alternative question of: whether the defendant's use of land has caused a *substantial* interference with the *ordinary* use of the claimant's land.[146]

Substantial Interference: This excludes minor annoyances, with 'real', 'significant' and 'material' all also used by the courts. Lord Wensleydale described this as:

> the law does not regard trifling and small inconveniences, but only regards sensible inconveniences, injuries which sensibly diminish the comfort, enjoyment or value of the property which is affected.[147]

The test is objective, asking not whether the claimant believes it is a substantial interference, but whether it is by the standards of an ordinary or average person in the claimant's position.[148]

Ordinary Use: Priority is afforded to general, normal and ordinary use of land, over more specific, particular and uncommon used. In *Ball v Ray*[149] the defendant used a residential house on a residential street as a stable to keep horses. In their judgement the court distinguished the noise of a horse in a stable from noise from a piano or children, noting the latter as ones which are to be reasonable expected and therefore put up with. In *Southwark London Borough Council v Tanner*[150] adjoining flats had been built without sound insulation, with the result that:

> The tenants can hear not only the neighbours' televisions and their babies crying but their coming and going, their cooking and cleaning, their quarrels and their love-making. The lack of privacy causes tension and distress.[151]

The House of Lords held that the normal use of a residential flat was not an actionable nuisance to the neighbours, noting that if it were 'we would have the absurd position that each, behaving normally and reasonably, was a nuisance to the other'.[152]

---

144 *Fearn and others v Board of Trustees of the Tate Gallery* [2024] AC 1, 13.
145 Ibid., 18–21.
146 Ibid., 21.
147 *St Helen's Smelting Co v Tipping* (1865) 11 HL Cas 642, 653–654.
148 *Fearn and others v Board of Trustees of the Tate Gallery* [2024] AC 1, 23.
149 *Ball v Ray* (1873) LR 8 Ch App 467.
150 *Southwark London Borough Council v Tanner* [2001] 1 AC 1.
151 Ibid., 7.
152 Ibid., 15F-G.

4.4.1.1.4 *Locality Principle*

In determining whether the land use is 'ordinary', consideration must be given to location, described by the court as the 'character of the locality'.[153] In *Sturges v Bridgman*[154] the Court of Appeal stated 'what would be a nuisance in Belgrave Square would not necessarily be so in Bermondsey'. This appears on the face of it to increase legal protection for the wealthy, but it was intended to contrast residential neighbourhoods (Belgrave Square) from industrial and manufacturing areas (Bermondsey, where leather manufacturing took place). The case concerned a doctor who built a consulting room at the end of their garden. The new consulting room backed on to the kitchen of their neighbour, which was used to make confectionary using large, loud equipment (and had been doing so for 20 years). The court found for the doctor, noting that the street was primarily residential, not one devoted to manufacturing and it was common for medical professionals on the street to conduct business from their homes.

4.4.1.1.5 *Coming to a Nuisance Is No Defence*

As evidenced in the case of *Sturges v Bridgman* above and confirmed in *Lawrence v Fen Tigers Ltd*[155] it is not, in itself, a defence to claim that land was already being used in the way alleged to be a nuisance prior to the claimant's occupation.

4.4.1.1.6 *Public Interest Is No Defence*

It is not a defence to a claim of private nuisance that the activity carried out by the defendant is one of public benefit.[156]

4.4.1.2 Fearn and Others v Board of Trustees of the Tate Gallery [2024] AC 1

A leading case in private nuisance is *Fearn and others v Board of Trustees of the Tate Gallery*[157] cited earlier in this section. The case saw an action brought for private nuisance by claimants who owned flats in a development adjacent to an art gallery, run by the defendants. The flat living areas had glass walls. The gallery had a public viewing platform which offered panoramic views of London. The court of first instance found that the 'living areas of the claimants' flats were under constant observation from the viewing gallery for much of the day, that the number of visitors was in the hundreds of thousands each year and that the visitors frequently took photographs of the interiors of the flats and sometimes posted them on social media'.[158] Both the court of first instance and the Court of Appeal found for the defendants, relying on the reasonableness of the gallery having a viewing platform, the construction of glass walls in a busy city and the claimant's failure to take steps to prevent the intrusion (by installing curtains, blinds or net-curtains). However the Supreme Court (with two judges dissenting) found in favour of claimants, concluding:

---

153 *Fearn and others v Board of Trustees of the Tate Gallery* [2023] UKSC 4, 38.
154 *Sturges v Bridgman* (1879) 11 Ch D 852, 865.
155 *Lawrence v Fen Tigers Ltd* [2014] AC 822.
156 See *Clerk & Lindsell on Torts*, 23rd ed., para 19–107.
157 *Fearn and others v Board of Trustees of the Tate Gallery* [2024] AC 1.
158 Ibid., para 48.

the viewing and photography which took place from the defendant's building caused a substantial interference with the ordinary use and enjoyment of the claimants' properties and (ii) operating a public viewing gallery as the defendant did was not an ordinary use of the defendant's land; that, therefore, the defendant was liable in nuisance to the claimants;[159]

4.4.1.3 Remedies

4.4.1.3.1 Damages

If the defendant is liable the claimant is entitled to claim damages which can include consequential losses as long as they are foreseeable. This includes any losses sustained because of physical damage to the land and any business losses. Any decrease in the value of the land is recoverable. In *Hunter v Canary Wharf Ltd*[160] it was stated that damages should be measured by the effect which the nuisance has on the value of the land. It was also stated, by a majority of judges, that damages for personal injury could not be recovered in private nuisance.[161] Where an injunction is claimed, as in the vast majority of private nuisance actions, the court has a discretion to refuse the injunction and award damages instead. This is an order for damages in lieu of injunction.[162]

4.4.1.3.2 Injunction

This is the principal remedy claimed, in the majority of cases, and it requires the offending activity to be terminated. It will normally be granted except where the offending activity is slight or irregular in occurrence. It is an equitable remedy and therefore discretionary in nature. An injunction may be perpetual in which case the activity must be stopped completely or it may be partial in which case time limits will be imposed on when the activity can take place. A good example of the latter arose in *Kennaway v Thompson*[163] where the Court of Appeal put a limit on the times when a motor boat club could hold their activities. This case is also a good example of the rule that 'coming to the nuisance' is no defence. In *Dennis v Ministry of Defence*[164] the claimants owned a country house, with adjoining land, in the vicinity of an airbase where pilots were trained to fly jet aircraft. The claimants alleged that the noise involved in these operations amounted to a nuisance and a successful claim was brought for the decrease in the value of the land due to the nuisance.

4.4.1.3.3 Abatement

A claimant may stop the nuisance by remedying the cause. This is the process of self-help. Cutting back overhanging branches or foliage are examples. The claimant must ensure that no unnecessary damaged is caused and no damage is inflicted on an innocent third

159 Ibid., see paras 7, 9–12, 16–17, 20–27, 31, 34–35, 38, 47–50, 52, 65, 72, 88, 133.
160 *Hunter v Canary Wharf Ltd* [1997] 2 All ER 426.
161 See also *Transco plc v Stockport MDC* [2003] UKHL 61.
162 See *Shelfer v City of London Electric Lighting Co* [1895] 1 Ch 287.
163 *Kennaway v Thompson* [1980] 3 WLR 361.
164 *Dennis v Ministry of Defence* [2003] EWHC 793.

party. Unless there is an emergency, the offending occupier should be informed and given a reasonable time to remedy the situation. Care should be taken when exercising this remedy as the abator may find that they have become a trespasser or caused a breach of the peace.

4.4.1.4 Defences

The general defences of 'volenti' and contributory negligence will apply but where the claimant's action is based on the unreasonable use of land by the defendant they are of little relevance.

The following specific defences may have application.

4.4.1.4.1 Prescription

Prescription means long use. The continuance of a private nuisance, for at least 20 years, entitles the defendant to exercise the nuisance as long as the claimant was aware of the nuisance *before* the 20 years period began and an actionable nuisance has existed throughout that time. The leading case is *Sturges v Bridgman*[165] discussed above. The defendant's argument that they had been pursuing their trade in confectionary for more than the prescription period failed because the interference did not become actionable, as a nuisance, until the claimant constructed their consulting room adjacent to the defendant's premises.

4.4.1.4.2 Statutory Authority

Where the act which gives rise to the nuisance is authorised by statute that authority will give the defendant a defence if it can be shown that the interference with the claimant's rights was permitted, expressly or impliedly, by the statute. What the alleged defendant is authorised to do, or not do, depends on the interpretation of the specific provisions.[166]

4.4.1.4.3 Planning Permission

Where a local authority grants planning permission for development within its area, and authorises a change in the character of land, the consent may act as a defence, in a similar way to statutory authority, but only if it is the consequence of the permission being granted. In *Gillingham BC v Medway [Chatham] Dock Co Ltd*[167] planning permission was granted to operate a busy commercial dock enterprise 24 hours each day. Heavy lorries passed through the residential neighbourhood surrounding the commercial dock. The local authority's attempt to obtain an injunction failed. If the planning permission does not change the character of the neighbourhood a nuisance may arise and it was emphasised in *Wheeler v Saunders Ltd* that as a general rule planning permission does not act as

165 *Sturges v Bridgman* (1879) 11 Ch D 852.
166 *Allen v Gulf Refining* [1981] AC 1001.
167 *Gillingham BC v Medway [Chatham] Dock Co Ltd* [1993] QB 343.

a defence.[168] In *Derek Watson v Promosport Ltd*[169] the claimants brought an action based on nuisance against the defendants who operated a motor racing circuit. The defendants had permission for the designated use subject to conditions. The court took the view that a change in the character of the area would be found if there had been a 'strategic' planning decision affected by considerations of public interest.

4.4.2 Public Nuisance

Public nuisance is primarily a criminal offence. It was a common law offence until 2022, when, following recommendations from the Law Commission[170] in 2015, it was made a statutory offence. Public nuisance is now found in S78 Police, Crime, Sentencing and Courts Act 2022:

S78 (1) A person commits an offence if—
- **a.** the person—
  - **i.** does an act, or
  - **ii.** omits to do an act that they are required to do by any enactment or rule of law,
- **b.** the person's act or omission—
  - **i.** creates a risk of, or causes, serious harm to the public or a section of the public, or
  - **ii.** obstructs the public or a section of the public in the exercise or enjoyment of a right that may be exercised or enjoyed by the public at large, and
- **c.** the person intends that their act or omission will have a consequence mentioned in paragraph (b) or is reckless as to whether it will have such a consequence.

2. In subsection (1)(b)(i) 'serious harm' means—
- **a.** death, personal injury or disease,
- **b.** loss of, or damage to, property, or
- **c.** serious distress, serious annoyance, serious inconvenience or serious loss of amenity.

3. It is a defence for a person charged with an offence under subsection (1) to prove that they had a reasonable excuse for the act or omission mentioned in paragraph (a) of that subsection.

An offence is therefore committed if a person's act or omission creates a risk, or causes serious harm to the public or obstructs the public in their exercise of enjoyment.

A single act may be sufficient to incur liability. Public nuisance is concerned with interferences with the lives and activities of a community although a private individual may bring an action in tort if they can prove so called 'special damage'. There is no requirement for the public nuisance to have any connection with the actual use of the land. It is not possible to indicate how many people need to be affected before an action can be brought as this is an issue of fact in each case depending upon how any representative cross-section of

---

168 Ibid.

169 *Derek Watson v Promosport Ltd* [2008] EWHC 759.

170 The Law Commission (LAW COM No 358) Simplification of Criminal Law: Public Nuisance and Outraging Public Decency, 2015.

the population in the particular locality is affected.[171] It may well be that a particular set of circumstances gives rise to claims both in private and public nuisance.[172]

4.4.2.1 Pre Police, Crime, Sentencing and Courts Act 2022

As noted above, prior to 2022 the offence of public nuisance was a common law offence. Despite S78 (6) Police, Crime, Sentencing and Courts Act 2022 abolishing the common law offence, in the first case under the new Act, the Court of Appeal adopted the following position:

> whilst we accept that the statements of principle in the case law predating the Act may sometimes be of some assistance, we emphasise that those statements related to a common law offence which has been abolished and replaced by the new statutory offence. We therefore do not accept that s78 must be interpreted precisely in accordance with what was said in the case law relating to the common law offence.[173]

Because of this, it remains imperative to understand both the common law position prior to S78 coming into force, alongside case authorities and guidance arising post S78.

In *Trevett v Lee*[174] the defendant was required to use a hosepipe to connect their premises to the water supply as there was no mains connection. The claimant, who suffered personal injury when tripping over the pipe, failed in their claim as the defendant's conduct was considered to be reasonable. Other highway examples include picketing on the road,[175] positioning a tee on a golf course in such a position that golfers hit balls onto a nearby highway,[176] and organising a pop festival in such a way that it causes traffic congestion, noise and general inconvenience to the public at large.[177] It is a public nuisance to allow property to fall into such a state that users of the highway are endangered, and in such circumstances liability would appear to be strict.[178] A defendant cannot avoid liability by delegating tasks to independent contractors where danger arises from works being carried out to the highway or from the state of the highway itself. Damage caused by something falling onto a highway can be a public nuisance. An owner of land adjoining a highway is liable for injuries caused by the collapse of a natural projection, such as a tree, if they knew of the defect or ought to have known of it.[179] In the case of an artificial projection, such as a lamp or a hoarding, liability is strict.[180] The sale of food and drinks which are not pure have been deemed to amount to a public nuisance.[181] In *Dollman v Hillman Ltd*[182] a successful claim was made where the claimant suffered injury because of fat left on the pavement

---

171 See *Att-Gen v PYA Quarries* [1957] 1 All ER 894.
172 See *Halsey v Esso Petroleum Co Ltd* [1961] 1 WLR 683.
173 *R v Smith and others* [2024] EWCA Crim 1040 Para 43.
174 *Trevett v Lee* [1955] 1 All ER 406.
175 *Thomas v National Union of Mineworkers* [1985] 2 All ER 1.
176 *Castle v St Augustine's Links* [1922] 38 TLR 615.
177 *Att-Gen of Ontario v Orange Productions Ltd* [1971] DLR 257.
178 *Wringe v Cohen* [1940] 1 KB 229.
179 *Noble v Harrison* [1926] 2 KB 332.
180 *Tarry v Ashton* (1876) 1 QB 314.
181 *AB v South West Water Services* [1993] 1 All ER 609.
182 *Dollman v Hillman Ltd* [1941] 1 All ER 355.

outside a butcher's shop. In *R v Johnson*[183] the making of obscene telephone calls to a large number of women constituted public nuisance while in *R v Rimmington*[184] there was no public nuisance committed when the actions of the defendant caused no common injury to a section of the public. In this case over five hundred packages were sent to members of the public containing racially offensive material. The addressees were chosen at random and on an ad hoc basis.

4.4.2.2 Post Police, Crime, Sentencing and Courts Act 2022

The first case to try persons under the new statutory offence, S78 was *R v Smith & Ors,* which reached the Court of Appeal.[185] The defendants were protesters with the movement Just Stop Oil, and in 2022, they staged a protest at the British Grand Prix Formula 1 motor race. They entered the race track itself, in a prohibited area, and sat down in a line, obstructing half of the track during the formula 1 race. They were convicted at first instance of causing a public nuisance contrary to S78 (1) and (4). Their convictions under S78 were upheld by the Court of Appeal, who provided the following guidance on the new statutory offence:

- the focus must be on the risk of harm which was created, not on whether any harm was in fact caused. The risk must be real, not fanciful.[186]
- It is a question of fact whether the persons put at risk of serious harm can properly be described as 'a section of the public'. (...) If an offender creates a risk of harm to only a single person, it would not be possible to find a risk to 'a section of the public'. The greater the number of persons placed at risk, the easier it is likely to be to conclude that they can properly be regarded as 'a section of the public'. But (...) there is no minimum number. A 'section of the public' is, in our view, simply a group of persons within a larger group or body of persons.[187]
- (It) remains necessary to distinguish a 'section of the public' from a series of individuals. Conduct which is specifically directed against, or gives rise to a risk of serious harm specific to, an individual will not be sufficient; and that will be so, even if the conduct is repeated on separate occasions against a number of individuals. The important consideration is whether it can properly be said that the conduct is directed generally and collectively against a group of persons who can fairly be regarded as 'a section of the public', or puts such a group generally and collectively at risk of serious harm, without discriminating between individual members of the group.

4.4.2.3 Proving Special Damage

Unless a claimant can prove special damage there will be no *civil* cause of action available. Special damage is damage over and above the inconvenience and annoyance suffered by the public at large. If it cannot be established there will only be the possibility of criminal liability on the defendant's part. Before special damage can be proved the loss

183 *R v Johnson* [1997] 1 WLR 367.
184 *R v Rimmington* [2006] 1 AC 459.
185 *R v Smith & Ors* [2024] EWCA Crim 1040.
186 Ibid., 46.
187 Para 49.

to the claimant needs to be of a different variety than that suffered by other individuals or there needs to be a significant difference in the extent of the damage. In *Benjamin v Storr*[188] the proprietor of a coffee house was affected by horses and carts, belonging to the defendant, which obstructed the highway outside their premises and blocked out light from all the shops in the row. The claimant could prove special damage, in excess of the other businesses, as customers had difficulty reaching the coffee house and the smell of the horses put customers off visiting the premises. Likewise in *Halsey v Esso Petroleum Co Ltd*[189] smuts from the defendant's oil depot caused actual damage to the claimant's car and the noise from the oil tankers caused them to have sleepless nights. The claimant was able to prove that they had suffered more than other residents who had been affected by the defendant's activities. Special damage may also arise where the nuisance results in the claimant having to incur greater expenditure. In *Rose v Miles*[190] the defendant obstructed a creek trapping the claimant's barges. The claimant was able to recover the cost of unloading the cargoes from the barges and transporting the items by land. Similarly, in *Tate & Lyle Industries v GLC*[191] the defendants received a licence to operate ferry terminals on the River Thames. The claimants had a new jetty constructed by the river from where they loaded sugar onto merchant ships. Because of an abundance of silt on the river bed, caused by the construction of the ferry terminals, the claimants had to spend a considerable amount of money having the riverbed dredged to remove the obstruction. The claimants successfully sued for special damage. In *News Group Newspapers v Society of Graphical Trades etc.*[192] the cost of providing transport and extra security for workers was recoverable as damages in public nuisance.

4.4.2.4 Remedies

Although public nuisance is primarily a criminal matter it is possible, in some circumstances, for damages to be claimed by an individual. The case is brought in the name of the Attorney General who in such circumstances is acting as the upholder of public rights. The claim for damages is known as a relator action. This enables an injunction to be obtained on behalf of those affected by the nuisance. An alternative is for the local authority to apply for the injunction on behalf of the local community. In *Hunter v Canary Wharf*[193] doubt was raised as to whether damages for personal injury which had resulted from public nuisance could be recovered. In *Corby Group Litigation v Corby BC*[194] the Court of Appeal confirmed that damages for personal injuries can be recovered in public nuisance cases.

188 *Benjamin v Storr* (1874) LR 9 CP 400.
189 *Halsey v Esso Petroleum Co Ltd* [1961] 1 WLR 683.
190 *Rose v Miles* (1815) 4 M & S101.
191 *Tate & Lyle Industries v GLC* [1983] 2 AC 509.
192 *News Group Newspapers v Society of Graphical Trades etc* [1987] ICR 181.
193 *Hunter v Canary Wharf* [1997] 2 All ER 426.
194 *Corby Group Litigation v Corby BC* [2008] EWCA Civ 463.

4.4.3 Statutory Nuisance

Because the process of bringing actions based on private nuisance is cumbersome, expensive and slow it was decided that the solution lay in putting the most common examples of nuisance into statutory form. The process dates from Victorian times when it was originally devised to deal with sanitation problems. The object of the law is to provide an expedited method of bringing nuisances to an end where the common law is too slow and where the activity is so serious that the cost should be borne by the local authority. Where a nuisance can be dealt with by this process it is known as a statutory nuisance. The current law is to be found in part 3 Environmental Protection Act 1990 (EPA). The system is operated by local authorities via their Environmental Health Officers (EHOS). By S79 of the 1990 Act every local authority has a duty to inspect its areas for statutory nuisances and to take steps to abate them.

4.4.3.1 How the System Works

S79 Environmental Protection Act 1990 states the circumstances which give rise to a statutory nuisance:

- Premises.
- Smoke from premises.
- Fumes or gases from premises.
- Dust, steam or other effluvia, arising on industrial/business premises.
- Accumulations or deposits.
- Animals.
- Noise emitted from or caused by a vehicle, machinery or equipment in the street (Added by the Noise and Statutory Nuisance Act 1993).
- Any other matter declared by any enactment to be a statutory nuisance.

To constitute a statutory nuisance, it must do one of the following:

- unreasonably and substantially interfere with the use or enjoyment of a home or other premises
- injure health or be likely to injure health[195]

4.4.3.2 Injure Health or Be a Nuisance

This means that the act complained of must either be a nuisance (public or private), in the common law sense, or an actual threat to the health of persons affected by it.[196] To 'injure health or be likely to injure health', it must be injurious to physical health whether actual or anticipated. In *Coventry City Council v Cartwright*[197] a rubbish dump owned by the local authority, in a residential area, was held not to be a statutory nuisance where there was no likelihood of disease or of vermin being attracted to it to spread disease.

---

195 Department for Environment, Food & Rural Affairs, Guidance, Statutory Nuisance: How councils deal with complaints (2015).

196 *National Coal Board v Thorne* [1976] 1 WLR 543.

197 *Coventry City Council v Cartwright* [1975] 1 WLR 845.

4.4.3.3 Abatement

If the local authority is considering taking enforcement action Environmental Health Officers will have to evaluate the extent to which the local population are being affected by the alleged statutory nuisance. In particular the nature and location of the activity together with its duration and utility will need to be considered. An abatement notice must be served on the 'appropriate person'. It should require abatement of the nuisance or restrict its occurrence. It may require works to be carried out or other steps be taken to comply with the notice. The notice should also state the penalties for non-compliance with the notice. Once a person has been served with the notice any contravention of it, without reasonable excuse, renders that person guilty of a criminal offence. An appeal against the notice can be made and in limited circumstances it is a defence to show reasonable excuse. The test here is an objective one and is not available where the notice has been contravened deliberately or intentionally. Businesses and trades may put forward the defence of best practicable means in that they did the best they could to prevent or counteract the nuisance. Special defences apply to noise on construction sites.

4.4.3.4 Penalties for Non-compliance

If someone does not comply with an abatement notice they can be prosecuted and fined:

- a lump sum (the amount is set by the court)
- further fines for each day they fail to comply (the amount is set by the court)

Councils can also take action to stop or restrict the nuisance by:

- carrying out works and making the person given the notice pay for them (this can include seizure and confiscation of equipment)
- applying to the High Court for an injunction (if a prosecution is not adequate)[198]

4.4.4 Rylands v Fletcher [1861–73] All ER Rep 1

In this case, the defendant mill owner employed independent contractors to construct a reservoir on their land to supply water to run the mill. Unknown to the defendant, and the contractors, an old mine shaft lay underneath the land. When the reservoir was filled the water escaped through the unsealed shafts and flooded the claimant's coal mine. Although it was established that the defendant had not been negligent, and that the contractors were competent, the defendant was held liable by the House of Lords. The case established a legal principle and is known as 'the rule in *Rylands v Fletcher*'. The Court of Appeal (upheld by the House of Lords) held:

> A person who for his own purposes brings onto his land and collects and keeps there anything likely to do mischief if it escapes, must keep it in at his peril, and if he does not do so, is prima facie answerable for all the damage which is the natural consequence of its escape.[199]

---

198 Department for Environment, Food & Rural Affairs, Guidance, Statutory Nuisance (2015).
199 *Rylands v Fletcher* (1866) LR 1 Exch 265 at 279 per Blackburn J.

The House of Lords, in confirming the Court of Appeal decision, qualified the rule to the effect that the defendant was only liable if they brought the thing on to their land in the course of a non-natural use of the land. This qualification has been accepted in later cases as an essential part of the rule and, in practice, usually a considerable obstacle towards a successful claim.

The Irish case of *Hanrahan v Merck Sharpe and Dohme*[200] provided the following overview of the rule, which was confirmed in *John Donnelly and Sons LTD v Hoey and another*[201]:

> We think that the true rule of law is that the person who for his own purposes brings on his land and collects and keeps there anything likely to do mischief if it escapes, must keep it in at his peril, and if he does not do so is prima facie answerable for all the damage which is the natural consequence of its escape. He can excuse himself by showing that the escape was owing to the plaintiff's default; or, perhaps, that the escape was the consequence of vis major or the act of God (...)[202]

4.4.4.1 Essentials of the Tort

4.4.4.1.1 Control of the Land

The defendant must be in control of the land but need not have an interest in it – a licence is sufficient.[203] This would cover utilities contractors laying pipes, cables or sewers beneath the highway. In contrast, by analogy with the position in private nuisance, the established principle is that a claimant must have an estate in land to have the necessary *locus standi* to bring the action.

4.4.4.1.2 Accumulation

The item must not be naturally present on the land. The escape of vermin, weeds or rock from the defendant's land will not be actionable.[204]

4.4.4.1.3 Dangerous Things

The defendant must have accumulated on their land an item that they realised would give rise to a high risk of danger or 'mischief' if it escaped. This has included fire, water, oil, gas and electricity. A falling flagpole,[205] fairground chair,[206] and a landowner who allowed caravan dwellers to live in his field who 'escaped' and committed minor criminal offences within the locality[207] have come within the definition.

---

200 *Hanrahan v Merck Sharpe and Dohme* [1988] ILRM 629.
201 *John Donnelly and Sons LTD v Hoey and another* [2024] IEHC 52.
202 *Hanrahan v Merck Sharpe and Dohme* [1988] ILRM 629.
203 *Charing Cross Electric Supply Co v Hydraulic Power Co* [1914] 3 KB 772; *Rainham Chemical Works Ltd v Belvedere Fish Guano Co Ltd* [1921] AC 465.
204 *Giles v Walker* (1890) 24 QBD 656; *Pontardawe RDC v Moore-Gwyn* [1929] 1 Ch 656.
205 *Shiffman v Order of St John* [1936] 1 All ER 557.
206 *Hale v Jennings* [1938] 1 All ER 679.
207 *Att-Gen v Corke* [1933] Ch 89.

4.4.4.1.4 Escape

There must be an escape from the place controlled or occupied by the defendant to other land. In *Read v Lyon*[208] the claimant munitions inspector was killed when an explosion took place in a shell-filling shop. As there was no escape from the premises there was no liability under the tort. Although the escape will normally be accidental the tort may cover intentional releases of dangerous things.[209] It may be that the 'thing' itself does not actually escape but the consequences of the event causes injury. In *Miles v Forest Rock Granite Co Ltd*[210] a blast of explosives on the defendant's land caused rocks to fall onto an adjoining highway resulting in damage.

4.4.4.1.5 Non-natural Use of Land

The courts have traditionally refrained from laying down specific examples of what would be a natural use of land, and conversely what would be a non-natural one, preferring to consider the issue on a case by case basis. However, they have increasingly been ready to hold that a use is natural with the result that the defendant escapes liability. In *Transco v Stockport MDC*[211] it was held that to be considered non-natural, the use had to be something which is out of the ordinary in that place and at that time. The judges found that the supply of water for domestic purposes in large pipes did not amount to a non-natural use. A different result was reached in *LMS International v Styrene Packaging and Insulation*[212] where *Transco* was followed. The case concerns an explosion, where in the process of manufacturing polystyrene, a spark ignited an inflammable gas at the defendant's factory and caused a fire damaging the claimant's premises. The process was deemed to be non-natural as it involved a high risk of such an incident happening. In *Transco v Stockport MDC*, Lord Bingham noted:

> the rule in *Rylands v Fletcher* is engaged only where the defendant's use is shown to be extraordinary and unusual. This is not a test to be inflexibly applied: a use may be extraordinary and unusual at one time or in one place but not so at another time or in another place (although I would question whether, even in wartime, the manufacture of explosives could ever be regarded as an ordinary user of land (...))[213]

4.4.4.1.6 Foreseeability and Damage

The case of *Cambridge Water v Eastern Counties Leather*[214] gave the first opportunity to review the law for many years. The case concerns the defendant leather manufacturers who in the process of greasing pelts for tanning purposes used toxic chemical solvents. Over a 20-year period there were frequent spillages of the chemicals through the concrete floor in

---

208 *Read v Lyon* [1947] AC 156.
209 *Crown River Cruises Ltd v Kimbolton Fireworks Ltd* [1996] 2 WLR 533.
210 *Miles v Forest Rock Granite Co Ltd* [1918] 34 TLR.
211 *Transco v Stockport MDC* [2003] UKHL 687.
212 *Transco v Stockport MDC* [2006] BLR 30.
213 *Transco* 11.
214 *Cambridge Water v Eastern Counties Leather* [1994] 2 WLR 53.

their warehouse where the solvents were stored. This had the effect of contaminating the local domestic water supply. When changes in the law required water companies to inspect their water resources, the claimants made a routine inspection and discovered the contamination. As a consequence the water authority was forced to move their pumping station and tried to recover the cost of so doing from the defendants. An action was brought which included claims under the rule in *Rylands v Fletcher.* It was stressed by the House of Lords that foreseeability of harm is a necessary requisite of any successful claim in either tort. On that basis the action failed. The case established that a defendant can only be liable for a type of damage which was reasonably foreseeable. If proved, a defendant will be liable for all the damage which is the natural consequence of the escape. Economic losses are not recoverable, and the modern view is that damages for personal injuries are not recoverable under the rule.[215] In *Transco v Stockport MDC,*[216] the House of Lords resisted the call to integrate the *Rylands v Fletcher* rule in negligence. With regard to foresight, Lord Bingham stated:

> It must be shown that the defendant has done something which he recognised, or judged by the standards appropriate at the relevant place and time, he ought reasonably to have recognised, as giving rise to an exceptionally high risk of danger or mischief if there should be an escape, however unlikely an escape may have been thought to be.

In the same judgment, Lord Bingham noted '(c)onsideration of the reported English case law over the past 60 years suggests that few if any claimants have succeeded in reliance on the rule in *Rylands v Fletcher* alone'.[217]

4.4.4.2 Defences

4.4.4.2.1 Volenti

Where there is consent, express or implied, to the defendant bringing the substance or accumulation on to their land, this will be a good defence. Consent is normally implied where the existence of the item offers some advantage to the claimant. A good example is buildings of multiple occupation where the presence of the item offers some benefit to the occupiers. Water tanks and sprinkler systems to protect buildings from fire have come within this category.[218]

4.4.4.2.2 Default of the Claimant/Contributory Negligence

If the claimant contributes to the escape of the dangerous thing, their damages will be reduced by an apportionment of liability under the Law Reform (Contributory Negligence) Act 1945. If the escape is entirely the fault of the claimant, or damage occurs because of the sensitivity of the claimant's property, it appears, by analogy with nuisance, that the defendant should not be liable.[219]

---

215 Lord Bingham in *Transco plc v Stockport MDC* [2003] UKHL at page 66.
216 Ibid.
217 *Transco* 5.
218 *Carstairs v Taylor* (1871) LR 6 Exch 217; *Peters v Prince of Wales Theatre Ltd* [1943] KB 73.
219 *Eastern & South Africa Telegraph Co v Cape Town Tramways Co* [1902] AC 381; *Ponting v Noakes* [1894] 2 QB 281.

4.4.4.2.3 *Statutory Authority*

Whether or not the defence applies is a matter of construction in each case; however, the issue is normally whether the defendant was acting under a duty. In *Green v Chelsea Waterworks*[220] the defendants were not liable when a water main burst as they were under a statutory duty to maintain a water supply. In *Charing Cross Electricity Co v Hydraulic Co*,[221] on similar facts, the defendants were only acting under a power which did not oblige them to provide a water supply so the defence did not apply.

4.4.4.2.4 *Act of God*

If the escape is a natural catastrophe which the defendant could not have foreseen or guarded against, this defence may apply. In *Nichols v Marsland*[222] it was successfully pleaded in a destructive storm but in *Greenock Corporation v Caledonian Railway*,[223] on similar facts, the court refused to accept the defence.

4.4.4.2.5 *Act of a Stranger*

If the escape is caused by the act of a third party over whom the defendant has no control, the defendant will not be liable. In practice it will be the actions of a trespasser. In *Box v Jubb*[224] the defence applied where a third party was responsible for causing a flood. A defendant may however be liable in negligence if the act of the stranger is foreseeable.

4.5 Trespass

Although often associated with criminal law, trespass is the oldest of all the existing torts. It can occur to land, or to a person. Trespass protects interests in land, protects interests in personal property and protects an individual's interest in their personal security. All types of trespass are actionable *per se* – it is not necessary for a claimant to prove damage to succeed. Another feature relating to all categories of trespass is that any interference must be direct to be actionable. It is an intentional tort. If a defendant can show that they had no intention of entering the land, then they have not committed the tort of trespass to land. Although statute has created criminal offences in connection with trespass to land such circumstances are rare.[225] There is a greater overlap with the criminal law in connection with trespass to the person particularly in connection with crimes of assault. Sometimes, other factors have to exist before there can be criminal as well as civil liability. Trespass to personal property is a civil matter unless criminal intent can be shown. This section of the chapter will deal primarily with trespass to land.

---

220 *Green v Chelsea Waterworks* (1894) 70 LT 547.
221 *Charing Cross Electricity Co v Hydraulic Co* [1914] 3 KB 772.
222 *Greenock Corporation v Caledonian Railway* (1876) 2 Ex D 1.
223 *Greenock Corporation v* [1917] AC 556.
224 *Box v Jubb* (1876) 4 Ex D 76.
225 See Public Order Act 1986. Criminal Justice and Public Order Act 1994.

4.5.1 Trespass to Land

This tort is a direct interference upon land in the possession of the claimant. It can be contrasted with private nuisance where the interference is indirect. If your neighbour throws dead flowers or tree branches on to your land that is a trespass while if tree roots spread to your land from next door that will amount to nuisance.[226]

4.5.1.1 Examples of Trespass to Land

The interference can occur in a number of ways but the most obvious are set out in the following text.

4.5.1.1.1 Entry Onto the Land by the Defendant Without the Claimant's Permission

The slightest crossing of the boundary is sufficient but there must be some contact with the fabric of the property.

4.5.1.1.2 Directly Causing Objects to Enter Onto the Claimant's Land

Leaning a ladder against a wall on the claimant's land has been held to be a trespass.[227] Placing items on a boundary would be actionable. Throwing stones, dumping rubbish or placing projections over neighbouring land would come into this category. Shared driveways can be a problem. In *Anderson v Bryan*[228] the laying of a driveway over the holes in which fence posts had been placed amounted to a trespass. If there is contact with the claimant's property, that is sufficient to constitute a trespass. Leaning a bicycle against a shop window would be sufficient. It is not necessary to cross the actual boundary of the premises.

4.5.1.1.3 Refusing to Leave the Land When Asked to Do So or Abusing the Position for Which the Visitor Is Present

A trespass may be intentional at its outset, or it may arise where a person's lawful right to remain on land has been revoked. If the permission to be on the land has expired, or the right to be there has been withdrawn, a person will become a trespasser if they do not exit the land within a reasonable period of time. A similar result arises where a person originally enters land lawfully but then abuses the position for which they are there. A person who lawfully enters land to deliver post or goods may become a trespasser if they extend their visit by entering a garage or outhouse. This may have important consequences if they are injured by the state of the premises which they have entered without permission.[229] If the trespass is not an isolated incident, and it continues on a regular basis, it gives rise to a new cause of action from day to day as long as it lasts. This is known as a continuing trespass. It arises where a person fails to remove something which was initially on the land lawfully but has ceased to be so. If a person is given a licence to keep their caravan on a piece of land but the licensor then revokes the licence it will be a continuing trespass to keep the item there.

---

226 *Lemmon v Webb* [1894] 3 Ch 1.

227 *Westripp v Baldock* [1939] 1 All ER 279.

228 *Anderson v Bryan* [2000] Unreported CA.

229 See Occupiers Liability. Paragraph 3.13.

4.5.1.2 The Extent of the Tort

Possession, not ownership, gives rise to a cause of action in trespass. What actually amounts to possession depends on the type of property. It is usually straightforward in connection with a house or commercial premises but possession of open land may depend on evidence of actual use. A licensee will normally lack the exclusive possession which is necessary to found an action based on trespass.[230] A hotel guest or a lodger will not have the *locus standi* to bring a successful action. Possession of land carries with it the right to the soil and things under it together with such amount of airspace as is needed for the normal use and enjoyment of the property.[231] It is long established that trespass can be committed in respect of the subsoil.[232] In *Kelsen v Imperial Tobacco Co Ltd*[233] an advertising sign which extended by a few inches over the claimant's property was actionable as a trespass. Overhead cables have attracted litigation as have crane 'jibs'. In *Woollerton & Wilson Ltd v Costain Ltd*[234] the defendant's crane swung over the claimant's land resulting in a trespass while in *Anchor Brewhouse Developments Ltd v Berkley House [Docklands Developments] Ltd*[235] crane booms were left to swing in the air when unused causing them to pass over neighbouring property. Overflight by aircraft is governed by the Civil Aviation Act 1982 which prevents any claim in trespass or nuisance as long as the flight is at a reasonable height and appropriate flying conditions have been adhered to. Similar rules apply as far as light aircraft, microlights and gliders are concerned. In practice this means adhering to the rules laid down by the Civil Aviation Authority (CAA). Similar rules apply to military aircraft. The 1982 Act imposes strict liability in respect of physical damage to property which arises from an overflight.[236]

Where damage occurs to property adjoining a highway, an action in trespass will fail unless negligence is also present from the person using the highway. This was confirmed *in Esso Petroleum Co Ltd and Another v Southport Corporation*,[237] a case concerning damage caused by oil being discharged from a tanker, the discharge taking place to 'save the crew and vessel from grave danger'.[238] The House of Lords held:

> the person who has suffered damage cannot recover in trespass in the absence of negligence on the part of the person who has caused the damage. See per Lord Blackburn in *River Wear Comrs v Adamson* (1877) (2 App Cas at p 767), where he says:
>
> > My Lords, the common law is, I think, as follows:—Property adjoining to a spot on which the public have a right to carry on traffic is liable to be injured by that traffic. In this respect there is no difference between a shop, the railings or windows of which may be broken by a carriage on the road, and a pier adjoining to a harbour or a navigable river or the sea, which is liable to be injured by a ship. In

---

230 *Hill v Tupper* (1863) 2 H & C 121; *Manchester Airport plc v Dutton* [2000] QB 133.
231 *Bernstein v Skyviews etc Ltd* [1977] 2 All ER 902.
232 *Cox v Moulsey* (1848) 5 CB 334.
233 *Kelsen v Imperial Tobacco Co Ltd* [1957] 2 QB 334.
234 *Woollerton & Wilson Ltd v Costain Ltd* [1970] 1 WLR 411.
235 *Anchor Brewhouse Developments Ltd v Berkley House [Docklands Developments] Ltd* [1987] 38 BLR 82.
236 See S76 [2] Civil Aviation Act 1982 and *Southgate v Commonwealth of Australia* [1987] 13 NSWLR 188.
237 *Esso Petroleum Co Ltd and Another v Southport Corporation* [1955] 3 All ER 864.
238 Ibid., para 867.

either case the owner of the injured property must bear his own loss, unless he can establish that some other person is in fault, and liable to make it good.

This was the principle applied by McCardie J in *Gayler & Pope Ltd v B Davies & Son Ltd* ([1924] 2 KB 75), in rejecting the contention that the plaintiffs in that case could succeed in trespass in the absence of negligence.

4.5.1.3 Remedies

4.5.1.3.1 Damages

The object is to restore the claimant to the position they were in before the tort was committed. If no loss has been sustained no damages are recoverable. If damage has occurred the amount of compensation will be the cost of restoring the property to its former condition. If the cost of reinstating the property to its original condition is out of all proportion to the loss suffered, damages should only represent the decrease in the value of the property. In an appropriate situation a claim for the loss of use of the property will be upheld.

4.5.1.3.2 Injunction

Where the trespass is a continuing problem, which is likely to be the case if the claimant has resorted to litigation, an injunction is more likely to be the appropriate remedy. Trespasses over land, or into airspace, are most likely to be dealt with in this manner. In *Costain*[239] the operation of the injunction was suspended when the offending party offered a substantial sum as compensation. An additional factor in the case was that the work was near completion.[240] This tends to be a factor which the courts bear in mind when granting the remedy. Damages can be awarded in lieu of an injunction but only if the requirements laid down in *Shelfer v City of London Electric Lighting Co*[241] are satisfied. These consist of minimal injury to the claimant, which can be estimated in monetary terms, adequate compensation can be made by a small monetary payment and the situation is one where it would be oppressive to grant an injunction.

4.5.1.3.3 Action for Recovery of the Land

If the claimant is not in possession of the land, and has an immediate right to possession, a claim can be made for repossession of the land. At one time there were procedural problems involved in obtaining repossession of the land but nowadays it is possible to enforce the right to possession even if the defendant's identity is not known. A person seeking to recover land in this way will frequently claim for mesne (pronounced 'mean') profits. This is any profit gained by the defendant while in unlawful occupation together with reasonable costs incurred by the claimant in obtaining possession.

4.5.1.3.4 Distress Damage Feasant

Where a chattel is unlawfully on the claimant's land, and has done actual damage to the claimant's property, the claimant may keep the item until the damage has been paid for. Damage caused by cricket and golf balls is a good example. In such circumstances the ball

239 See Paragraph 3.23.2.
240 *See Jagger v Sawyer* [1995] 2 All ER 189.
241 *Shelfer v City of London Electric Lighting Co* [1895] 1 Ch 235.

may be lawfully retained until the damage has been paid for. The remedy does not give the claimant the right to use the property or to sell it.

4.5.1.3.5 Self Help

As an alternative to taking legal action the occupier may use reasonable force to eject a trespasser. As self help is not encouraged by the courts the rightful occupier must act carefully so as not to be in breach of the criminal law.[242] In *Arthur v Anker*[243] the claimant was deemed to have consented to run the risk of having her car clamped where notices on private land prominently displayed the risk of clamping and indicated that a release fee would be payable.

4.5.1.4 Defences

4.5.1.4.1 Statutory Authority

A wide range of officials have powers of entry laid down by statute. Examples include Health and Safety Inspectors, Trading Standards Officers and Environmental Agency officials. If they are acting beyond the scope of their authority they will be trespassers.

4.5.1.4.2 Volenti

The consent may be express or implied. If consent is express, it is a question of fact depending upon the circumstances. If there is no express consent a visitor has a right to proceed to the front door of premises to state the nature of their business but nothing more. The occupier, in such circumstances, has the option of revoking the visitor's right to be there and if there is non-compliance the visitor will be a trespasser.

4.5.1.4.3 Third Party Rights

A person who enjoys a third party right over an estate in land, such as an easement or a *profit a prendre*, will not be a trespasser. A person who enjoys a customary right over land will also come into this category as will a licensee unless the permission is revoked. Those who exercise their right to pass and repass over the highway, or have the benefit of rights over a private road, will not be liable in trespass.[244]

4.5.1.4.4 Necessity

The necessity may relate to the preservation of life or property. There must be no negligence on the defendant's part.[245]

4.5.2 Trespass to Goods

As with other torts, trespass to goods is actionable *per se* and must be direct and intentional to be actionable. The tort is an interference with the possession so the owner, or a lawful borrower of the goods, may instigate proceedings except against anybody else who has a

---

242 See Criminal Law Act 1977 and Protection from Eviction Act 1977.

243 *Arthur v Anker* [1997] QB 564.

244 *DPP v Jones* [1999] 2 All ER 257.

245 *Rigby v Chief Constable of Northamptonshire* [1985] 2 All ER 285; *Monsanto plc v Tilly* [2000] Env LR 313.

better legal title. Examples include a bailee of goods to whom the chattels are entrusted to carry out work, such as a car repairer who has the vehicle in their workshops while carrying out repairs, or a dressmaker who is making alterations to a wedding dress. The tort may be committed by taking or destroying the goods or by simply touching them, although this will rarely arise in practice.[246] Related to the tort of trespass to goods is the tort of conversion. This is governed by the Torts (Interference with Goods) Act 1977 but the common law rules relating to this area of law remain relevant of relevance. Conversion arises where somebody deals with another's property in such a way to act as to be a denial of that person's rights or acts in such as way to be inconsistent with the rights of the claimant. If goods are found the finder will have a right of possession against everyone except someone with a better title. Case law has assisted the finders of jewellery in this respect.[247] Liability can arise in respect of any act which amounts to a denial of title. Not only does it include taking, disposing or destroying the goods but also where the bailee refuses to restore goods on demand or where goods are wrongfully delivered to a third party. If a person has lawful authority to be in possession of the goods there is no trespass or conversion. It is no defence that the defendant is mistaken as to their rights. The injured party may retake the goods as long as they act with no more force than is necessary in the circumstances. If the defendant is no longer in possession of the goods, damages can be claimed representing their value and possibly consequential damages as well.

4.5.3 Trespass to the Person

This is a tort which protects a person's interest in their security and well-being. As is the case of the other types of trespass, the interference must be direct and physical, while the tort is again actionable *per se.* There is an overlap with criminal law as the conduct of the defendant may also give rise to a criminal offence. There are three main aspects of the tort. The first is assault which arises where a threat is made against somebody else. The second is battery which amounts to the actual use of force against another person. Finally there is false imprisonment where the defendant causes the claimant's freedom to be totally restrained. As far as any assault is concerned the claimant must be in apprehension of an immediate battery before the tort can be committed. If the defendant does not have the capacity to carry out the tort then no assault will have taken place.

The traditional view was that words alone would not constitute an assault but there is now authority from the criminal law that it can be.[248] A battery amounts to a use of force against another person. It must be a direct and intentional act. Self-defence may be a defence to assault and battery as long as it is proportionate. The police may rely on statutory powers in this respect but any force used must be proportionate. Consent is relevant. Where the consent is express that will be a matter of fact and it will be a defence. Consent may also be implied. Where a person has capacity, they may consent to, or refuse, medical treatment. In the case of sporting activities consent will only be applicable to activities which come within the rules of the game. Necessity may also be a defence, and nowadays

---

246 *Kirk v Gregory* (1876) 1 Ex D 55.

247 *Armory v Delamirie* (1721) 1 Strat 505; *Parker v British Railways Board* [1982] QB 1004.

248 *R v Ireland* [1997] 4 All ER 225.

it plays a more prominent part in medical cases than implied consent. False imprisonment is concerned with unlawful detention. It arises where the defendant causes the claimant's freedom to be totally restrained. There must be no safe means of escape. It is a strict liability tort and can arise even though the claimant is unaware of the detention. If the defendant is carrying out a lawful arrest no tort is committed. Where a person is detained under the Mental Health Act 1983, with a mental illness, a tort is not committed. The Protection from Harassment Act 1997 made harassment both a criminal offence and a civil matter. It is widely drafted and the conduct of the defendant can amount to anything which a reasonable person may equate with harassment. There is no requirement to show actual loss.

4.6 Defamation

This tort protects interests in reputation. If the defendant makes a defamatory statement about the claimant, which is published, the claimant will have a right of action against the defendant unless the latter can establish a defence. The major issue for this area of law is to find a compromise between the protection of a person's reputation and the right to freedom of speech. The case of *Lachaux v Independent Print Ltd and another*[249] provided a useful introduction to this area of law:

> The tort of defamation is an ancient construct of the common law. It has accumulated, over the centuries, a number of formal rules with no analogue in other branches of the law of tort. Most of them originated well before freedom of expression acquired the prominent place in our jurisprudence that it enjoys today. Its coherence has not been improved by attempts at statutory reform. Statutes to amend the law of defamation were enacted in 1888, 1952, 1996 and 2013, each of which sought to modify existing common law rules piecemeal, without always attending to the impact of the changes on the rest of the law. The Defamation Act 2013 is the latest chapter in this history.[250]

The law governing defamation is found in the Defamation Act 2013. S1 Defamation Act 2013 defines defamation in the negative:

1. A statement is not defamatory unless its publication has caused or is likely to cause serious harm to the reputation of the claimant.
2. For the purposes of this section, harm to the reputation of a body that trades for profit is not 'serious harm' unless it has caused or is likely to cause the body serious financial loss.

The common law prior to the enactment of the 2013 statute remains relevant, although altered. Defamation has a number of peculiarities. The cases are among the most expensive forms of litigation. They tend to continue for a long time and many go to appeal. Damages are often higher than in personal injury cases, with legal costs taking up large proportions

---

249 *Lachaux v Independent Print Ltd and another* [2019] UKSC 27.
250 Ibid., 1.

of the claim. Cases often involve people in the public eye.[251] An unusual characteristic of these actions is that they are still tried by jury. In practice they are the only type of High Court civil action that is. The use of juries makes the outcome of cases unpredictable. Jurors, in these cases, are notorious for awarding inflated sums by way of damages. It is only in the last 20 years that the Court of Appeal has been able to vary the amount of damages awarded by a jury in defamation actions.[252] There have been attempts to expedite proceedings by introducing a summary process whereby cases can be dealt with by judge alone. In practice the more substantial cases are still dealt with by judges and jury.

In English and Welsh law, defamation consists of two categories – libel and slander.

4.6.1 Distinguishing Libel and Slander

Libel is defamation in a 'permanent' form, i.e. written or printed. It is always actionable *per se* (the act alone is enough, no proof of damage is required) and is injury to the claimant's reputation and the associated injury to their feelings. Slander is temporary i.e. an oral statement, and is, for the most part, not actionable *per se*. The law does not presume injury to reputation by mere oral statements and treats injury to feelings as insufficient to found a cause of action. Here, special damage, representing pecuniary loss rather than injury to reputation, must be proved for an action rooted in slander.[253] There are exceptions to this, where a statement is actionable without proof of special damage when –

1. it is calculated to disparage the claimant in any office, profession, calling, trade or business held or carried on by him at the time of the publication;
2. it is published of the claimant in the way of his office or calling and in relation to his conduct in it, and imputes unfitness for or misconduct in that office or calling; or
3. it imputes that the person of whom the words are published has committed a crime punishable by imprisonment.[254]

4.6.2 Establishing a Claim

A claimant must prove the following to succeed in a defamation action.

4.6.2.1 Defamatory Statement

The test, which tends to be used to ascertain whether the statement is defamatory or not, was that laid down by Lord Atkin in *Sim v Stretch*.[255] The judge said that a statement will be defamatory if its effect is to 'lower the claimant in the minds of right thinking people, or

---

251 *Jason Donovan v The Face* [1998] Unreported; *Cruise v Express Newspapers plc* [1999] 2 WLR 327; *Vardy v Rooney* [2022] All ER (D) 28 (August); *Depp II v News Group Newspapers Ltd and another* [2020] All ER (D) 01 (November); *Schofield v Politicalite Ltd and another* [2024] All ER (D) 56 (March).
252 Courts & Legal Services Act 1990; see *John v Mirror Group Newspapers* [1996] 2 All ER 35 and *Kiam 11 v MGN Ltd* [2002] EWCA Civ 43; *Blake and others v Fox* [2022] 4 WLR 77; *Duke of Sussex v Associated Newspapers Ltd* [2023] EWHC 3120 (KB).
253 *Lachaux v Independent Print Ltd and another* [2019] UKSC 27 paras 4 and 5.
254 Halsbury's Laws of England Defamation (Volume 32 (2023)) (1) (iv) (517) Slander actionable per se.
255 *Sim v Stretch* [1936] 52 TLR 669.

cause them to be shunned or avoided'. Halsbury's Laws provides a statement as defamatory of the person of whom it is published if:

- it tends to lower him in the estimation of right-thinking members of society generally[256] or
- if it exposes him to public hatred, contempt or ridicule[257] or;
- if it causes him to be shunned or avoided.[258]

A claimant cannot select potentially libellous statements to rely on if the written passage overall is not defamatory.[259] Another relevant issue is that of an innuendo where words do not appear to be defamatory, if taken at face value, but the claimant asserts that they have an inner meaning.[260]

4.6.2.1.1 Libel

Although libels are generally in writing (or print), case law has confirmed that statues, a caricature, waxwork, effigy, chalk marks on a wall, signs, pictures and film sound-track are all capable of being libellous.[261]

4.6.2.1.2 Slander

A slanderous statement can be made or conveyed by spoken words, sounds, looks, signs, gestures or in some other non-permanent form.[262]

4.6.2.2 Statement Must Refer to the Claimant

If the claimant is named the position is straightforward. It is sufficient that the claimant can show that people think it refers to them. This may be so even though a fictional name is used or if two people have the same name.[263] It can also arise if there is nobody named but it is evident in the circumstances that there is a reference to the claimant.[264] It is not enough that the words reflect on the claimant's property; there must also be an imputation against the claimant personally, for example, that they have knowingly or negligently sold defective goods.[265]

---

256 *Sim v Stretch [1936] 2 All ER 1237* at 1240, HL, per Lord Atkin.

257 *Parmiter v Coupland (1840) 6 M & W 105* at 108 per Parke B.

258 *Youssoupoff v Metro-Goldwyn-Mayer Pictures Ltd (*1934) 50 TLR 581, CA. Cf Thornton v Telegraph Media Group [2010] EWHC 1414 (QB), [2011] 1 WLR 1985, [2010] EMLR 25 (applied in *Daniels v British Broadcasting Corpn* [2010] EWHC 3057 (QB), [2010] All ER (D) 263 (November)).

259 *Charleston v News Group Newspapers* [1995] 2 All ER 315.

260 *Byrne v Dean* [1937] 1 KB 818.

261 See *Monson v Tussauds Ltd, Monson v Louis Tussaud* [1894] 1 QB 671 at 692, CA. Com Dig, Libel (A), and Bac Abr, Libel (A), instancing (on the authority of *Case de Libellis Famosis (1605) 5 Co Rep 125*a at 125b) *Jefferies v Duncombe* (1809) 11 East 226; *Du Bost v Beresford (1810) 2 Camp 511*; and *Levi v Milne (1827) 4 Bing 195; Austin v Culpeper (1683) Skin 123; Spall v Massey (1819) 2 Stark 559; Smith v Wood (1812) 3 Camp 323; Monson v Tussauds Ltd, Monson v Louis Tussaud; Ralston v Ralston [1930] 2 KB 238*; *Tolley v JS Fry & Sons Ltd [1931] AC 333*, HL; *Youssoupoff v Metro-Goldwyn-Mayer Pictures Ltd (1934) 50 TLR 581*, CA.

262 See Halsbury's Laws of England Defamation (Volume 32 (2023)) (1) (iv) (511) and *Amersi v British Broadcasting Corpn* [2024] EWHC 774 (KB).

263 *Newstead v London Express Newspapers Ltd* [1940] 1 KB 377.

264 *Dwek v Macmillan Publishers* [2000] EMLR 284.

265 Halsbury's Laws of England Defamation (Volume 32 (2023)) (1) (iv) (519).

4.6.2.3 Publication to a Third Party

To be actionable there must be publication to at least one person who is not the defendant's spouse or the claimant. This can be extensive in nature and can include every sale of a newspaper, every lending of a book from a library and each time the statement appears on the internet. Even speaking in a loud voice about the claimant so that people can hear can be actionable.[266]

4.6.2.4 Serious Harm

This requirement was introduced through S1 Defamation Act 2013. The common law position prior to the coming into force of the Act was that the statement had an inherent tendency to cause *some harm* to reputation, whereas the Act now requires the statement to have caused or be likely to cause harm which is *serious*. The interpretation of this requirement was considered at length in *Lachaux v Independent Print Ltd and another*.[267] With regards serious harm caused, the Supreme Court confirmed that this is a fact which 'can be established only by reference to the impact which the statement is shown actually to have had'.[268] The court continued that it is a 'combination of the inherent tendency of the words and their actual impact on those to whom they were communicated'.[269] In *Banks v Cadwalladr*, the Court of Appeal provided the following interpretation of S1(1) 'serious harm':

> A statement is defamatory *only if and to the extent* that its publication causes serious harm to reputation or is likely to do so, and not otherwise. This is entirely consistent with the language of section 1(1) which does not contain an exhaustive definition of what is defamatory but an exclusionary criterion. It does not say that a statement *is* defamatory *if* its publication causes serious harm. It says a statement is *not* defamatory *unless* its publication has that effect.[270]

4.6.3 Remedies

4.6.3.1 Damages

The normal rules relating to damages will apply. The Court and Legal Services Act 1990 allowed the Court of Appeal to review damages awards in defamation cases in circumstances where they considered them inappropriate.[271] There is a ceiling on general damages of £200 000. Exemplary damages may be awarded in circumstances where the claimant can prove that the defendant knew that the tort was being committed or was reckless in that respect. The award of damages will often be accompanied by a suitable apology or correction.

---

266 *McManus v Beckham* [2002] EWCA Civ 939.
267 *Lachaux v Independent Print Ltd and another* [2019] UKSC 27.
268 Ibid., para 14.
269 Ibid., para 14.
270 *Banks v Cadwalladr* [2023] EWCA Civ 219 para 45.
271 Paragraph 3.24.

4.6.3.2 Injunction

An injunction may be granted to prevent publication of a defamatory statement or a statement being repeated. The remedy is an equitable one and the normal rules applicable to such remedies apply.

4.6.3.3 An Apology

The publication of an apology by the defendant is not a remedy awarded by the courts, and instead arises primarily when the parties settle by agreement. Under S12 Defamation Act 2013, when the courts find for the claimant, they can order the defendant to publish a summary of the judgment.

4.6.3.4 Removal of the Statement

Under S13 Defamation Act 2013, where the court finds for the claimant, they can order a website operator to remove the statement or to stop distributing, selling or exhibiting that which contains the statement.

4.6.4 Defences

4.6.4.1 Truth

It is a complete defence under S2(1) Defamation Act 2013 for a defendant to show that the statement complained of is substantially true. This abolishes the common law defence of justification.

4.6.4.2 Absolute Privilege

There are some circumstances where freedom of expression is essential, and these are protected by the defence of absolute privilege. It only applies to occasions and reports of high public importance, where words published or reported on such occasions can never be the subject of an action in defamation, even if the defendant was motivated by express malice.[272] The most important examples are statements made in either of the two Houses of Parliament, statements made in the course of judicial proceedings, including tribunals, and communications made between officers of state. The statement cannot be relied upon in a court of law.

4.6.4.3 Qualified Privilege

The defence of qualified privilege protects statements made which are untrue and defamatory but made in good faith. As confirmed in *Davies v Snead*[273] 'where it is right in the interests of society that a person should tell to another certain facts, then, if in good faith and without malice he does tell them, it is a privileged communication'. There are three categories of qualified privilege:

1. limited communications between persons having a common and corresponding duty or interest to make and receive the communication;

---

272 *Munster v Lamb (1883) 11 QBD 588* at 600, CA, per Brett MR; Halsbury's Laws of England Defamation (Volume 32 (2023)) (1) (iv) (593).
273 *Davies v Snead* (1870) LR 5 QB 608 at 611.

2. communications to the public at large, or to a section of the public, made pursuant to a legal, social or moral duty to do so, in reply to a public attack, or in the form of peer-reviewed statements in scientific or academic journals (whether published in electronic form or otherwise);
3. fair and accurate reports, published generally, of the proceedings of specified persons and bodies.[274]

4.6.4.4 Honest Opinion

Under S3 (1) Defamation Act 2013, it is a defence to an action for defamation where the defendant can show that the defamatory statement was an honestly held opinion. This abolishes the common law defence of fair comment. There are three conditions under the Act which must be fulfilled:

1. Statement complained of was a statement of opinion
2. Statement complained of indicated the basis of the opinion
3. An honest person could have held the opinion on the basis of:
   a. A fact which existed at the time the statement was published
   b. Anything asserted to be a privileged statement published prior to the defamatory statement.

Under S3(5), the defence is defeated if the claimant can show that the defendant did not hold the opinion.

4.6.4.5 Public Interest

Under S4 Defamation Act 2013, it is a defence to a claim of defamation to show that

a. The statement was or formed part of a statement on a matter of public interest
b. The defendant reasonably believed that publishing the statement was in the public interest.

This section abolishes the common law defence known as the Reynolds defence, although the explanatory notes in the Act alongside *Economou v de Freitas*[275] confirm that the new defence is 'based on the existing common law defence established in *Reynolds* ...and ... is intended to reflect the principles in that case and subsequent case law'. The *Reynolds* defence[276] was summarised in *Bonnick v Morris*[277]:

> (t)he Reynolds privilege is concerned to provide a proper degree of protection for responsible journalism when reporting matters of public concern. Responsible journalism is the point at which a fair balance is held between freedom of expression on matters of public concern and the reputations of individuals. Maintenance of this standard is in the public interest and in the interests of those whose reputations are involved. It can be regarded as the price journalists pay in return for the privilege.[278]

274 Halsbury's Laws of England Defamation (Volume 32 (2023)) (1) (iv).
275 *Economou v de Freitas* [2018] EWCA Civ 2591.
276 *Reynolds v Times Newspapers and ors* [2001] 2AC 127.
277 *Bonnick v Morris* [2002] UKPC 31.
278 Ibid., para 23.

4.6.4.6 Responsibility for Publication

This defence protects printers, distributors and other secondary publishers. It is a defence if one can show that:

1. they were not the author, editor or publisher of the statement complained of;
2. they took reasonable care in relation to its publication; and
3. they did not know, and had no reason to believe, that what he did caused or contributed to the publication of a defamatory statement.[279]

S5 Defamation Act 2013 provides a specific defence for operators of websites where defamatory statements are posted. Under S5 (2) it is a defence for the operator to show that it was not the operator who posted the statement on the website. However the defence is defeated if the claimant can show that:

a. it was not possible for the claimant to identify the person who posted the statement,
b. the claimant gave the operator a notice of complaint in relation to the statement, and
c. the operator failed to respond to the notice of complaint in accordance with any provision contained in regulations.[280]

4.6.4.7 Offer to Make Amends

This aligns with the making of an apology, as detailed in Section 4.6.3.3 but is formulated through compliance with a statutory provision. Under S2 (1) Defamation Act 1996, a person who has made a defamatory statement may offer to make amends. The offer must be in writing, must call itself an offer to make amends under the Act and must state whether it is qualified or not. The offer must

1. make a suitable correction of the statement complained of and a sufficient apology to the aggrieved party;
2. publish the correction and apology in a manner that is reasonable and practicable in the circumstances; and
3. pay to the aggrieved party such compensation (if any), and such costs, as may be agreed or determined to be payable.[281]

4.7 Breach of Statutory Duty

The tort of breach of statutory duty arises where a statute is regulatory or criminal, but also gives rise to duties in torts. The majority of statutes are essentially regulatory in nature and the question of civil liability sometimes does not exist or is minimal. Much depends on the intention of the legislature. The operation of this area of law is based on statutory interpretation which often involves policy considerations. The relevant statute must be intended to create civil liability otherwise no claim for damages will exist. Much of the law

---

279 Halsbury's Laws of England Defamation (Volume 32 (2023)) (1) (iv) 655.
280 S5 (3) Defamation Act 2013.
281 See Defamation Act 1996 S2 (4) (a)–(c).

relating to breach of statutory duty is concerned with accidents at work while the presence of Health and Safety legislation is important in this context. Some Acts specifically exclude civil liability. The Health and Safety at Work etc. Act 1974 states that the Act gives rise to no civil liability but some of the Regulations made under the Act do. The Building Act 1984 does give rise to civil liability. Frequently the statute does not indicate whether it gives rise to a claim for damages or not.

4.7.1 The Requirements

- The proper construction of the statute was intended to confer private rights of action upon a class of persons of which the claimant is one;[282]
- The claimant must establish an injury or damage of a kind against which the statute was designed to give protection; and
- They must establish that the breach of statutory obligation caused, or materially contributed to, that injury or damage, or (exceptionally) to the risk of that injury or damage.[283]

4.7.1.1 Duty of Care Owed to the Claimant Was Imposed on the Defendant

The claimant must show that the statute was intended by Parliament to confer a civil remedy for its breach and the duty owed by the defendant to the claimant was broken. A duty must be identifiable from the precise wording of the statute.[284]

4.7.1.1.1 Injury of a Kind That the Statute Was Intended to Prevent

In *Ginty v Belmont Building Supplies Ltd*[285] statutory regulations required those involved in the roofing business to use crawling boards when at work. The defendants supplied the boards but the claimant, an experienced roofer, failed to use them and fell through the roof. Although technically in breach of the statute, the defendants were acquitted as they had done everything that could be expected in the circumstances. The breach of duty must be the cause of the damage which must not be too remote. In *Young v Charles Church [Southern] Ltd*[286] an electrician succeeded in a claim based on psychiatric damage when a pole on which they and their colleague were standing struck a live wire resulting in the death of the other workers. The defendants were in breach of the relevant construction regulations which contemplated such damage. If the courts consider that an alternative remedy was intended by the relevant statute they will not impose a duty.

A defence a breach of statutory duty may be specially provided by statute (e.g. See the Highways Act 1980 S58(1)). Contributory negligence on the part of the claimant may be established by the defendant as a partial defence, however *volenti non fit injuria*, is not

---

282 *X (minors) v Bedfordshire County Council* [1995] 3 All ER 353 at 364, *Poole Borough Council v GN* [2019] UKSC 25.
283 *Bonnington Castings Ltd v Wardlaw* [1956] 1 All ER 615, *Fairchild v Glenhaven Funeral Services Ltd* [2002] UKHL 22.
284 *Chipchase v British Titan Products Co Ltd* [1956] 1 QB 545.
285 *Ginty v Belmont Building Supplies Ltd* [1959] 1 All ER 414.
286 *The Times* 1 May 1997.

generally applicable by way of defence to a claim founded on breach by an employer of his statutory duty.[287]

4.8 Employers Liability

The liability of employers to those who work for them may arise in a number of ways. Where appropriate, an employer may be vicariously liable for a tort committed by an employee during the course of employment (see Section 4.3). If there has been a breach of statutory duty, and the relevant statute imposes civil liability, the employer may incur liability (see S69 Enterprise and Regulatory Reform Act 2013). An employer owes a non-delegable duty in respect of the health and safety of employees irrespective of any conditions imposed by statute. The leading case is *Wilson & Clyde Coal Co Ltd v English*[288] where four main 'duties' were identified, with Lord Wright describing them as 'fundamental obligations of a contract of employment which lie outside the doctrine of common employment, and for the performance of which employers are absolutely responsible'[289]: *Wilson* confirmed an employer as holding a duty to exercise reasonable care and skill when providing the following to their employees:

- Safe place of work.
- Safe system of work.
- Competent staff.
- Safe plant and equipment.

4.8.1 The Obligations

4.8.1.1 Safe Place of Work

Alongside obligations contained in secondary legislation,[290] employers have a common law duty to maintain equipment, provide adequate ventilation, temperature, and lighting, maintain furniture, fittings, floors, walls, and ceilings, arrange workstations and access to work areas and have in place measures to prevent injury. At common law the employer must take steps to try to ensure that the system which has been installed is known to employees and is complied with.

4.8.1.2 Safe System of Work

A safe system of work concerns the duty to ensure the structure employees work under is safe. It is dependent on each place of work, but may include the sequence in which tasks are carried out, the method through which employees are required to work, and the provision of instructions.

---

287 Halsbury's Laws of England, Tort (Volume 97A (2021)), General Tortious Liabilities, Unlawful Conduct, Breach of Statutory Duty, Nature of the Cause of Action, Breach of statutory duty: essentials of cause of action (para 99).

288 *Wilson & Clyde Coal Co Ltd v English* [1938] AC 57.

289 Ibid., para 640.

290 *Workplace (Health, Safety and Welfare) Regulations 1992, SI 1992/3004.*

4.8.1.3 Competent Staff

Employers have a duty to ensure that their employees are competent to carry out the tasks which are entrusted to them. This includes taking the best practicable steps to eliminate unsafe practices and not to condone bad behaviour.

4.8.1.4 Safe Plant, Materials and Equipment

Any equipment which is provided must be safe and properly maintained. To avoid misuse of equipment by employees, it is often sensible for employers to give training and updating to their workforce. Employers' obligations have now been extended to cover psychiatric injuries covered by negligent work practices. It seems that a successful claimant must now show that it was reasonably foreseeable that he would suffer a psychiatric illness as a result of the employer's breach of duty.[291] Statutory obligations are found in secondary legislation, including Provision and Use of Work Equipment Regulations 1998 (SI 1998/2306) and Personal Protective Equipment at Work Regulations 1992 (SI 1992/2966)).

4.8.2 Defences

4.8.2.1 Volenti

In *Smith v Baker*[292] it was held that volenti would only be relevant if the claimant accepted freely and understood the specific risks involved. There must be no coercion. The defence will not apply where there is a breach of statutory duty.

4.8.2.2 Contributory Negligence

Where appropriate, an apportionment of damages may be made under the Law Reform (Contributory Negligence) Act 1945. If the employee is considered 100% responsible for their misfortune there may be a full reduction and no damages will be awarded to them.[293]

4.9 Product Liability

The law of negligence has greatly assisted injured parties who suffer damage where there is no privity of contract between the parties. However the difficulties encountered in proving negligence have always been considerable in connection with defective products especially proving fault and causation.

4.9.1 Consumer Protection Act 1987

The difficulties experienced with defective products was addressed at European Community level in 1985 by Product Liability Directive 85/374/EEC. Member states were required to comply with the Directive within 3 years. The result in the UK is the

291 *Barber v Somerset County Council* [2004] UKHL 13.
292 *Smith v Baker* (1891) AC 325.
293 *Jayes v IMI [Kynoch] Ltd* [1985] ICR 55.

Consumer Protection Act 1987. Following the withdrawal of the UK from the European Union, the Act still applies but is subject to amendments made by the Product Safety and Metrology etc. (Amendment etc.) (EU Exit) Regulations (SI 2019/696). The Act no longer needs to be interpreted in line with the EU Product Liability Directive or in line with decisions of the European Court of Justice.

The Act imposes strict liability on producers for harm caused by defective goods. People injured by faulty products can sue for compensation without having to prove negligence provided they can prove the product was defective and the defect in the product was responsible for the harm. Regulations were introduced in 2005 to supplement the Act. The Act and Regulations leave untouched claims in contract against the retailer of the product, any action in negligence and, where appropriate, any claim for breach of statutory duty. Case authorities, including *Gee & Others v DePuy International Limited*,[294] approved by the UK Supreme Court in *Hastings v Finsbury Orthopaedics Ltd*[295] confirm the assessment of the defect in goods depends on the facts of the case, and include compliance with regulations and potential to avoid risk. The claimant need only establish that a defect was present and a causal relationship between the defect and the injury caused.

By S1(2) of the Act, liability is imposed on the 'Producer'. This will include the manufacturer but will also cover minerals which are 'won or abstracted'. Where a product does not fall within these categories, but the development of the item is attributable to an industrial or related process, it will be covered by the Act. This would cover crop production and those involved in similar processes. Those who brand-name products, import products into the European Community or hold themselves out as being producers are covered by the Act. A supplier will normally not be liable under the Act as long as they do not come under any of the former categories. They do have obligations to name producers in circumstances where consumers suffer damage covered by the Act otherwise they will be personally liable. The products covered by the Act are extensive. All consumer goods and those used in the workplace are included. This includes component parts and certain raw materials. Food is covered. Buildings themselves are not covered by the Act but building materials are included.[296]

S3 of the Act provides that there is a defect in a product if the safety of that product is not as persons generally are entitled to expect. All the circumstances are to be taken into account including packaging and any instructions relating to use. The Act has no application if the item is safe but useless. The Act only provides for claims in relation to death, personal injury and damage to private property. Small claims are excluded (less than £275) while no claim can be made in respect of damage to the respective product itself. Damage to business property and economic losses resulting from defective products are excluded.

294 *Gee & Others v DePuy International Limited* [2018] EWHC 1208 (QB) *Hastings v Finsbury Orthopaedics Ltd*, 2022 S.C. (U.K.S.C.) 43 (2022).

295 *Hastings v Finsbury Orthopaedics Ltd* [2022] UKSC 43.

296 S46.

4.9.2 Consumer Rights Act 2015

Consumer contracts are governed by the Consumer Rights Act 2015, which requires all contracts to supply goods include a term that the goods are of satisfactory quality and comply with their respective description and/or sample supplied. S9 (2) sets the standard for satisfactory quality as:

> The quality of goods is satisfactory if they meet the standard that a reasonable person would consider satisfactory, taking account of—
> **a.** any description of the goods,
> **b.** the price or other consideration for the goods (if relevant), and
> **c.** all the other relevant circumstances (see subsection (5)).

(5) The relevant circumstances mentioned in subsection (2)(c) include any public statement about the specific characteristics of the goods made by the trader, the producer or any representative of the trader or the producer.

Where goods are unsatisfactory but the issue was drawn to the customers attention prior to contract, or where an examination is made or the goods themselves or a sample which ought to have revealed the issue, the Act cannot be relied on.

4.10 Remedies

As discussed within this chapter, the law of tort provides a number of remedies depending on the category of tort committed by the defendant. Remedies may be judicial, provided by the court, or extra-judicial, available to party themselves. Judicial remedies include damages and injunctions whilst extra-judicial include expulsion of a trespasser from land and re-entry to land.

4.10.1 Judicial Remedies

Judicial remedies are those granted by the court to a claimant following a successful action brought in the law of torts.

4.10.1.1 Damages

Damages are the principal remedy in tort. They are compensatory in nature and their aim is to put claimants into the position they would have been in had the wrong not been committed- the claimant should not be worse or better off as a result of the tort being committed. This is the principle of *restitution in integrum.* Damages may be either general or special. General damages include matters such as loss of future earnings, pain and injury suffered, losses which result from the decrease in value of a house because a surveyor negligently failed to recognise defects when carrying out a valuation and loss of the ability to enjoy life as you did before the tort was committed. This is sometimes called amenity loss. General damages are not capable of being precisely quantified. Special damages relate to costs which can be precisely identified such as itemised repair costs.

Also classed as general damages, but non-compensatory in nature, are contemptuous damages. These are awarded where the claimant's rights have been infringed but the court considers that the claimant was wrong to bring the action. Nominal damages are awarded where little damage has been caused but the court considers that the claimant was correct to bring the action. Exemplary damages are awarded where the court disapproves of the defendant's conduct and are awarded to deter others from similar behaviour. Another category, known as aggravated damages, may be awarded to compensate for injury to feelings and distress caused by the defendant's bad behaviour. This last category is compensatory in nature but recognises that the claimant's position has been made worse by the defendant's malice.

Compensatory damages can be divided into pecuniary and non-pecuniary losses. This relates respectively to financial and other losses suffered. In *Farley v Skinner*[297] the defendant surveyor was asked to prepare a report relating to a house which the claimant was buying. The claimant specifically asked the surveyor if the subject property was troubled by noise from aircraft as he wanted a house in a quiet location. The surveyor said that this would not be a problem, and the purchase went ahead with the claimant spending a considerable amount of money improving the property. The claimant went into occupation but found that aircraft noise was a major problem. The House of Lords awarded the claimant £10,000 by way of damages. The House of Lords[298] stated that when calculating damages for breach of duty it is necessary to ascertain exactly what the duty consists of. The defendant will only be liable for consequences arising from the negligent performance of that duty. The *South Australian Assett Management* case concerns the 'classic' situation of claimants lending money for the purchase of property based on valuations made by defendants which turn out to be vastly optimistic. In this case the House of Lords took the view that the defendants did not owe a duty to the claimants to advise whether or not to make the loans but simply to make a valuation of the subject property. Their liability was limited to the consequences of their advice being wrong and not for the overall drop in property prices in the market. There are policy considerations here while the case does not lay down how the courts identify the duty which is being owed.

In the case of compensation in respect of damage to land and buildings a court can take the approach of awarding a sum equal to the decrease in the value of the property or award the cost of reinstating the property to its original condition. The latter has tended to be the approach which the courts have favoured except where the claimant has no intention of repairing the building or where the cost of reinstatement would be out of all proportion to the loss suffered. In addition, a claimant will be entitled to compensation for loss of use during the time that the repairs are being carried out and this will extend to loss of profits in the case of a business. If a property is destroyed the award will be the market value of the property at the time of destruction. There is a duty on the claimant to take reasonable steps to mitigate any tortious losses sustained.

---

297 *Farley v Skinner* [2001] UKHL 49.

298 Paragraph 3.8 and *South Australian Asset Management Corp v York Montague Ltd* [1997] AC 191.

4.10.1.2 Injunction

This is an equitable remedy which prohibits a wrongful act or sometimes requires a defendant to take steps to put matters right.[299] The usual rules relating to equitable remedies apply. It is discretionary in nature and must be appropriate to the circumstances. It is awarded if the court considers it 'just and equitable' in the circumstances. It tends to be used where there is a course of conduct rather than a single act, so it is particularly appropriate in trespass and nuisance cases. There are cases where a court may decide to award damages in lieu of an injunction[300] but these rules are stringently applied to prevent wrongdoers with means being able to pay for the injury they inflict. Injunctions are normally perpetual and prohibitory in nature but an injunction may be interlocutory (interim). This is where the order is granted before the case is heard in an attempt to prevent further harm. The grant of such an injunction is not an indication that the claimant has won their case. Increasingly, modern courts try to effect a compromise between the parties in the manner in which the order operates.[301] Failure to obey an injunction is a contempt of court which may result in the imposition of a fine or imprisonment.

4.10.1.3 Specific Restitution of Property

This is a legal remedy which restores goods to their owner. There are a number of circumstances where the restoration of property is the preferred remedy:

1. when the asset is that which the claimant originally was entitled and the claimant wants that asset rather than the monetary value of it,
2. when the defendant's gain exceeds the claimant's loss, and/or
3. when the defendant is insolvent.[302]

4.10.2 Extrajudicial Remedies

On occasions, the law does allow a certain degree of self-help. The recapture of goods, abatement of a nuisance and re-entry onto land are good examples. It is tolerated, but self-help is not popular with the courts although it is recognised that its use does help to limit potential litigation. The problems associated with it can be illustrated by the decision in *Revill v Newberry*.[303]

---

299 *Redland Bricks Ltd v Morris* [1970] AC 652.
300 *Shelfer v City of London Electric Lighting* [1895] 1 Ch 287.
301 *Kennaway v Thompson* [1981] QB 88.
302 C.P. Murphy, 'What is Specific About "Specific Restitution"?' *Hastings L.J* (2009): 853 60.
303 *Revill v Newberry* [1996] QB 567.

5

Land Law

CONTENTS

5.1 Introduction

Land law provides a legal framework that governs land and our interaction with it. It is concerned with rights, obligations, interests and uses of land, and provides a structure under which they are recognised and can be enforced. The reason land law has its own legal framework, distinct from general rights and ownership in property, is that it is unique. Several features assist in creating this unique status:

- It is all around us, we interact with it every day of our lives, it is finite, and it is permanent.
- Property ownership is an essential part of the UK economy and land is often one of the most, if not the most expensive asset one will ever own.
- Land is capable of supporting simultaneous rights, uses and interests – on one piece of land you may have an owner, a tenant, a restriction on the front door colour, a mortgage and a neighbour who can only access their land via yours. Several people have rights over a single piece of land in this example, and land law enables these rights to coexist.
- Interests and rights in land may run consecutively (one after the other, for example a life interest) or concurrently (at the same time, such as the example above).

- It is possible to bind a future owner with the rights and interests which currently exist over a piece of land – for example, a current owner allowing a neighbour to use part of a property to park their car may continue to bind future owners. Under contract law, ordinarily a contract binds only the parties to it; however, with land, interests can bind future third parties. Such a right or interest is considered as attached to the land (proprietary right in or over land) and can be for the benefit of, or burden to, both current and future owners of the property.

The current legal regime governing land in England and Wales is a mixture of historic and modern statute and common law, with the current structure finding its roots in the feudal system introduced by William the Conqueror in 1066. Major land reform took place on 1 January 1926 in a raft of legislation which received royal assent in 1925. Societal change has rendered reform necessary in some areas; however, the 1925 Acts provided the foundational building blocks of our current system, and some remain in force and integral to the land law regime today, most notably the Law of Property Act 1925.

5.2 Defining Land

Whilst land is a form of property, the law makes a distinction between it and other types of property, described as real property (land) and personal property (everything else). The courts have long distinguished between the two, in particular with regard to remedies. Birk describes this historic distinction:

> A judgment in money can be called personal because it gives the victorious claimant no right in or to any particular thing, but merely a right that a (...) defeated defendant pay the sum in question... in some actions you could recover the thing itself. Those actions came to be called 'real actions' 'real' meaning thing related in the simplest sense that the person claiming would recover the very thing they claimed. The subject matter of real actions became real property.[1]

The Latin for these remedies is a right *in rem*, in the thing, real property, and a right *in personam*, against a person, personal property, for which the remedy would be damages. Land law is primarily concerned with rights *in rem*, rights in the land itself, as opposed to those held by the people who created them. As land is both unique and finite, damages are an insufficient remedy and instead remedying the wrong (for example, where the owner had been incorrectly dispossessed) requires the return of land itself.

An everyday definition of land may include the surface around us, all which is not water, and/or areas of ground and physical property. S205 (1) (ix) Law of Property Act 1925 provides a much more comprehensive definition:

---

1 P. Birks, 'Before We Begin: 5 Keys to Land Law,' in *Land law: Themes and Perspectives*, ed. S. Bright and J. Dewar (Oxford University Press, 1998), 470.

> "Land" includes land of any tenure, and mines and minerals, whether or not held apart from the surface, buildings or parts of buildings (whether the division is horizontal, vertical or made in any other way) and other corporeal hereditaments; also a manor, an advowson, and a rent and other incorporeal hereditaments, and an easement, right, privilege, or benefit in, over, or derived from land; . . . and "mines and minerals" include any strata or seam of minerals or substances in or under any land, and powers of working and getting the same . . .; and "manor" includes a lordship, and reputed manor or lordship; and "hereditament" means any real property which on an intestacy occurring before the commencement of this Act might have devolved upon an heir;

5.2.1 Dissecting the Definition

5.2.1.1 The Extent of Land

Although the language of S205 is far from common parlance, the definition retains its importance, not least as it confirms that, in law, land includes not only the tangible and physical (corporeal hereditaments) but also the intangible (incorporeal hereditaments). Corporeal hereditaments are physical, such as a field or building, whereas incorporeal hereditaments are invisible rights in land, such as leases, mortgages and easements. The definition also includes mines and minerals, which extend land from that on the surface to include that beneath the surface. This encapsulates the Latin maxim of *cuius est solum, eius est usque ad caelum et ad inferos* (whoever owns the soil, it is theirs up to Heaven and down to Hell). Practical difficulties are immediately apparent with this wide maxim – utility pipes under land and aeroplanes flying above are two simple examples where, under this maxim, trespass would take place constantly. Common law and statute have therefore sought to limit the extent of ownership to account for the practical impact. In the case of *Bernstein v Skyviews and General Ltd*[2] an aeroplane flying several hundred feet above land for the purposes of taking photographs may be entitled to do so, providing it does not infringe the reasonable enjoyment of the land affected. In a similar vein, section 76(1) Civil Aviation Act 1982 provides civil aircraft with immunity from trespass as long as they are flying at a reasonable height above ground. Statute has also limited ownership of land beneath the surface, exampled with regard to the extraction of coal and oil.[3]

5.2.1.2 That Growing on the Land

The common law distinguishes between different categories of things growing on the land. As stated above, naturally occurring vegetation forms part of the land. However, following the sale of land, disputes have arisen over the ownership of crops and trees that have been planted by the previous owner. If forming part of the, they will obviously be transferred to the new owner automatically at the time of the sale, whereas if they retain their status as separate chattels the original owner will retain ownership in them, and therefore be entitled to remove them. The common law resolves this problem by drawing a distinction between

---

2 *Bernstein v Skyviews and General Ltd* [1978] QB 479.
3 SS1(1) & 7(3) Coal Industry Act 1994; SS1(a) & 2(1) Petroleum Act 1994.

what it describes as *fructus naturales* and *fructus industriales*. *Fructus naturales* are things which grow naturally on land (for example vegetation) but also things planted which then produce a crop each year without any further human intervention (for example, fruit trees). These form part of the land on which they grow and will pass to the new owner on a sale of the land. These are distinguished from *fructus industriales* which the law regards as chattels rather than land. These are cultivated crops which require annual human intervention (for example wheat or potatoes). As items of personal property, the owner of the land retains ownership in them and is therefore entitled to remove them before parting with the land to the new owner.

5.2.1.3 Attachment to the Land

A fixture is a chattel which has become (in a legal sense) a part of land by being attached to it. This is important on a sale of land, as the basic rule is that fixtures pass with the land, but chattels do not. On a transfer of land, chattels may be removed but fixtures which have become a constituent part of the land may not. In order to ascertain whether an object is a fixture or a chattel, the courts have traditionally applied two tests.

5.2.1.3.1 The Degree of Annexation Test

This is the primary test, applied to show how permanently the object has been attached to the land. If something is physically fixed to land (for example by nailing, screwing, being set in concrete or similar) it is presumed to be a fixture and the more firmly it is fixed the stronger the presumption becomes. Conversely, if something is not fixed to land it is presumed to be a chattel.

In *Smith v City Petroleum Co Ltd*[4] petrol pumps on a filling station forecourt were deemed to be fixtures in a dispute over their status. Similarly, in *Buckland v Butterfield*,[5] a wooden balcony which had been bolted to the side of a house was also held to be a fixture. Conversely, in *TSB v Botham*[6] where electrical 'white goods' slotted into standard holes in a fitted kitchen but not fixed in any way were held to be chattels. Some quite significant objects have been held to retain their status as chattels as a result of applying the logic of this test. For example, the case of *Berkley v Poulett*[7] concerned the status of a statue in the grounds of a stately home. Although weighing approximately half a ton, it was not fixed down in any way but was simply secured in position by its own weight. On this basis it was held to be a chattel. The status of an even larger and heavier object was considered in *Royal Bank of Canada v Beyak*[8] where a mobile home was held to be a chattel.

The degree of annexation test is, however, only a *prima facie* test. It is not conclusive about the status of the particular item under consideration but raises a presumption. This presumption can sometimes be rebutted by applying another test, the purpose of annexation test.

---

4 *Smith v City Petroleum Co Ltd* [1940] 1 All ER 260.
5 *Buckland v Butterfield* (1820) 2 Brod & Bing 54.
6 *TSB v Botham* [1994] 1 All 3R 272.
7 *Berkley v Poulett* [1977] 1 EGLR 86.
8 *Royal Bank of Canada v Beyak* (1981) 119 DLR 505.

5.2.1.3.2 The Purpose of Annexation Test

This test is used if the degree of annexation test is difficult to apply. In the event of a conflict between the two rules, degree of annexation test will prevail. Unlike the degree of annexation test, this test is not concerned with the physical way in which the item has been placed in position; instead it addresses the *intention* with which it was placed there. If it was placed with the intention of effecting a permanent improvement of the land or building in question, it is a fixture. If, on the other hand, it was placed in position simply for its better enjoyment as a chattel, or for security purposes, then it remains a chattel. Each situation depends very much on its own facts. Is the intention to improve the use of the land or enhance the item itself? The principle is illustrated by the comments of Blackburn J in *Holland v Hodgson*[9] where they stated that a pile of stones stacked together in a yard would be considered as chattels but the same set of stones forming a wall would be part of the land.

The way in which the application of the purpose of annexation test can rebut the presumptions generated by the degree of annexation test can be seen in the following two cases. In *Hulme v Brigham*[10] two printing machines, each weighing 12 tons, were bolted to a workshop floor to prevent vibration when they were in use. Despite the extent of their physical annexation to the building they were nevertheless held to be chattels in view of the purpose of this annexation. The presumption and rebuttal operated in entirely the opposite direction in *D'Eyncourt v Gregory*,[11] where small, free-standing stone statues were placed in niches in the façade of a house. Although they were not physically attached to the building they were held to be fixtures because they were an integral part of the house's architectural design.

In *Elitestone Ltd v Morris*[12] the House of Lords approved the use of this twofold test approach when deciding on the status of certain objects but felt that it was less helpful when deciding on the status of others. In that case the Law Lords had to decide whether a wooden bungalow resting on, but not attached to, concrete pillars was a chattel. If so, the defendant's tenancy of the site could not be one of a dwelling house and they would not enjoy security of tenure under the Rent Act 1977. Overruling the Court of Appeal, they took the view that decisions about the status of a house itself needed to be considered on a more common-sense basis rather then being subject to the precise analysis suggested by the twofold approach. It was therefore unnecessary to apply the degree of annexation test at all. The purpose of annexation was held to be the defining question and it was to be determined objectively, according to the facts of the case. In deciding that the bungalow formed part and parcel of the land, the judges were influenced by the fact that a house which was constructed in such a way that it could not be removed except by destruction could not have been intended to remain a chattel but must always have been intended to form part of the land.

The *Elitestone* approach was also followed in *Chelsea Yacht and Boat Club Ltd v Pope*[13] where the status of a houseboat had to be considered. It was argued that the boat had become a fixture and would therefore automatically be transferred on a sale of the land as it had all mains services connected. However, as it could easily be moved to another mooring without causing damage to its fabric, it was held to be a chattel.

9 *Holland v Hodgson* (1872) LR 7 CP 328.
10 *Hulme v Brigham* [1943] KB 152.
11 *D'Eyncourt v Gregory* (1866) LR 3 Eq 382.
12 *Elitestone Ltd v Morris* [1997] 2 All ER 513.
13 *Chelsea Yacht and Boat Club Ltd v Pope* [2001] 2 All ER 409.

5.3 Owning Land

The general concept of 'ownership' involves the exclusive right to use, possess, control, destroy or dispose of property within one's ownership. In a theoretical legal sense we might describe ownership as indicating that one has all the rights in a particular item of property that are capable of existing. If, for example, you own a pen (an item of personal property) no one else can stop you using it and you are free to destroy it or give it away if you choose to do so. You own all the rights in it. Applying this general concept, it is not possible to own land in English law. Instead, it is only possible to own *rights* in land. Some of these rights are bundled together to form packages of rights known as legal estates. It is therefore possible to own a *legal estate* in land which will bear a strong resemblance to the familiar concept of ownership of property which applies to personal property. The rights within this package will include the following:

- Exclusive possession – the right to control and manage the land including the right to exclude everyone else from it.
- Enjoyment – the right to enjoy all the benefits which the land has to offer (this includes the right to draw percolating water from the ground and certain rights over neighbouring land, including a right to support for the soil).
- Alienation – the right of the estate owner to sell or otherwise dispose of the legal estate in the land.

An estate owner is said to hold the land rather than own it. This concept of holding land finds its origins in the Feudal System and is known as *tenure*. Historically there were many different types of legal, however as a result of section 1 Law of Property Act 1925, there are now only two, the freehold and the leasehold.

5.3.1 Freehold Ownership

The legal term for the freehold legal estate is the 'fee simple absolute in possession'. This rather complicated expression was used to distinguish it from other legal estates that could also exist before the enactment of the Law of Property Act 1925. The various parts of the expression have the following meanings:

- Fee – the estate can be inherited.
- Simple – the freeholder can pass the estate to anyone.
- Absolute – the grant will continue forever.
- In possession – the person who has the benefit of the estate is entitled to immediate possession of the land or, if the land has been let, is entitled to rent from the land.

Perhaps unsurprisingly the expression is rarely used in full and is often abbreviated to 'fee simple' (or just 'freehold'). The fee simple is characterised by the fact that it is of indefinite duration. Should they choose to do so an owner of a fee simple can therefore own it in perpetuity, and dispose of it how they see fit, through transfer in life or upon death. The majority of houses in England and Wales are freehold.

5.3.2 The Leasehold Estate

The legal term for the leasehold legal estate is the term of years absolute. A leasehold estate, like the freehold estate, is a package of rights in the land itself. It is, however, characterised by the fact that it is granted by another estate owner who grants these rights for a term of lesser duration than they themselves are entitled to. Because a freeholder's estate is of unlimited duration, they may grant a lease for any period they like and, in practice, one can often encounter leases of 999 years as well as many shorter terms. A leaseholder can only grant a lease (described as a 'sub-lease') for a lesser term than that which has been granted to them. The owner of a 999-year leasehold term therefore has considerable scope to grant leases, for example, for 5 weeks, 5 months, 5 years, 50 years or 500 years. The estate owner who grants a leasehold estate to another obviously retains some rights in the land themselves, including an entitlement to receive rent and, crucially, for the land to revert back to them at the end of the term. The rights retained are therefore collectively referred to as the 'reversion'.

The term of the lease does not have to be for a fixed 'term of years' but can be measured by reference to some shorter time interval, for example, weeks or months. Equally, it does not have to be what is described as a 'fixed-term tenancy'. It can instead take the form of a 'periodic tenancy'. Under this arrangement, the length of the term is not fixed at the outset but continues on a rolling basis until terminated by the service of an agreed period of notice. Periodic tenancies may be described, for example, as weekly tenancies, monthly tenancies, quarterly tenancies or yearly tenancies, depending on the agreed period that has been used to define them. Either party can terminate such a tenancy by serving notice to quit on the other party to expire at the end of the agreed period. If notice is not served, the tenancy simply rolls on from agreed period to agreed period.

In practice the leasehold estate is sometimes described as a term of years, a lease, a demise, or a tenancy. The person who grants a leasehold estate is known as the lessor or landlord. The one who takes the lease is known as the lessee or tenant. It is important to understand that the leasehold estate is not necessarily an inferior estate to the freehold estate. The two estates are simply legal vehicles for the economic activities of property management and investment. For example, consider a situation where a freehold owner grants a lease of a property for 999 years at a rent of £50 per annum. Which is the more valuable legal estate? The leasehold estate, and its practical implications for particular types of property, is addressed in greater detail in Chapter 6, which deals with the law of landlord and tenant. In a residential context, in England and Wales, leasehold is primarily seen with regard to flat ownership. This is particularly prevalent where one property has been demised, or divided into multiple dwellings, for example, a block of flats or property which was once a single dwelling and has been subdivided into two or more flats.

5.3.2.1 Criticisms of Leasehold Ownership

In January 2023, Michael Gove, The Secretary of State for Levelling Up, Housing and Communities, told *The Sunday Times* newspaper, 'I don't believe leasehold is fair in any way. It is an outdated feudal system that needs to go. And we need to move to a better system and to liberate people from it'.[14] Common criticisms include uncertainty of ownership as lease term diminishes, cost of lease extensions, payment of service charges and a lack of regulation of freeholders. Criticism intensified following the Grenfell Tower fire tragedy in 2017 and the use of leases with doubling ground rent clauses by numerous national housebuilders. The Competition and Markets Authority in England and Wales noted '(f)or years leaseholders have been plagued by what we believe are unfair practices'.[15]

5.4 Co-ownership of Land

It is quite common for two or more people (for example, those in personal, business or familial relationships) to jointly own the same legal estate in land. This can be either freehold or leasehold ownership. Where this occurs, the law describes this as a co-ownership, and the owners as co-owners. Co-ownership is governed by both statute and common law, with the Law of Property Act 1925 (LPA 25) and the Trusts of Land and Appointment of Trustees Act 1996 (TOLATA 96) the main statutes governing this area of law. The Law of Property Act 1925 determines that there are only two ways in which land can be held simultaneously by two or more people – as joint tenants or as tenants in common.

5.4.1 Joint Tenants

A joint tenancy exists where two or more people own the whole property, as opposed to each owning a specific share of its total value. The individual owners are treated in law as one single owner.

The two main characteristics of the joint tenancy are the presence of what are known as 'the four unities' and the operation of the 'right of survivorship' on the death of one of the co-owners. The first of these is a theoretical concept which the law has developed to assist in identifying the existence of a joint tenancy, whilst the second is an entirely practical consequence.

5.4.1.1 The Four Unities

The textbook rule is that a joint tenancy can only exist if the four unities are present. These are:

- Unity of interest – as each co-owner is collectively entitled to the whole, the interest of each of them must, by definition, be identical.
- Unity of possession – the land must not be physically divided up but each co-owner must have a right to possession of the whole.

---

14 S. Swinford, 'Michale Gove to Scrap Feudal Leasehold System,' *The Times (UK)* 30 January 2023.
15 Sarah Cardell, interim chief executive of the CMA, quoted in J. Gardiner, 'CMA Drags More National Housebuilders Into Leasehold Investigation,' *Housing Today* August 2022.

- Unity of title – there must be a single deed that vests the property in all co-owners.
- Unity of time – the single deed must vest the property in all the co-owners at the same time rather than making provision for some of them to join the group at a later date.

5.4.1.2 The Right of Survivorship

The right of survivorship determines that when one joint tenant dies, ownership automatically passes to the remaining joint tenants. A joint tenant is therefore unable to bequeath the joint tenancy to another.

5.4.2 Tenants in Common

Where property is held as a tenancy in common, each co-owner has a recognised share of the property. In contrast to joint tenants, where all own the property equally, for tenants in common, shares in the property can be allocated as the tenants in common see fit, identifying their respective portions. This allows tenants in common to allocate equal or unequal shares amongst each other. It is most common where the parties contribute differing amounts of capital to the purchase. The land itself is still owned as a single unit by the tenants in common – the land is not divided, just its ownership. The property is not, therefore physically divided and, for this reason, the Law of Property Act 1925 refers to a tenancy in common as 'land held in undivided shares'. There is no right of survivorship with tenants in common, meaning that upon the death of a tenant in common, ordinarily rules of inheritance or intestacy will apply, and each tenant in common is free to bequeath their share as they wish.

5.4.3 Identifying the Type of Co-ownership

Ordinarily, upon purchase of land, intending co-owners will be asked how they wish to hold the land – as joint tenants or as tenants in common. If the deed fails to state the capacity in which they intend to hold the property, the common law presumes a joint tenancy. However, the presumption can be rebutted if there is evidence of a contrary intention. This will be the case where:

- The deed includes words (described as 'words of severance') which indicate that the parties intended to have separate shares in the land. The following examples have been held to be words of severance: 'in equal shares'; 'equally'; 'divided between'; 'amongst'; 'respectively';
- The co-owners are business partners; and/or
- The co-owners have contributed to the purchase price in unequal shares.

5.4.4 Converting a Joint Tenancy to a Tenancy in Common

It is possible to convert a joint tenancy into a tenancy in common by a process of severing the joint tenancy. As highlighted in *Harris v Goddard:*

> Severance is, as I understand it, the process of separating off the share of a joint tenant, so that the concurrent ownership will continue but the right of survivorship

> will no longer apply. The parties [who decided to sever] will hold separate shares as tenants in common.[16]

The main practical effect of severance is to defeat the right of survivorship. A couple who hold their matrimonial home as joint tenants might decide to sever the joint tenancy when contemplating divorce. Although other methods of severance are possible the normal way would be through the service of a written notice by one joint owner on all other tenants clearly expressing their intention to sever.

5.5 Evidencing Ownership of Land

If an owner wishes to sell their legal estate in land they must first prove to the buyer that they are the owner, and therefore able to sell it. This process of proving ownership is referred to as proving the 'title' to land. This is an important aspect of the whole process of transferring ownership of a legal estate which is itself described as the conveyancing process. There are two systems of conveyancing in England and Wales, depending on whether the land is registered or unregistered. Unregistered land accounts for approximately 20% land ownership, with 80% of land ownership being registered. Whether land is registered or unregistered determines the legal system used for sale and purchase.

5.5.1 The Nature and Role of Deeds

Deeds are documents which comply with certain legal formalities to ensure that their authenticity can be easily proved than would be the case with an ordinary written document. They are used in many legal and business situations but have a particular role within land law. The reason for this is that in almost all cases the only way that a legal estate or legal interest (one of the third-party rights in land, see Section 5.7) can be created or transferred is by deed.[17]

The traditional common law formalities required that a deed had to be signed, sealed and delivered to be valid. This meant that the person to be bound by the deed had first to sign the document, then to add their personal seal to it in sealing wax, and finally that they had to personally and formally hand it over to the other party. In practice, deeds were also signed by a witness to the parties' signature although this was not strictly required for a deed to be valid. Over time some of these formalities, notably the requirement for a wax seal, were relaxed. There was briefly a period when a small self-adhesive red sticker was used instead of sealing wax. Eventually even this was dispensed with and documents simply included a small pre-printed circle containing the letters 'LS' (*locus sigilli* or 'the place of the seal') alongside the parties' signatures.

16 *Harris v Goddard* [1983] 3 All ER 242.
17 Law of Property Act 1925, S52(1).

The formalities for the creation of a deed are now contained in section 1 Law of Property (Miscellaneous Provisions) Act 1989. This no longer requires a document to be sealed in order to be a valid deed but does set out three additional requirements. Firstly the face of the document must make it clear that it is intended to be a deed. This will typically be achieved by the document describing itself as a deed or expressing itself to be executed or signed as a deed. Secondly, the document must be signed by the person to be bound by it in the presence of a witness who must then also sign. Finally, the document must be delivered to the person who can rely upon it although this need not be done formally and can take place by post or by someone on behalf of the person who is to be bound by it.

Deeds can take many forms, according to the purpose for which they are created. In the context of the creation or transfer of a legal estate in land, the following would be the most common:

- Conveyance – transferring a legal estate on sale.
- Deed of Gift – transferring an estate where there is no consideration.
- Assent – transferring a legal estate to a beneficiary by the personal representatives of a deceased estate owner.
- Mortgage Deed – granting a mortgage to a lender over a legal estate in land in return for a loan (secured on the legal estate).
- Lease – granting a new leasehold estate.
- Deed of Assignment – transferring an existing leasehold estate.

5.5.2 Unregistered Land

When someone acquires a legal estate in unregistered land, all the old deeds relating to the property are handed to them, together with a new deed (for example, a conveyance) through which the previous owner transfers the estate to them. Traditionally, the way in which someone proved ownership of a legal estate was simply by being able to produce the deed transferring the estate to them, along with some of the old deeds that proved that the previous owners had good title at the time that they transferred the estate in the past. The process is referred to as *deducing title* and is illustrated by the following simple example.

In the year 2010, Helen wishes to purchase the freehold in Blackacre from George. George has a large bundle of old deeds relating to the property including the following:

Conveyance from Charles to David dated 1930.
Conveyance from David to Elaine dated 1957.
Conveyance from Elaine to Fiona dated 1985.
Conveyance from Fiona to George dated 1989.

George can therefore prove their ownership of the freehold to Blackacre by producing the 1989 conveyance to them and also some of the earlier deeds which prove that Fiona was entitled to transfer the estate, and that the earlier estate owners were similarly entitled to effect the transfers which they made. George deduces title in this way by demonstrating an unbroken chain of ownership stretching back into the past.

The earliest deed which an estate owner produces in the chain of ownership is referred to as the root of title, and a question arises about how far back in time it is reasonable to go in order to be sure that the current owner is the rightful owner of the estate. This is a matter for the parties to agree but in the absence of contrary agreement, S23 Law of Property Act 1969 provides that it should be 15 years. In practice this means that one should go back to the first document in the chain that is older than this minimum period. In the above example, if we go back 15 years, we reach the date 1995. The first document which is older than this is the 1989 conveyance from Fiona to George. Therefore, in this example, because because of the length of time George has owned the property, they only need to produce this single conveyance to Helen as evidence of their title.

In practice, an estate owner is unlikely to want to part with the original deeds until a purchaser is ready to hand over the purchase price to them, so they initially evidence title by producing copies of the relevant documents. Before the invention of photocopiers these had to be typed or handwritten in the form of summaries of various documents called 'abstracts of title'. Because of the laborious nature of this process the clerks who produced them did so using an abbreviated form of language. In later years photocopies of the documents attached to a schedule (called an 'epitome of title') replaced the use of abstracts. However produced, these copy documents are mailed to the purchaser (or their legal advisor) at some point in advance of the completion of the transfer.

5.5.3 The Land Registration System

5.5.3.1 Principles of Registration

The traditional unregistered system was extremely inefficient. It relied on bundles of title deeds that could easily be lost, stolen or damaged. It was also unnecessarily time consuming as title had to be investigated on the occasion of every transaction affecting the title.

The Land Registration Act 1925, one of the number of Acts which revolutionised land law, introduced a system of land registration with the aim of simplifying the conveyancing process. It established a Land Registry, with the intention that all titles should eventually be registered in a series of district registries. The current legislation is now contained in the Land Registration Act 2002.

The estates which are capable of registration at the Land Registry (the 'registerable estates') are freeholds and leaseholds granted for more than 7 years. Their owners are free to register them voluntarily; however, to encourage land registration, registration of title is compulsory when unregistered freeholds or leaseholds are:

- Transferred (through gift, inheritance or sale)
- Mortgaged
- Upon the death of the sole owner

On application for first registration, the estate owner must evidence their title to the Land Registry in the same way that they would do for a purchaser of unregistered land, establishing root of title. If satisfied, the Land Registry will prepare a register for the estate which will mirror the legal situation disclosed by the preregistration deeds and will allocate a unique title number to it. From this point on the deeds cease to have any significance and the register, rather than the deeds, provides conclusive evidence of the ownership of the estate. Once registered, the State guarantees the title, and there are provisions for the payment of compensation to those who suffer loss as a result of any errors on the register.

5.5.4 Why Register Land?

Bevan contextualises land registration through considering the reasoning for registering births, deaths and marriages – registration provides an opportunity for people to understand their community. Thus land registration:

> (p)rovides interested parties, including those intending to purchase a piece of land, with the opportunity to find out more about a particular plot of land and to determine whether the party selling has the power to do so and whether the land to be purchased will be acquired free from or encumbered by ore-existing rights (...) registration allows interested parties to mitigate or guard against risks in dealing with land.[18]

The benefits and aims of land registration include:

- Providing a complete and accurate reflection of land, enabling titles to be easily investigated
- Removing the cost of investigating a title when discovering whether a seller has the right to sell
- Reducing the risk of fraud where a seller does not have the right to sell
- Informing buyers of any burdens on the land
- Assisting the conveyancing process, increasing conveyances through increased confidence
- Supporting the market and the economy through increased land transfers

5.5.4.1 The Form of the Register

The registers exist in electronic format and are public documents. On payment of a small fee anyone can obtain a copy of the register for a particular title, either by post, or online through the Land Registry website. The register comprises three parts.

5.5.4.1.1 Property Register

This part of the register contains the description of the property. It states whether the title is freehold or leasehold and describes the property by reference to its postal address, and to a plan filed at the registry showing the extent of the property edged in red. If the property has the benefits of any rights over neighbouring properties (for example a right of way) this will also be recorded in this part of the register.

---

18 C. Bevan, *Land Law* (3rd ed.) (Oxford University Press, 2022), 50.

5.5.4.1.2 Proprietorship Register

The proprietorship register contains three types of information. Firstly it includes the names and addresses of the estate owners (who are described as the 'registered proprietors'). Secondly it states the class of title that the registry has awarded to the estate, according to the strength of the application for first registration or subsequent upgrading. The following four possible classes of title can be awarded:

- Title Absolute
- Good Leasehold Title
- Possessory Title
- Qualified Title

Finally, the proprietorship register also contains details of any restrictions that have been placed on the way in which the registered proprietor is free to dispose of the property in order to protect the interests of certain third parties who have rights in the property, for example those of beneficiaries under a trust.

5.5.4.1.3 Charges Register

The charges register contains notices of certain third-party rights to which the estate is subject and which will bind a purchaser (see Section 5.7).

5.5.4.2 Subsequent Dealings

Once an estate has been registered, subsequent sales and other dealings are dealt with according to the requirements of the Land Registration Act 2002. There is no requirement to produce historic deeds, as the register provides conclusive evidence of title, meaning all that is required is an official Land Registry copy to the purchaser in advance of the sale.

The way in which a transfer of the legal estate takes effect is also slightly different for a registered title. The document giving effect to the transfer is still a deed but (in the case of a freehold estate) is referred to as deed of transfer rather than a conveyance. Once the deed has been executed, unlike the situation with unregistered title, the transfer of the estate is not immediately effective. Section 27(1) Land Registration Act 2002 provides that dispositions of registered land only become effective once they are registered. Following a completion of their purchase the purchaser must therefore lodge the deed of transfer with the registry and apply for the name of the registered proprietor to be amended in the proprietorship register. There is a strong incentive to do so as a failure to complete the registration within 2 months results in the legal title reverting to the former owner.

5.6 Adverse Possession

5.6.1 The Nature of Adverse Possession

Adverse possession is a legal mechanism which allows a trespasser to acquire an estate in land after being in possession of it for a certain amount of time, displacing the rights of the paper owner. The concept is sometimes colloquially known as squatters' rights.

Although capable of producing some harsh results for those who are deprived of their land, it is justified on grounds of public policy. It provides a mechanism for encouraging the efficient use of society's limited land resources in circumstances where affected land has been neglected, or perhaps abandoned, by its paper owner for a considerable period of time.

The legal framework applicable to claims of adverse possession depends on whether the land is registered or unregistered. Prior to the coming into force of the Land Registration Act 2002, both registered and unregistered land followed the same legal framework; however, the Act introduced a different regime for registered land.

5.6.2 Adverse Possession of Unregistered Land

Adverse possession has traditionally been based on the principle of a statutory time limit for actions, whereby an action in the courts becomes 'statute-barred' after a certain period of time. This continues to be the case with unregistered land. The limitation period for actions for the recovery of land is 12 years (S15 Limitation Act 1980). Once a trespasser has been in possession of unregistered land for 12 years, the paper owner is statute-barred from recovering possession. From this moment the trespasser, as the person in possession of the land, has a better right to the land than the paper owner.

The 12-year time period starts to run from the moment the trespasser adversely possesses the paper owner's land. The paper owner is then regarded as having been 'dispossessed' or as having 'discontinued their possession' (Limitation Act 1980, schedule 1, paragraphs 1 & 8). It is not necessary for the same person to be in adverse possession for the whole 12-year period. A trespasser may transfer their started but uncompleted right to adverse possession to another trespasser who would then be entitled to rely on the combined periods of adverse possession when establishing the 12-year time period. Once the 12-year period has started to run, if they are aware, paper owners often seek ways to 'stop the clock' in order to prevent the trespasser acquiring title once the full 12 years has elapsed. Mere assertions of their legal rights by the paper owner, or requests that the trespasser leaves the property, are insufficient. However, the following mechanisms may be effective.

5.6.2.1 Action for Possession

If the paper owner brings an action for possession, and is successful in removing the trespasser, this will bring the adverse possession to an end. However, if the paper owner is not seeking an immediate end to the trespasser's possession but simply wishes to preserve their own title to the land the following two alternative options are available.

- Written acknowledgement of the paper owner's title
  A written acknowledgement, by the trespasser, of the paper owner's title will stop the clock. If the trespasser remains, the 12-year limitation period will start running again (Limitation Act 1980, SS29 & 30). Such an acknowledgement may be express, or implied from some other written statement. For example, in *Lambeth LBC v Bigden*,[19]

19 *Lambeth LBC v Bigden* (2000) 33 HLR 478.

the trespasser was held to have provided such an acknowledgement when they wrote to the paper owner requesting them not to sell the property. A paper owner may protect their position by retaining, or obtaining, appropriate written acknowledgements from the trespasser.

- Unilateral licence

  Possession cannot be 'adverse' if it is lawful, for example if the paper owner has granted permission for the trespasser to remain on the land. The Court of Appeal's decision in *BP Properties Ltd v Buckler*[20] suggests that the paper owner may be able to prevent time running in favour of a trespasser simply by granting them a unilateral licence to occupy the property. In *BP Properties v Buckler*, Buckler lived in a farmhouse with his elderly mother. She had formerly had a tenancy of the house but this had expired and the family had continued in possession as trespassers. BP (who owned the freehold) attempted to gain possession of the house before the expiry of the 12 year limitation period. Because of local hostility to them they withdrew the action and wrote to the old lady telling her that she could live in the house rent-free for the rest of her life. On her death, BP sought possession from Buckler who then himself claimed title by adverse possession. The Court of Appeal granted possession to BP. The mother, Mrs Buckler, had been in possession by virtue of the licence and this had stopped time running. Consequently, Buckler had only himself been in adverse possession from the date of his mother's death and BP were not statute-barred from bringing the action against him.

The decision has been criticised as allowing paper owners to prevent time running against them by a unilateral act of giving permission, without having to incur the expense of court proceedings. However, in *Buckler* the mother hadn't responded to BP's letters. If she had expressly rejected the offer of the licence the adverse possession would, presumably, not have been interrupted.

5.6.3 Adverse Possession of Registered Land

Following the enactment of the Land Registration Act 2002 it has become more difficult to acquire title to registered land by adverse possession. Title can only now be acquired by following a two-stage procedure laid down in the Act rather than by acquiring it automatically after 12 years' adverse possession. Under S96 of the new Act the 12-year limitation period in S15 Limitation Act 1980 no longer applies to registered land, meaning a trespasser can have been in adverse possession for considerably longer than 12 years without the paper owner's right to possession becoming statute-barred.

However, if a trespasser has been in adverse possession of land for the last 10 years, they can apply to be registered as proprietor of the relevant title (schedule 6). Their application triggers a notification, by the Land Registry, to the registered proprietor who then has 3 months in which to object.

If they fail to object to the application within the 3-month time period, the trespasser will automatically be registered as the new proprietor. If they do object within 3 months,

20 *BP Properties Ltd v Buckler* (1987) 55 P & CR 337.

the trespasser's application will automatically be rejected (unless one of the three special circumstances considered in the following text exist). If rejected, they must wait a further 2 years before making a further application and, if the paper owner wishes to recover possession, they will bring an action for possession within this 2-year period. At the end of 2-years, if the trespasser is still in possession, they are able to make a second application, and this will automatically be successful.

The three circumstances, referred to above, where the trespasser's first application will not be rejected automatically on receipt of an objection from the paper owner, relate to complicated matters of law. If the trespasser alleges that one of these applies, then the matter would be determined by the Adjudicator (an independent judicial officer created by the Land Registration Act 2002 with responsibility for determining contested land registration applications). The three circumstances are:

Estoppel

The trespasser may be registered as the new owner in circumstances where the doctrine of estoppel applies. This will be the case where they have acted to their detriment in the belief, encouraged or acquiesced in by the paper owner, that they owned the land in question. For example, if they have built a garage on land which they believe to be their own with the acquiescence of the paper owner, the paper owner will then be estopped from denying the trespassers entitlement to the land.

Some other entitlement to be registered

The trespasser may be registered if, irrespective of their adverse possession, they are entitled to be registered as proprietor for some other reason. These cases are rare but will include situations:

Where the trespasser is entitled to the land under a will but is in possession of the land without the consent of the deceased's executors.

Where the trespasser has contracted to buy the land and has paid the purchase price, but where the legal estate has not been transferred to them.

Reasonable mistake as to boundary

Where the physical boundaries between two properties have not been fixed by the Land Registry, this ground provides a mechanism for correcting the register through the mechanism of adverse possession. If the trespasser has reasonably believed, for at least 10 years, that the land to which their application relates has belonged to them then they may be registered as the proprietor. If they have knowingly encroached on the registered proprietor's land then it is unlikely that the test of reasonable belief would be satisfied. Claims are therefore more likely to be successful where the encroachment was by the trespasser's predecessor in title, or where fences were inaccurately placed on the initial development of the land.

5.6.4 Requirements for Adverse Possession

A trespasser cannot acquire title by adverse possession, either to registered or unregistered land, unless they can show that they have *adversely possessed* the paper owner's land for the required time period. Cases demonstrate that the following three requirements must all be present for adverse possession to exist.

5.6.4.1 Factual Possession

The trespasser must, as a matter of fact, be 'in possession' of the land. This concept is synonymous with the concept of exclusive possession – the trespasser must have control of the land to the exclusion of all other persons, including the paper owner. If you remember, exclusive possession is one of the key aspects of land ownership.

> The general concept of 'ownership' involves the exclusive right to use, possess, control, destroy or dispose of property within one's ownership.

In *Powell v McFarlane*[21] Lord Justice Slade articulates this notion, that only one person can be in possession at any one time, in the following terms:

> Factual possession signifies an appropriate degree of physical control. It must be a single and [exclusive] possession Thus an owner of land and a person intruding on that land without his consent cannot both be in possession of the land at the same time. The question what acts constitute a sufficient degree of exclusive physical control must depend on the circumstances, in particular the nature of the land and the manner in which land of that nature is commonly used or enjoyed.

Generally, clear evidence of exclusion of other persons is required and any continued use by the paper owner will usually defeat the trespasser's claim. A mere trespass is not sufficient – for example the occasional walking over the land could not amount to adverse possession. In *Powell v McFarlane* grazing a cow, coupled with making hay and limited repairs to fencing, did not suffice. Enclosing the land by erecting a new fence[22] or fitting new locks to doors[23] are generally the types of actions that will be required.

Where land is suitable for very limited uses it will be easier to demonstrate the required degree of physical control. In *Red House Farms (Thornton) Ltd v Catchpole*[24] a small island had been formed when a river changed course. The island was unsuitable for any significant agricultural purpose. In these circumstances a trespasser was able to establish adverse possession by regularly using it for shooting.

5.6.4.2 Adverse to the Rights of the Paper Owner

The whole notion of adverse possession is that possession must be inconsistent with and contrary to the rights of the paper owner. This does not mean that possession must necessarily cause an inconvenience or annoyance to the paper owner.[25] There is not even a requirement that the paper owner should be aware that the trespasser is in possession.[26] However, if the possession is enjoyed by virtue of some legal entitlement then it cannot be adverse. Hence, the existence of a lease or licence will defeat a claim as the possession,

---

21 *Powell v McFarlane* (1977) 38 P & CR 452 at 470–471.
22 *Buckinghamshire County Council v Moran* [1989] 2 All ER 225.
23 *Lambeth LBC v Blackburn* (2001) 82 P & CR 494.
24 *Red House Farms (Thornton) Ltd v Catchpole* [1977] 2 EGLR 125.
25 *Treloar v Nute* [1976] 1 WLR 1295.
26 *Rains v Buxton* (1880) 14 ChD 537.

even if exclusive, is by the agreement of the paper owner. The case discussed above, *BP v Buckley* evidences this – the mother was granted a licence for life, which stopped the clock running during their lifetime.

5.6.4.3 The Intention to Possess

There can be no adverse possession unless the trespasser has an intention to possess the land (Latin: *animus possidendi*). The trespasser's attitude to *ownership* is irrelevant. They may know that the land belongs to someone else or they may mistakenly believe that it is theirs. Alternatively, they may never have thought about the question of ownership but simply treated the land as theirs because it suited their purposes. Whatever the trespasser's understanding about the *ownership* of the land, they must intend to *exclusively possess* it – in other words they must intend to take control of it as if it were their own and to exclude everyone else from it. Once again, this is clear from Lord Justice Slade judgment in *Powell v McFarlane*[27]

> the *animus possidendi* involves the intention, in one's own name and on one's own behalf, to exclude the world at large, including the owner with the paper title if he be not himself the possessor, so far as is reasonably practicable and so far as the processes of the law will allow.

It will always be a question of evidence as to whether the trespasser had the necessary *animus possidendi*. In many circumstances this will be inferred from acts of factual possession – for example, enclosing land by erecting a new fence or fitting new locks to doors will usually be taken as convincing evidence that the trespasser intends to establish exclusive possession. Many adverse possession cases arise where land is vacant and awaiting future development and a trespasser takes up possession in the interim. It is now clear that the trespasser will have the necessary *animus possidendi* in these circumstances even if they take up possession with the understanding that the paper owner may wish to use the land in the future – they do not have to have the intention to exclude the paper owner in all future circumstances. Lord Justice Slade emphasises this in *Buckinghamshire County Council v Moran*[28]:

> What is required for this purpose is not an intention to own or even an intention to acquire ownership but an intention to possess, that is to say an intention for the time being to possess the land to the exclusion of all other persons, including the owner with the paper title.

5.6.5 Adverse Possession and Human Rights

As we saw in Chapter 1, the UK is currently a signatory to the European Convention on Human Rights and Fundamental Freedoms (ECHR). The rights within the Convention have been enacted into English law by the Human Rights Act 1998 and are therefore

---

27 *Powell v McFarlane* (1977) 38 P & CR 452 at 471–472.
28 *Buckinghamshire County Council v Moran* [1989] 2 All ER 225.

directly enforceable in the English courts. Article 1 of Protocol 1 to the Convention contains an entitlement to the protection of property and, for several years, there was much debate as to whether the law of adverse possession was incompatible with this.

The debate centred on the case of *J.A. Pye (Oxford) Ltd v Graham*.[29] In that case the claimants were property developers who owned some fields adjacent to the defendants' farm. The claimants' long-term aim was to develop the fields but, in the meantime, they allowed the defendants to use them for grazing. The fields were totally enclosed and access to them was gained through a padlocked gate for which only the defendants had a key. The parties had originally entered into a licence agreement for the use of the fields, but when this expired in 1984 the defendants continued to use the fields for a further 13 years. During this time, they had made a number of requests for the formal licence to be renewed and had been willing to pay for the use of the fields, but their requests were ignored. In 1997 the defendants sought to formalise their rights to adverse possession. In response to this, the claimants commenced the proceedings for possession of the fields, arguing that the defendants lacked the necessary intention to possess. The House of Lords ruled in favour of the defendants, holding that they had been in adverse possession of the land for the requisite 12 years. There was no requirement that they should have had an intention to acquire ownership of the land but simply to use it for their own benefit. In the circumstances they had demonstrated the necessary *animus possidendi* and their willingness to pay for the use of the land if so requested was irrelevant.

Following the loss of the case in the House of Lords, the claimants commenced proceedings against the UK government in the European Court of Human Rights (ECtHR) in Strasbourg. They alleged that, by depriving them of their property, the law of adverse possession violated Article 1 of Protocol 1 to the European Convention on Human Rights. The case was decided by the Grand Chamber of the ECtHR which ruled that the law of adverse possession was, in fact, entirely compatible with Article 1.[30]

> Every. . . . . .person is entitled to the peaceful enjoyment of his possessions. No one shall be *deprived of his possessions* except in the public interest and subject to the conditions provided for by law and by the general principles of international law. The preceding provisions shall not, however, in any way impair the right of a State to enforce such laws as it deems necessary to *control the use of property* in accordance with the *general interest*. . . . . .

Within the wording of the Article, the Grand Chamber took the view that the law of adverse possession was not actually a mechanism for depriving a person of their possessions. In common with similar provisions in other European countries, its purpose was instead to regulate the use of property via the limitation period. The deprivation of possessions was simply a consequence of this, and could be justified as being in the general interest under Article 1 if the adverse possession mechanisms were 'proportionate', achieving

29 *J.A. Pye (Oxford) Ltd v Graham* [2003] 1 AC 419.
30 *J.A. Pye (Oxford) Ltd v United Kingdom* [2007] ECHR 700.

a balance between the general interest and the rights of the paper owner. The Grand Chamber was satisfied that the law was proportionate as:

- The law had been in force for many years so the paper owner would have been aware of the limitation period.
- The limitation period was not excessively short.
- Relatively little action would have been required by the paper owner to have 'stopped the clock' from running against them.

5.7 Third-party Rights in Land

Thus far, this chapter has been concerned with ownership and the rights associated. The other category of rights which can exist in land are third-party rights. These are rights held over land by someone who does not own the land. Third-party rights are described as 'interests' in land rather than estates. They can exist as either legal interests or as equitable interests.

5.7.1 Legal Interests

Section 1 Law of Property Act 1925 provides that only five legal interests are capable of existing. Only two are of any practical significance for our purposes and these will be considered in detail in this chapter. They are:

- Easements
- Mortgages

5.7.2 Equitable Interests

As discussed in Chapter 1, equity developed because of the deficiencies of the common law. As a consequence of this, a set of separate courts emerged alongside the common law courts, granting different remedies such as injunctions and specific performance. Equity was more flexible and recognised the existence of certain rights which the common law did not. These are the rights which, in a land law context, we refer to as 'equitable interests'. A restrictive covenant is an example of an equitable interest.

The classification of a right as being either a legal or an equitable interest has little significance in terms of its substance. However, the distinction has traditionally been crucial in determining the extent to which a right is binding on future owners of the land. Although the situation is now complicated by the introduction of land registration, the basic rule is:

Legal interests – will *always* be binding on a purchaser of the land.

Equitable interests – will *only* be binding on a purchaser of the land providing certain requirements have been complied with.

These issues are primarily the responsibility of lawyers rather than built environment professionals. There are a large number of equitable interests but the following are of particular importance:

5.7.2.1 Trusts

The defining characteristic of a trust is the separation of the title to property from the right to enjoy its benefits. The person holding the title (for example the freehold estate) is known as the trustee. The person who is entitled to enjoy the benefits (for example, to occupy it, or to receive the rent from it) is known as the beneficiary. Historically, the common law did not recognise this distinction. It would only protect the rights of a person holding title to property, even where they had agreed to hold the property for the benefit of someone else (the beneficiary). If the title owner subsequently failed to honour their obligations under such an arrangement the beneficiary was consequently unable to obtain redress from the common law courts. The law of equity intervened to protect the interests of the beneficiary through the device of the trust. For this reason a trust is an equitable interest rather than a legal one. The rights which the beneficiary owns in the property are variously described as the 'equitable interest, the 'beneficial interest' or simply the 'equity'. Trusts can be created expressly, by implication, or by statute.

5.7.2.1.1 Express Trusts

An express trust arises where the legal estate is transferred to someone on terms that they are to hold it on trust for a third party. Alternatively, an existing owner of a legal estate can expressly declare that they hold it on trust for a third party. In either case the declaration of trust should generally be in writing (Law of Property Act 1925, S53(1)(b)).

5.7.2.1.2 Implied Trusts

Implied trusts will typically arise where a third party contributes to the purchase price of a property being bought by a purchaser. In such circumstances, although the legal estate will be transferred into the name of the purchaser, they will generally hold the land on trust for themselves and the third party in the proportions in which they contributed to the purchase price. The same principles would operate where a property is bought in joint names but the parties contribute unequal shares of the purchase price.

5.7.2.1.3 Statutory Trusts

Although beyond the scope of this chapter, readers should be aware that statutes often use trusts in hidden ways to achieve particular legal outcomes. For example, although few would be aware of it, all co-owners of land are actually joint tenants of the legal estate, holding the beneficial interest in the property on trust for themselves, either as joint tenants, or as tenants in common (Law of Property Act 1925, SS34(2) & 36(1)).

5.7.2.2 Contractual Rights in Land

Section 2 Law of Property (Miscellaneous Provision) Act 1989 requires a contract to create or transfer a legal estate or interest to be in writing, and to be signed by the parties. Providing these formalities have been complied with the contract is binding as a matter of contract law. If one party fails to honour the contract the other will therefore be entitled to damages in respect of their losses. However, as the law regards every piece of land as unique, these types of contract will normally be enforceable by the equitable remedy of specific performance (see Chapter 2).

Where this is the case, under the principle that 'equity regards as done that which ought to be done' the purchaser of the legal estate or interest acquires an equitable interest in the land from the moment that the contract is entered into. On the signing of a contract for the creation or transfer of a legal estate the purchaser is therefore said to acquire an 'estate contract' in the land. In the same way, where the transaction relates to a legal interest (for example an easement or a mortgage) an 'equitable easement' or an 'equitable mortgage' would come into existence.

Providing the requirements of section 2 Law of Property (Miscellaneous Provision) Act 1989 have been satisfied the same principles can also operate to create equitable interests where there is some deficiency in the parties' attempts to create or transfer legal rights. This might arise if, for example, a deed has been improperly executed or, where the land is registered, upon a failure to effect registration of a transaction at the Land Registry. Once again, depending on the substance of the transaction, the following equitable interests are capable of being created in this way:

- Estate contract
- Equitable easement
- Equitable mortgage
- Restrictive covenants

5.7.3 Easements

5.7.3.1 The Nature of Easements

An easement can exist as a legal interest in land. It is defined as the right to make limited use of a neighbour's land. An example of an easement is where a house is built in the middle of a farmer's field. Originally, the farmer allowed a worker to live there, and later sold it to a third party with a small garden around it. The farmer still owns the land surrounding the house, rendering the property landlocked and inaccessible without crossing the farmer's field. Here, a right of way across the farmer's land is essential to access the property – without it, the use of the property would be impossible.

Many rights have been recognised as easements, and it is helpful to categorise them as being either positive or negative in their effect.

5.7.3.1.1 Positive Easements

Positive easements are a class of rights that entitle the owner of the right to perform some positive act on the other piece of land. The best known example is a right of way over a neighbour's land (as exampled above).

5.7.3.1.2 Negative Easements

In contrast, negative easements are rights which entitle their owner to stop the owner of the other land from behaving in a particular way on their own land. The classic example of a negative easement is a right to light. This is a right for one owner to receive light through their windows. The effect of this would be to prevent their neighbour from building on their land in such a way as to restrict the flow of light to their neighbour's windows.

Although we can categorise easements in this way, and can list particular examples of rights that have been held to be easements, one of the leading land law textbooks for law students[31] notes that 'easements are rather like elephants: easy to recognise but very difficult to define'. For this reason, the courts do not actually attempt to define them. Instead, they decide if a particular right is capable of existing as an easement by asking if it satisfies certain essential characteristics.

5.7.3.2 Essential Characteristics of an Easement

The essential characteristics of an easement were first described in the case of *Re Ellenborough Park*.[32] The original owners owned a park and surrounding land in Weston-Super-Mare. They sold the surrounding land in individual plots for building purposes, granting the purchaser of each plot the right to use the park for recreational purposes. They subsequently sold the park itself to a developer who planned to build upon it. The owners of the surrounding plots claimed that their rights to use the park were binding on the developer and that they were prevented from building on it. The court had to decide whether these rights were easements, and therefore binding, or simply personal rights which the developer could ignore. The Court of Appeal identified four essential characteristics of an easement. As these all existed, it held that the plot purchasers' rights to use the park were easements, and binding on the developer. The four essential characteristics were identified as follows.

5.7.3.2.1 There Must Be a Dominant and a Servient Tenement

This means that there must be a piece of land which benefits from the easement (the dominant tenement) and another area of land which has the burden of the interest over it (the servient tenement). Although the two properties must be near to each other, they need not necessarily be adjacent to each other.

5.7.3.2.2 An Easement Must Accommodate the Dominant Tenement

The right must improve the usefulness or amenity of the dominant tenement rather than simply conferring a personal benefit on its owner. The test is whether any possible owner of the dominant tenement would regard the right as a benefit and therefore if it has the effect of increasing the value and saleability of the land. In *Hill v Tupper*[33] the owner of a canal which adjoined Hill's land granted him a right to let out pleasure boats on it. The court in that case held that this was not a right that was capable of existing as an easement. It was not a benefit to Hill's land but simply conferred a commercial benefit on him as an individual. This case can be contrasted with *Moody v Steggles*[34] where the owner of a public house had a right to place an advertisement for the business on neighbouring land. The public house had existed on the plot for hundreds of years so the land and the business carried on there had become intertwined. In these circumstances, the court held that the right was capable of existing as an easement.

---

31 J.-A. MacKenzie and M. Phillips, *Textbook on Land Law* (12th ed.) (Oxford University Press, 2008), 501.
32 *Re Ellenborough Park* [1956] Ch 131.
33 *Hill v Tupper* (1863) 2 H&C 121.
34 *Moody v Steggles* (1879) 12 Ch D 261.

5.7.3.2.3 The Dominant and Servient Owners Must Be Different Persons

Even if the previous two characteristics are present, any right benefiting the dominant tenement cannot be an easement during any period when the two tenements are owned by the same person. The reason for this is that one cannot have rights against oneself. During such periods any such right falls into abeyance and is referred to as a 'quasi-easement', ready to spring into life in certain circumstances under the rule in *Wheeldon v Burrows*[35] if the two tenements subsequently become owned by different persons (see Section 5.7.3.3.3).

5.7.3.2.4 The Right Claimed Must Be Capable of Forming the Subject Matter of a Grant

This final characteristic means that the right must be one which the law recognises as capable of being granted by deed. This embraces a number of practical and policy requirements, including the following:

It must be specific and capable of precise definition

If the nature of a right is too vague to be clearly described in a deed then it cannot be an easement. The following examples illustrate the approach taken by the courts in this context.

Rights of way – A right of way is capable of existing as an easement as it is possible to define the right with precision. The location of the affected road or path can be clearly described (for example by reference to a plan). Any restrictions on the extent of the right (for example limiting it to passage on foot or at certain times of the day) are also capable of being identified in a deed. However, in *Chaffe v Kingsley*,[36] the Court of Appeal considered that a reference in a deed to a right of way over an 'intended road' which was not yet in existence was not sufficiently precise to be recognised as an easement.

Rights of drainage – Rights of drainage are also a common form of easement, the location of which are typically marked on deed plans.

Rights to light – Rights to light are capable of existing as easements. However, an easement of light cannot exist for the benefit of land with no buildings on it[37] but only in respect of a window or other aperture in a building which is primarily designed to admit light.[38]

Rights to air – Under the same principle there can be no general easement to the flow of air over one's property, for example for the benefit of a windmill,[39] but only one capable of definition by reference to some defined channel or ventilation shaft.[40]

Rights of support – Although an estate owner is entitled to a natural right of support from the soil of neighbouring property for their land in its natural state there is no such right for the benefit of buildings which have been built upon it. Nevertheless, such a right is capable of existing as an easement[41] and is extremely common in the case of terraced or semi-detached properties.

---

35 *Wheeldon v Burrows* (1879) 12 Ch D 31.
36 *Chaffe v Kingsley* (2000) 79 P & CR 404.
37 *Roberts v Macord* (1832) 1 Mood & R 230.
38 *Levet v Gas Light & Coke Co Ltd* [1919] 1 Ch 24.
39 *Webb v Bird* (1861) 10 CBNS 268.
40 *Wong v Beaumont Property Trust Ltd* [1965] 1 QB 173.
41 *Dalton v Angus* (1881) 6 App Cas 740.

Rights to use facilities – The rights to use facilities on neighbouring property are capable of existing as easements, including a right to use a toilet.[42]

Rights of storage – In *Wright v Macadam*[43] the court held that a right to store coal on a neighbour's land is capable of existing as an easement. Although easements of storage are capable of existing in respect of all types of goods and materials there are important limitations to this.

Rights to a pleasant view – It is well-established that there can be no easement to enjoy a pleasant view over neighbouring property because it is incapable of precise definition.[44] Similar principles would also prevent the existence of an easement of privacy.[45]

It must not amount to exclusive possession of the servient tenement

Rights which would have the effect of excluding the servient owner from possession of their land cannot exist as easements. The assertion of such rights is more akin to a claim to the servient owner's estate itself than to the more limited rights associated with an easement. In *Copeland v Greenhalf*[46] a wheelwright claimed to be entitled to an easement to store vehicles on a 150 foot long strip of land belonging to their neighbour. The court rejected the claim on the basis that it amounted virtually to a claim to possession, or at any rate to one for the joint use of the land.

If storage on the servient land is seen as ousting its owner from possession it is difficult to reconcile the above decision with that in *Wright v Macadam*[47] where, as we have seen, a right to store coal on a neighbour's land was held to be an easement. The courts have sought to reconcile the apparent contradiction in a series of cases relating to car parking. Since *London & Blenheim Ltd v Ladbroke Parks Ltd*[48] it has been established that a right to park a car is capable of existing as an easement, at least where the right does not amount to a claim to the possession of a defined parking space. However, that case also established that it will always be a question of degree as to whether the nature of the right claimed is so extensive as to leave the servient owner without any reasonable use of their land.

The *London & Blenheim* test was applied in *Hair v Gillman*[49] where a right to park a single car on a forecourt that could accommodate four cars was held to be an easement. In contrast, the Court of Appeal came to a different conclusion when applying the same test in *Batchelor v Marlow*.[50] In that case a right to park up to six cars on Mondays to Fridays for the whole of the working day was held to be incapable of being an easement as it so deprived the servient owner of the use of their land that it rendered their ownership 'illusory'. More recently, the House of Lords has cast doubt on the *London & Blenheim* test in the case of *Moncrieff v Jamieson*.[51] Although their

42 *Miller v Emcer Products Ltd* [1956] Ch 304.
43 *Wright v Macadam* [1949] 2 KB 744.
44 *William Aldred's Case* (1610) 9 Co Rep 57b.
45 *Browne v Flower* [1911] 1Ch 219.
46 *Copeland v Greenhalf* [1952] Ch 488.
47 *Wright v Macadam* [1949] 2 KB 744.
48 *London & Blenheim Ltd v Ladbroke Parks Ltd* [1992] 1 WLR 1278.
49 *Hair v Gillman* (2000) 80 P & CR 108.
50 *Batchelor v Marlow* [2003] 1 WLR 764.
51 *Moncrieff v Jamieson* [2007] 1 WLR 2620.

Lordships' comments in that case were made *obiter*, they suggested that the correct test should not be about the extent to which the servient owner retains *use* of the land, but about the extent to which they retain *possession* and therefore *control*. If this approach is followed in subsequent cases it suggests that the courts may tolerate a much greater level of interference in the servient land than has previously been the case.

It must not involve the servient owner in expenditure

An easement is a right to do something (a positive easement) or a right to prevent something being done (a negative easement). It is not a right to have something done so the law will not recognise a right as an easement if it requires any positive action, and therefore the expenditure of money, on the part of the servient owner. In *Regis Property Co Ltd v Redman*[52] the court rejected a claim that a right to receive hot water amounted to an easement.

It must not amount to the creation of a new negative easement

Rights to light and rights of support are negative easements as they prevent the use of the servient land in certain ways. However, the courts are extremely reluctant to recognise any further negative easements because of their effect in restricting development of the land affected. In *Phipps v Pears*[53] the court therefore rejected a claim to an easement of weather protection following the demolition of a building which had previously sheltered another from the elements.

5.7.3.3 Acquisition of Easements

A right does not automatically come into existence as an easement simply because the law recognises that it is capable of existing as such. Easements must be acquired by the owner of the dominant land, either by 'grant' or 'reservation'. A grant takes place where a landowner *grants* an easement over their land to the owner of other land. This will typically occur where the landowner sells part of their land and grants easements to the purchaser over the part they retain. A reservation only ever takes place *on a sale* of part. Here, the landowner reserves easements over the part being sold for the benefit of the land they are retaining.

- Express grant or reservation

  This arises where the grant or reservation is expressly stated in a deed, typically the deed transferring a part of the landowner's land to a purchaser.
- Implied grant or reservation

  In certain circumstances where a landowner transfers part of their land to a purchaser but the deed is silent about the question of easements the law will impliedly grant or reserve them. Both implied grant and reservation are possible although, as we will see, the latter is less common. Easements can be implied in four different ways.

52 *Regis Property Co Ltd v Redman* [1956] 2 QB 612.

53 *Phipps v Pears* [1965] 1 QB 76.

5.7.3.3.1 Easements of Necessity – Grant or Reservation

The courts will imply an easement where transferred or retained land would otherwise be completely unusable. In *Nickerson v Barraclough*[54] the court held that a right of way had been impliedly granted in respect of a 'landlocked' piece of land that had no access to the road otherwise than across neighbouring land.

5.7.3.3.2 Intended Easements – Grant or Reservation

Where the parties obviously intend that the transferred or retained land should have some specific use, the law will give effect to the presumed intention of the parties and will imply an intended easement. In *Wong v Beaumont Property Trust Ltd*[55] a lease was granted for the use of a cellar as a restaurant. However, for health and safety reasons, the cellar could not be used in this way without the installation of a ventilation duct over land retained by the landlord. In order to give effect to the parties' shared intentions, the court held that an easement had been impliedly granted permitting its installation.

5.7.3.3.3 The Rule in Wheeldon v Burrows *[1879] 12 ch 131 – Grant Only*

Under this rule, where a person sells part of their land, the purchaser will obtain the benefit of any rights (the so-called 'quasi-easements') which the seller was enjoying over the land at the time of sale. The right must be necessary for the reasonable enjoyment of the land and also be continuous and apparent, which means that the right must be of a permanent nature and discoverable with relative ease. Where the rule applies, it converts any existing quasi-easements into easements for the benefit of the land being transferred.

5.7.3.3.4 Section 62 Law of Property Act 1925 – Grant Only

This provision was included in the Law of Property Act 1925 as a word-saving provision so that, on the sale of a property, all existing easements would automatically be transferred to the purchaser without the need to specifically refer to them in the conveyance. However, the courts have interpreted it as actually granting new easements in certain circumstances by converting existing licences. The case of *Wright v Macadam*[56] illustrates the operation of this rule. During the course of a lease, the landlord had informally agreed that the tenant could store coal in a shed on neighbouring land. When the lease expired, a new lease was granted which, like the first one, made no mention of any right to store coal. The court held that the grant of the new lease converted the existing licence to store coal into an easement under section 62.

5.7.3.3.5 Prescription (Presumed Grant)

General Rules Where a landowner can demonstrate, in effect, that they have continuously exercised an easement over other land for a minimum period of time (typically 20 years) the law will presume that such an easement has been granted at some point in the past, notwithstanding the absence of any evidence to this effect (for example, in a deed).

54 *Nickerson v Barraclough* [1981] Ch 426.
55 *Wong v Beaumont Property Trust Ltd* [1965] 1 QB 173.
56 *Wright v Macadam* [1949] 2 KB 744.

In *R v Oxfordshire County Council, ex p Sunningwell Parish Council*[57] Lord Hoffmann noted: 'Any legal system must have rules of prescription which prevent the disturbance of long-established de facto enjoyment'.

In order to demonstrate that the enjoyment of the land in question arises from their entitlement to an easement, they must demonstrate that they have behaved as if they have an absolute right to such enjoyment rather than, for example, having to do so by force, under cover of darkness or with the consent of the landowner. The law describes this as proving that their enjoyment was 'as of right' and this requires them to demonstrate that such enjoyment was *nec vi, nec clam, nec precario* (without force, without secrecy, without permission). In *Dalton v Angus*[58] it was noted that 'the whole law of prescription and the whole law which governs the presumption of inference of the grant... rest upon acquiescence'. In *Winterburn v Bennett*,[59] the owners of fish and chip shop claimed an easement by prescription over the car park of a neighbouring Conservative Club which had been used by their customers and for deliveries. The Club steward had verbally asserted ownership of the land on a number of occasions, and a sign was erected which read 'Private car park. For the use of Club patrons only. By order of the Committee'. The owners of the fish and chip shop claimed an easement over the car park by prescription. The question for the court was whether the sign was sufficient to prevent the easement occurring. The court held:

> in circumstances where the owner has made his position entirely clear through the erection of clearly visible signs, the unauthorised use of the land cannot be said to be, "as of right"... Protest against unauthorised use may...take many forms...but I reject the notion that it is necessary for the owner, having made his protest clear, to take further steps of confronting the wrongdoers... still less to go to the expense and trouble of legal proceedings.[60]

The judgment concludes:

> The erection and maintenance of an appropriate sign is a peaceful and inexpensive means of making clear that property is private and not to be used by others. I do not see why those who choose to ignore such signs should thereby be entitled to obtain legal rights over the land.[61]

The usual way of acquiring an easement by prescription is under the Prescription Act 1832. Under section 2 a period of 20 years' uninterrupted enjoyment as of right immediately prior to bringing an action in court will be sufficient to establish an easement. Although the enjoyment must be 'uninterrupted', section 4 provides that nothing shall be deemed to be an interruption unless 'submitted to or acquiesced in for one year' by the dominant owner. Thus, in practice, it is sometimes said that enjoyment as of right for 19 years and one day is sufficient to establish the easement.

---

57 *R v Oxfordshire County Council, ex p Sunningwell Parish Council* [2000] 1 AC 335, 349.
58 *Dalton v Angus* (1881) 6 app. Cas.740, 773.
59 *Winterburn v Bennett* [2016] EWCA Civ 482.
60 Ibid 40.
61 Ibid 41.

Other mechanisms exist for acquiring an easement by prescription including a 40-year period under section 2 which operates in a slightly different way to that described above. It is also possible to rely on common law prescription or the doctrine of lost modern grant, both of which, in practice, provide alternative ways for calculating a 20-year period.

Rights to Light

Although an easement of light can also be acquired by prescription in any of the ways described above, S3 Prescription Act 1832 provides an additional mechanism which, in practice, is the most frequently used. This provides that 20 years' uninterrupted enjoyment of light immediately prior to action will automatically result in an easement being acquired unless it has been enjoyed on the basis of a written agreement. The significance of this provision is that the dominant owner need not demonstrate that enjoyment has been 'as of right' and only the existence of a written agreement will defeat a claim after an uninterrupted period of 20 years.

The rules previously discussed as to the nature of an interruption also apply to the acquisition of easements under S3. Previously the only way to interrupt the acquisition of an easement of light was to physically obstruct the light to the affected window. Historically, this took the form of erecting a hoarding adjacent to the window although this would now be difficult due to the requirement to obtain planning permission. The Rights of Light Act 1959 therefore now provides that the registration of a light obstruction notice will have the same effect.

5.7.3.4 Extinguishment of Easements

Once acquired, easements become permanent rights in land, capable of binding successive purchasers of the servient tenement. However, there are a number of ways in which they can be extinguished.

5.7.3.4.1 Express Release

This arises where the dominant tenement owner expressly gives up their right to the easement by deed.

5.7.3.4.2 Implied Release (Abandonment)

Extinguishment may be implied from the circumstances. However, non-use of the easement is insufficient to extinguish an easement. The circumstances must be such that they demonstrate a clear intention by the dominant tenement owner to permanently abandon the easement. In *Stokoe v Singers*[62] the owner of an easement of light had bricked up the affected windows for over 20 years. Nevertheless, the infill had not been bonded into the surrounding wall and the iron bars on the outside of the window were left in place. The appearance of the window remained and the court held that these circumstances did not amount to abandonment. In contrast, an easement of light was held to have been abandoned in *Moore v Rawson*[63] where the wall containing the windows was demolished and replaced with a new wall containing no windows.

62 *Stokoe v Singers* (1857) 8 EL&BL 31.

63 *Moore v Rawson* [1824] 3 B&C 332.

5.7.3.4.3 Unity of Seisin

If the dominant and servient tenements are owned by the same person, any easement is extinguished. This is because one cannot have rights against oneself and one of the essential characteristics of an easement is that the dominant and servient tenements must be owned by *different* people.

5.7.3.4.4 Statute

In contrast to the situation with restrictive covenants, there is no general statutory mechanism for extinguishing an easement. However, a number of statutes do make provision for the extinguishment of easements in particular circumstances, for example, the Town and Country Planning Act 1990 and the Commons Registration Act 1965.

5.7.3.5 Easements Distinguished from Certain Other Rights

A number of other rights have similarities with easements and some of these are described in the following text.

5.7.3.5.1 Licences

A licence is simply a permission to do something which would otherwise amount to a trespass, for example to walk across someone else's land, or to occupy their land in some way. In contrast to an easement, a licence is personal right rather than a right in land. It therefore exists only between the original parties, the licensor and licensee, and will not be binding on a purchaser of the land.

5.7.3.5.2 Natural Rights

Natural rights are the package of rights that the owner of a legal estate is entitled to exercise. Unlike easements, they arise automatically and do not have to be acquired. Estate owners are entitled to a natural right of support for the soil on their land they have no right of support for the buildings erected upon it unless this has been acquired as an easement.

5.7.3.5.3 Public Rights, Customary Rights and Town or Village Greens

Easements are private rights which can only be exercised by the owner of a dominant tenement. Certain other rights can exist which benefit groups of people, and do not require the existence of a dominant tenement. Public rights are one such category and the most frequently encountered is the public right of way. This can exist at common law or under statute and entitles members of the public to use roads, footpaths and certain other land. This now includes the 'right to roam' under the Countryside and Rights of Way Act 2000. Customary rights exist for the benefit of the inhabitants of a particular locality rather than the public at large whilst rights can also exist for the public to use land as a town or village green if registered under the Commons Act 2006.

5.7.3.5.4 Profits à Prendre

Like easements profits, à prendre are private property rights. However, unlike them, they entitle their owner to take some item from the land of another. A right to cut and take timber or to catch fish comes into this category. They can be acquired in similar ways to easements and have traditionally been treated as forming part of the same area of law.

They were of great significance historically but are much less so today following the industrial revolution and change from a rural to an urban society.

5.7.3.5.5 Party Wall etc. Act 1996

The Party Wall etc. Act 1996 was enacted in order to facilitate certain categories of construction operations in the vicinity of property boundaries. It achieves this by enabling the most appropriate construction solutions to be employed on affected structures irrespective of their location in relation to the boundary or to any common law rights affecting them. Subject to compliance with a procedure described in the Act building owners are given a statutory right to undertake construction work at the boundary and this replaces any previous common law right to do so.

The Act's procedures apply to construction operations in three different situations. They are most frequently encountered where works ('party wall works') are carried out to a party wall or other shared boundary structure. They also apply to the erection of a new boundary structure ('line of junction works') and to excavations which have the potential to interfere with the stability of an adjacent building or structure ('adjacent excavations').

There are minor differences between the procedures in each of these three situations. However, they all commence with the service of an originating notice by a building owner wishing to undertake construction work on an adjoining owner whose property will be affected by it. The adjoining owner can respond in a number of different ways, but in most cases, a dispute will arise between the parties within the meaning of the legislation. Although there is then scope for this to be resolved by a single agreed surveyor, the parties will usually each appoint a surveyor and the two surveyors will publish a joint award which will regulate the conduct of the works. Providing the building owner undertakes the work in accordance with the terms of the award this will be lawful, notwithstanding the fact that it involves interference with property owned by the adjoining owner.

5.7.3.5.6 Access to Neighbouring Land Act 1992

Landowners have no general common law right of entry onto adjoining land to carry out maintenance to their own property. The Access to Neighbouring Land Act 1992, therefore provides a mechanism for an owner to obtain a court order granting access in these circumstances. The right of access is limited to the carrying out of 'basic preservation works' and does not apply to alteration or improvement work.

5.7.4 Mortgages

5.7.4.1 The Nature of Mortgages

Simply put, a mortgage is a loan which is secured on land. The majority of property purchases in the UK are facilitated with the assistance of a mortgage. Somewhat confusingly the legal definition is entirely the opposite. The mortgage, in a legal sense, is not the money that is loaned but the *rights* created in the land in order to provide the security for the loan. It is therefore the borrower ('mortgagor') who grants the mortgage to the lender ('mortgagee') rather than the other way round. As with an easement, the mortgage can exist as a legal interest in land. Mortgages are created by deed and are often described as a 'legal charge' on the land affected.

Mortgage deeds will contain a large number of terms in addition to the one which actually charges the property. One of these will specify a date for the repayment of the loan and this is known as the legal date for redemption (sometimes also described as the contractual date for redemption). We will see that this has a particular legal significance. In modern day domestic mortgages, whatever the actual length of the mortgage term, the legal date for redemption is typically 6 months after the date that the mortgage was granted. This is not as alarming as it sounds for, as we will see, the borrower is protected from the literal effects of this provision as long as they are not otherwise in breach of the mortgage.

5.7.4.2 Borrower's Rights

For historical reasons the borrower's continuing rights in the property are collectively referred to as the equity of redemption. Although this is no longer the case, mortgages used to be created by transferring the legal estate to the lender for the term of the loan and the borrower's remaining rights therefore existed only in equity. We still refer to 'the equity' in a property, meaning the value of the property to the estate owner after payment of all monies owed under the loan secured by a mortgage.

5.7.4.2.1 The Equitable Right to Redeem

The most important aspect of the equity of redemption is the equitable right to redeem the mortgage. At common law the borrower only had a right to redeem on the legal date for redemption. If they failed to do so, the right to redeem was lost forever. The lender was entitled to keep the property and the borrower remained liable to repay the loan. These harsh rules were exacerbated by the fact that some lenders would reputedly go into hiding on the legal date for redemption making it impossible for borrowers to repay on the due date. Equity intervened to modify the harsh common law rules by recognising that the lender's interest was simply a security for a loan and that the borrower retained rights in the land (the equity of redemption). It applied the maxim 'once a mortgage, always a mortgage' and permitted redemption at any time after the legal date for redemption had passed.

Because of the importance it placed on the right to redeem, equity also took the view that the terms of the mortgage, including any related business transactions, should not prevent or impede the borrower's right to do so. There should, in the words of equity, be 'no clogs on the equity of redemption'.

5.7.4.2.2 Freedom from Clogs on the Equity of Redemption

If any 'clogs' are identified they will be struck out. Options for the lender to purchase the mortgaged land have been treated in this way as the exercise of the option prevents the borrower from ever redeeming the mortgage. In *Jones v Morgan*[64] the Court of Appeal struck out such a clause where the lender was given an option to purchase one half of the mortgaged land.

For the same reason the courts are also wary of clauses which purport to postpone the legal date of redemption as illustrated by the decision in *Fairclough v Swan Brewery Co Ltd*.[65]

64 *Jones v Morgan* [2002] 1 EGLR 125.

65 *Fairclough v Swan Brewery Co Ltd* [1912] AC 565.

Fairclough had a 20-year lease of a hotel. They subsequently borrowed money from the brewery secured by mortgaging the hotel to them. The mortgage deed contained a clause requiring them to purchase beer only from the brewery and a further term postponing the contractual date for redemption until the final 6 weeks of the lease. Three years into the mortgage Fairclough wished to purchase beer elsewhere. They therefore sought to pay off the loan and to redeem the mortgage early but the brewery refused. The Privy Council struck out the clause postponing redemption as it prohibited discharge of the mortgage until the lease was virtually valueless and redemption, at that point, was simply not worth having, despite the brewery's assertion to the alternative.

This decision can be contrasted with *Knightsbridge Estates Trust Ltd v Byrne*[66] where the mortgage of several freehold properties contained a clause postponing the contractual date for redemption for 40 years. In that case, where the two parties were both large companies with equal bargaining strength, the Court of Appeal held that the clause was valid.

5.7.4.2.3 Freedom from Ongoing Collateral Advantages

The courts are also suspicious of terms in a mortgage which purport to provide the lender with some collateral advantage over and above the repayment of the principal and interest under the loan. *Solus* agreements, where a business agrees to obtain all its supplies from a particular wholesaler, are a particular example of this and are common between breweries and publicans. This is exampled in *Fairclough v Swan Brewery Co Ltd.*[67]

The courts have traditionally struck out such agreements where the advantage is designed to last beyond the time when the mortgage will be redeemed. In *Noakes & Co v Rice*[68] a publican's obligation to buy beer from the brewery was to continue until the end of his lease, even if the mortgage was redeemed at an earlier date. The House of Lords held that the agreement was unenforceable as the publican would otherwise only recover a tied property on redemption in place of the untied property which they had mortgaged. However, as occurred in the case of *Biggs v Hoddinott*,[69] the courts will generally be unwilling to strike out collateral advantages which terminate on redemption as long as they are not otherwise oppressive or unconscionable.

5.7.4.2.4 Freedom from Oppressive or Unconscionable Terms

The courts will also strike out other terms which they consider to be particularly unfair to borrowers. This occurred in *Cityland & Property (Holdings) Ltd v Dabrah*[70] where the mortgage secured a loan of £2,900. There was no provision for payment of interest but simply a requirement to repay a total sum of £4,553 by regular instalments over the 6 year term of the mortgage. The mortgage also contained the usual clause that the whole of the capital sum would become due if the borrower defaulted on the repayments. The borrower experienced financial difficulties within the first year and went into arrears with their repayments. The lender demanded immediate payment of the £4,553. This represented 157% of

66 *Knightsbridge Estates Trust Ltd v Byrne* [1939] Ch 441.
67 *Fairclough v Swan Brewery* [1912] AC 565
68 *Noakes & Co v Rice* [1902] AC 24.
69 *Biggs v Hoddinott* [1898] 2 Ch 307.
70 *Cityland & Property (Holdings) Ltd v Dabrah* [1968] Ch 166.

the loan and an annual interest rate of 38%. The court held that this requirement was unfair and substituted an interest rate of 7%.

A different outcome occurred in *Multiservice Bookbinding Ltd v Marden*[71] where the mortgage repayments were calculated in Swiss francs. Due to a massive devaluation of the pound there was a dramatic increase in the amount payable under the mortgage. This equated to an interest rate of 33% over the 10 year term of the mortgage – significantly more than the 38% over a single year in *Cityland*. Nevertheless, the court upheld the relevant clause in the mortgage. The transaction was a commercial one between businesspersons of equal bargaining power who were each legally represented. There was no evidence that the lender had an unfair advantage over the borrower. Although the transaction might be seen as unreasonable, this was not sufficient for the court to set it aside. This should only occur in situations where the mortgage terms are 'oppressive or unconscionable', meaning that the lender has behaved in a 'morally reprehensible manner'.

5.7.4.2.5 Statutory Protection

Borrowers also have statutory protection against extortionate charges in mortgages. Most first mortgages of residential property will be regulated by the Financial Services Authority under the Financial Services and Markets Act 2002. Other mortgages are protected under the Consumer Credit Act 2006.

5.7.4.3 Lender's Rights

The lender has a number of rights in the property to enable them to enforce payment of the monies due in the event of the borrower's default.

5.7.4.3.1 Possession

A lender might wish to seek possession in order to sell a defaulter's property with vacant possession, or perhaps to let it out if the current state of the market is such that a sale would not realise the full value of the loan.

In theory, possession can be obtained by the lender from the moment that the mortgage has been entered into, and without any fault on the borrower's part.[72] In practice, this right will usually be restricted by a term in the mortgage stating that it can only be exercised in the event of the borrower's default.

The right can be exercised without a court order if it does not involve the use of force. However, to prevent misunderstandings, and to avoid the possibility of criminal liability under the Criminal Law Act 1977, it is advisable to obtain a court order, at least where the property is still occupied.

Section 36 Administration of Justice Act 1970 gives the court a discretionary power to adjourn or postpone proceedings for possession of a dwelling house. It can, however, only do so if it considers that the borrower is likely to be able to pay off the arrears within a reasonable period.

71 *Multiservice Bookbinding Ltd v Marden* [1979] Ch 84.
72 *Four-Maids Ltd v Dudley Marshall (Properties) Ltd* [1957] Ch 317.

5.7.4.3.2 Sale

The lender has a statutory power of sale and it is not necessary for this to be provided for in the mortgage. To be effective the power of sale must have *arisen* and it must also have become *exercisable*. Once a power of sale arises the lender is generally capable of giving a good title to a purchaser. However, if it is not also exercisable, they may have to pay damages to anyone who suffers loss as a result of their actions.

Under section 101 Law of Property Act 1925 the power of sale arises as soon as the legal date for redemption has passed (see paragraph 4.8.1). Section 103 then provides that it will not be exercisable until:

- There has been 3 months' default following the service of a notice requiring payment, or;
- Two months' interest is in arrears, or;
- There has been a breach of some other term in the mortgage deed.

The sale may be by auction or by private treaty. There is, however, an obligation on the lender to obtain the true market value of the property as at the date of sale. In *Cuckmere Brick Co Ltd v Mutual Finance Ltd*[73] a lender was held to be in breach of this duty of care for failing to advertise before an auction that the land had planning permission for 100 flats. The land sold for £44,000, whereas its true market value with planning permission would have been around £65,000.

Once the land has been sold the lender holds the proceeds of sale on trust. They must then apply them in the order described in section 105 Law of Property Act 1925:

1. Discharge of any prior mortgages.
2. Expenses of the sale.
3. Discharge of the lender's mortgage.
4. Discharge of any subsequent mortgages.
5. Remaining balance to the borrower.

5.7.4.3.3 To Appoint a Receiver

A receiver is a person who is appointed to manage the property and to receive its income on the lender's behalf. The power to appoint a receiver arises and becomes exercisable in the same circumstances as the power of sale. The lender may wish to appoint a receiver to recover mortgage arrears instead of selling the property where it is income producing. This might occur where, for example, it is a business and is producing a profit, or where it is tenanted and therefore producing rent.

5.7.4.3.4 Foreclosure

Foreclosure is a draconian remedy and is rarely used. It allows a lender to apply to the court for a foreclosure order. If granted the effect is to extinguish all the borrower's rights in the property, putting an end to the equity of redemption. Title passes to the lender who becomes the new owner. The lender is therefore free to sell the property but no monies

73 *Cuckmere Brick Co Ltd v Mutual Finance Ltd* [1971] Ch 949.

are then due to the borrower, even if there is a surplus on the sale. There is, however, little point from a lender's point of view, in seeking a foreclosure order as:

- Under section 91(2) Law of Property Act 1925 the court has discretion to order a sale instead of a foreclosure. Wherever there is positive equity in the property it is likely to do so.
- The process takes longer than a sale. Unlike the situation with a sale it is necessary to obtain a court order to be able to foreclose. Even if successful a final order is not made immediately. An order nisi is first made, giving the borrower 6 months to pay the arrears and this period can be extended. The order will not be made absolute until this period has expired and the borrower has still failed to pay.

5.7.4.3.5 To Bring an Action for Breach of Contract

This becomes relevant in a negative equity situation, where there is insufficient money from the proceeds of sale to pay off the lender's debt. The mortgage deed contains a contract between the borrower and the lender. Irrespective of whether a sale has taken place a breach of this contract entitles the injured party to sue the other for breach of contract. If the borrower has failed to pay all monies owed to the lender then they are in breach of contract and can be sued. A sale of the property will not, therefore, wipe out the borrower's indebtedness.

5.7.4.4 Further Mortgages

It is possible for a single legal estate to be subject to more than one mortgage at the same time. If the borrower defaults and one of the lenders sells the property there may be insufficient proceeds of sale to repay all the loans. If this occurs, rather than sharing the available proceeds equally between all lenders, money is paid according to a pecking order described in rules for the priority of mortgages.

All mortgages of registered land are required to be registered in the charges register of the affected title. The priority of mortgages is therefore simply governed by the order in which they were entered on the register. Mortgages of unregistered land are now rare. However, where this occurs a first mortgage is protected by the lender taking possession of the title deeds and this will always have priority over all other mortgages. Subsequent mortgages have to be registered as a land charge (see Section 5.7.6.1.1) and their priority is governed according to the order in which they were registered.

5.7.5 Restrictive Covenants

5.7.5.1 The Nature of Covenants

A covenant is a legally binding promise contained in a deed. The person making the promise is referred to as the 'covenantor' whilst the person to whom it is made is the 'covenantee'. Covenants can take many different forms; however, in a land law context, there are two broad types. The first relates to the covenants made between the landlord and the tenant in leasehold property and these will be considered in Chapter 6. The other type, which we are concerned with here, consists of those covenants which are made between the owners of neighbouring land, whether they hold that land under a freehold or a leasehold estate.

These types of covenants are generally entered into when an estate owner is selling off part of their land and they wish to exercise some control over the way in which the part being sold will be used following the sale. They are therefore sometimes referred to as 'vendor and purchaser covenants' or 'freehold covenants'. The purchaser may be required to enter into covenants restricting the way in which they can use the land in the future ('restrictive covenants') or promising to perform some positive act in respect of it ('positive covenants'). By way of example, restrictive covenants might limit the height of fences that can be erected or prohibit certain colours of paint being used when painting the property. In contrast, positive covenants might require the purchaser to paint the property annually or to erect and maintain a fence. For reasons which will become clear only restrictive covenants can exist as rights in land and fall into the category of equitable interests. As with easements (see Section 5.7.3), a restrictive covenant can only exist where there is both dominant and servient land.

5.7.5.2 Enforceability of Covenants

The relationship between the covenantor and the covenantee is contractual, and will always be enforceable between the original parties to the deed in which it appears. If a purchaser of land covenants to maintain a boundary fence but then fails to do so, they will be in breach of contract. This will entitle the covenantee to sue them, and to obtain damages or an injunction on normal contract law principles. In theory, because there is privity of contract between them, the covenant continues to be enforceable between the original parties even after each of them has sold their respective pieces of land.

The more difficult question, and the one which is governed by land law, is whether the covenant is enforceable between subsequent owners of the dominant and servient land, possibly many years after the original owners have sold their land. In seeking to answer this question the law asks whether the burden and benefit of the covenant are capable of 'running with the land'. If the burden runs with the land this means that a purchaser buys it subject to the covenant and the covenant can therefore be enforced against them even though the promise was not made by them. Similarly, if the benefit runs with the land, a purchaser receives an entitlement to require someone else to comply with the covenant and is entitled to take them to court if they fail to do so.

5.7.5.2.1 Does the Burden Run with the Land?

At Common Law At common law the burden of the covenant does not run with the land, and a purchaser of the servient land is not bound by it. This principle was established in *Austerberry v Oldham Corporation.*[74] In that case Austerberry sold some of their land to a company to build a road. The company covenanted that they would build the road and then keep it in a good state of repair. Following construction of the road they sold it to Oldham Corporation. When the road required maintenance Austerberry sued the Corporation for breach of the covenant. The Court of Appeal rejected the claim, holding that the burden of a covenant does not run with the land.

---

74 *Austerberry v Oldham Corporation* (1885) 29 Ch D 750.

In Equity Equity has intervened to alleviate the harshness of the common law position in certain situations and recognises that the burden of a covenant can run with the land providing that certain conditions are satisfied. This position has its origins in the case of *Tulk v Moxhay*[75] which concerned land in Leicester Square.

Tulk owned houses and vacant land in the square. They sold the land to Elms but retained the houses. In the conveyance of the land, Elms covenanted that they would not build on it (a restrictive covenant). However, they subsequently sold the land to Moxhay. There was no covenant against building in the conveyance from Elms to Moxhay but Moxhay was aware of the existence of the earlier covenant that Elms had made. Moxhay nevertheless proposed to erect buildings on the land so Tulk issued injunction proceedings to prevent it. The court granted the injunction on the basis that Moxhay was subject to the covenant as they had notice of it. The case established that, at least in equity, the burden of a covenant could run with the land in certain circumstances (and therefore could exist as an equitable interest in land).

The necessary conditions for this were developed in later cases:

The Covenant Must Be Negative (Restrictive) in Substance

In *Haywood v Brunswick Permanent Benefit Building Society*[76] a covenant to repair some houses had been entered into. The servient land was later sold and subsequently mortgaged to the building society by the purchaser. The purchaser defaulted on the mortgage and the building society, which had notice of the repairing covenant, took possession of the property. The question for the court was whether the building society was bound by the covenant. The Court of Appeal held that it was not. The rule in *Tulk v Moxhay* only applied to covenants that were negative in substance, meaning that they must not require the expenditure of money in order to be complied with. This is the origin of the rule that only the burden of a restrictive covenant (but not a positive covenant) can run with the land in equity.

The Covenant Must Have Been Imposed for the Benefit of Land Retained by the Original Covenantee

This relates to the requirement that, as with easements, there must be both dominant and servient land. The concept, in the law of easements, of 'accommodating' the dominant tenement is expressed in this context as a requirement for the covenant to 'touch and concern' the dominant land. This means that the covenant must provide a benefit to the land rather than a personal benefit for the original covenantee. The leading case establishing the requirement for the covenantee to retain land which is benefitted by the covenant is *London County Council v Allen*,[77] in which the LCC sold a large plot of land to a builder who covenanted that they would not build upon part of the land which had been designated for use as a road. The builder subsequently sold the plot to Allen. Although Allen had notice of the covenant, they nevertheless started to build some houses on it. The LCC applied for an injunction to restrain the work. The Court of Appeal refused the injunction as the LCC had not retained any

75 *Tulk v Moxhay* (1848) 2 Ph 774.

76 *Haywood v Brunswick Permanent Benefit Building Society* (1881) 8 QBD 403.

77 *London County Council v Allen* [1914] 3 KB 642.

land capable of benefiting from the covenant, which was therefore not binding on Allen when she purchased the plot, even though she had notice of it. The rationale for the rule in *Tulk v Moxhay* had been to provide protection for landowners who chose to sell part of their land. The existence of the retained land was therefore an essential condition for the operation of the rule.

The Original Parties Must Have Intended the Burden of the Covenant to Run with the Land

This will usually be apparent from the wording of the covenant in the deed, which will typically be expressed to be made by the covenantor 'on behalf of himself and his successors in title'. In the absence of such express wording, section 79 Law of Property Act 1925 provides that the parties are deemed to have so intended unless they express some contrary intention.

The Purchaser of the Servient Land Must Have Notice of the Covenant

This was central to the decision in *Tulk v Moxhay* but, as we will see, this requirement will today more usually be satisfied by registration.

5.7.5.2.2 Does the Benefit Run with the Land?

At Common Law We have seen that, under ordinary contract law principles, the covenant will continue to be enforceable against the original covenantor whether the covenant was positive or restrictive. However, if the original covenantee has sold the dominant land, the question arises as to whether his entitlement to enforce the covenant against the original covenantor passes to his successors in title. The law says that it will, as long as (a) the covenant 'touches and concerns' the dominant land and (b) the parties intended the benefit to run with the land (and this requirement is now implied by section 78 Law of Property Act 1925). In most cases where a covenant has genuinely been made for the benefit of other land a successor in title to the original covenantee will, therefore, be able to enforce against the original covenantor.

In Equity We have seen that in certain circumstances the burden of a restrictive covenant (but not of a positive covenant) can run with the land in equity under the rule in *Tulk v Moxhay* and that the covenant will then also be enforceable against a successor in title to the original covenantor. Under these rules the original covenantee will always be able to enforce the covenant against the covenantor's successors in title. However, for this entitlement to pass to the original covenantee's successors in title, they must themselves demonstrate that the *benefit* of the covenant has passed to them *in equity*. As long as the covenant 'touches and concerns' the dominant land this will almost always be the situation following the case of *Federated Homes Ltd v Mill Lodge Properties Ltd*.[78] Contrary to what had previously been thought, the Court of Appeal held in that case that the benefit of a covenant is automatically annexed to dominant land by section 78 Law of Property Act 1925 without the need for any additional evidence or formality.

Building Schemes Building schemes (also sometimes known as 'schemes of development') are housing estate developments where a developer imposes identical restrictive

78 *Federated Homes Ltd v Mill Lodge Properties Ltd* [1980] 1 WLR 594.

covenants on each plot with the aim of maintaining the quality of the estate. Where the legal requirements of a building scheme are satisfied the benefits and burdens of all the covenants automatically pass to the purchasers of each of the plots, and to their successors in title. This means that, at any time in the future, every plot owner is always entitled to enforce any of the covenants against any other owner who fails to comply with them. Significantly therefore, there is no requirement for the developer to have retained dominant land capable of being benefited by the covenants as each of the plots has the benefit of them. Examples include paint colour for external walls, maintaining the property, not erecting fences, not drying washing outside, etc.

Although the situation has been refined by subsequent cases, the traditional legal requirements for the existence of a building scheme were set out in *Elliston v Reacher*.[79] In that case a building society sold off a large number of plots. It imposed identical restrictive covenants on each purchaser but did not, itself, retain any land once the last plot had been sold. One of the covenants prevented the houses on the estate being used for the purposes of a hotel. Almost 50 years later, two of the plot owners on the estate were Elliston and Reacher. Reacher owned two plots, which they used for a hotel business. Elliston, therefore, brought injunction proceedings against Reacher to enforce the restrictive covenant. The Court of Appeal awarded the injunction, holding that both the benefit and the burden of the covenant had run with the land due to the existence of a building scheme. The following legal requirements for a building scheme were identified:

- All the plots must derive their title from a single seller.
- Before any of the sales took place, the seller must have laid out the land as separate plots.
- The seller must have imposed identical restrictions on the purchasers of each of the plots with the intention that these were to be for the benefit of all the other plots.
- The original purchasers must have acquired their plots on the understanding that there were common restrictions on all the plots, and that they were intended to be mutually enforceable.

Discharge and Modification of Restrictive Covenants Because the burden of restrictive covenants can run in equity they are capable of preventing an owner from making effective use of their land. It is, however, possible for restrictive covenants to be discharged in a number of ways, including the following.

- By agreement
  Owners of the dominant and servient land can agree to discharge the covenant, They would give effect to this by entering into a deed of discharge.
- By extinguishment
  A covenant will automatically be extinguished where the dominant and servient land come into the same ownership. This does not, of course, apply to the plots in a building scheme.

79 *Elliston v Reacher* [1908] 2 Ch 374.

- By the lands tribunal
  The role of the Lands Tribunal was introduced in Chapter 1, paragraph 1.12.1. Under section 84 Law of Property Act 1925 an application can be made to the Tribunal to discharge or modify a restrictive covenant. In order to be successful the applicant must establish one of the following four statutory grounds.
- The covenant has become obsolete due to changes in the character of the property or the neighbourhood.
- The covenant impedes some reasonable use of the land and:
  - it does not provide any practical benefit of substantial value to anyone, or;
  - it is contrary to the public interest, and in each case;
  - that money will be an adequate compensation for anyone suffering loss as a result of its discharge or modification.
- The parties have expressly or impliedly agreed to its removal.
- The discharge or modification will not injure anyone entitled to the benefit of the covenant.

If the Tribunal orders the discharge or modification of a covenant it may also require the servient owner to pay compensation to the dominant owner. The Tribunal is required to take the current planning policies of the relevant local authority into account when deciding whether to discharge or modify a covenant.

5.7.6 The Enforceability of Third-party Rights

Third-party rights in land were introduced at Section 5.7. These consist of 'legal interests' (including easements and mortgages) and 'equitable interests' (including restrictive covenants, trusts, estate contracts, equitable easements and equitable mortgages). In addition, a leasehold 'legal estate' will also be a third-party right with regards its relationship with the freehold estate (or any superior leasehold estate) within the same piece of land.

Here we are concerned with the circumstances in which a third-party right will be binding on a purchaser of the land to which it relates, and therefore enforceable against them. This depends on whether the land is registered or unregistered.

5.7.6.1 Unregistered Land

Historically, the enforceability of third-party rights depended on whether they were legal or equitable. If they were legal, they were always enforceable against a purchaser. If they were equitable, enforceability depended on what is known as the 'doctrine of notice'. Under this doctrine, equitable interests were binding on a purchaser *unless* they were a 'bona fide purchaser for value without notice'. This is someone who acting in good faith who buys the legal estate and, crucially, does so *without* having any knowledge of the existence of the equitable interest. Such a purchaser would take the land free from the equitable interest (which would then cease to exist). The doctrine of notice resulted in great uncertainty as to whether equitable interests were binding in a particular situation, and carrying risks both for their owners and for purchasers.

5.7.6.1.1 The Post 1925 System

Parliament intervened in 1925 to introduce a greater degree of certainty. The distinction between legal and equitable interests remained. The rules relating to the enforceability of legal rights remained substantially unchanged. However, in the context of equitable interests, the doctrine of notice was largely replaced by two new procedures.

1. Under the Law of Property Act 1925, the interests of beneficiaries under a trust in the land were said to be 'overreached'. This means that, as long as the purchaser pays purchase monies to at least two trustees, they take the land free from the beneficiary's interest. The interest would not be destroyed but would instead be transferred to the proceeds of sale. Following the sale, the trustees would hold the proceeds of sale, rather than the land itself, on trust for the beneficiary.
2. The Land Charges Act 1925 (now replaced by the Land Charges Act 1972) introduced a system of 'land charges registration'. Land charges largely correspond to the equitable interests. The legislation provided a facility for those with an entitlement to an equitable interest to register them at a central land charges registry (not to be confused with the Land Registry) in Plymouth. In so doing, they protected their interest, which would then be automatically binding on a purchaser of the land, whether or not they had notice of it. The legislation also established a search facility so that purchasers could check whether any interests had been registered in advance of their purchase. Equally, a failure to register resulted in a purchaser taking the land free from the interest. Under this system the enforceability of equitable interests depended entirely on whether or not they had been registered as a land charge.

5.7.6.2 Registered Land

The system of registration of title to land was described in Section 5.5.3. Where land is registered, the enforceability of third-party rights against a purchaser are governed by the Land Registration Act 2002. The significance of the distinction between legal and equitable interests has effectively disappeared. Instead, a purchaser will be bound by interests (whether legal or equitable) which are either protected by an entry on the register or which are capable of overriding the register.

5.7.6.2.1 Interests on the Register

Almost all the legal and equitable interests we have considered in this chapter are capable of being protected by an entry on the charges register of the title they relate to. Once protected in this way they will bind a purchaser of the land contained in the title. As the register is a public document, it is, however, possible for purchasers to inspect it in advance of their purchase, and therefore to be fully aware of these interests. If an interest has not been registered, then it will not be binding on a purchaser unless it is one of a limited number of rights which are capable of overriding the register.

Overriding Interests One of the principles of land registration is that the contents of the register should mirror the actual state of a title, including any third-party rights to which it is subject. The existence of overriding interests, which cannot be discovered from an inspection of the register and are nevertheless binding on a purchaser, is often described as a crack in this mirror. The rationale for their existence is that the nature of some interests is such that it would not be reasonable or practical for them to be entered on the register. The most important overriding interests are described in the following text.

- Leases of 7 years or less
  Leases for terms in excess of 7 years are capable of registration as a title in their own right. As part of that process, they will also be entered in the charges register of the superior title and are therefore fully protected. Leases of 7 years or less are protected by being categorised as overriding interests and will also be binding on a purchaser of the superior title.
- Interests of persons in actual occupation
  Where someone has a legal or equitable interest in land, and they are in actual occupation of that land, they have an overriding interest which will be binding on a purchaser. This typically occurs where a cohabitee contributes money towards the purchase of a house which they subsequently reside in with their partner; however, only their partner's name appears on the title. In these situations the law considers that an implied trust arises. The cohabitee has an equitable interest in the property which is converted into an overriding interest by virtue of their occupation. Equally, a purchaser of land acquires an estate contract in the land from the moment that they enter into a purchase contract. If they go into occupation before completion of the purchase their equitable interest would also be converted into an overriding interest.

5.7.6.3 Easements Created by Implication or by Prescription

Legal easements can be created expressly, by implication or by prescription. Where created by express grant or reservation they must be protected by an entry on the charges register in order to be enforceable against a purchaser. However, it will often not be practical to protect an informally created easement in this way, whether this has occurred by implied grant or reservation or by prescription. These types of easement will bind a purchaser as an overriding interest in any one of the following circumstances:

- Where the purchaser actually knows about its existence.
- Where they do not know about it but its existence would have been obvious from a reasonably careful inspection of the property.
- Where the easement has actually been exercised during the year immediately prior to the date of the purchase (for example, the use of drainage easements or other 'invisible' easements that could not have been discovered by an inspection of the land).

5.7.6.4 Other Interests

A small number of interests in land are not capable of protection on the charges register of the title to which they relate. Some of these are instead capable of existing as overriding interests so are protected in this way. Leases of 3 years or less are an example of this.

However, one of these interests deserves special mention. This is the interest of a beneficiary under a trust. This is neither capable of being protected by an entry on the register, nor (unless the beneficiary is in occupation as discussed above) of existing as an overriding interest. Instead, the beneficiary's interest is protected by being overreached in the same way as described in the context of unregistered land. The beneficiary's interest is transferred from the land to the proceeds of sale. As with unregistered land, this will only occur if the purchaser pays the purchase monies to at least two trustees. Although this is not essential, it is usual to insert a restriction in the proprietorship register preventing any transfer of the land from being registered unless this requirement has been complied with.

5.8 Commonhold

We have seen how positive covenants, entered into by the owners of neighbouring land, cannot be enforced against the original covenanting party's successors in title. This can create a problem for the owners of units (for example flats or business units) forming part of a larger building. The value and amenity of their individual units are dependent on the owners of all other parts of the building properly maintaining their respective parts. Because of the difficulty of enforcing positive covenants, this effectively means that there is no way to enforce repairing obligations of other owners, once the original covenanting parties have sold their interest in these properties.

The solution to this problem has traditionally been for developers to grant long leaseholds of flats and other such units to purchasers due to the different rules governing the enforceability of covenants between landlords and tenants in leases (see Chapter 6). The tenants of each unit will then covenant with the landlord to repair their original unit. The landlord covenants with the tenants of each flat to repair the common parts of the building (including the structural parts, entrances, stairways and other shared areas) and to enforce the repairing covenants of other tenants if they fail to undertake their repairing obligations. In theory this ensures that the tenant of each individual unit always has a mechanism by which they can enforce the repairing obligations of others in respect of the other units and the common parts.

In practice, there are two major problems with using long leaseholds in this way. The first is that a lease is, by definition, a diminishing asset. As the end of the term approaches, lenders become increasingly unwilling to make mortgage loans on the security of the property which therefore becomes unmarketable. The second is that landlords may act in their own interest rather than in that of the tenants. They may not take their obligations to maintain the building seriously or, conversely, they may be overzealous in doing so, resulting in excessive service charge demands to the tenants.

Commonhold was introduced by the Commonhold and Leasehold Reform Act 2002 in an attempt to overcome these problems. It provides a mechanism whereby the individual units can be sold as freehold properties in circumstances where the owners can always enforce the repairing obligations of others in respect of all other parts of the building. It achieves this by establishing the 'commonhold' as an entirely new form of landholding, capable of registration at the Land Registry. Freehold titles are registered for each of the 'units' and also for the 'common parts' within the commonhold. Commonhold does not create a new form of ownership- there are still only two recognised by law – freehold and leasehold. It allows unit owners to own the freehold of their flat and, jointly with the other unit owners, own the freehold of any communal areas. The owner of each individual unit owns the freehold in their unit but is also a member of a 'commonhold association'. This is a company which is owned collectively by all the unit owners, and which itself owns the freehold in the common parts, as well as having the responsibility for their maintenance. The division of the building into units and common parts, and the detailed arrangements and responsibilities for maintaining every aspect of it are described in a document called the 'commonhold community statement' (CCS) which also forms part of the commonhold title registered at the Land Registry. This document contains all the legal rules relating to the operation of the building and, crucially, is binding on all existing and future unit owners for as long as they retain their interest in their unit. At present, uptake of commonhold is low, described as 'woeful',[80] with reports of only 20 commonhold developments having been built since the legislation came into force in 2002.

80 Bevan, *Land Law*, 2022, 381.

6

The Law of Landlord and Tenant

CONTENTS

6.1 The Leasehold Estate

A leasehold, introduced in Chapter 5, is one of two legal estates that can exist in land (the other being the freehold). Leases (also called 'tenancies') exist in many forms. They can involve, for example, a private individual paying weekly rent for living accommodation, a farmer working a farm which is let to them by the freeholder, or a company leasing an office block for the purposes of its business. Long leases (for example, for 999 years) are also used for certain types of owner-occupied residential property. Leases are characterised by an ongoing relationship between the owner of the leasehold estate (the 'tenant' or 'lessee') and the owner of the superior estate (the 'landlord' or 'lessor'), out of which the lease has been created. The law of landlord and tenant is a specialist branch of land law which is concerned with the legal rights and obligations that exist between these two parties.

6.1.1 Types of Leases

6.1.1.1 Fixed-term Tenancy

A fixed-term tenancy is one which lasts for a defined period of time as stated at the outset. It can be for any length of time specified by the parties, whether for a few days or for hundreds of years.

In September 2024, the UK government introduced the Renters' Rights Bill 2024, which, as of April 2025, is moving through Parliament. It seeks to significantly alter the position of private rental agreements, so although not yet in force, it is important that you are aware of it, as it may affect a number of different aspects of the law of landlord and tenant once passed.

The Bill, currently in the House of Lords, is applicable only to England, and is restricted to private rental agreements – it does not legislate for commercial leases. As described by the Ministry of Housing, Communities and Local Government, the aim of the Bill is to 'transform the experience of private renting (...) improve the current system for both the 11 million private renters and 2.3 million landlords in England (...) give renters much greater security and stability so they can stay in their homes for longer, build lives in their communities, and avoid the risk of homelessness'.[1] If passed, S1 (1) Renters Rights Bill will remove fixed-term tenancies for private renters. Instead, all tenancies will be periodic, with a 2-month notice period applicable to both landlord and tenant.

6.1.1.2 Periodic Tenancy

In contrast to a fixed-term tenancy, the length of a periodic tenancy is not determined at the outset. These tenancies are instead defined by reference to a particular time period and simply continue on a rolling basis, from period to period, until terminated by a valid notice to quit by one of the parties at the end of a period. The period can be for any length of time, for example a weekly, monthly, quarterly or yearly tenancy.

6.1.1.3 Tenancy at Will

A tenancy at will is said to exist where a tenant has exclusive possession of the property, but on terms where either party is entitled to terminate the tenancy at any time. It is typically an interim arrangement where a tenant is in possession pending the negotiation of the terms of a more formal lease. Despite its name it is not strictly a tenancy at all as it lacks certainty of term, which, as we will see in the following text, is one of the essential elements of a valid lease. A tenancy at will is therefore similar to a licence, but with the added ingredient of exclusive possession.

6.1.2 Essential Elements of a Valid Lease

6.1.2.1 Exclusive Possession

We saw in Chapter 5 that the right to exclusive possession is one of the defining characteristics of a legal estate in land. Exclusive possession entitles the estate owner to control and manage the property, which includes the right to exclude every other person from it (including, in the case of a leasehold estate, the landlord). A lease cannot exist unless this feature is present. If someone has been granted the right to occupy and use land but does

1 Ministry of Housing, Communities and Local Government 'Guidance; Guide to the Renters' Rights Bill' (January 2025).

not have the right to exclusive possession, they only have a licence (permission) to do so and not an estate in land.

The distinction between a lease and a licence is important, as a number of statutory benefits are only available to those with a lease (tenants/lessees) not those with a licence (licensees). Historically landlords have attempted to deny the status of 'tenant' (with its associated statutory benefits) to occupants by granting licences instead of tenancies. The leading case on the lease/licence distinction is *Street v Mountford*[2] where the parties entered into a document called a 'licence agreement'. Under the agreement Mr Street allowed Ms Mountford to occupy a furnished room at the top of a house in return for the payment of a weekly 'licence fee'. The House of Lords held that, despite its label as a licence, the arrangement in fact created a weekly tenancy. The case established that an occupier's status as either a tenant or licensee is normally decided by answering the factual question of whether exclusive possession is present, rather than by following the expressed intention of the parties. In *Street v Mountford*, the occupier was held to have exclusive possession despite a provision in the agreement entitling the house owner to have access to the room for inspection purposes. *Street* can be contrasted with *AG Securities v Vaughan*[3], which concerned another titled 'licence agreement' to occupy a room in a house shared by three other people. Three other occupants signed identical agreements under which they each agreed that the owner of the house could introduce new licensees for each of the rooms as and when they became vacant. The House of Lords held that the house owner's entitlement to introduce new occupants indicated that the owner retained exclusive possession of the property. Therefore, the occupants in this case were licensees rather than tenants.

The courts are wary of landlords' attempts to deny tenancy status to their tenants by the use of sham means to exclude the entitlement to exclusive possession. In *Aslan v Murphy*[4], the occupier was given a 'licence' to occupy a tiny basement room, within which the owner was allowed to introduce other occupiers to share the room with the 'licensee'. As the room was barely big enough even for a single bed, the Court of Appeal was unconvinced that this provision was genuine. It therefore held that the occupier had exclusive possession, and they were a tenant. The House of Lords came to the same conclusion in *Antoniades v Villiers*[5] which concerned another titled 'licence agreement' for a cohabiting couple to occupy a one-bedroom flat. A provision purporting to entitle the property owner to move other people into the flat was regarded as a sham and the couple were held to be tenants with exclusive possession.

Although exclusive possession is a prerequisite for the existence of a tenancy, its presence does not automatically mean that a tenancy exists. Where exclusive possession is present, it is then necessary to consider whether there are any circumstances which prevent the creation of a tenancy. This might be the case if, for example, there was no intention between the parties to create legal relations, for example, in a family arrangement. Equally, the existence of exclusive possession might be explained on other grounds, for example, where

---

2 *Street v Mountford* [1985] AC 809.
3 *AG Securities v Vaughan* [1990] 1 AC 417.
4 *Aslan v Murphy* [1990] 1 WLR 766.
5 *Antoniades v Villiers* [1990] 1 AC 417.

premises are occupied through a contract of employment, or under a contract for the purchase of land where a purchaser has possession of the land prior to completion of the sale.

6.1.2.2 Certainty of Term

The law requires all leases to have a certain start date, and for the end date to be ascertainable. Unless stated to the contrary the start date will be the date on which the tenant goes into possession.

It is common for the parties to enter into a contract for a lease to start at some time in the future, or indeed for them to enter into an immediately binding lease which starts at some future date (a 'reversionary lease'). However, when they do so, it is important to ensure that the start date is clearly stated. In *Harvey v Pratt*[6] the parties entered into an agreement for a 21 year fixed tenancy of a garage. The agreement contained detailed provisions about the terms of the lease but did not state the date of commencement of the term. The Court of Appeal held that the agreement was not a valid lease due to the absence of a start date. Any attempt to create a lease with a start date more than 21 years in the future will also be void under S149 Law of Property Act 1925.

As well as having a certain start date, leases must also have an end date which can be identified at the start of the term. In a fixed-term tenancy the length of the term must be clearly stated. In *Brilliant v Michaels*[7] the claimant entered into an agreement to take the tenancy of a flat when it became vacant. The agreement was held to be void for uncertainty, as it was not ascertainable when the flat would become vacant. This was also the case in *Lace v Chantler*[8] where an agreement was entered into in 1940 'for the duration of the war'. As it was unclear how long the Second World War would last, the agreement was held to be void. A similar result was reached in *Prudential Assurance Co Ltd v London Residuary Board*[9] where a letting was to continue 'until the land was required by the London County Council for road widening'. The House of Lords held that the end date of the proposed term was insufficiently certain for it to come into existence. However, in this case, it was held that a yearly tenancy had been created as the tenant had actually entered into possession and paid a yearly rent. This raises the question of how a periodic tenancy can be said to satisfy the requirement for certainty of term, as its end date is not ascertainable at the commencement. The answer is that the law treats periodic tenancies as a series of fixed term tenancies rather than as a single open-ended one. Each period of the tenancy equates to a fixed term and on this basis the law is satisfied that the requirement for certainty is satisfied.

One final point concerns so-called 'perpetually renewable leases'. These arise where the lease inadvertently contains an option for the tenant to renew the term at the end of the lease 'on the same terms as those contained in the original lease'. By definition this form of wording would also require the option to renew to be included in the new lease and this would have the effect of making the lease forever renewable. In the interests of creating certainty, S145 Law of Property Act 1922 converted such leases into 2000 year terms, which are also capable of early termination by the tenant.

6 *Harvey v Pratt* [1965] 1 WLR 1025.
7 *Brilliant v Michaels* [1945] 1 All ER 121.
8 *Lace v Chantler* [1944] KB 568.
9 *Prudential Assurance Co Ltd v London Residuary Board* [1992] AC 386.

6.2 Formalities for the Creation of Leases

6.2.1 The Creation of Legal Leases

We have seen in Chapter 5 that, under S52(1) Law of Property Act 1925, legal estates and interests can generally only be created by deed. As a legal estate in land, the general rule is that a lease must be made by deed. However, under S54(2) Law of Property Act 1925, a lease with a duration of 3 years or less can be created either orally or in writing, provided as it is at full market rent and the tenant is immediately entitled to go into possession. Periodic tenancies also fall into this exception to the general rule, even though they may ultimately continue for longer than 3 years. Note, however, that this exception only applies to the *grant* of a lease. The transfer ('assignment') of an existing lease must always be by deed, even if it is for less than 3 years and was initially created without a deed.

In addition to the requirement for creation by deed, leases of over 7 years must be registered at the Land Registry with their own separate title. Leases of between three and 7 years can be protected by an entry on the charges register of the superior title (be that freehold or leasehold) and all leases of 7 years or less exist as overriding interests.

6.2.2 Failure to Comply with Creation Formalities

6.2.2.1 At Common Law

If the parties fail to comply with any requirements for a deed or registration, the intended lease will be void at law. However, if they were unaware of the requirements, it is likely that the tenant will still go into possession and start paying rent, and that the landlord will accept the rent and otherwise behave as if there is a valid lease. Where this occurs, the law may assume that the parties have instead entered informally into a periodic tenancy under the exception contained in S54(2) Law of Property Act 1925.

6.2.2.2 In Equity

In certain circumstances, equity may intervene to assist the parties. It can do nothing for them if their attempt to create the fixed-term lease was simply an oral agreement. However, if there is something in writing (perhaps a deed that was improperly executed, or a valid deed followed by a failure to register it with the Land Registry) it might treat this as a contract to create the lease, satisfying S2 Law of Property (Miscellaneous Provisions) Act 1989. Either of the parties could, therefore, bring court proceedings to enforce the contract by seeking the equitable remedy of specific performance. If granted, this would compel the parties to complete the required formalities, which would have the effect of converting the agreement into a valid legal lease. However, if neither party brings court proceedings to enforce the contract, equity may assist the parties in another way. Under the equitable maxim 'equity regards as done that which ought to be done', the contract to create the lease will be regarded as a lease with immediate effect. Although void as a legal lease, it will instead take effect as an equitable lease.

The combined effect of the legal and equitable rules is that a tenant might end up with both a legal tenancy and an equitable one. The potential conflict between the two was considered in *Walsh v Lonsdale*.[10] The case concerned a contract for the grant of a 7-year

10 *Walsh v Lonsdale* (1882) 21 ChD 9.

lease of a mill where rent was to be paid 1 year in advance. Pending the formal grant of the lease the tenant went into possession and started paying the agreed yearly rent quarterly in arrears. No deed was ever drawn up, and 3 years later a dispute arose between the parties as to the basis on which rent was payable. The tenant claimed to be in possession as a legal yearly tenant subject to payment of the quarterly rent in arrears. The landlord, however, argued the existence of the equitable lease requiring rent to be paid yearly in advance. The Court of Appeal held that the rent was payable in advance. The terms of the equitable lease took precedence because, since the Judicature Act 1873,[11] equity prevails where there is a conflict between the rules of equity and law.

Since the decision in *Walsh v Lonsdale* it is sometimes said, as between the parties, that an equitable lease is as good as a legal lease. However, it should be remembered that an equitable lease will only exist in circumstances where specific performance is available as a remedy. The courts will not grant this discretionary remedy to someone who has themselves behaved badly and who does not therefore 'come to equity with clean hands' (another equitable maxim). If the remedy would not be available, it follows that the principle that 'equity regards as done that which ought to be done' will not assist as the equitable interest will not be created. Finally, it should be noted that, an equitable lease is less likely to be enforceable against a purchaser than a legal one.

6.3 Termination of Leases

Leases can be terminated (also called 'determined') in a number of ways and the most important ones are described here. As will be discussed further in the text, some of these are subject to statutory provisions providing security of tenure for particular types of tenants.

6.3.1 Notice to Quit

This is the conventional method by which a periodic tenancy is terminated. Unless the parties have agreed to the contrary, notice equal in length to the period of the tenancy must be served. The notice may be served by either party and must expire at the end of a period of the tenancy.

6.3.2 Passing of Time

A fixed-term tenancy will automatically terminate at the end of the term by a process of 'effluxion of time'. No notice is required.

6.3.3 Break Clause

Fixed-term tenancies sometimes contain a break clause (or 'option to determine'). These clauses might allow either or both parties to bring the tenancy to an end before the expiry

11 The relevant provision is now contained in S49(1) Supreme Court Act 1981.

of the term at a particular time or on the happening of a particular event. The exercise of a break clause will only be effective if it is exercised strictly in accordance with the relevant clause in the lease. The notice to exercise the option must be in the correct form, served at the correct time, and in the correct manner.

6.3.4 Surrender

This arises where the tenant gives up their interest in the property to their immediate landlord. The surrender may be express, in which case a formal deed must be used, or it can arise by operation of law where the tenant does some act which is inconsistent with the continued existence of the tenancy and the landlord concurs. The giving up of possession by the tenant and the return of the keys to the landlord is a classic example.

6.3.5 Forfeiture

As will be discussed further in the text, forfeiture is a remedy available to a landlord in the event of a tenant's breach of covenant. Where it is available, it will bring a lease to an end.

6.3.6 Merger

If the tenant acquires the estate out of which their lease has been granted (the reversion) the two estates will merge and the tenancy will come to an end.

6.4 Removal of Tenants' Fixtures

Chattels can sometimes become classed as a 'fixtures' by being attached to land. At the end of a tenancy the general rule is that the tenant may remove chattels but that they must leave any fixtures, as these will have become part of the land, and therefore the landlord's property. This rule is relaxed in landlord and tenant situations in the case of what are referred to as 'tenant's fixtures'. These consist either of those items that can be described as 'ornamental and domestic fixtures' or as 'trade fixtures'. The tenant is free to remove these types of fixtures at the end of the term provided they make good any damage caused in doing so.

6.5 Covenants in Leases

6.5.1 Express Covenants

Covenants in the law of landlord and tenant refers to any promise made between the parties concerning the terms of the lease, whether in a deed, in a written tenancy agreement, or made orally. Where the promises are expressed by the parties in any of these ways, they are referred to as express covenants.

6.5.2 Implied Covenants

In a limited number of areas, the law will imply covenants in circumstances where the parties have neglected to address them by express covenants. However, if an express covenant deals with an areas, it will almost always take precedence over the implied covenant, even if it is more limited in scope than the implied covenant.

Worthy of note is that during the COVID-19 pandemic, a number of temporary changes were introduced by the UK Government which impacted landlord and tenant rights and responsibilities. In particular, residential tenancies and protection from eviction (S81 Coronavirus Act 2020) and protection from forfeiture (explained in detail later in this chapter) for business tenancies (S82 Coronavirus Act 2020). Non-statutory guidance was also provided with regard to rent, mortgage payments and possession proceedings, health and safety obligations, repairs and inspections, which was withdrawn on 25 March 2022.

6.5.2.1 Landlords Implied Covenants

6.5.2.1.1 Quiet Enjoyment

Despite its name, the covenant for quiet enjoyment is not a promise that the tenant will be allowed to enjoy the property free from noise. In *Southwark LBC v Mills*[12] a claim by tenants in a local authority housing block about inadequate soundproofing between the flats failed. The covenant is a promise by the landlord that the tenant will be allowed to enjoy the possession of the property without physical interference by the landlord, or by those deriving title from the landlord, such as the tenants of adjoining properties.

Harassment by the landlord amounts to a breach of this covenant. This was held to be the case in *Kenny v Preen*[13] where the landlord sent threatening letters to a tenant, banged on their door and shouted threats to the effect that they would physically throw the tenant and their possessions into the street. The harassment of a tenant will also have other legal consequences as well as being a breach of this covenant. The Protection from Eviction Act 1977 (as amended by the Housing Act 1988) and the Protection from Harassment Act 1997 render the harassment of a residential tenant a criminal offence. S27 Housing Act 1988 also creates a new tort of unlawful eviction if a residential occupier is driven out of their home as a result of harassment by the landlord. The Act provides for the payment of substantial damages, representing the difference between the value of the property with the tenant in occupation and their value with vacant possession.

Physical interference with the tenant's enjoyment of the property which does not constitute harassment can also be a breach of the quiet enjoyment covenant. In *Owen v Gadd*[14] the covenant was held to have been breached where the landlord erected scaffolding outside the tenant's shop, obstructing the shop window, interfering with access and causing a loss of trade. However, where the tenant suffers inconvenience which falls short of a physical interference with the property, this will not amount to a breach of the covenant. This question arose in *Browne v Flower*[15] where the tenant complained to the court about

---

12 *Southwark LBC v Mills* [2001] AC 1.
13 *Kenny v Preen* [1963] 1 QB 400.
14 *Owen v Gadd* [1956] 2 QB 99.
15 *Browne v Flower* [1911] 1 Ch 219.

a new external staircase which ran past their bedroom window. The court held that a loss of privacy was not sufficient to constitute a breach of the quiet enjoyment covenant and rejected the claim.

6.5.2.1.2 Not to Derogate from Grant

This covenant is an implied promise by the landlord that they will not do anything which detracts from the value of the lease they have granted. It is not appropriate for a landlord to take with one hand that which they have granted with the other. The practical application of the covenant concerns the use of adjacent land by the landlord, or perhaps by persons deriving title from them. A landlord must not use the adjacent land, or permit it to be used, in a way that is inconsistent with the purpose for which the property has been let. The leading case is *Aldin v Latimer, Clark, Muirhead*[16] where the landlord was held in breach of this covenant when, having let premises for the purposes of timber drying, they built on adjoining land and interrupted the flow of air to the tenant's premises. A similar conclusion was reached in *Grosvenor Hotel Co v Hamilton*[17] where the landlord leased an old house to a tenant and then used machinery on adjoining land which caused the house to be unstable.

A landlord is not liable under this covenant if nearby property is let for a similar purpose and, as a consequence, a tenant suffers financial loss. Nevertheless, there is some obligation on the landlord to ensure that tenancies of adjacent properties are let for purposes which are compatible with the use of the subject property. For example, in *Chartered Trust plc v Davies*[18] the Court of Appeal held that the landlord was in breach of the covenant to the tenant of a gift shop in a narrow shopping arcade. In that case the landlord had breached the covenant by letting the tiny adjoining shop to a pawnbroker, resulting in queues of people in the arcade spilling over into the tenant's gift shop.

6.5.2.1.3 Covenants to Repair

Fitness for Human Habitation Where residential premises are let on a furnished basis, there is an implied promise by the landlord that they are fit for human habitation at the start of the tenancy. This is a very limited promise, as it involves no continuing obligation to maintain the premises, and no obligation at all in the case of unfurnished premises. The extent of the covenant is also extremely limited. The rule was established in *Smith v Marrable*[19] where a landlord was held to be in breach in circumstances where a house was infested with bugs. There is no requirement that the premises should be comfortable, and the basic test of habitability requires that the occupants should be free from risk of physical injury or damage to health. Other cases where landlords have been held to be in breach have related to defective drains,[20] poor quality water supply[21] and contamination by tuberculosis.[22]

---

16 *Aldin v Latimer, Clark, Muirhead* [1894] 2 Ch 437.
17 *Grosvenor Hotel Co v Hamilton* [1894] 2 QB 836.
18 *Chartered Trust plc v Davies* [1997] 2 EGLR 83.
19 *Smith v Marrable* (1843) 11 M & W 152.
20 *Wilson v Finch Hatton* (1877) 2 Ex D 336.
21 *Chester v Powell* (1885) 53 LT 722.
22 *Collins v Hopkins* [1923] 2 KB 617.

S8 Landlord and Tenant Act 1985 Obligations

This section imposes obligations on the landlords of residential premises let at very low rents. The obligations are that the premises will be fit for human habitation at the commencement of the lease and that they will continue to be so for the length of the term. Unfortunately, the provision is of little use because it only covers lettings where the rent does not exceed £80 per year in London and £52 elsewhere. As there has been no revision of these rental levels since 1957, there will, no doubt, be very few people covered by the provision. Further, the landlord must be notified of the defects, and it will not apply if the defects cannot be rendered fit at reasonable expense.

S11 Landlord and Tenant Act 1985 Obligations

This provision applies to 'short leases' of residential properties (including flats) of less than 7 years. It requires the landlord to keep the structure and exterior of the property in repair and also to keep the services in the property in working order. The landlord is only liable if they have notice of the defect, but the parties cannot 'contract out' of the provision, except with the consent of the court.

Common Parts In cases of flats in multistorey blocks, the landlord is subject to an obligation to take reasonable care to keep the means of access to each flat in reasonable repair. This common law duty was established in *Liverpool City Council v Irwin*[23] which concerned the claimant's tenancy of a flat on the ninth floor of a 15-storey block. As a result of vandalism, the lifts were constantly out of order, the staircases and passages were unlit and dangerous, access to the rubbish chutes was dangerous, and the chutes themselves were constantly blocked. The House of Lords held that, as all these facilities were essential to the use of the flats, the landlord had a duty to take reasonable care to keep them in repair. Nevertheless, it emphasised that this was not an absolute obligation to repair, and in this particular case, the landlord had exercised reasonable care. The extent of the problem was due to the scale of the vandalism rather than a failure by the landlord to fulfil their obligations.

6.5.2.2 Tenant's Implied Covenants

6.5.2.2.1 To Pay Rent

In those cases where the rent is not agreed between the parties expressly and it is obvious that the parties envisage a tenancy coming into being, it is implied that the landlord is entitled to a reasonable sum for the use and enjoyment of the land.

6.5.2.2.2 To Pay Rates and Taxes

Unless the lease provides to the contrary, such payments are the responsibility of the tenant.

6.5.2.2.3 Covenants to Repair

To Use the Premises in a Tenant-like Manner This obligation requires the tenant:

a. to take reasonable care of the premises; and
b. to undertake minor odd jobs or day-to-day maintenance that is consistent with this duty of care.

---

23 *Liverpool City Council v Irwin* [1977] AC 239.

It does not include any liability for fair wear and tear. The classic statement of the tenant's duties is found in Lord Denning's judgment in *Warren v Keen*[24]:

> The tenant must take proper care of the premises. He must, if he is going away for the winter, turn off the water and empty the boiler; he must clean the chimneys when necessary and also the windows; he must mend the electric light when it fuses; he must unstop the sink when it is blocked by his waste. In short, he must do the little jobs around the place which a reasonable tenant would do. In addition he must not, of course, damage the house wilfully or negligently. . . . . .but, apart from such things, if the house falls into disrepair through fair wear and tear or lapse of time or for any reason not caused by him, the tenant is not liable to repair it.

Duty Not to Commit Waste This is not strictly a covenant as it is an obligation that arises in tort. As such, it applies whatever the parties expressly agree. Waste is the causing of damage to property which reduces the value of the reversion. The duty not to commit waste overlaps with the obligation to use the premises in a tenant-like manner. The most important types of waste in this context are:

- Voluntary waste – positive acts which destroy or damage or alter the premises.
- Permissive waste – acts of negligence or omission which allow the building to fall into disrepair due to neglect.

A tenant for a fixed term is liable for voluntary and permissive waste. A periodic tenant is likely only liable for voluntary waste although they must, of course, also use the property in a 'tenant like manner'.

Duty to Allow the Landlord to Discharge Their Repairing Obligations Where the landlord is subject to an obligation to maintain the property they have an implied licence:

- To view the state of repair.
- To execute the necessary repairs.

6.5.3 The Usual Covenants

If the parties enter into an *agreement* for a lease before the creation of the lease itself, it will contain an implied term that the lease will contain 'the usual covenants'. What is 'usual' will depend on the type of premises, the purpose for which they are let and the geographical location. However, subject to any contrary agreement, this will always include the landlord's covenants for quiet enjoyment and non-derogation from grant, as well as the tenant's covenants to pay rent, rates and taxes and to allow the landlord to enter and view the state of repair of the premises. In addition, also subject to any contrary agreement, the following provisions will be included:

- A covenant by the tenant to keep the premises in repair.
- A forfeiture clause, entitling the landlord to re-enter and terminate the lease in the event of the tenant failing to pay the rent (but not for breach of other covenants).

24 *Warren v Keen* [1954] 1 QB 15, at 20.

This can be of particular significance if the parties subsequently fail to enter into a formal lease. Under the equitable principles discussed above, the parties could nevertheless be bound by the 'usual covenants' implied in the earlier contract.

6.5.4 Rent

Rent is the payment by a tenant for the right to exclusive possession of the property. All leases will invariably contain an express covenant for the tenant to pay rent, but as we have seen, in the rare situations where this is overlooked, this will be implied. Where an express covenant is included in the lease, the amount of the rent must be clearly stated (or capable of being ascertained if a fixed sum is not stated) or the whole lease will be void for uncertainty.

Where the rent payable under the lease represents the full market rent for the property, it is described as a 'rack rent'. However, in some cases the rent might be capitalised and a lump sum consideration (known as a 'fine' or a 'premium') paid at the beginning of the term instead. Where this occurs, it is also usual that a small amount of rent will be paid during the term, known as a 'ground rent'. This is common where a developer sells off leasehold flats or houses on an estate to owner occupiers. In circumstances where no rent is really expected over and above the payment of a premium, the lease would nevertheless still contain a requirement for payment of a nominal financial sum, or possibly for payment of a peppercorn ('peppercorn rent'). Indeed, for long residential leases granted following the coming into force of the Leasehold Reform (Ground Rent) Act 2022, if any ground rent is demanded, it cannot be for more than one literal peppercorn per year.

If there is no contrary provision in the lease, the rent will be payable in arrears at the end of each period of a periodic tenancy, or at the end of each year of a fixed term tenancy. In order to improve the landlord's cash-flow, leases usually contain express provisions that rent will be payable in advance. Because rent is paid in return for the exclusive possession of the land, it continues to be payable even if the buildings are damaged or destroyed and become unusable by the tenant. Because of this, it is commonplace for leases to contain an express term to the effect that payment of rent becomes suspended on the occurrence of certain events, including damage or destruction by fire.

If the Renters Rights Bill (as introduced at Section 6.1.1.1) is passed as currently sits in the Bill, under sections 9 and 10, it will prohibit landlords or letting agents from mandating or accepting payment of rent in advance of the tenancy being entered into.

6.5.4.1 Rent Review

6.5.4.1.1 Nature and Purpose of Rent Review

It is common practice, in leases of commercial premises, for the level of rent payable by the tenant to be reviewed periodically rather than remaining static throughout the term. The purpose of rent review is to enable the landlord to obtain the market rent for the property from time to time throughout the term rather than being locked into a rent based on market conditions at the time the lease was granted. Upwards only rent reviews are the norm so that, on review, if the market rent is higher than the amount currently payable, then the existing provision will be replaced by the higher sum. If not, the former sum will continue to be payable.

The mechanism for a rent review will be contained in a rent review clause within the lease. If you remember, the rent must be capable of being ascertained with certainty or the lease itself will be void for uncertainty. The clause must provide a clear mechanism for determining the new rent and it will typically deal with the following five issues:

- Frequency of rent reviews.
- Method of valuation of the market rent.
- Method of initiating rent reviews.
- Provision for agreement of market rent between the parties.
- Procedure in default of agreement.

Frequency of Rent Reviews The review periods vary from lease to lease. Five years is common, but it is not unusual to find shorter periods.

Valuation of Market Rent

The Hypothetical Letting

The purpose of the rent review is to provide the landlord with a rent that they could obtain if they offered the property for rent on the open market with vacant possession. This is obviously an artificial situation, as they are not actually free to do so until the current lease expires. However, in order to satisfy the purpose of rent review, the valuation must be based on this artificial situation. This is an important principle of rent review. Property valuers do not value the property itself. They value an *interest* in property. In a rent review it would make no sense to value the current tenant's interest in the property. The valuation must be of a hypothetical letting to a new tenant in a situation where the existing tenancy is not currently in existence. This hypothetical letting will typically be described in the rent review clause in similar terms to the following:

> Market rent means the rent at which the demised property might reasonably be expected to be let as a whole in the open market with vacant possession by a willing landlord to a willing tenant without a premium upon the terms of this lease (other than the amount of rent).

The Presumption in Favour of Reality

Precisely because the actual letting to be valued is so hypothetical, it can sometimes be extremely difficult to know how to define every single aspect of the imaginary situation that the valuer is being asked to consider. The courts therefore take the view that anything specifically referred to in the rent review clause must be taken into account but that, apart from this, the valuation should be on the basis of the reality of the situation as it actually affects the property being valued. In *Cooperative Wholesale Society Limited v National Westminster Bank plc*[25] this was described by Lord Justice Hoffman in the following terms:

> This approach has produced what is sometimes called the 'presumption in favour of reality' in the construction of rent review clauses. In the absence of clear contrary

25 *Cooperative Wholesale Society Limited v National Westminster Bank plc* [1995] 1 EGLR 97, at 99J.

words or necessary implication, it is assumed that the hypothetical letting required by the clause is of the premises as they actually were, on the terms of the actual lease and in the circumstances as they actually existed.

By way of example, a question will often arise regarding the length of the term to be valued. Traditionally, the longer the term, the greater the security for the tenant and therefore the higher the rent would be. However, in a recession the opposite might be the case as tenants might be reluctant to take on long-term commitments in those circumstances. In the absence of a clear statement in the lease regarding the length of the term to be valued the valuer might legitimately decide to undertake their valuation on the basis of either:

- The original term of the lease, or;
- The period until the next rent review, or;
- The unexpired term of the lease at the review date.

Although the correct approach will depend in the precise wording of the rent review clause, the decision in *Norwich Union Life Assurance Society v TSB*[26] is indicative of the approach often taken by the courts. In that case the review took place in the twelfth year of a 22-year term with valuation being required 'on the terms of this lease'. The court applied the presumption in favour of reality and held that the unexpired term of 10 years should be valued rather than the original 22-year term.

Assumptions and Disregards

If the valuation was simply to be made on the basis so far described the presumption in favour of reality would lead to injustice in a number of situations. For this reason, in addition to describing the hypothetical letting, it is also common for rent review clauses to require the valuer to take account of certain 'assumptions' and 'disregards', which include the following:

Common assumptions:

- The tenant has complied with their covenants
- The premises are fully fitted out and ready for immediate occupation and use

Common disregards:

- Tenant's occupation
- Goodwill
- Improvements

Whilst rent reviews are more common with commercial leases, the Renters Rights Bill (introduced at Section 6.1.1.1) will prohibit rent review clauses being included in private rental agreements. Instead, the Ministry for Housing provides the following overview for the proposed procedure for private sector rental agreement rent increases, as included in S7 Renters Rights Bill amending the Housing Act 1988:

---

26 *Norwich Union Life Assurance Society v TSB* [1986] 1 EGLR 136.

- All rent increases in the private rented sector will be made using the same process.
- Landlords will be able to increase rents once per year to the market rate – the price that would be achieved if the property was newly advertised to let.
- To do this, they will need to serve notice, setting out the new rent and giving at least 2 months' notice of it taking effect.
- If a tenant believes the proposed rent increase exceeds market rate, they can then challenge this at the First-tier Tribunal, who will determine what the market rent should be.[27]

6.6 Repairing Covenants

6.6.1 Nature of Repairing Covenants

If there is no express repairing covenant in a lease, subject to the law of waste and the limited circumstances in which a landlord impliedly agrees to repair, neither party is liable for repairs. However, most leases contain express covenants imposing repairing obligations on the landlord, the tenant, or dividing the responsibility between them. In addition, S11(1) Landlord and Tenant Act 1985 implies a covenant into most residential leases of less than 7 years that the landlord is to:

a. keep in repair the structure and exterior of the dwelling house (including drains, gutters and external pipes),
b. keep in repair and proper working order the installations in the dwelling-house for the supply of water, gas and electricity and for sanitation (including basins, sinks, baths and sanitary conveniences, but not other fixtures, fittings and appliances for making use of the supply of water, gas or electricity), and
c. keep in repair and proper working order the installations in the dwelling-house for space heating and heating water.

Following amendments made by the Housing Act 1988, for tenancies granted after 15 January 1989, the S11(1) covenant is extended to cover any part of the building in which the tenant has an estate or interest (ss11(1A), (1B)).[28] The Supreme Court, in *Edwards v Kumarasamy*[29] held that S11 should not be given an unnaturally wide meaning, noting that as 'the section imposes obligations on a contracting party over and above those which have been contractually agreed, one should not be too ready to give an unnaturally wide meaning to any of its expressions. Quite apart from that (...)'.[30]

6.6.2 Awaab's Law

Awaab Ishak lived with his parents in Rochdale, UK in a property owned by a housing association. The presence of mould in the flat had been reported to the housing association, both by Awaab's parents and a health visitor. Awaab sadly passed away shortly after his

27 Ibid.
28 See *Anchor Hanover Group v Cox* [2023] UKUT 14 (LC) and Housing Act 1988.
29 *Edwards v Kumarasamy* [2016] UKSC 40.
30 Ibid., para 18.

second birthday. The coroner reported 'Awaab Ishak died as a result of a severe respiratory condition due to prolonged exposure to mould in his home environment. Action to treat and prevent the mould, was not taken'.[31] Following his death, Awaab's parents campaigned for legislative changes with regard to hazards and repair responsibilities in social housing. The result is the Social Housing (Regulation) Act 2023. The Act strengthens the regulation of social housing, including regular inspections, increased enforcement powers, time limits for landlords to address hazards, right of information requests by tenants and standard setting for housing providers.

6.7 User Covenants

6.7.1 Nature of User Covenants

If there are no restrictions as to use in the lease, the tenant may use the premises as they wish, subject to compliance with planning regulations, any covenants affecting a superior title, and any other legal restrictions (for example, the law of nuisance). However, in practice, the landlord will generally also have a desire to control the way the tenant uses the premises by imposing what are known as 'user covenants'. These will either require the property to be used for a particular purpose (e.g. as a dwelling), or will impose restrictions on certain types of use. As with other types of covenant, they may be 'absolute' or 'qualified'.

- Absolute covenants impose an absolute requirement on the tenant to behave (or not to behave) in a certain way.
- Qualified covenants impose a similar obligation but provide that the tenant may be permitted to depart from the obligation with the landlord's prior (usually written) consent.

6.7.2 Restriction on Charging for Consent

S19(3) Landlord and Tenant Act 1927 provides that the landlord is not entitled to demand payment for the giving of consent to a change of use where this is required as part of a qualified covenant. The section applies notwithstanding any contrary provision in the lease, meaning the parties cannot 'contract out' of this requirement. Note, however, that the section does not prevent the landlord from charging for consent in certain circumstances:

- In the case of absolute covenants, or;
- Where the change of use also involves the making of structural alterations.

It also does not prevent the landlord from requiring the tenant to pay:

- A reasonable sum by way of compensation for any diminution in the value of the reversion that will be caused by the change of use, and;
- Legal expenses.

31 Regulation 28 Report to Prevent Future Deaths, available at: https://www.judiciary.uk/wp-content/uploads/2022/11/Awaab-Ishak-Prevention-of-future-deaths-report-2022-0365_Published.pdf

6.8 Covenants Against Alterations

6.8.1 Nature of Covenants Against Alterations

An alteration is a change in the fabric or form of a building, such as converting a house into flats or subdividing existing rooms. A change in appearance, on its own, will not suffice if it does not affect the fabric. In *Bickmore v Dimmer*[32] the erection of a large external clock supported by iron stays and bolted to the side of a building was held not to amount to an alteration.

Unless the lease contains a provision to the contrary the tenant is free to carry out alterations to the property. However, in practice, the landlord will want more control over the tenant's actions than this and covenants against alterations are commonly included. As with user covenants these can be either absolute (imposing a prohibition on alterations) or qualified (requiring the landlord's consent for alterations).

The case of *Duval v 11-13 Randolph Crescent Ltd*[33] concerned absolute covenants over a block of nine flats in Maida Vale, London. Each lease contained a covenant preventing the tenant from making any alteration or improvement to the premises without the prior written consent of the landlord (which could not be unreasonably withheld) (clause 2.6), a qualified covenant. Each lease also contained a covenant preventing the tenant from cutting into any roofs, walls, ceilings or service media (clause 2.7), an absolute covenant. One tenant, Ms Winfield sought the landlord's permission to remove part of a wall under clause 2.6 (the qualified covenant). Another tenant (Dr Duval) opposed the work, relying on clause 2.7 (the absolute covenant). The question for the court was whether a landlord could authorise work under the qualified covenant which would be in breach of the absolute covenant. The Supreme Court held that the landlord did not have the right to modify, vary, or authorise work which would be in breach of clause 2.7, the absolute covenant. Only a consensus of all tenants could do so.

6.8.2 Unreasonable Withholding of Consent

Where a qualified covenant requires the landlord's consent for the making of alterations, and an alteration amounts to an improvement to the property, S19(2) Landlord and Tenant Act 1927 provides that the landlord's consent shall not be unreasonably withheld. Once again, the parties cannot 'contract out' of this requirement by including a contrary provision in the lease. The question of whether an alteration is indeed an improvement, triggering the section, has to be considered from the tenant's point of view rather than from that of the landlord. In *Woolworth & Co v Lambert*,[34] a tenant wished to remove the back wall of the shop in order to connect it to another shop leased from a different landlord. The landlord argued their entitlement to refuse consent to the alteration as its effect would be to reduce the value of their reversion and it could not therefore be an improvement. The Court of Appeal rejected this argument, holding that any alteration which increases

---

32 *Bickmore v Dimmer* [1903] 1 Ch 158.

33 *Duval (Respondent) v 11-13 Randolph Crescent Ltd (Appellant)* [2020] UKSC 18.

34 *Woolworth & Co v Lambert* [1937] Ch 37.

the value or usefulness of the premises from the *tenant's* point of view is an improvement, whatever its effect on the landlord's reversion. S19(2) therefore applied and, in the circumstances, the landlord had unreasonably withheld consent. The section does, however, include some protection for the landlord by providing that they are entitled to make consent conditional upon the tenant:

- Paying a reasonable sum by way of compensation for any diminution in the value of the reversion caused by the improvement, and;
- Undertaking to reinstate the premises at the end of the term.

The section does not apply to absolute covenants, only qualified.

6.9 Assignment and Sub-letting

An 'assignment' of a lease occurs when a tenant transfers their rights in the premises to another tenant for the remainder of the term of the lease. The original tenant no longer has any interest in the legal estate. This is distinguished from 'sub-letting' (or 'under-letting') which arises where a tenant retains their leasehold estate but lets the whole or part of the premises to another tenant. In such circumstances the sub-letting must be for a period less than the initial lease. Here the original tenant retains their interest in the legal estate. Assignment and sub-letting are collectively referred to as 'alienation'. An assignment must always be made by deed; however, the formalities for the creation of a sub-lease are exactly the same as for the creation of any other form of lease.

By way of example:

Assignment: Lease has 99 years remaining and is transferred to another for the remaining 99 years.

Sub-letting: Lease has 99 years remaining and is sub-let to another for 50 years.

6.9.1 Nature of Assignment and Sub-letting

Unless the lease contains a provision to the contrary, the tenant is free to dispose of their interest in the property in any way they choose. However, it is common for express covenants to be imposed on the tenant which prevent alienation altogether (an absolute covenant), or which require the tenant to obtain the landlord's consent before being allowed to assign or sublet (a qualified covenant).

A common absolute covenant may read:

> The tenant covenants that it will not assign, sub-let or part with possession.

A common qualified covenant may read:

> The tenant covenants that it will not assign, sub-let or part with possession without the consent of the landlord. Such consent will not be unreasonably withheld.

6.9.2 Unlawful Discrimination

In most circumstances it is unlawful to refuse to allow someone to occupy a property on the grounds of their sex, race, religion or disability (Equality Act 2010). However Schedule 5 Equality Act 2010 provides a number of exceptions, along with examples:

- A single woman owns a large house in London and lives on the top floor, although the bathroom and toilet facilities are on the first floor. The ground floor is unoccupied and she decides to take in a lodger, sharing the bathroom and toilet facilities. Various prospective tenants apply but she chooses only to let the ground floor to another woman. This would be permissible under this exception.
- A Jewish family owns a large house but only lives in part of it. They decide to let out an unoccupied floor but any new tenant will have to share kitchen and cooking facilities. The family choose only to let the unoccupied floor to practising Jews as they are concerned that otherwise their facilities for keeping their food kosher may be compromised. This would be permissible under this exception.[35]

6.9.3 Restriction on Charging for Consent

Parliament has intervened to prevent landlords charging for the granting of consent to alienation in certain circumstances in S144 Law of Property Act 1925. This section only applies to qualified covenants. The parties are however free to 'contract out' of the provision by inserting a contrary provision in the lease. Where the provision applies, no form of charging is permitted, although the landlord is still permitted to require the tenant to pay associated legal expenses.

6.9.4 Unreasonable Withholding of Consent for Assignment and Sub-letting

6.9.4.1 S19(1)(a) of the Landlord and Tenant Act 1927

Where a covenant requires the landlord's consent for alienation, S19(1) Landlord and Tenant Act 1927 provides that the landlord's consent shall not be unreasonably withheld.

The parties cannot 'contract out' of this requirement by including a contrary provision in the lease.

6.9.4.2 Landlord and Tenant Act 1988

Where a covenant prohibits alienation without a landlord's consent, it is important to the tenant that the landlord deals with the request for consent fairly and quickly. If the landlord fails to do so, the prospective assignee or subtenant is unlikely to wait around for things to be sorted out. In practical terms, the landlord's failure to act can deprive a tenant of their right to alienate, even where this right is contained in the lease. Tenants had very little power in these situations at common law so Parliament enacted the Landlord and

---

35 S773 Schedule 5, Equality Act 2010.

Tenant Act 1988 to provide protection. Where the tenant has served a written application for consent, S1(3) of this Act imposes the following duties on the landlord:

- To serve a notice on the tenant within a reasonable time setting out their decision about the granting or withholding of consent.
- To grant consent where it is reasonable to do so (and to only impose such conditions on that consent as are reasonable to impose).
- To set out the reasons for withholding consent in the notice where consent is withheld.

S1(6) places the onus on the landlord to prove that they have complied with these duties rather than on the tenant to prove that they have breached them. There is a powerful incentive for the landlord to comply, as a failure to do so would render them liable to the tenant in damages for breach of the statutory duty.

6.9.4.3 Reasonableness of Landlord's Withholding of Consent

The purpose of alienation covenants is to prevent the property being used in an undesirable way and/or by an undesirable tenant. The reasonableness of a landlord's decision to withhold consent will therefore be judged according to the extent to which it relates to these purposes. In order to be reasonable a withholding of consent must also be based on some aspect of the landlord and tenant relationship. The landlord has no right to withhold consent in order to achieve some 'collateral' advantage which is unconnected with the parties or the terms of the lease.

By way of example, in *Parker v Boggon*[36] an unreasonable withholding of consent was held to have occurred where this was due to the proposed assignee having diplomatic immunity from legal proceedings. In *Bates v Donaldson*[37] the withholding of consent in order to enable the landlord to obtain possession for their own use was also unreasonable. The landlord was also held to have unreasonably withheld consent in *Re Gibbs and Houlder Brothers and Co Ltd's Lease.*[38] In that case the proposed assignee had a tenancy of an adjoining property from the same landlord and planned to serve notice to quit this tenancy following the assignment. The landlord refused consent as this would leave them with a vacant property which would be difficult to let. Not surprisingly the court held that the landlord's refusal of consent was unreasonable. The reason for refusal had no reference either to the personality of the proposed assignee or to the subject matter of the lease.

Examples of reasonable withholdings of consent include *Ashworth Frazer Ltd v Gloucester City Council*[39] where the proposed assignee had already applied for planning permission to use the premises for recycling metal, indicating an intention to breach the user covenant in the lease. Equally, in *British Bakeries (Midlands) Ltd v Michael Tester & Co Ltd*[40] the landlord was held to have acted reasonably in withholding consent due to the incomplete and unreliable nature of the financial references provided by the proposed assignee. The withholding was also held to be reasonable in *Pimms v Tallow Chandlers Co*[41] where

36 *Parker v Boggon* [1947] KB 346.
37 *Bates v Donaldson* [1896] 2 QB 241.
38 *Re Gibbs and Houlder Brothers and Co Ltd's Lease* [1925] Ch 198.
39 *Ashworth Frazer Ltd v Gloucester City Council* [2002] 1 All ER 377.
40 *British Bakeries (Midlands) Ltd v Michael Tester & Co Ltd* [1986] 1 EGLR 64.
41 *Pimms v Tallow Chandlers Co* [1964] 2 QB 547.

the proposed assignee wanted to exploit the lease to obtain participation in the landlord's future development of the property.

Traditionally, the question of what amounts to a reasonable withholding of consent by the landlord has been a matter for the courts. In *Ashworth Frazer Ltd v Gloucester City Council*[42] the court held:

> the question whether the landlord's conduct was reasonable or unreasonable will be one of fact to be decided by the tribunal of fact.

Likewise, in *International Drilling Fluids Ltd v Louisville Investments (Uxbridge) Ltd*[43]:

> it is in each case a question of fact, depending upon all the circumstances, whether the landlord's consent to an assignment is being unreasonably withheld.

In *Hicks v 89 Holland Park (Management) Ltd*[44] the court held:

> What is or is not reasonable is in every case a question of fact and degree, to be assessed at the date when the relevant consent is sought – (...) with the reasonableness concept being given a broad common sense meaning (...) tested by asking whether '... a notional hypothetically reasonable person in ... the position of the defendant might have arrived at the conclusion under challenge (...)'.[45]

For an in-depth discussion on reasonableness of consent refusal, see *Davies-Gilbert v Goacher & Ors.*[46]

For commercial leases granted on or after 1 January 1996, S22 Landlord and Tenant (Covenants) Act 1995 provides that a withholding of consent to assign shall not be unreasonable where the reasons had been specified in the lease or some other prior agreement. It has become standard practice for commercial leases to include a list of circumstances in which consent to an assignment can be refused, and of conditions to which any consent may be subject. Typical stated reasons for refusing consent might include:

- Where the proposed assignee is not a public company quoted on the London Stock Exchange.
- Where the proposed assignee's pre-tax profits are less than three times the rent payable under the lease.
- Typical stated conditions to which consent may be subject might include:
- A requirement that the assignee must provide a rent deposit or guarantor.
- A requirement that the former tenant must enter into an authorised guarantee agreement.

---

42 *Ashworth Frazer Ltd v Gloucester City Council* [2001] 1 WLR 2180 at [4], per Lord Bingham.
43 *International Drilling Fluids Ltd v Louisville Investments (Uxbridge) Ltd* [1986] Ch 513 at 521, per Balcombe LJ.
44 *Hicks v 89 Holland Park (Management) Ltd* [2021] EWHC 930 (Comm).
45 Ibid., at [16](b), per HHJ Pelling QC.
46 *Davies-Gilbert v Goacher & Ors* [2022] EWHC 969 (Ch).

Finally, a device which can assist landlords in alienation cases is the use of a so-called '*Bocardo*' clause (named after the decision in *Bocardo SA v S & M Hotels Ltd*[47]). This is where the lease provides that the tenant must offer to surrender the tenancy as a precondition to any dealing, whether assignment or sub-letting. If the landlord does not approve of the identity of the proposed assignee, they can accept a surrender of the lease. Such a provision is not invalidated by S19(1) of the 1927 Act.

6.10 Enforceability of Covenants in Leases

6.10.1 Leases Granted Before 1 January 1996

The enforceability of leases granted before 1 January 1996 depends on the traditional rules relating to 'privity of contract' and 'privity of estate'. Privity of contract exists between the original parties to the lease and all covenants are therefore mutually enforceable between them, in theory, for the whole of the term of the lease. However, once one or both of the original parties has assigned their interest in the lease, the question of enforceability will be of more concern to the new landlord or tenant than to the original parties. Although there will be no privity of contract between them, there is nevertheless always said to be privity of estate between the parties for the time being to a lease. In these situations the covenants will be mutually enforceable as long as they touch and concern the land.[48] This means that they must affect the land itself rather than being merely personal covenants between the parties. All the normal covenants in a lease will be included within this requirement but a tenant's covenant to pay money to someone other than landlord[49] and a landlord's covenant to repair property not included within the lease[50] have been held to fall outside it.

6.10.2 Leases Granted on or After 1 January 1996

The Landlord and Tenant (Covenants) Act 1995 applies to leases commencing after 1 January 1996. Enforceability of covenants in these leases is no longer governed by the rules relating to privity of contract and privity of estate. Instead the general rule is that covenants are mutually enforceable between the landlord and tenant for the time being and the original or former parties to the lease generally cease to have any liability once they part with their interest in the property. In practice the situation is slightly more complicated than this. Former landlords are not automatically released from liability under the covenants but have to follow a notice procedure laid down by the Act. The Act also introduces the concept of the authorised guarantee agreement, where a tenant can be made to guarantee the performance of their assignee when the landlord requires this as a condition of granting consent to the assignment.

47 *Bocardo SA v S & M Hotels Ltd* [1980] 1 WLR 17.
48 *Spencer's Case* (1583) 5 Co Rep 16a.
49 *Mayho v Buckhurst* (1617) Cro Jac 438.
50 *Dewar v Goodman* [1909] AC 72.

6.11 Remedies for Breach of Covenant

Remedies are the mechanisms used by an injured party to enforce their legal rights, either through the courts, or in some other way. A variety of remedies are available, according to the nature of the covenant which has been breached.

6.11.1 Landlord's Remedies for Non-payment of Rent

6.11.1.1 Action for Recovery of Rent

The landlord can bring a court action against the tenant for rent arrears. Under S19 Limitation Act 1980, the action must be brought within 6 years from the date it fell due or will be statute barred.

6.11.1.1.1 Distress and Commercial Rent Arrears Recovery (CRAR)

The common law right of distress (an ancient remedy enabling landlords to seize goods where a tenant was in rent arrears) was abolished in 2014 by S71 Courts, Tribunals and Enforcement Act 2007.[51] For commercial landlords, a new procedure was introduced – the CRAR procedure. Established by the Tribunals, Courts and Enforcement Act 2007, CRAR applies exclusively to commercial properties with a written tenancy agreement, rent arrears must exceed a minimum threshold, and landlords must serve a Notice of Enforcement on the tenant, providing at least 7 days' notice before seizing goods.

6.11.1.1.2 Forfeiture

Forfeiture is the right of the landlord to terminate the lease following a breach of covenant by the tenant. It is sometimes called a proviso for re-entry. The right to forfeiture will generally only exist if the lease expressly provides for it.

For residential properties, S2 Protection from Eviction Act 1977 provides that the right of forfeiture can only be exercised by court proceedings. Further, S146 Law of Property Act 1925 requires the landlord to serve a notice on the tenant outlining the breach of covenant and providing the tenant with a reasonable period of time to remedy it.[52] Where possession is obtained by a landlord, tenants have 6 months under S138 County Courts Act 1984 to apply to the court for relief. In *Golding v Martin*,[53] a tenant with a long lease moved overseas, failed to pay service charges due and did not receive the notice, sent to the property in question. The landlord took possession of the property and the tenant sought relief from the forfeiture. The County Court held that the tenant was barred by statute, as way over 6 months had passed. The judge ended their judgment noting:

> The endnote to the final chapter in this cautionary tale must be that a non-resident and absentee leaseholder who provides no correspondence address other than that of the property itself must either (a) make proper arrangements for forwarding or

---

51 art. 2(1)(a) Tribunals, Courts and Enforcement Act 2007 (Commencement No. 11) Order 2014 SI 2014/768.

52 *Freeholders of 69 Marina, St Leonards on Sea v Oram* [2011] EWCA Civ 1258; [2012] H.L.R. 12.

53 *Golding v Martin* [2019] 3 W.L.R. 138.

diverting the mail addressed to the premises or (b) entrust the task of 'keeping an eye' on their property to persons who are actually committed to that task.

If, following a breach of covenant by the tenant, the landlord nevertheless elects to treat the lease as continuing, they are said to have waived their right to forfeiture. Waiver typically takes the form of a landlord demanding or accepting rent falling due after the date of the breach. In *Central Estates (Belgravia) v Wolgar*[54] this was held to have occurred where the rent was demanded due to a clerical error by the landlord's managing agents. Similarly, in *Segal Securities Ltd v Thoseby*[55] where the landlord accepted rent 'without prejudice to the landlord's right to forfeit', they were nevertheless held to have waived the right to forfeiture.

6.11.1.2 Landlord's Remedies for Breach of Other Covenants

6.11.1.2.1 Forfeiture

As discussed above, before a landlord can exercise their right to forfeiture for breach of a covenant (including other than for payment of rent), they must first serve a notice on the tenant under S146 Law of Property Act 1925 (a 'section 146 notice'). The notice must specify the breach complained of, require the breach to be remedied and, if desired, require the tenant to pay compensation. The purpose of the procedure is to give the tenant an opportunity to put things right, and hence to avoid the lease being forfeited. Once the notice has been served the landlord must allow the tenant a reasonable time to comply with it before exercising their right to forfeiture.

The tenant has a right, under S146, to apply for 'relief' against forfeiture at any time between the service of the notice and the landlord actually re-entering the property. The court has a wide discretion to grant relief and may, for example, order a stay of any forfeiture proceedings upon condition that the tenant remedies the breach within a specified period of time.

Parliament has provided additional protection for tenants where breaches of repairing covenants are alleged. Section 1 Leasehold Property (Repairs) Act 1938 applies to leases of at least 7 years with at least 3 years left to run. In these situations a S146 notice must also advise the tenant of their right to serve a counter-notice within 28 days. If the tenant does then serve a counter-notice, the landlord is prevented from exercising their right to forfeiture without the leave of the court. This will only be granted if the landlord can prove that one of the following statutory grounds applies:

- That the value of the reversion has already been substantially diminished, or;
- That the immediate remedying of the breach is required in order, either:
- to prevent such substantive diminution;
- to comply with statutory requirements;
- to protect the interest of an occupier other than the tenant;
- to avoid a much heavier repair cost in the future.

The purpose of the 1938 Act is to protect tenants from pressure from landlords to carry out non-essential repairs during the course of their lease. As the lease nears its end (in the

54 *Central Estates (Belgravia) v Wolgar* [1972] 1 QB 48.
55 *Segal Securities Ltd v Thoseby* [1963] 1 QB 887.

final 3 years) the landlord has a greater interest in the state of the property and the tenant loses this protection. Protection is also available under S147 of the 1925 Act where the section 146 notice relates only to internal decorative repairs. In these circumstances the tenant has an additional right to apply for relief and, if the court considers that the notice is unreasonable, it has the power to relieve the tenant from liability for these repairs entirely.

6.11.1.2.2 Damages

A landlord might choose to bring an action against the tenant in order to obtain an award of damages to compensate for the financial losses suffered. These would be assessed on ordinary contract law principles (see Chapter 2). Where the claim relates to the breach of a repairing covenant, S1 Leasehold Property (Repairs) Act 1938 applies in exactly the same way as it does to forfeiture. The landlord must therefore serve a S146 notice advising the tenant of their right to serve a counter-notice and, if necessary, seek leave of the court before they can commence proceedings for damages.

To protect tenants from excessive claims at the end of the lease in circumstances where the landlord might have plans for redevelopment rather than for repair, S18 Landlord and Tenant Act 1927 imposes a statutory ceiling on the amount of damages that can be awarded. It provides that damages shall never exceed the diminution in the value of the reversion caused by the breach and, in particular, that no damages shall be recoverable at the end of a term where the landlord intends to demolish or structurally alter the premises in such a way that the effect of the repairs would be negated.

6.11.1.2.3 Repairs Notice

In the absence of an express provision in the lease, the landlord has no right to enter the property to carry out repairs which the tenant has failed to undertake. However, leases will often include such a right, following service upon the tenant of a notice (described by as a 'repairs notice'). The landlord can then undertake the repairs and recover the costs incurred from the tenant in the courts. The case of *Jervis v Harris*[56] established that such costs are recoverable as a debt, rather than by an action for damages and the Leasehold Property (Repairs) Act 1938 does not therefore apply. The remedy is particularly appealing to landlords as it allows them to dispense with the need to serve a S146 notice and the possibility of having to obtain the leave of the court before commencing proceedings.

6.11.1.2.4 Specific Performance

Specific performance will rarely be a suitable remedy. Ordinarily, forfeiture or damages will be the most appropriate remedy, in part as specific performance places an obligation on the tenant to carry out the repairs. It is however available in rare, and appropriate circumstances. In *Rainbow Estates Ltd v Tokenhold Ltd*[57] the court ordered the specific performance of the tenant's covenant where a Grade II listed building was in serious disrepair and, unusually, the lease contained no forfeiture clause or clause entitling the landlord to undertake repairs under a repairs notice. An order for specific performance was therefore the only remedy available to bring about the necessary repairs.

---

56 *Jervis v Harris* [1996] 1 EGLR 78.

57 *Rainbow Estates Ltd v Tokenhold Ltd* [1998] 2 EGLR 34.

Following *Rainbow Estates*, the courts have reiterated the limited circumstances in which specific performance would be appropriate with regard to landlord and tenant. In *Blue Manchester Ltd v North West Ground Rents Ltd*,[58] the judge noted:

> It is well-established that specific performance is a discretionary remedy which will only be granted where it appears to the court in all the circumstances to be just and equitable. The court must always proceed with caution since it is a draconian remedy in the sense that failure to comply with an order for specific performance is a contempt of court.[59]

In *Airport Industrial GP Ltd v Heathrow Airport Ltd*[60] the court provided the following guidance as to when specific performance may be suitable:

1. the remedy should be made available where it is the appropriate remedy and, in particular, where damages are not an adequate remedy;
2. it will be relevant that the person with the benefit of the contract cannot enter upon the relevant land and carry out, or procure the carrying out of, the work;
3. in the case of an obligation to build contained in a lease, it will be relevant to consider whether the landlord with a right to forfeit the lease should be left to pursue that remedy, to recover possession of the premises and then to have the ability to carry out the building works;
4. the court's order should contain sufficient definition of what is to be done

6.11.2 Tenant's Remedies

6.11.2.1 Damages

Where a tenant suffers financial and/or other losses as a result of a landlord's breach of covenant, damages might be an appropriate remedy. Damages will be awarded according to the actual amount of the losses suffered by the tenant as a result of the landlord's breach of covenant. Where a landlord breaches a repairing covenant, a residential tenant will be entitled to the cost of carrying out the necessary repairs. In addition, damages will include the cost of restoring any internal decorations, the cost of alternative accommodation and compensation for living in unpleasant surroundings. However, where the tenant holds the lease as an investment, damages will be calculated on the basis of the diminution in value of their estate which has been caused by the landlord's failure to repair.

6.11.2.2 Specific Performance

Under S17 Landlord and Tenant Act 1985, the court has discretion to order the specific performance of a landlord's repairing covenant in a lease of a dwelling. The remedy is also available for business leases under the court's general equitable jurisdiction.[61]

---

58 *Blue Manchester Ltd v North West Ground Rents Ltd* [2019] EWHC 242 (TCC).

59 Ibid., 53.

60 *Airport Industrial GP Ltd v Heathrow Airport Ltd* [2015] EWHC 3753 (Ch).

61 *Jeune v Queens Cross Properties Ltd* [1974] Ch 97.

6.11.2.3 Self-help

Where a landlord is in breach of their repairing covenant, the tenant can give notice that they intend to do the repairs. If they do so, undertaking repairs that were the landlord's responsibility under the covenant, the tenant is entitled to deduct the reasonable costs of the repairs from future payments of rent.[62] If the landlord subsequently brings an action against the tenant for failure to pay the rent, the tenant can counterclaim for the repair costs which they have incurred.[63] This principle was applied by the court in *Loria v Hammer*[64] wherein Dr Loria, the tenant, undertook repair work to rectify dampness, inflow of water and dry and wet rot in their property following the landlord's (Mr Hammer's) failure to repair. The court held that following breach by the landlord:

> Dr Loria was justified in concluding that if the remedial steps necessary to restore the premises to good and substantial repair and condition were to be taken at an appropriate speed then the matter could not be left in the hands of Mr Hammer or Mr Kritzler but that she, with or without her fellow lessees, would have to make her own or their own arrangements.[65]

6.12 The Statutory Codes

We have thus far considered the various legal rules affecting the landlord and tenant relationship. In addition to these rules, there are also a number of major statutory codes that affect certain types of tenancies. Where these codes apply the legal rules have to be read in the context of the detailed statutory arrangements imposed by them. There are separate codes affecting residential, business and agricultural tenancies. They operate in different ways but they all provide tenants with security of tenure (the right to a new lease or to stay in possession of the premises at the end of the lease). In addition, some of them have also provided mechanisms for the control of rent, for succession by relatives, for the payment of compensation at the end of the lease, and for leasehold extension and enfranchisement. In the remainder of this chapter, we consider the operation of the relevant statutory codes for private sector residential tenancies and for business tenancies.

6.12.1 Private Sector Residential Tenancies

6.12.1.1 Introduction

Between 1915 and 1977 legislation was enacted which gave qualifying residential tenants in the private sector unprecedented levels of protection in terms of rent control, security of tenure and succession by relatives. From 1980 onwards a distinct change of policy emerged due to a perception that the existing legislation leaned too far in favour of tenants, and that

62 *Lee-Parker v Izzet* [1971] 1 WLR 1688.
63 *British Anzani (Felixstowe) Ltd v International Marine Management (UK) Ltd* [1980] QB 137.
64 *Loria v Hammer* [1989] 2 EGLR 249.
65 Ibid., at 260.

this had limited the availability of residential property being placed on the rental market by landlords. A number of reforms were introduced over time, which progressively eroded the tenants' rights in this area and the relevant legislation is now contained in the Rent Act 1977, the Housing Act 1988 and the Housing Act 1996. As a result of these Acts, the level of protection afforded to a residential tenant depends on the date on which their tenancy was created.

As introduced at Section 6.1.1.1, the Renters Rights Bill 2024 will affect private residential tenancies in a number of ways. As, at the time of drafting, this Bill is not yet in force, the following reflects the position prior to the Renters Rights Bill. However, at the close of this section is an overview of the proposals included in the Bill.

6.12.1.2 Tenancies Commencing Prior to 15 January 1989

Tenancies created prior to 1989 are still subject to the Rent Act 1977 and provide high levels of protection for tenants. Although of decreasing significance over the years, thousands of properties are still subject to Rent Act tenancies. They are called 'protected tenancies' or 'regulated tenancies'. Once the original agreement comes to an end (including those ending after 1989), a regulated tenancy becomes a 'statutory tenancy' as long as the tenant continues to live in the property. Regulated and statutory tenancies have the following characteristics:

- The landlord cannot evict the tenant unless they obtain a possession order from the courts, and the courts can grant an order only in certain circumstances.
- Succession rights: If the tenant dies their tenancy could pass to a spouse, civil partner or cohabiting partner.
- Either the landlord or the tenant can apply for a fair rent to be registered.
- If a rent is registered, it is the maximum the landlord can charge until it is reviewed or cancelled.
- If a rent is not registered, the landlord can only increase the rent in certain circumstances.[66]

6.12.1.3 Tenancies Commencing Between 15 January 1989 and 27 February 1997

Tenancies created during this period are regulated by the Housing Act 1988. Unless certain requirements were complied with these tenancies take effect as 'assured tenancies'. Assured tenancies have the following characteristics:

- Most assured tenancies are periodic tenancies, often operating on a rolling month-month basis without an end date.
- They therefore continue until either the tenant or landlord brings it to an end.
- Evictions can take place only through the landlord providing reasoning to the court. A possession order will only be granted by the court on certain statutory grounds.

66 See Communities and Local Government, Regulated Tenancies, available at: https://assets.publishing.service.gov.uk/media/5a74b61740f0b61df4777da1/138295.pdf.

- Rights in an assured tenancy can be lost if the property is no longer the tenant's main home.
- Rent could be increased in a number of ways, including via rent review clauses, agreement or a S13 notice. The basic principle under the 1988 legislation is that the rent payable should be the market rent, preferably one agreed between the parties.
- Succession rights: If the tenant dies, their tenancy could pass to a spouse, civil partner or cohabiting partner.

6.12.1.4 Assured Shorthold Tenancies

During the period under consideration (15 January 1989 to 27 February 1997) it was also possible to create an 'assured shorthold tenancy'. These differ from assured tenancies in two respects:

- The landlord is entitled to possession at the end of the contractual tenancy without having to prove any of the statutory grounds required to obtain possession of an assured tenancy. This, of course, is the major attraction of this type of tenancy from a landlord's point of view.
- The tenant has a limited right to apply to the rent assessment committee for the rent to be reduced. Where they do so, the committee will reduce the rent only if it is satisfied that the rent is too high by comparison with similar properties let on assured shorthold tenancies in the locality of the subject property. If there are no comparable properties it will take no action.

During the period under consideration a tenancy could only become an assured shorthold tenancy if:

- It was for a fixed term of 6 months or more, and;
- The landlord had served a notice in prescribed form before the commencement of the tenancy, warning the tenant about the nature of the tenancy and providing advice about the entitlement to apply for a rent reduction.

If a landlord failed to comply with these requirements (and many landlords got them wrong) an assured tenancy would be created inadvertently and the tenant would obtain security of tenure. If a validly created assured shorthold tenancy came to an end and a new tenancy of the same premises was then granted to the same tenant the new tenancy would also be an assured shorthold tenancy regardless of the fact that no notice had been served.

6.12.1.5 Tenancies Commencing After 27 February 1997

These tenancies are regulated by the Housing Act 1988 as amended by the Housing Act 1996. Changes were introduced by the 1996 Act to prevent assured tenancies from being created inadvertently instead of assured shortholds. From 27 February 1997 the two conditions for the creation of assured shorthold tenancies (fixed term of at least 6 months and prior service of notice) no longer apply.

Residential tenancies automatically became assured shorthold tenancies unless the landlord served notice before the tenancy to the effect that it will be an assured tenancy. All tenancies (including periodic tenancies and very short fixed terms) now come within the definition of assured shortholds. Note, however, that, as an order for possession of an assured shorthold tenancy cannot be made earlier than 6 months after the beginning of the tenancy, the 6 months minimum term still exists in practice if not in theory.

6.12.1.6 Changes to Residential Tenancy Law Under the Renters Rights Bill 2024

If the Bill remains in its current form, once in force it will abolish both fixed-term assured tenancies and assured shorthold tenancies, and prevent new ones being created. Instead, all new residential tenancies granted once the Bill is an Act will be periodic, running from month to month, as opposed to a fixed term. With regards existing tenancies, the fixed term stated within any assured or assured shorthold tenancies will be removed, and replaced with a periodic term, running from month to month.

'Awaab's Law', introduced at Section 7.6.2, will be extended under the Bill to include properties let under private tenancies and licences.

6.13 Leasehold Enfranchisement and Extension

Leasehold enfranchisement is a process which leaseholders can go through to either extend their lease or to buy a share of the freehold. There are two pieces of legislation which will impact leasehold extension and enfranchisement which, at time of writing, are not yet in force. The first is the Leasehold and Freehold Reform Act 2024, which received Royal Assent in May 2024 but it is largely not yet in force, and the second is the Leasehold and Commonhold Reform Bill. As such, the following will consider the existing law before introducing proposed changes.

6.13.1 Existing Law

The Leasehold Reform Act 1967, along with the Leasehold Reform, Housing and Urban Development Act 1993, allows residential tenants holding under a long lease and at a low rent either to purchase the freehold (enfranchisement) or to the grant of an extended lease for a period of 50 years (extension). To obtain the benefit of the Act, the tenant must have a lease which was originally granted for a term exceeding 21 years and be paying a rent of less than two-thirds of the property's rateable value. Houses under leasehold are governed by the Leasehold Reform Act 1967 and flats under the Leasehold Reform, Housing and Urban Development Act 1993.

The laws were passed to circumvent the problems caused to leaseholders where the original tenant had bought the property as an owner occupier, but with leasehold rather than a freehold title. Towards the end of the lease, a tenant could easily end up with little in the way of a saleable asset because of the diminishing nature of the leasehold estate and the reluctance of mortgage lenders to lend on such assets. A tenant can therefore use the Act to ensure their home continues to be a saleable asset.

The price for the freehold or extended term will be as agreed between the parties, or as determined by the Leasehold Valuation Tribunal in default of agreement. The basis of the valuation for the purchase of the freehold is that the leaseholder is morally entitled to the ownership of the building, while the freeholder has similar rights to the ownership of the land on which it stands. This provides individual tenants of flats with an entitlement to a 90-year extension of their leases. It also grants a right to the enfranchisement of the freehold by the tenants on a collective basis.

The Commonhold and Leasehold Reform Act 2002 is also in force, and was designed to address some of the same problems as the legislation considered here. Commonhold ownership, as an alternative to leasehold, was introduced in the 2002 Act, which allows each flat owner (unit owner) to do so as a freeholder under a structure to manage common areas. This form of ownership remains relatively uncommon, and so is not considered in detail in this chapter.

6.13.2 Proposed Law

6.13.2.1 Leasehold and Freehold Reform Act 2024

The Government describes the Act as providing homeowners with 'more rights, power and protections over their homes'.[67] It will do so by:

- Reducing the cost of, and simplifying the process for lease extensions
- Reducing the cost of, and simplifying the process for buying the freehold
- Increasing the standard lease extension term to 990 years (up from the 50 noted above)

6.13.2.2 Leasehold and Commonhold Reform Bill

This Bill, if passed, is likely to be much further reaching, introducing significant changes such as:

- Prohibiting new leasehold flats
- Ending forfeiture rights for freeholders for small debts
- Shifting focus to commonhold

6.14 Business Tenancies

The commercial leasehold market in the UK is a very large market, with a 2025 survey reporting that 94.9% of businesses lease their property, leaving only 5.1% owning.[68] Business tenancies are predominately regulated by Part II, Landlord and Tenant Act 1954 (as amended by the Regulatory Reform (Business Tenancies) (England and Wales) Order 2003). Under the Act, a business is defined as to include 'a trade, profession or employment and include any activity carried on by a body of persons, whether corporate or unincorporate'.[69]

67 See Department for Levelling Up, Housing and Communities, 24 May 2024, News Story, Leasehold reforms become law, gov.uk.

68 Dutton Gregory Solicitors, February 2025 Survey – 618,149 leaders, interviewed 24–25 February. Full data set available at https://www.duttongregory.co.uk/site/blog/commercial-news/commercial-property-market-statistics-uk (accessed 29 April 2025).

69 S23 (2) Landlord and Tenant Act 1954.

6.14.1 Tenancies to Which the 1954 Act Applies

The 1954 Act applies to tenancies where:

1. The premises are occupied by the tenant for the purposes of its business (as defined in S23 (2) cited above);
2. It is either a periodic tenancy or one for a fixed term with a duration of at least 6 months; and
3. It is not otherwise excluded from the protection of the Act[70]

The requirement for a tenancy to exist therefore excludes licences from the Act's protection. As noted above, business purposes are defined within the Act as including 'any trade, profession or vocation'. The courts have, however, interpreted this widely to include any activity which is carried on for payment. By way of example, in *Addiscombe Garden Estates Ltd v Crabbe*[71] a private tennis club, and in *Parkes v Westminster Roman Catholic Diocese Trustee*,[72] a charitable recreational club for children and the elderly, were each held to satisfy the definition of business purposes.

6.14.2 Security of Tenure

Security of tenure in this context is the right to remain in a property after the term of the lease expires. Business tenancies are afforded security of tenure under Part II Landlord and Tenant Act 1954, which means that, unless a landlord can show a permitted reason to remove them, a business tenant can remain in the premises after the expiry of their original lease.

6.14.2.1 Tenancies Not Protected by the Act

Apart from those tenancies which fail to satisfy the requirements above, there are others which are excluded from the Act's protection, either by the Act itself, or because of cases decided in the courts. These include:

- Fixed-term tenancies of 6 months or less
- Tenancies at will (agreement with consent of both parties which can be terminated at any time)
- 'Contracted out' tenancies

6.14.2.1.1 Contracted Out Tenancies

As a general rule, parties cannot 'contract out' of the Landlord and Tenant Act 1954, and any agreement which attempts to exclude or modify the tenant's security of tenure will be void (S38). The default position is that business tenants have security of tenure, however,

70 See 1954 Act, ss43 and 43ZA, exclude various tenancies from the scope of the Act, including tenancies of agricultural holdings, farm business tenancies, and mining leases.
71 *Addiscombe Garden Estates Ltd v Crabbe* [1958] 1 QB 513.
72 *Parkes v Westminster Roman Catholic Diocese Trustee* (1978) 36 P&CR 526.

section 38A provides a statutory mechanism which allows the parties to agree to contract out. To do so, they must comply with the following requirements:

- Before the tenancy is entered into the landlord must serve a notice (colloquially called a 'health warning') on the tenant advising them of the consequences of entering into the contracting out agreement.
- The tenant must then sign a declaration acknowledging service of the notice and confirming their understanding of, and consent to, the agreement. Where the notice was served less than 14 days before the commencement of the tenancy the declaration must be in the form of a statutory declaration (sworn in front of a solicitor).
- The lease document must contain a reference to the notice and the declaration.

6.14.2.2 The Nature of Continuation

If the contractual tenancy comes to an end by a method which is not prescribed by the Act (for example, by effluxion of time for a fixed-term tenancy or by a landlord serving a notice to quit in the case of a periodic tenancy) the tenancy simply continues. Continuation is, in principle, a continuation of the contractual term (rather than a new 'statutory tenancy') and hence the tenancy continues on substantially the same terms as the original tenancy.

6.14.2.3 Termination of Tenancies Protected by the Act

The Act provides that the only ways that the contractual tenancy (or the continuation tenancy, if it has already started) can come to an end are as follows:

a. Forfeiture
b. Surrender
c. Tenant's (but not landlord's) notice to quit a periodic tenancy
d. Tenant's notice to terminate under section 27. In the case of fixed-term tenancies a tenant can prevent the continuation tenancy from running by serving not less than 3 months notice to this effect on the landlord. They can therefore prevent the continuation tenancy from ever starting by serving the notice towards the end of the contractual term. Alternatively, once it has started, they can still serve notice in order to bring the continuation tenancy to an end.
e. Agreement for the grant of a new tenancy under section 28. If the parties agree to enter into a new tenancy the old tenancy will terminate on the date of commencement of the new tenancy.
f. Landlord's notice under S25 Landlord and Tenant Act 1954
g. Tenant's request under S26 Landlord and Tenant Act 1954

6.14.3 Reform

In November 2024, the Law Commission published the first of two consultation papers which focused on security of tenure in business tenancies.[73] The issue addressed was

73 Law Commission, Business Tenancies: The right to renew Consultation Paper 1: models of security of tenure (November 2024) Consultation Paper 266.

whether business premises should have security of tenure at all, and if so, whether the 'contracting out' model should be retained or substituted for a 'contracting-in' model. They describe the option as such:

> Under a contracting-out model, the default position is that tenants have security of tenure (in other words, the default position is that tenants have protected tenancies) unless the parties agree otherwise and go through a prescribed statutory process to contract out of security. Under a contracting-in model, that position is reversed so that the default position is that tenants do not have security of tenure (in other words, the default position is that tenants have unprotected tenancies) unless the parties agree otherwise and go through a statutory process to contract into the scheme.[74]

At time of writing, the consultation is taking place, seeking responses from 'all businesses – whether large or small, whether landlord, tenant or both, and whatever sector[75] in which they may operate – and their advisors, to take the time to let us know their views'.[76]

74 Ibid., 42.
75 In the commercial property field, a reference to a 'sector' commonly refers to the nature of the business undertaken at a property – in other words, the 'use' made of the premises. So, a business on a trading estate might be wholesale or retail units, or manufacturing units. Large out of town premises might be 'retail' (for example, supermarkets or large furniture stores), or warehousing (for example, the distribution hubs of supermarkets or online retailers), or related to the electricity supply (for example, solar or windfarms) (p. 6, fn 20 Law Commission consultation, Ibid.).
76 Ibid., 6.

7

Public Law

CONTENTS

7.1 Introduction

Public law governs both the relationship between the state and individuals or organisations, and relations between different branches of the state. Criminal law is an example of public law – the state determines which acts or omissions are considered criminal, and brings an action when persons or organisations are suspected of committing them. Another aspect of public law is called administrative law. Administrative law regulates the bodies that administer government policies. For ease, in this chapter, these bodies will be called 'public bodies', which includes government bodies, central government departments, local authorities and regulators. Administrative law is concerned with the composition of public bodies, their powers, duties, rights and responsibilities. Judicial review, where the court reviews decisions made by public bodies, is a very important aspect of administrative law.

The chapter begins with an overview of judicial review. The grounds for a judicial review are considered with reference to relevant case law and an outline of the judicial review procedure is provided. Certain selected areas of public law are then considered. These include the planning process and areas of state regulation that are of particular relevance to those operating within the built environment such as building regulations and environmental law. Health and Safety law and the regulations that relate to safety in the workplace and occupational health are also an important feature of public law, and these are also considered in this chapter.

7.2 Judicial Review

Judicial review is a court proceeding within which a judge reviews the legality of a decision or action by a public body. It is concerned with the *way* in which a decision or action has been taken by public bodies, as opposed to challenging the decision itself, focusing on the procedure followed rather than the conclusion reached. Judicial review can only be taken against a public body, as decisions against private bodies are dealt with by private law. The extent of the power held by a public body can be reviewed as well as the procedural correctness of a decision and the fairness of the process. In reviewing a decision or action by a public body, the court will consider the statute that grants the power alongside principles derived from previous cases to determine firstly, what the rule is and secondly, whether it has been correctly applied. The rules concerned can be contained in a wide variety of statutory provisions and in a range of areas, including housing, planning, environment, education and immigration.

Where a right of appeal exists, it should be exhausted first before resorting to judicial review. This was confirmed by Baroness Hale in *R (on the application of Cart) v The Upper Tribunal*:

> Where there was a right of appeal, of course, an aggrieved party would be expected to use that rather than judicial review. Judicial review was always a remedy of last resort[1]

There are currently more judicial reviews of immigration decisions than in any other area. A case of such which attracted significant media attention in the UK was *R (on the application of AAA and ors) v The Secretary of State for the Home Department (UNHCR intervening).*[2] It concerned the UK Government's immigration policy to relocate selected asylum seekers to Rwanda for processing and resettlement. A judicial review was filed by a coalition of immigration rights groups to block the first scheduled flights to Rwanda on the basis that it would be 'unlawful to remove anyone to Rwanda because there are "substantial grounds for believing that they would be at real risk" of treatment in Rwanda contrary to article 3 European Convention on Human Rights ("ECHR")'.[3] Another judicial review which received significant media attention was one brought by the UK Government challenging the scope of COVID-19 inquiry chair's powers under the Inquiries Act 2005 to require the disclosure of documents. Such documents included WhatsApp messages between former Prime Minister Boris Johnson and others, notebooks and diaries.[4]

In 2018, the Institute for Government reported that:

- 3,597 claims for judicial review were brought;
- Only 5% of those brought reached a full hearing; and

---

1 *R (on the application of Cart) v The Upper Tribunal* [2011] UKSC 28 Para 19.

2 *R (on the application of AAA and ors) v The Secretary of State for the Home Department (UNHCR intervening)* [2023] EWCA Civ 745.

3 Ibid., Para 460.

4 *R (on the application of the Cabinet Office) v The Chair of the UK COVID-19 Inquiry* [2023] EWHC 1702 (Admin).

- Of those which reached a full hearing, the court found for the public body in 50% of cases, and against in 40%. The remaining cases were ongoing (at time of statistics) or withdrawn.

7.2.1 Grounds for Judicial Review

In *CCSU v Minister for the Civil Service*[5] Lord Diplock identified three grounds for judicial review: illegality, irrationality and procedural impropriety. In addition, the Human Rights Act 1998 allows for judicial review to protect ECHR rights.[6]

A judicial review can be of the decision (substantive grounds) or of the procedure adopted (procedural grounds). Under substantive grounds, there are two main areas of challenge; that the decision-maker has gone outside the powers given or that the decision-maker has abused a discretionary power. Procedural grounds include certain rules of fairness, called 'natural justice', and requirements laid down in statute.

7.2.1.1 Substantive Grounds

7.2.1.1.1 Acting Outside Powers (Ultra Vires)

The term given to acts exceeding powers granted by statute is *ultra vires*, meaning literally outside powers. Any such act will be invalid. The doctrine cannot, however, be applied to the validity of an Act of Parliament. In *R v Richmond upon Thames Council ex parte McCarthy and Stone Ltd*[7] the local authority planning department had started to charge a £25 fee for informal consultations between developers and planning officers prior to planning applications made for new developments. There was no provision in the law for such a consultation. The House of Lords held that the fee was unlawful as the charge was not incidental to the council's planning functions. It is evident from this case that no charge can be levied by a public body on the public without clear statutory authority.

7.2.1.1.2 Abuse of Discretionary Powers

Statute often provides very broad discretion to a decision-making body. However, not all decisions made when exercising such discretion will be lawful. There are a series of grounds upon which exercise of discretion can be reviewed:

- Taking into account irrelevant considerations.
- Not taking into account relevant considerations.
- Using powers for improper purposes.
- Making an error of law.
- Delegating power without authorisation.
- Fettering discretion.
- Breaching financial duties.
- Acting unreasonably.

---

5 *CCSU v Minister for the Civil Service* [1985] AC 374, 410.

6 Sections 6 and 7.

7 *R v Richmond upon Thames Council ex parte McCarthy and Stone Ltd* [1992] 2 AC 48.

- Breaching the proportionality principle (in cases where rights under EU law or ECHR exist).
- Acting incompatibly with ECHR rights.
- Making a material error of fact.

One case may encompass a number of grounds, as was seen in *R v Home Secretary ex parte Venables and Thompson*.[8] In this case, the Home Secretary increased the tariff (the period before release from prison will be considered) for two prisoners (Venables and Thompson) from 10 to 15 years. The Home Secretary stated that the young offenders would be dealt with in the same way as adult offenders. The House of Lords held that there had been an *error of law*:

> His legal premise was wrong: the two sentences are different. A sentence of detention during Her Majesty's pleasure requires the Home Secretary to decide from time to time.......whether detention is still justified. The Home Secretary misunderstood his duty. This misdirection by itself renders his decision unlawful.

They also held that *irrelevant considerations* had been taken into account in the form of public petitions to increase the tariff and that the Home Secretary had failed to take into account *relevant matters* (in this case the progress and development of Venables and Thompson whilst in prison).

The *fettering of discretion* refers to an over-rigid adherence to policy. It does not mean that a public body cannot adopt a policy and apply it in most circumstances, but the opportunity for the policy not to be applied must be available. For example, an authority could not adopt a rule that certain applications will always be refused. Policies cannot be treated as binding rules. In *British Oxygen Company v Board of Trade*,[9] there was a scheme in operation by the Board of Trade, which allowed for discretionary grants to be made. The Board introduced a rule that no grants were payable for items costing less than £25. British Oxygen spent more than £4 million on gas cylinders, but each one only cost £20. The House of Lords held that the Board was entitled to make the £25 rule, but it had to take into account individual arguments with regard to its discretion.

The standard of *unreasonableness* required for a decision to be set aside owing to public body acting unreasonably is a very high one. The test was laid down in the case of *Associated Provincial Picture Houses Ltd v Wednesbury Corporation*.[10] Lord Greene, MR, in setting out the test, said that for a decision to be set aside as unreasonable, the decision had to be 'so unreasonable that no reasonable authority could ever have come to it'. Unreasonableness has also been referred to as irrationality.[11] The standard has been toned down, and in *R v Chief Constable of Sussex ex parte International Trader's Ferry Ltd*,[12] Lord Cooke expressed it as the decision taken must be 'one which a reasonable authority could reach'.

---

8 *R v Home Secretary ex parte Venables and Thompson* [1998] AC 407.
9 *British Oxygen Company v Board of Trade* [1971] AC 610.
10 *Associated Provincial Picture Houses Ltd v Wednesbury Corporation* [1948] 1 KB 223.
11 Lord Diplock in *CCSU v Minister for Civil Service* [1985] AC 374, 410.
12 *R v Chief Constable of Sussex ex parte International Trader's Ferry Ltd* [1999] 2 AC 418.

7.2.1.2 Procedural Grounds

Procedural requirements include those laid down in statute and certain rules of fairness (termed 'natural justice'), which must be adhered to in the decision-making of public bodies. Decisions can be challenged if the correct procedure has not been followed or if they have been unfairly reached. *Ridge v Baldwin*[13] examples of statutory procedure not being followed. The Chief Constable of Brighton Police was dismissed following an acquittal on charges of conspiracy. The Police Act 1919 set out the procedure for dismissal of a Chief Constable, and this included a formal inquiry into the charges brought, which had not taken place. The Committee that dismissed the Chief Constable argued that the dismissal had taken place under other powers (The Municipal Corporations Act 1882), which rendered the inquiry unnecessary. The House of Lords held that the 1919 Act applied and, as the procedure of an inquiry had not been followed, the decision was void.

The rules of natural justice derive from the common law and have been built up by the courts over centuries to determine procedural fairness in the courts. Alongside the common law rules, Article 6 (1) ECHR guarantees the right to a fair hearing, as incorporated in the Human Rights Act 1998. The rules of natural justice are more commonly referred to as *fairness*. The duty to act fairly applies to the *procedure* and not to the substantive *decision*. There are two main components to fairness; the rule against bias and the right to a fair hearing. When a decision is found to have been reached unfairly, it is void.

7.2.1.2.1 The Rule Against Bias

The rule derives from common law and is now codified in Article 6 (1) ECHR and the Human Rights Act 1998, requiring an 'independent and impartial tribunal'. It is not necessary for an individual to prove that bias has occurred, instead they can show a *real possibility* of bias. Decision-makers must also be seen to be unbiased. In the words of Lord Hewart in *R v Sussex Justices ex parte McCarthy*,[14] 'justice should not only be done but should manifestly and undoubtedly be seen to be done'. It is, therefore, not just a question of whether the decision-maker has an interest in the matter of the decision, but also of them not coming to the decision with an open mind. An example of the rule against bias is in the case of *R v Secretary of State for the Environment ex parte Kirkstall Valley Campaign Ltd*,[15] where the planning authority itself had private interests in the relevant planning permission.

7.2.1.2.2 The Right to a Fair Hearing

There is no prescriptive content to this right in part owing to the word 'fair'. As Lord Mustill acknowledged in the case of *R v Secretary of State for the Home Department ex parte Doody*,[16] standards of fairness change over time and what fairness demands will differ from case to case. Fairness will often require that an individual can make representations either before or after the decision is made and that they are aware of the case to answer. Although there is no overarching right to an oral hearing or to know the evidence against oneself, where disciplinary procedures result in the loss of employment or of a benefit, there is a

13 *Ridge v Baldwin* [1964] AC 40 HL.

14 *R v Sussex Justices ex parte McCarthy*, [1924] 1 KB 256.

15 *R v Secretary of State for the Environment ex parte Kirkstall Valley Campaign Ltd* [1996] 3 All ER 304.

16 *R v Secretary of State for the Home Department ex parte Doody* [1994] 1 AC 531, 557.

right to a decision before an unbiased tribunal, the right to notice and the right to be heard. There is no universal right to representation, regardless of the proceedings in question.

Fairness often requires that reasons be given for a decision, but this is decided on a case by case basis. As a general rule, if the decision significantly impacts person or property, it is more likely that reasons will be required. If reasons are required, they must be proper and adequate, be understandable and deal with the relevant points.[17] The leading case on the giving of reasons is *Doody*,[18] wherein Doody and three other prisoners were serving mandatory life sentences for murder. The Home Secretary had consulted with the trial judge and set the penal element (the period before parole can be considered). Judicial review was sought on the ground that the Home Secretary had followed an unfair procedure. One of the main arguments was that fairness required the Home Secretary to give reasons when he decided to impose a different penal element to that recommended by the judiciary. Lord Mustill, in this case, posed a simple question 'Is the refusal to give reasons fair?' He concluded in the circumstances of this case that it was.

7.2.1.2.3 Legitimate Expectations

Grounds for judicial review can also arise from the legitimate expectations of a party. Legitimate expectations are an aspect of legal certainty, first articulated by Lord Denning and recognised in English law from the 1970s.[19] Legitimate expectations can arise in a number of situations:

- An indication has been given that a certain procedure will apply (for example, an oral hearing).
- There is pre-existing policy or guidelines upon which an individual or group relies.
- There is consistency of practice, which is relied upon.

In the case of *Attorney General of Hong Kong v Ng Yuen Shiu*,[20] Ng Yuen Shiu had entered Hong Kong illegally from Macau. Following a change in immigration policy, it was announced that 'all illegal immigrants from China would be liable to be repatriated'.[21] When asked about those from Macau, the office of the Secretary for Security stated 'Those illegal immigrants from Macau will be treated in accordance with procedures for illegal immigrants from anywhere other than China. They will be interviewed in due course. No guarantee can be given that you may not subsequently be removed. Each case will be treated on its merits'.[22] Ng Yuen Shiu reported to an immigration officer, was detained, and a removal order was made against him. He appealed to an immigration tribunal, which dismissed his appeal without a hearing. Ng Yuen Shiu applied for judicial review on the basis of a legitimate expectation, derived from the statement given by the office of the Secretary for Security that each case would be considered on its own merits. The Privy Council held:

---

17 *Re Poyser and Mills' Arbitration* [1964] QB 467.
18 At no. 12.
19 *R v Liverpool Corporation ex parte Liverpool Taxi Fleet Operators Association* [1972] 2 QB 299.
20 *Attorney General of Hong Kong v Ng Yuen Shiu* [1983] 2 All ER 346.
21 Para 349.
22 Ibid.

> when a public authority has promised to follow a certain procedure, it is in the interest of good administration that it should act fairly and should implement its promise, so long as implementation does not interfere with its statutory duty. The principle is also justified by the further consideration that, when the promise was made, the authority must have considered that it would be assisted in discharging its duty fairly by any representations from interested parties and as a general rule that is correct.[23]

A fair inquiry was to be held, during which the respondent was to be given an opportunity to make such representations as they saw fit as to why they should not be removed from Hong Kong.[24]

Re Liverpool Taxi Owners' Association[25] concerned an increase in the number of taxicab licences, a policy which the Liverpool Taxi Owner's Association were against. An undertaking had been made by the licensing authority that interested parties would be fully consulted before any decision was taken on increases. The increase, and eventual removal of the limit in licences, took place without consulting the Taxi Owners Association. The court held:

> The corporation in considering applications for hackney carriage licences under the 1847 Act were under a duty, in exercising that administrative function, to act fairly; the court was concerned to see that the policy adopted by the corporation with regard to licences was adopted after due and fair regard to all the conflicting interests, for even where the corporation's function was administrative the court would not hesitate to intervene if it was necessary to secure fairness. The duty to act fairly meant that the corporation should be ready to hear persons or bodies whose interests were affected which included the association.

The Court of Appeal held that no action should be taken with regard to licences issued without first hearing representations made by or on behalf of any interested parties.

7.2.2 Procedure for Judicial Review

The Civil Procedure Rules 1998 (CPR) allow single judges of the High Court to decide judicial review cases, and S15 Tribunals Courts and Enforcement Act 2007 allows the Upper Tribunal jurisdiction to grant relief in certain classes of judicial review case. The specified classes are to be determined by directions of the Lord Chief Justice (or their nominee) with agreement of the Lord Chancellor. The full procedure for judicial review (including pre-action protocols) can be found in the Administrative Court's Notes of Guidance on Applying for judicial review.[26]

---

23 Ibid., 352.
24 Ibid., 352.
25 *Re Liverpool Taxi Owners' Association* [1972] 2 All ER 589.
26 http://www.hmcourts-service.gov.uk/cms/1220.htm

7.2.2.1 Time Limits

Applications for judicial review must be brought promptly, and the civil procedure rules provides that this must be within 3 months of the decision unless a shorter time period is specified in statute.

7.2.2.2 Permission

There is no automatic right to judicial review and permission (referred to as *leave*) must be sought. This is a procedural hurdle. To obtain permission, an application has to be served on the defendant and anyone else who the claimant considers to be an interested party. It is necessary to present an arguable case to gain permission. A decision to refuse permission can be subject to reconsideration on the request of the claimant, and there is a right of appeal to the Court of Appeal. Permission will not be granted unless the applicant has *sufficient interest* in the matter to which the application relates. This is also referred to as *standing* or *locus standi.*

7.2.2.2.1 Standing

The requirement for a claimant to demonstrate sufficient interest in the matter is designed to filter out frivolous and unauthentic applications. The personal rights and interests of an individual have to be affected or the individual has to be concerned with official decisions that affect the interests of society as a whole. Alternatively, the applicant can be an interest or pressure group whose members' rights and interests are affected or those of society at large.

The original test for sufficient interest was laid down in the case of *R v Inland Revenue Commissioners ex parte National Federation of Self-Employed and Small Businesses Ltd.*[27] The House of Lords set out two stages:

1. Leave to apply, which Lord Scarman said 'prevents abuse by busybodies, cranks and other mischief makers'.
2. When the merits of the case are known, then the original decision to grant leave can be reviewed.

   Individual Standing: Students of Scientology, in a challenge to the Home Office's refusal to allow them to remain in the country, were found to have sufficient interest and granted leave.[28] A gypsy seeking direction to the local authority to provide an adequate site was also held to have standing.[29] In the case of *Gillick v West Norfolk and Wisbech Area Health Authority,*[30] a parent sought to challenge the health authority's policy on contraception and was granted standing. However, in the case of *Holmes v Checkland,*[31] an anti-smoker was found not to have standing to challenge the BBC broadcast of a snooker contest sponsored by a tobacco company as they had no more interest in the matter than any other member of the public.

---

27 *R v Inland Revenue Commissioners ex parte National Federation of Self-Employed and Small Businesses Ltd* [1982] AC 617.

28 *Schmidt v Secretary of State for the Home Department* [1969] 2 Ch 149.

29 *R v Secretary of State for Environment ex parte Ward* [1994] 1 WLR 834.

30 *Gillick v West Norfolk and Wisbech Area Health Authority,* [1986] AC 112.

31 *Holmes v Checkland* [1987] TLR, 15 April.

Pressure and Interest Groups: A group's *own* interests can be affected as in the case of the Liverpool taxi owners[32] and the Royal College of Nursing, in a challenge to a circular on the role of nurses in abortion.[33] In these cases, individual members would also have had sufficient interest in the matter. The *public* interest can also be at stake. In the Inland Revenue[34] case, those engaged in casual labour for newspapers had provided false names to avoid income tax. The Inland Revenue Commission had declared an amnesty, where if details were supplied for the past 2 years, they would not pursue tax due for previous years. The National Federation of Self-employed and Small Businesses (a tax-payers' association) sought to challenge the agreement. The House of Lords held that the National Federation did not have sufficient interest to pursue the case, although their members would have had standing as individual taxpayers.

The courts have, on occasions, found that public interest groups do have sufficient interest in the matter at stake and on others that they do not. For example, in the case of *R v Secretary of State for the Environment ex parte Rose Theatre Trust Co Ltd*,[35] a company that was specifically incorporated to save the historic Globe Theatre site was found not to have standing. The same judge in the case of *R v Poole BC ex parte BeeBee*[36] found that the WWF and the British Herpetological Society did have sufficient interest to challenge the grant of planning permission by the Borough Council to itself for the development of protected heathland. The difference appears to be that, in the latter case one of the pressure groups in question had a financial interest in the matter. The decision whether or not to grant standing to an interest group will depend on the individual circumstances of the case. However, generally speaking, reputable pressure groups of long-standing and with a wide membership are more likely to be seen as having sufficient interest. In the case of *R v Secretary of State for Environment ex parte Greenpeace Ltd (No. 2)*,[37] Greenpeace brought a challenge against the siting of a nuclear reprocessing plant at Sellafield. They were found to have standing, although they were unsuccessful in their challenge. A significant factor in the decision was the strength of Greenpeace's support in the UK.

7.2.3 Remedies

In actions for judicial review, remedies are awarded at the discretion of the court. Even if a challenge is successful, a remedy is not automatic, and the court can refuse to give a remedy for a variety of reasons. Examples include delay in commencing proceedings, unreasonable behaviour of the claimant or if the grant of a remedy is contrary to the public interest.

---

32 At no. 15.
33 *Royal College of Nursing v DHSS* [1981] AC 800.
34 At no. 20.
35 *R v Secretary of State for the Environment ex parte Rose Theatre Trust Co Ltd* [1990] 2 WLR 186.
36 *R v Poole BC ex parte BeeBee* [1991] 2 PLR 27.
37 *R v Secretary of State for Environment ex parte Greenpeace Ltd (No. 2)* [1994] 4 All ER 352.

7.2.3.1 Prerogative Remedies

Example prerogative remedies include:

- A quashing order (formerly known as *certiorari*) which quashes a decision. If part of the decision is good, then an order can be granted to quash only the offending section.
- A prohibiting order (previously prohibition), which is similar to a quashing order but affects future action. It prevents a body from making a decision which would be capable of being quashed.
- A mandatory order (which used to be referred to as *mandamus*) which compels action. It can be used against ministers and departmental officials and prevents unlawful failure to act. This type of order is often used in conjunction with a quashing order. Failure to abide by any of the prerogative orders amounts to contempt of court.

7.2.3.2 Declaration

This is not a legal remedy, but a statement of the positions of the parties. As with a mandatory order, it can be used to encourage government ministers to take a particular action. Although there are no legal consequences, public bodies usually respond to a declaration of the court and modify any deficiencies in their decision.

7.2.3.3 Injunction

An injunction can be of an interim or a permanent nature and can be positive or negative. They can be used against the Crown or a government minister, and non-compliance can amount to contempt of court. Injunctions are rarely utilised because the end result can normally be achieved by a quashing order or a mandatory order. An injunction can, however, be useful as an interim remedy whilst waiting for another order.

7.2.3.4 Damages

Damages are rarely granted in judicial review actions and are only recoverable if they would have been available through a private law action.

7.3 Building Regulations

Building Regulations are secondary legislation which set standards for constructing and amending buildings. Their purpose is to ensure buildings are safely constructed and not a danger to the health and safety of occupants. A national system of building control (except in inner London) has existed since 1965 and was radically revised by the Building Regulations 1985. Building regulations are made under the Building Act 1984, and the current regulations are the Building Regulations 2010 (SI 2010/2214), which apply in England and Wales to 'building work'. They include the inner London area which was previously subject to the London Building Acts 1930–78. A separate system of building control applies in Scotland and Northern Ireland. The term 'building work' includes 'building new buildings, making buildings bigger, altering buildings and changing what they are used for. It also covers installing a "controlled service" or a "controlled fitting". A replacement window is an example of a controlled fitting. A boiler is an example of a controlled service. 'Renovation of thermal elements' is also building work'.[38]

7.3.1 Content of Regulations

Building Regulations promote:

- Standards for most aspects of a building's construction, including its structure, fire safety, sound insulation, drainage, ventilation and electrical safety;
- Energy efficiency in buildings; and
- The needs of all people, including those with disabilities, in accessing and moving around buildings. They set standards for buildings to be accessible and hazard-free wherever possible.[39]

The general performance requirements are set out in Parts A–P of Schedule 1 and each Part is supported by an approved document that contains non-binding guidance on how to comply. Although use of the approved documents is not mandatory, the documents can be relied upon in legal proceedings where breach of the Regulations is alleged.

Schedule one sets out the requirements in relation to design and construction of buildings:

Part A – Structural safety
Part B – Fire safety
Part C – Site preparation and resistance to contaminants and moisture
Part D – Toxic substances
Part E – Resistance to the passage of sound
Part F – Ventilation
Part G – Sanitation, hot water safety and water efficiency
Part H – Drainage and waste disposal
Part J – Combustion appliances and fuel storage systems
Part K – Protection from falling, collision and impact
Part L – Conservation of fuel and power
Part M – Access to and use of buildings
Part N – Glazing safety
Part P – Electrical safety
Part Q – Security, and
Part R – Communications infrastructure

There is a duty on persons undertaking work that falls within the scope of Building Regulations to submit plans, together with specifications and particulars. They apply to the initial construction of a building, extensions and any material alteration or change of use. Temporary buildings, those not open to the public and agricultural buildings are exempt.

---

38 HM Government, Manual to the Building Regulations: A code of practice for use in England.
39 LexisPSL Construction Overview.

7.3.2 Building Control Process

The building control process is the approval of certain aspects of building work by a building inspector. It may be checked by:

- Building control body (local authority or an approved inspector) or
- 'Competent person' (where work is carried out by someone who works under a government approved scheme)

7.3.2.1 Building Control Body

7.3.2.1.1 Local Authority Building Control

If building work is intended which needs to be checked by a building control body, there are two routes:

1. Deposit full plans (Regulation 14) or
2. Submit a building notice (Regulation 13).

Only in exceptional circumstances (Regulation 12(8)) can work start without either full plans deposited or a building notice submitted (Regulation 12).

Full Plans: Full plans involve submitting architectural drawings, specifications and other detailed documents. Building work which requires full plans to be submitted includes work on commercial buildings, flats above shops and building work taking place near or which will cross public sewers. Where full plans are needed (Regulation 12, (3), (4) and (5)) the local authority must pass or reject the plan within 5 weeks (Regulation 14A (6)), or 2 months if an extension has been agreed with the applicant in writing (S16 Building Act 1984). Plans may be rejected, with reasons, where the work would contravene the Building Regulations or the plans are defective.

Building Notice: Building notices are most appropriate where the work to be carried out is straightforward, often where drawings are not required. Regulation 13 contains the information needed in the application, and building work can start on the third day after the notice is submitted. Under Regulation 13 (5), the notice is invalid where work has not started within 3 years of the notice being submitted. The local authority is not required to pass or reject a building notice, however, if the work contravenes the Building Regulations, they can require it to be removed or altered as appropriate.

Following Commencement of Work: The local authority must be given notice when work reaches certain prescribed stages, allowing them time to inspect as required. If, during the work or within a year of completion, the local authority deems it to contravene the Building Regulations, they may serve notice under S36 Building Act 1984 requiring the work to be altered or removed within 28 days. Under S37 Building Act 1984, where a disagreement as to compliance occurs, the local authority can be given notice that an independent expert is to be appointed, and the deadline extended to 70 days. If the local authority does not agree with a contrary independent report, an appeal may be made to the Magistrates' Court under S40 Building Act 1985.

7.3.2.1.2 Approved Inspector Building Control

Approved inspectors are companies or individuals that are licensed through CICAIR Ltd (Construction Industry Council Approved Inspectors) under the Building Act 1984.

Approved inspectors must be financially and professionally independent of the work they inspect, with the exception of minor works (as defined in Regulation 9(5) Approved Inspectors Regulations).

An initial notice must be provided to the local authority, containing the following (Schedule 1, Approved Inspectors Regulations)

- Description of the work
- Connection of any drainage
- Where a new building or extension is proposed
  - Site plan showing boundaries and location
  - Statement confirming consultation with sewerage undertaker where necessary

The local authority has 5 days to consider the initial notice. If it is not rejected within 5 days of receipt, it is deemed to have been accepted. When the work is complete, the inspector must provide the local authority with a final certificate providing evidence that the work complies with the Building Regulations. The local authority has 10 days to reject the final certificate, otherwise it is deemed to have been accepted after this time has passed.

7.3.2.2 Competent Person Schemes

Building Regulations do not need to be applied for where work is to be carried out by a tradesperson working under a 'competent person scheme'. Tradespersons recognised by the scheme are able to self-certify, once work is complete, that it complies with Building Regulations, and where necessary, inform the local authority of the work completed and a certificate of compliance is issued. Schedule 3 Building Regulations contains a table of self-certification schemes, which includes:

- Installation of heat-producing gas appliances;
- Installation of hot water or heating systems;
- Installation of air conditioning systems;
- Installation, as a replacement, of a window, rooflight, roof window or door in an existing dwelling or building other than a dwelling; and
- Insertion of insulating material into the cavity walls of an existing building.

7.4 The Planning System

The national planning system in England operates primarily under a combination of local and national policies which dictate what can be built and where. Government planning policies are contained in the National Planning Policy Framework, with which local plans (prepared by local planning authorities), and neighbourhood plans (prepared by parish or town councils or local groups) must comply. Planning law is contained in a series of key statutes supplemented by extensive central guidance (in the form of planning policy statements); however, there is a very limited role for the courts in planning issues. The only criminal offences arise from non-compliance with a notice. There is no third-party right of appeal, so the only route for someone, other than the applicant, to challenge a determination of planning permission is by judicial review if the decision-making process has not been correctly followed. Governmental and statutory roles are relatively minimal, with the majority of planning decisions made by the local planning authority (LPA).

The key statutes are:

- Levelling-up and Regeneration Act 2023
- Town and Country Planning Act (TCPA) 1990
- Planning and Compensation Act 1991
- Planning and Compulsory Purchase Act (PCPA) 2004
- Planning Act 2008
- Localism Act 2011

7.4.1 When Is Permission Needed?

7.4.1.1 Development

The law places an obligation on a landowner to obtain planning permission before certain work takes place. This is different, and if needed, in addition to the Building Regulations discussed above. S57 (1) Town and Country Planning Act 1990 (TCPA) states 'Planning permission is required for the carrying out of any development of land'. The definition of 'development' is broad,[40] and includes:

- building operations (e.g., structural alterations, construction, rebuilding, most demolition);
- material changes of use of land and buildings;
- engineering operations (e.g., groundworks);
- mining operations;
- other operations normally undertaken by a person carrying on a business as a builder; and
- subdivision of a building (including any part it) used as a dwellinghouse for use as two or more separate dwelling houses.

7.4.1.1.1 Building Operations

Building operations are defined in S55 TCPA as including:

a. demolition of buildings;
b. rebuilding;
c. structural alterations of or additions to buildings; and
d. other operations normally undertaken by a person carrying on business as a builder.

It encompasses 'any activity that alters the physical or the functional characteristics of land or buildings'.[41]

40 S55(1) Town and Country Planning Act 1990.
41 A. Ransome, 'What is Operational Development in Planning?' ADP, March 2022.

7.4.1.1.2 Material Change of Use

The Town and Country Planning (Use Classes) Order 1987, as amended, groups common uses of land and buildings into classes for planning purposes. These groups include:

Part B (Schedule 1)
Class B2 – General Industrial
Class B8 – Storage and distribution
Part C (Schedule 1)
Class C1 – Hotels
Class C2 – Residential institutions
Class C2A – Secure residential institutions
Class C3 – Dwelling houses
Class C4 – Small Houses in multiple occupation
Part A (Schedule 2) Commercial, Business and Service
Class E – Commercial, Business and Service
Part B (Schedule 2) Local Community and Learning
Class F.1 Learning and non-residential institutions
Class F.2 Local community

For work to be classified as 'a material change of use' to an existing structure, there must be a substantial physical impact on the land which is relevant to town and country planning. There is no statutory definition of material change of use; however, it is linked to the significance of a change and the resulting impact on the use of land and buildings,[42] and intensification of use may amount to a material change.[43] Whether a material change of use has taken place is a matter of fact and degree which is determined on each individual case.

7.4.1.1.3 Exempted Activities

A list of activities that do not constitute development is provided in TCPA 1990.[44] Amongst these are activities that fall in the category of 'a change of use within the same class of the *Use Classes Order*'.[45] These are uses that have a similar land use impact. For example, a change from one type of office use to another type of office use or from one type of shop use to another shop use will not attract the need for planning permission.

7.4.1.1.4 Permitted Development

Development can be permitted under statute, in which case no express consent is required from the LPA, and planning permission is deemed to be automatically granted. There are 33 classes of permitted development listed in the General Permitted Development Order.[46] These cover minor developments, developments carried out by public services and

---

42 Ministry of Housing, Communities and Local Government, Ministry of Housing, Communities & Local Government (2018–2021) and Department for Levelling Up, Housing and Communities 'When is permission required?' Published 6 March 2014 Last updated 26 July 2023.
43 *Brooks and Burton v DOE* [1977] 1 WLR 1094.
44 S55 (2) (a)-(g)Town and Country Planning Act 1990.
45 Use Classes Order 1987 SI 1987/764.
46 TCPA General Permitted Development Order 1995 SI 1995/418.

favoured activities (agriculture and forestry). Development consent may still be needed if such projects exceed certain thresholds and the right to development can be withdrawn, for example, if an environmental impact assessment is required. Other developments are permitted in Special Development Orders, Local Development Orders, Enterprise Zones and Simplified Planning Zones.

7.4.2 Application for Planning Permission

The majority of developments require planning permission from the LPA. The LPA decides a planning application using relevant policies contained in its local plan, and, if it exists, its neighbourhood plan. They consult with a range of public bodies and any representations made to the authority will be *material considerations.* Whether a particular consideration is material to a planning application will depend on the circumstances of the case. It is for the LPA to decide in the first instance and the courts in case of a dispute. The courts have generally ruled that purely private interests (such as neighbouring property values) are not material considerations.[47] All applications must be publicised. Unless the parties agree to an extension, the planning authority has 8 weeks in which to come to a decision. The application may be refused, granted or granted subject to conditions. Reasons must be provided. If permission is granted, the development that is authorised must be started within 5 years of obtaining consent. Applicants for substantial projects must now consider the environmental aspects and whether or not the application is subject to an *Environmental Impact Assessment.* Major infrastructure projects are subject to the provisions of the Planning Act 2008. Nearly all applications are decided by planning officers, but the Secretary of State has unfettered power to call in any planning application.[48] On the infrequent occasions when an application is called in for determination by the Secretary of State, there is almost always a public inquiry.

7.4.2.1 Local Authority Development Plans

Planning determinations are led by the development plan, which includes local and neighbourhood plans in force and any spatial development strategies produced by combined authorities or elected Mayors.

7.4.2.2 Material Considerations

There is no statutory definition or guidance as to what constitutes a material consideration. Planning policy statements and representations by consultees and third parties are certainly material considerations as are a range of other matters determined by case law. For example, environmental issues can be material considerations.[49]

47 House of Commons, Overview of the planning system (England), August 2023.

48 S77 Town and Country Planning Act 1990.

49 See, for example, *West Coast Wind Farms Ltd v Secretary of State for the Environment and North Devon DC* [1996] JPL 767, where environmental considerations were just one of a number of material considerations brought into the balancing act.

7.4.2.3 Planning Conditions

S70(1)TCPA allows the LPA to impose such conditions 'as it thinks fit'. Guidance is provided in S72 and S75 and there is a policy on conditions published by the Secretary of State.[50] The courts have taken a restrictive view on planning conditions, and it is clear that these cannot be imposed for ulterior motives. In the case of *Newbury DC v Secretary of State for the Environment*,[51] it was held that conditions must:

- Be imposed for a planning purpose and not for an ulterior motive.
- Fairly and reasonably relate to the development permitted.
- Not be perverse (so unreasonable that no reasonable authority could have imposed them).

7.4.2.4 Planning Obligations and Contributions

Planning obligations are defined as 'legal obligations entered into to mitigate the impacts of a development proposal'.[52] These are primarily relevant to large developments. Under the Community Infrastructure Levy Regulations 2010, regulation 122 (2), a planning obligation may only constitute a reason for granting planning permission for the development if the obligation is –

a. necessary to make the development acceptable in planning terms;
b. directly related to the development; and
c. fairly and reasonably related in scale and kind to the development.

They are commonly entered into under S106 TCPA 1990 by a person with an interest in the land and the LPA. Once entered into, they are binding and run with the land. Example obligations include providing affordable housing, creating public open space, improving roads and providing educational facilities.

In addition to planning obligations, developers may be asked to provide contributions to infrastructure. One such contribution is via the Community Infrastructure Levy, a fixed charge placed on new development which is used to fund infrastructure improvements. The levy only applies where the local authority has an approved charging schedule, setting out its rates and publishing them on their website. The levy is regulated under the Community Infrastructure Levy Regulations 2010. See Table 7.1 for the levy costs in Watford, Hertfordshire (correct as of November 2024).

7.4.3 Appeals

There is a right of appeal to the Secretary of State on a planning determination and/or its conditions. Most appeals are dealt with on the basis of written representations made by the parties, but if either side requests it, the issue must be dealt with by public local enquiry before a planning inspector. The application is effectively heard afresh with both legal and

50 Circular 11/95.
51 *Newbury DC v Secretary of State for the Environment* [1981] AC 578.
52 Ministry of Housing, Communities and Local Government, Ministry of Housing, Communities & Local Government (2018–2021) and Department for Levelling Up, Housing and Communities, Guidance, Planning obligations, updated September 2019.

Table 7.1 Calculate the costs of CIL.

Watford charging schedule		
Type of development	**Base CIL rate**	**CIL rate 2024**
Residential (includes Houses in Multiple Occupation (HMOs), Co-living and Build to Rent)	£120 per square metre	£179.29
Hotel	£120 per square metre	£179.29
Specialist accommodations for the elderly and/or disabled including sheltered and retirement housing and nursing homes, residential care homes and extra care accommodation. (This does not include registered, not for profit care homes) (within use class C2 and C3)	£120 per square metre	£179.29
Retail (Class A1–A5)	£120 per square metre	£179.29
Retail – Within the primary shopping area (Class A1–A5)	£55 per square metre	£82.18
Office	£0 per square metre	£0
Industrial	£0 per square metre	£0
Other uses	£0 per square metre	£0
Major developed areas (MDAs)	£0 per square metre	£0

Source: https://www.watford.gov.uk/planning-information-1/community-infrastructure-levy-watford.

policy grounds open for consideration. Reasons must be given for the decision. There is a fast-track procedure for *householder appeals* which relies on copies of the planning application form, the decision letter form the LPA and a statement of case only.[53] An application can be made to the High Court to review the decision on appeal.[54] If planning permission has been refused or granted subject to conditions and the owner of the land can show that the land is incapable of reasonably beneficial use in its existing state, the owner may serve a purchase notice on the planning authority requiring them to buy the land at market value.[55]

7.4.4 Enforcement

A breach of planning control is defined in S171A Town and Country Planning Act 1990 as:

- Carrying out of development without the required planning permission; or
- Failing to comply with any condition or limitation subject to which planning permission has been granted.

53 Town and Country Planning (Appeals) (Written Representation Procedure) (England) Regulations 2009 SI 2009/452.
54 S288 Town and Country Planning Act 1990.
55 S137–148 Town and Country Planning Act 1990.

Table 7.2 What enforcement powers do local planning authorities have?

Type of notice	Required action	Right of appeal?
Planning contravention notice	Can be used to find out information about a reported or suspected planning breach.	✗
Enforcement notice	Require the person on whom it is served to take certain steps to address a planning breach, for example, to stop certain activities or to remove buildings or works from land.	✓
Breach of condition notice	Requires to person on whom it is served to comply with planning conditions set out in the notice.	✗
Temporary stop notice	Requires an activity that may be a planning breach to stop immediately for a period of 56 days.[14] A temporary stop notice can be issued independently of an enforcement notice.	✗
Stop notice	Requires activities that comprise a planning breach to stop. A stop notice can only be served alongside an enforcement notice.	✗
Enforcement warning notice (since 25 April 2024)[15]	Notifies a person that they breached planning control and invites them to submit a retrospective planning application within a certain time period.	✗

Source: Part 7 Town and Country Planning Act 1990; DLUHC and MHCLG, Enforcement and post-permission matters, last updated April 2024.

Responsibility for enforcement sits with the LPA, and they may take whatever enforcement action may be necessary, in the public interest, in their administrative areas.[56] Table 7.2 above lists the enforcement powers held by local planning authorities.

The most common enforcement mechanism utilised by local planning authorities for a breach of planning control is the issuance of an enforcement notice[57] on the owners and occupiers of the land and any other person who the authority considers is materially affected by the notice. If the breach occurs in a conservation area, or the building is listed, a listed building enforcement notice may be issued. The notice must specify the breach complained of, the steps to be taken to remedy the breach, the date upon which the notice will take effect and the period for compliance with the notice.

The time limits for enforcement action are laid down in S171B Town and Country Planning Act 1990 and the Levelling Up and Regeneration Act 2023. In most cases, development is immune from enforcement actions if no action is taken:

- within 10 years of substantial completion for a breach of planning control consisting of operational development where substantial completion took place on or after 25 April 2024

56 Enforcement and post-permission matter, UK Government, Guidance, August 2024.
57 See DLUHC, Live tables on planning application statistics: Table LT_P127, last updated 7 March 2024; DLUHC, Planning application statistics: Table CPS1, last updated 7 March 2024.

- within 10 years for an unauthorised change of use to a single dwelling house where the change of use took place on or after 25 April 2024
- within 4 years of substantial completion for a breach of planning control consisting of operational development where substantial completion took place before 25 April 2024;
- within 4 years for an unauthorised change of use to a single dwelling house where the change of use took place before 25 April 2024
- within 10 years for any other breach of planning control (essentially other changes of use)[58]

In the event of non-compliance with the notice, the planning authority may enter the land and carry out the steps required by the enforcement notice and recover any expenses due. Breach of planning control on its own is not a criminal offence but failure to comply with a valid enforcement notice is.

7.4.5 Human Rights and the Planning System

Provisions under the European Convention on Human Rights are relevant to the planning system, in particular article 1 (First Protocol) (right to own property), article 8 (right to respect for private and family life) and article 14 (prohibition of discrimination) (see *R (on the application of Devonhurst Investments Limited) v Luton Borough Council*).[59] However the government guidance notes:

> (i)n some instances there is a clear public interest in taking rapid action to address breaches of planning control. To ensure that this is a proportionate approach, before serving a stop notice, the LPA must be satisfied that there has been a breach of planning control and that the activity which amounts to the breach must be stopped immediately and before the end of the period allowed for compliance with the related enforcement notice.[60]

The route of appeal from planning determinations to the Secretary of State gave rise to a challenge under human rights law (Article 6, right to a fair trial). In the case of *R v Secretary of State for Environment Transport and the Regions ex parte Holding and Barnes plc and others*[61] (the *Alconbury* case) a submission was made that the decision made by the Secretary of State on appeal made him 'judge in his own cause where his policy is in play' and that 'He cannot be both policy maker and decision-taker'. The House of Lords found that Article 6 was not breached as the legality of the planning judgment is open to challenge by judicial review.

---

58 Ibid.
59 *R (On The Application of Devonhurst Investments Limited) v Luton Borough Council* [2023] EWHC 978 (Admin).
60 See Enforcement and post-permission matter, UK Government, Guidance, August 2024.
61 [2001] UKHL 23.

7.4.6 Planning and the Environment

The government's National Policy Planning Framework (NPPF) 2023 determines that the purpose of the planning system is 'to contribute to the achievement of sustainable development, including the provision of homes, commercial development and supporting infrastructure in a sustainable way'.[62] Chapter 14 NPPF asserts that the planning system should:

> support the transition to a low carbon future in a changing climate, taking full account of flood risk and coastal change. It should help to: shape places in ways that contribute to radical reductions in greenhouse gas emissions, minimise vulnerability and improve resilience; encourage the reuse of existing resources, including the conversion of existing buildings; and support renewable and low carbon energy and associated infrastructure.[63]

In *R (McLennan) v Medway Council*[64] planning permission had been rejected owing to the effect an extension would have on the light reaching a neighbour's solar panels. The court held that the mitigation of climate change is a material planning consideration.

The Levelling-up and Regeneration Act 2023 imposes an obligation on the Secretary of State to have regard to 'the need to mitigate, and adapt to, climate change' when preparing or modifying national development and management policies (which concern the development and use of land in England).[65]

The Environment Act 2021 introduced a 10% 'biodiversity net gain' condition for grant of planning permission for 30 years with associated powers for new conservation covenant.

7.4.6.1 Environmental Impact Assessment

Environmental impact assessments (EIA) in the context of planning in England is governed by the Town and Country Planning (Environmental Impact Assessment) Regulations 2017, which apply to development given planning permission under Part III Town and Country Planning Act 1990. The aim of an EIA is to protect the environment by ensuring that local planning authorities have knowledge of any projects which may have a significant effect on the environment, and take the effect into account when considering whether to grant planning permission. The 2017 regulations require the effect to be *significant* which means only a small number of projects fall under its remit.

There are five stages to the Environmental Impact Assessment process:

Stage	Title	Brief description
1	Screening	Determination of whether a proposed project is likely to have a significant impact on the environment
2	Scoping	Determination of the extent of the issues which need to be considered and reported in the Environmental Statement

(Continued)

62 Para 7 National Policy Planning Framework (NPPF) 2023.

63 Ibid Para 157.

64 *R (McLennan) v Medway Council* [2019] EWHC 1738 (Admin).

65 S38ZA (1) and (3) Levelling-up and Regeneration Act 2023.

(Continued)

Stage	Title	Brief description
3	Preparing an Environmental Statement	The Environmental Statement must be prepared by competent experts, and include information reasonably required to assess the likely significant environmental effects of the development
4	Publicise Environmental Statement and application	Allowing the public to give their views about the proposed project and the Environmental Statement
5	Decision-making	Environmental Statement, comments made and representations are to be taken into account by the LPA when deciding whether or not to award planning permission for the proposed project.

7.5 Water Pollution

The previous UK Government released a 25-year Environment Plan in 2018, within which clean water was a key aim. Water is identified as a 'priority area' under S1 (3) Environment Act 2021, with part 5 of the Act dedicated to water. Water pollution law in England is centred around a consent system for discharges into *controlled waters*. Controlled waters are defined in S104 Water Resources Act 1991 and cover virtually all inland and coastal waters (surface and ground water). However, discharges can be made into controlled waters where consent is sought. The consent system is to be found in Schedule 10 Water Resources Act 1991 and the Control of Pollution (Applications, Appeals and Registers) Regulations 1996. Consents are set on an individualised basis, taking into account local conditions and the status of the receiving waters. They are flexible and can be altered to respond to changes in the local environment. An application for a consent should be made to the Environment Agency (EA) for:

- Any discharge of trade or sewage effluent into controlled waters.
- Any discharge of trade or sewage effluent through a pipe from land into the sea outside the limits of controlled waters.
- Any discharge where a prohibition is in force.

There is no legal obligation to obtain a consent, but it is an offence to discharge into controlled waters without one or in breach of the conditions of one. The consent, therefore, acts as a defence to a potential prosecution under one of the general water pollution offences.

7.5.1 The General Water Pollution Offences

The general water pollution offences under S85 (1) Water Resources Act (WRA) 1991 are 'causing or knowingly permitting any poisonous, noxious, or polluting matter or any waste to enter controlled waters'. 'Poisonous, noxious or polluting' are not defined in the Act but the courts have interpreted the meaning of 'polluting' very broadly. For example, in the case of *R v Dovermoss Ltd*,[66] ammonia found its way into spring water used for water supply. The source was a field on which animal slurry had been spread. Heavy rain had resulted in the slurry seeping into the ground near the spring and entering the water supply. The defence argued that no harm had actually been done to the receiving waters and that ammonia levels did not exceed maximum concentrations permitted under drinking water regulations. The court held that it was not necessary for the prosecution to prove that the substance had actually caused any harm. It was sufficient that there was a likelihood or capability of causing harm to animal or plant life or those who use water. For a successful prosecution, therefore, actual pollution does not have to be proven, or, indeed, to have occurred.

Of the two offences contained in S85 (1) WRA 1991, the *causing* offence is strict liability and is the most commonly prosecuted of the two offences. All that is necessary, for a successful prosecution of this offence, is the entry of potentially polluting substances into controlled waters. The leading case on *causing* under S85 (1) is *Environment Agency v Empress Car Co (Arbertillery) Ltd*.[67] In the *Empress Cars* case, alleged vandalism of an oil storage tank caused entry of oil into controlled waters. A protective bund had been overridden by the owners and an unknown person had entered the premises and opened the tap. The entire contents of the tank overflowed across a yard, into a storm drain and into a nearby river. On appeal, the defence argued that there had been no positive act on the part of the company which amounted to 'causing' the entry and that it had been the act of a stranger. The House of Lords, rejecting the appeal, ruled that a person may be held to have caused the entry of polluting matter if that person did something with or without the occurrence of other facts, which produced a situation in which the polluting matter could escape.

There are limited defences available in S88 WRA 1991. Holding a consent is a defence, and there is a defence in cases of emergency, but the courts have taken a restrictive approach to this, and it will only apply when human life is threatened.[68]

Recent cases concerning breaches of pollution laws and regulations into waterways have been brought against large companies. Taylor Wimpey were fined just under £500,000 for polluting the River Llwyd[69] and Anglian Water were ordered to pay fines totalling £1.2 million for incidents of pollution across Cambridgeshire, Buckinghamshire and Northamptonshire [70] In 2021, Southern Water were fined a record £90 million fine after pleading guilty to 6,971 unpermitted sewage discharges.[71]

---

66 *R v Dovermoss Ltd* [1995] Env LR 258.

67 *Environment Agency v Empress Car Co (Arbertillery) Ltd.* [1998] All ER 481.

68 *Express Ltd v Environment Agency* [2003] Env LR 29.

69 See National Resources Wales, 'Taylor Wimpey prosecuted by NRW for river pollution offences', May 2023.

70 See Environment Agency, 'Water company hit with combined fines of over £1.2m for pollution incidents in East England', October 2022.

71 Gov.uk Press Release, Record £90m fine for Southern Water following EA prosecution, July 2021.

7.6 Contaminated Land

Land contamination is often a result of previous industrial use, requiring work be done to enable the land to be safely re-used. The regime for contaminated land is found in Part 2A Environmental Protection Act 1990 (EPA), which provides ways of identifying and remedying land which poses a significant risk to health and/or the environment, working with the planning system to make the land suitable for redevelopment.

7.6.1 Defining Contaminated Land

S78A (2) EPA 1990 defines contaminated land as:

any land which appears to the local authority in whose area it is situated to be in such a condition, by reason of substances in, on or under the land, that;

- significant harm is being caused or there is a significant possibility of such harm being caused; or
- pollution of controlled waters is being, or is likely to be, caused.

Harm is defined in S78 (4) as:

> harm to the health of living organisms or other interference with the ecological systems of which they form part and, in the case of man, includes harm to his property.

Under S78(5) to ascertain whether there is significant harm or the possibility of significant harm is provided in guidance issued by the Secretary of State, the most recent of which was issued in 2012.[72] Under Part 2A, there needs to be a contaminant pathway-receptor linkage. This means there must be contaminants present in, on or under the land that pose a hazard, and one of more pathways (routes) which they may harm people, the environment, property or pollute controlled waters.

Paragraph 4.5 of the Guidance notes:

> The following health effects should always be considered to constitute significant harm to human health: death; life threatening diseases (e.g., cancers); other diseases likely to have serious impacts on health; serious injury; birth defects; and impairment of reproductive functions.

7.6.2 Identifying Contaminated Land

Under the EPA 1990, local authorities have a duty to inspect land for the purposes of identifying contaminated land and special sites:

Under S78B(1):

Every local authority shall cause its area to be inspected from time to time for the purpose –

a. of identifying contaminated land; and
b. of enabling the authority to

---

72 Department for Environment, Food & Rural Affairs, Environmental Protection Act 1990: Part 2A Contaminated Land Statutory Guidance, April 2012.

decide whether any such land is land which is required to be designated as a special site.

Under S78B(2):

> In performing [these] functions... a local authority shall act in accordance with any guidance issued for the purpose by the Secretary of State.
>
> Special sites are those where there is a threat of serious harm or pollution and they come under the control of the Environment Agency.
>
> The statutory guidance (discussed above) provides the following when determining whether land is contaminated:
>
> The local authority has the sole responsibility for determining whether any land appears to be contaminated land. It cannot delegate this responsibility (except in accordance with section 101 Local Government Act 1972). However, in making such decisions the authority may rely on information or advice provided by another body such as the Environment Agency, or a suitably qualified experienced practitioner appointed for that purpose.

There are four possible grounds for the determination of land as contaminated land (with regard to non-radioactive contamination):

a. Significant harm is being caused to a human, or relevant non-human, receptor.
b. There is a significant possibility of significant harm being caused to a human, or relevant non-human, receptor.
c. Significant pollution of controlled waters is being caused.
d. There is a significant possibility of significant pollution of controlled waters being caused.[73]

7.6.3 Notification and Consultation

Once contaminated land is identified, owners, occupiers and potentially liable parties are notified.[74] There will normally be a minimum 3-month consultation period, which gives the opportunity for voluntary remediation to be undertaken. During this period, remediation methods will be identified, and a cost benefit analysis carried out. The standard of remediation is a suitable for use standard (including planned use under planning application).

7.6.4 Remediation

S78A(7) EPA 1990 defines remediation as:

a. the doing of anything for the purpose of assessing the condition of –
  i. the contaminated land in question; or
  ii. any controlled waters affected by that land; or
  iii. any land adjoining or adjacent to that land;

---

73 5.5-5.6 Environmental Protection Act 1990: Part 2A Contaminated Land Statutory Guidance, p. 30.
74 S78B (3) Environmental Protection Act 1990 Part 2A.

b. the doing of any works, the carrying out of any operations or the taking of any steps in relation to any such land for the purpose –
   i. of preventing or minimising, or remedying or mitigating the effects of, any significant harm (or significant pollution of controlled waters), by reason of which the contaminated land is such land; or
   ii. of restoring the land or waters to their former state; or
c. the making of subsequent inspections from time to time for the purpose of keeping under review the condition of the land or waters.

The statutory guidance lists the broad aims of remediation to be:

a. to remove identified significant contaminant linkages, or permanently to disrupt them to ensure they are no longer significant and that risks are reduced to below an unacceptable level; and/or
b. to take reasonable measures to remedy harm or pollution that has been caused by a significant contaminant linkage.[75]

7.7 Waste Management Law

Recent years have seen a shift in emphasis in waste management law. Initially the focus was upon the protection of public health; however, there has been a movement towards the prevention of waste in the first place, with the aim of helping combat climate change and optimise resources. With regard to the built environment and construction, the UK government cites the construction industry as producing 60% of total waste produced.[76]

7.7.1 Defining Waste

Unfortunately, no straightforward definition of 'waste' exists. The UK Government provides the following to assist in defining waste:

> A material is waste if the holder has discarded it. The holder is the person or legal entity who has the material at the time it's discarded. This may not be the owner – for example, if someone has leased the material, they become the holder. Assessment of whether a material has been discarded is based on the actions of the holder. A holder may unintentionally, involuntarily or accidentally discard a material. They may also be required to discard it.

The Environment Agency considers all the following factors when they assess if a material is discarded and therefore classed as waste:

- burden
- certainty of use

75 6.5 Environmental Protection Act 1990: Part 2A Contaminated Land Statutory Guidance, p. 35.
76 2.2.2 Government Commercial Function, Promoting Net Zero Carbon and Sustainability in Construction, Guidance Note, September 2022.

- fit for purpose
- a specific purpose
- management
- environmental harm
- common classification as waste
- disposal or recovery
- fuel or waste
- an item returned for a refund
- reuse

They also note when a material has not become waste, as a by-product or by reuse:
A material will not be waste if all the following apply:

- it is used for the same purpose for which it was designed – the use must not be subordinate or incidental to the original use
- the previous holder intended for it to be reused
- no repair, or no more than minor repair, is required to it when it is transferred from the previous holder to the new holder, and the previous holder knows this
- any necessary repair is going to be done
- its use is lawful
- it is not managed in a way that indicates that it is waste, for example it is not transported or stored in a way that could cause it to be damaged

If a material becomes waste before it is reused, you will have to apply the end of waste test to it.

7.7.2 Managing Waste

7.7.2.1 Duty of Care

A duty of care is imposed on persons responsible for handling waste under S34 EPA 1990. Those subject to the duty of care include any person who imports, produces, carries, keeps, treats or disposes of controlled waste – it applies to everyone in the waste chain. There is also a restricted duty on domestic waste producers. Any person is subject to the duty to take reasonable steps to:

- Prevent any other person contravening (S33)
- Prevent any other person contravening an environmental permit.
- Prevent the escape of waste.
- Ensure that the waste is transferred only to an authorised person.
- Ensure that an adequate written description of the waste is given to anyone to whom the waste is transferred (The Environmental Protection (Duty of Care) Regulations 1991).

There is a code of practice that gives guidance on reasonable steps, which must be taken into account in deciding whether the duty has been complied with. Breach of the duty is a criminal offence, even if no harm has been caused. The duty of care has the effect of making the system self-policing and encourages appropriate waste management systems.

7.7.3 Fly-tipping

Fly-tipping is the illegal dumping of liquid or solid waste on land or in water. Prosecutions may be brought for fly-tipping using one of the following provisions:

- S33 Environmental Protection Act 1990
- Regulations 12 and 38 Environmental Permitting (England and Wales) Regulations 2016
- Schedule 21 Environmental Permitting (England and Wales) Regulations 2016

For the year 2022–2023, local authorities in England dealt with 1.08 million fly-tipping incidents, 60% of which involved household waste.[77] Both local authorities and the Environment Agency have a responsibility with regard to fly-tipping, with local authorities primarily responsible for smaller scale incidents and the Environment Agency for those on a larger scale or which pose an immediate threat to human health or the environment.[78]

7.7.3.1 S33 Environmental Protection Act 1990

Under S33 EPA, it is an offence to:

a. deposit controlled waste in or on land, unless it is in accordance with an environmental permit;
b. submit controlled waste to any listed operation (other than a disposal operation mentioned above) unless it is under and in accordance with an environmental permit;
c. knowingly cause or knowingly permit either of the above;
d. treat, keep or dispose of controlled waste in a manner that is likely to cause pollution of the environment or harm to human health.

An environmental permit will serve as a defence in the case of a, b and c above. The primary activities for which an environmental permit is needed include:

- an 'installation' – an industrial facility, manufacturer or other business that produces potentially harmful substances, for example a landfill site, a large chicken farm, a food factory, a furniture factory, a dry cleaners, a petrol station
- a waste operation – a site where waste is recycled, stored, treated or disposed of
- a mining waste operation – a site which manages waste produced from mines or quarries
- a medium combustion plant or specified generator
- a small waste incineration plant – where certain types and quantities of waste are burned
- mobile plant – plant that's designed to move or be moved, for example a machine that's moved onto a site to clean contaminated soil
- a solvent emission activity – releasing organic solvents directly or indirectly into the air[79]

---

77 Department for Environment, Food and Rural Affairs, Official Statistics, Fly-tipping statistics for England 2022–2023 (updated March 2024).

78 Ibid., 10.2.

79 Guidance, Environmental Permits, Environment Agency and Department for Environment, Food and Rural Affairs (updated October 2020).

There is also a due diligence defence to an unpermitted activity.[80] The question of what constitutes a 'deposit' has given rise to some case law. In the case of *Leigh Land Reclamation Ltd v Walsall MBC*,[81] it was held that a deposit only occurs when the waste reaches its final resting place. This decision, however, proved problematic as it was easy to argue that a deposit was only temporary and thus avoid liability. The decision was overturned in *R v Metropolitan Stipendiary Magistrate, ex parte London Waste Regulation Authority*[82] when the court held that 'deposit' applied to temporary deposits.

As well as traditional sentences, courts can order compensation for clean up and the confiscation of vehicles and the Environment Agency has powers to order clean up on the occupier and in default, carry out the necessary work and recover expenses.

7.7.4 Site Waste Management

A site waste management plan (SWMP) is a document which outlines how waste will be managed throughout a construction project. In 2008, regulations mandated all UK construction projects over £300,000 had a SWMP; however, this was repealed in 2013, and they are now voluntary, although recommended.

7.8 Emissions from Buildings

The built environment contributes approximately 40% of UK carbon emissions.[83] The government has set a legally binding target (net zero target) to reduce the net emissions by 100% by 2050 when compared to 1990 levels. This is codified in S1(1) Climate Change Act 2008, with duty to do so placed on the Secretary of State. At COP26 the UK government committed to achieving 68% reductions in carbon emissions by 2030.

7.8.1 Construction and Emissions

The UK government acknowledges that greenhouse gases are emitted at every stage of the construction and use cycle, from the manufacture of materials through construction and maintenance to eventual demolition.[84] However, the government has also set a target of building 300,000 new homes a year.[85] In 2022, a Construction Playbook was released by the UK Government, aiming to *set out key policies and guidance for how public works projects and programmes are assessed, procured and delivered.* One of the aims of the playbook is

---

80 S33 (7) (a) Environmental Protection Act 1990.

81 *Leigh Land Reclamation Ltd v Walsall MBC* (1991) 155 JP 547.

82 *R v Metropolitan Stipendiary Magistrate, ex parte London Waste Regulation Authority* [1993] All ER 113.

83 2.2.2 Government Commercial Function, Promoting Net Zero Carbon and Sustainability in Construction, Guidance Note, September 2022.

84 House of Commons Environmental Audit Committee, *Building to Net Zero: Costing Carbon in Construction, First Report of Session 2022–23*, HC103.

85 The Conservative and Unionist Party, The Conservative and Unionist Party Manifesto, 2019; House of Commons Library, Tackling the under-supply of housing, CBP-7671 (4 February 2022).

to enable the construction sector to 'Take strides towards our 2050 net zero commitment, using whole life carbon approaches to reduce carbon emissions linked to buildings and infrastructure and within the construction supply chain'.[86]

The National Policy Procurement Policy Statement (PPN5/21) states that tackling climate change and reducing waste is a national priority outcome that Contracting Authorities should have regard to when formulating their procurement strategy (contracting authorities are defined in S2(1) Procurement Act 2023).[87]

Under Procurement Policy Note 06/21: *Taking account of Carbon Reduction Plans in the procurement of major government contracts*, suppliers who are bidding on central government contracts (over £5 million p/a in value) must commit to achieving net zero by 2050 and are to detail their organisation's UK greenhouse gas emissions via the publication of a Carbon Reduction Plan.[88]

7.8.2 Existing Homes and Emissions

In July 2024, the UK government reported:

> In 2022, emissions from residential buildings accounted for a fifth (20%) of greenhouse gas emissions in the UK. The Climate Change Committee, the government's advisory body, said the UK will not meet its emissions targets 'without near complete decarbonisation of the housing stock'.[89]

Data from 2020 cited that of the 29 million existing homes across the UK, at least 19 million still need to be made low carbon, low-energy and resilient to a changing climate.[90]

One way the energy performance of homes is assessed is through Energy Performance Certificates (EPCs). They do so using two ratings, an energy efficiency rating and an environmental impact rating, both on a scale of 1–100 and banded A-G. EPCs are governed by the Energy Performance of Buildings (England and Wales) Regulations 2012, which came into effect on 9 January 2013, and the Building Regulations 2010. The regulations require an EPC to be commissioned before a property is marketed for sale or rent, and once obtained, and EPC is valid for 10 years. However, in 2020 the UK government reported '(i)n England alone over ten million owner occupied homes and over three million private

---

86 HM Government, The Construction Playbook, Government guidance on sourcing and contracting public works projects and programmes, Version 1.1, September 2022, 3.

87 2.1.7 Government Commercial Function, Promoting Net Zero Carbon and Sustainability in Construction, Guidance Note, September 2022; S2 (1) Procurement Act 2023 'contracting authority' means – (a) a public authority, or (b) in the case of a utilities contract, a public authority, public undertaking or private utility, other than an excluded authority.

88 2.3.2 Government Commercial Function, Promoting Net Zero Carbon and Sustainability in Construction, Guidance Note, September 2022.

89 House of Commons Library, Research Briefing 'Environmental standards for new housing' September 2024.

90 House of Commons Environmental Audit Committee, *Energy Efficiency of Existing Homes Fourth Report of Session 2019–21*, HC 346, 5.

rented sector landlords need to upgrade the energy efficiency of their homes to become A, B or C rated by 2035 for the Government's to achieve its climate aspirations'.[91]

At present, only privately rented homes and those owned by local authorities and housing associations (in certain areas in the UK) are subject to regulations dictating energy efficiency. Under the Energy Efficiency (Private Rented Property) (England and Wales) Regulations 2015, a tenant may serve notice on their landlord requesting consent for making energy efficiency improvements to the property[92] to which a landlord must not unreasonably refuse consent. Since 2020, privately rented homes in England and Wales must have an EPC rating of at least E,[93] which is expected to rise to C by 2030.

7.9 Health and Safety at Work

Since the beginning of the nineteenth century, the law has sought to regulate how employers 'manage' safety at work. As new hazards emerged through the industrial age (mills, factories, offices, mechanised farming) so too did legislation to cover the worst abuses of employee safety.

By the early 1970s, it had become evident that insufficient emphasis was being placed on accident prevention. A committee was set up under Lord Robens to inquire into the recognised problems in health and safety at work and to make recommendations. The subsequent report recommended a lighter touch, goal-setting approach to legislation, with the law serving as a framework for self-regulation. The Robens Report,[94] which set out the findings of the Committee, had a significant impact on the development of health and safety law in the UK. Most of the 1972 report was accepted by Parliament and it formed the basis for the Health and Safety at Work etc. Act 1974 (HSWA). The HSWA is the primary piece of legislation covering occupational health and safety in the UK, setting out the duties which:

- employers have towards employees and members of the public
- employees have to themselves and to each other
- certain self-employed have towards themselves and others

In 2008, the Corporate Manslaughter and Corporate Homicide Act 2007 came into force. The legislation enables companies and organisations to be found guilty of corporate manslaughter as a result of serious management.

7.9.1 Health and Safety at Work etc. Act 1974

The HSWA replaced existing legislation and introduced a system of Regulations and Codes of Practice. The operation of the Act is in the hands of the Health and Safety Executive (HSE), while enforcement is the responsibility of Health and Safety Inspectors.

---

91 Ibid.

92 S8 (1) Energy Efficiency (Private Rented Property) (England and Wales) Regulations 2015.

93 Minimum Energy Efficiency Standards (MEES) 2018 under Energy Efficiency (Private Rented Property) (England and Wales) (Amendment) Regulations 2015 as amended.

94 Safety and Health at Work. The Report of the Robens Committee, Cmnd 5034, June 1972.

7.9.1.1 Duties

S2 (1) states: It shall be the duty of every employer to ensure, so far as is reasonably practicable, the health, safety and welfare at work of all his employees.

This includes, as far as is reasonably practicable:

- **a.** the provision and maintenance of plant and systems of work that are safe and without risks to health;
- **b.** arrangements for ensuring safety and absence of risks to health in connection with the use, handling, storage and transport of articles and substances;
- **c.** the provision of such information, instruction, training and supervision as is necessary to ensure the health and safety at work of his employees;
- **d.** the maintenance of any place of work it in a condition that is safe and without risks to health and the provision and maintenance of means of access to and egress from it that are safe and without such risks;
- **e.** the provision and maintenance of a working environment for his employees that is safe, without risks to health, and adequate as regards facilities and arrangements for their welfare at work.[95]
- **f.** Prepare and revise as necessary a written statement containing a policy with regard to health and safety at work, arrangements for carrying out the policy and the drawing of attention to it to employees.

7.9.1.2 Inspectors

Inspectors have extensive rights to enter premises to make investigations and require the production of documents and information. An Improvement Notice may be served where a particular practice is required to be remedied, while in serious cases a Prohibition Notice may be served if there is a risk of serious personal injury. The Act provides for criminal penalties in cases of breach and in some instances allows for a civil action for breach of statutory duty.

7.9.2 The 1992 'Six-pack' Regulations

The 1974 Act is an enabling Act and regulations can be made under it relating to almost any matter connected to health and safety. Thus, the bulk of health and safety law is to be found in the form of regulations. Some regulations that pre-dated the Act were brought under its ambit when it came into force and further regulations were brought in to operationalise the framework provided by the Act.

There are a number of regulations which govern health and safety:

- Management of Health and Safety at Work Regulations 1999
- Workplace (Health, Safety and Welfare) Regulations 1992
- Provision and Use of Work Equipment Regulations 1992
- Personal Protective Equipment at Work Regulations 2018
- Manual Handling Operations Regulations 1992 (amended 2002)
- Health and Safety Display Screen Equipment Regulations 1992 (amended 2002)

95 See S2 (2) (a)–(e) Health and Safety at Work etc Act 1974.

Most of these regulations have since either been updated by revocation and replacement or amendment. A later addition is the Reporting of Injuries, Diseases and Dangerous Occurrences Regulations 2013.

7.9.2.1 Management of Health and Safety at Work Regulations 1999 (as Amended)

The original 1992 regulations were replaced and revoked by these 1999 regulations. The Regulations are supplemented by an Approved Code of Conduct (ACoP) containing guidance on the Regulations.[96] The central feature of the Regulations is the duty on employers to undertake suitable and sufficient assessment of the risks to employees in the workplace. The Regulations require measures to be identified to comply with health and safety duties and impose general duties on planning, monitoring, reviewing and providing health surveillance. Competent persons must be appointed to assist in the undertaking of measures and information provided to employees about health and safety risks. There is a new provision in the 1999 Regulations that did not appear in the original 1992 version. Regulation 4 of the new Regulations requires that preventive measures are implemented in accordance with a hierarchy set out in Schedule 1. The top priority is the avoidance of risk.

7.9.2.2 Workplace (Health, Safety and Welfare) Regulations 1992 (as Amended)

These regulations apply to most workplaces (excluding construction sites) and cover a wide range of basic health, safety and welfare issues. The regulations are supported by an ACoP, which is published together with guidance. The provisions of the Code are admissible as evidence in criminal proceedings and are often received in evidence in civil actions. The focus of the Regulations is upon elements of the structure and layout of the workplace that affect employees and the facilities that are provided for the workforce. As such, it includes provisions on ventilation, temperature, lighting, cleaning, workstations, floors, traffic routes, doors, walls, windows, etc., as well as sanitary conveniences, washing facilities, drinking water, changing and rest facilities.

7.9.3 Construction (Design and Management) Regulations 2015

The Construction (Design and Management) Regulations 2015 (CDM 2015) came into force on 6 April 2015, replacing CDM 2007. CDM 2015 provides a legal framework for the management of health, safety and welfare on construction projects. The Health and Safety Executive lists the following as key elements to securing construction health and safety:

- **a.** managing the risks by applying the general principles of prevention;
- **b.** appointing the right people and organisations at the right time;
- **c.** making sure everyone has the information, instruction, training and supervision they need to carry out their jobs in a way that secures health and safety;
- **d.** dutyholders cooperating and communicating with each other and coordinating their work; and[97]
- **e.** consulting workers and engaging with them to promote and develop effective measures to secure health, safety and welfare.

---

96 Management of Health and Safety at Work (L21, 2000).

97 Health and Safety Executive, Managing health and safety in construction: Construction (Design and Management) Regulations 2015, L153, published 2015, 4.

7.9.3.1 Client Duties

Regulations 4 and 5 provide the client's duty to make suitable arrangements for managing a construction project, and for maintaining and reviewing the arrangements throughout, in order to manage the health and safety risks. Projects involving more than one contractor impose a duty on the client to appoint a principal designer and a principal contractor, and to ensure they carry out their duties. Regulation 6 defines projects that require notification to enforcing authorities and places a duty on a client to notify.

7.9.3.2 Health and Safety Duty Roles

Regulation 8 sets out the requirements on anyone working on a project with certain responsibilities. They relate to appointing designers and contractors, the need for cooperation between dutyholders, reporting anything likely to endanger health and safety and ensuring information and instruction is understandable.

7.9.3.3 Duties of Others Within a Project

Regulations 9–11 are concerned with the duties of designers, 12 details the duties on principal designers and/or contractors with regard to construction phase plans and health and safety files. Regulation 13 details the principal contractor's duties during the construction phase, their main being to plan, manage, monitor and coordinate health and safety. Other duties include making sure suitable site inductions and welfare facilities are provided.[98]

7.9.3.4 General Requirements for All Construction Sites

Part 4 of CDM 2015 details provisions applicable to work carried out on a construction site. They include ensuring a safe place to work, good order and site security, stability of structures, provisions concerning use, transportation and storage of explosives, fresh air, temperature and weather protection, fire and lighting.[99]

7.9.4 The Control of Substances Hazardous to Health (COSHH) Regulations 2002 (as Amended)

The COSHH Regulations introduced another approach to safety on site, based on limiting the risks of exposure to hazardous substances. Hazardous substances are defined as 'any natural or artificial substance whether solid, liquid, gas or vapour (including micro-organisms)'.[100] The Regulations are supported by an Approved Code of Practice.[101] A breach of the Regulations is a potential criminal offence under s33 (1) Health and Safety etc. Act 1974 and can also give rise to civil liability in so far as it causes damage.[102]

The Regulations prohibit exposure to certain substances and aim to protect the health of persons exposed to other hazardous substances. This is achieved by means of the

98 Ibid., 36.

99 See regulations 16–35.

100 Reg 2 (1).

101 The Control of Substances Hazardous to Health Regulations 2002 (as amended) Approved Code of Practice and Guidance, L5.

102 HSWA s47 (2) and see Chapter 3, paragraph 3.10.

requirement for risk assessments to be carried out when exposure may occur. Employers are then required to either prevent or control exposure. Control systems are to be maintained, examined and tested and exposure in the workplace is to be monitored. In addition, the Regulations require that health surveillance is in place and that information, instruction and training is provided for persons who may be exposed to substances hazardous to health and that arrangements are in place to deal with accidents, incidents and emergencies.

7.9.5 The Control of Asbestos at Work Regulations 2012

Asbestos has been responsible for more work-related deaths than any other cause and the mortality rate is still rising.[103] Asbestos is a material made of tiny fibres, which when disturbed and inhaled, can cause serious health problems and death. It was used in many industries and buildings, including as insulation material for buildings, boilers and pipes; car brakes and floor tiles, insulating board to protect buildings and ships against fire; asbestos cement for roofing sheets and pipes.[104] All types have been under an import ban since 1999; however, its widespread use and expense in safely removing means much remains in situ across the UK. These regulations place legal duties on employers responsible for licensable and non-licensable work with asbestos. They also place a specific duty to manage asbestos on the owners and/or those responsible for maintenance in non-domestic premises. The regulations set minimum standards for the protection of employees from risks related to exposure to asbestos. Employers should also take account of people not directly employed by them but who could be affected by the work being done on asbestos (including employees of other employers, people occupying buildings, members of the public, etc.).[105]

7.9.6 The Work at Height Regulations 2005 (as Amended)

Falls from height remain one of the single biggest causes of workplace deaths and major injuries. The Regulations apply to all work at height where there is a risk of a fall liable to cause personal injury. The Regulations place duties on employers, the self-employed and any person that controls the work of others. They are supplemented by the Work at Height Regulations 2007, which apply to those who work at height providing instruction or leadership in caving, climbing, sporting, recreation or team-building activities. As part of the Regulations, duty holders must ensure:

- All work at height is properly planned and organised.
- Those involved in work at height are competent.
- The risks from work at height are assessed and appropriate work equipment is selected and used.
- The risks from fragile surfaces are properly controlled.
- Equipment for work at height is properly inspected and maintained.

---

103 The Health and Safety Executive reports that approximately 5,000 people die each year from asbestos-related diseases.

104 UK Health and Safety Authority, Guidance, Asbestos: general information, March 2024.

105 Health and Safety Executive, Managing and working with asbestos, Control of Asbestos Regulations 2012, L143, published 2013, 9.

The overriding principle is that a person to whom the Regulations apply must do all that is reasonably practicable to prevent anyone from falling. The regulations set out a hierarchy for managing and selecting equipment for work at height. Duty holders must:

- Avoid work at height where they can.
- Use work equipment or other measures to prevent falls where they cannot avoid working at height.
- Where they cannot eliminate the risk of a fall, use work equipment or other measures to minimise the distance and consequences of a fall should one occur.

The Regulations include Schedules giving requirements for existing places of work and means of access for work at height, collective fall prevention (e.g. guardrails and working platforms), collective fall arrest (e.g. nets, airbags, etc.), personal fall protection (e.g. work restraints, fall arrest and rope access) and ladders.

8

Dispute Resolution

CONTENTS

8.1 Causes of Disputes

The industry can be very contentious due to the nature of the work, technical disagreements can arise based on designs, specifications and methods of construction. Problems with contracts being poorly written with the potential for ambiguity are another common problem. Common disputes arise in relation to the standard of workmanship, quality of materials, payment mechanisms and processes, delay and management of time and occasionally arguments about whether or not a contract is in place, or what the exact terms of it are. For more information regarding the issues in these areas, please refer to Chapter 3 on Construction Law. There are two categories of disputes: technical and legal.

Technical disputes require the parties to ascertain the facts of what has happened and, once ascertained, apply the law to those facts. However, ascertaining such facts isn't always as easy as one might expect, as demonstrated by the case of *Independent Broadcasting Authority v EMI Electronics Ltd and BICC Construction Ltd.*[1] The case concerned a television mast on Emley Moor in West Yorkshire. The structure was over 385 metres high and should have been able to withstand heavy ice loading and strong winds. However, it collapsed in March 1969, more than 2 years after completion, due to ice formation and strong winds. A lengthy investigation was required to ascertain the reason for the collapse.

Legal issues relate to the contract and the obligations agreed by the parties. Sometimes it is that parties have different understandings of the meaning of the contractual clause, but at other times it can be that the law has yet to decide responsibility on a particular issue. Advancements in technology are ever quicker, and the law needs to catch up. There can never be a statute for every situation, which leaves the courts applying existing law and principles to new situations.

1 [1978]11 WLUK 72.

Some disputes will be quite simple and of types which frequently occur and can therefore be reasonably quickly and easily resolved by informal dispute resolution methods. The less serious, or more straightforward, matters can often be resolved by adjudication, but for very complex cases (such as the *EMI v BICC*), or cases relating to novel situations, or with several connected parties and contracts, litigation may be the best or only forum for resolution.

8.2 Litigation

Litigation is the legal term for court actions. To sue a party is to litigate. Companies or parties that are frequently suing others are often referred to as litigious. A company known for being litigious may be seen as a strong party, but the flip side is that others may be put off from doing business with them, which ultimately could make business more difficult or more expensive.

The benefits of a court decision, in addition to being able to enforce it (see the following text), are that it provides a definitive answer (subject to appeals – see the following text) which helps with development of the law and understanding of the contract clauses in common use. As explained in Chapter 1, judicial precedence means that once a question of law has been decided by a court, it must be followed in all future cases. This is particularly helpful when questions arise over the meaning of standard form contracts (see Chapter 3) as it allows the parties greater clarity of their obligations and procedures.

Litigation is often viewed as a last resort, not just due to reputational damage from such a public forum, but also due to the length of time it can take to resolve a dispute this way. Cases can take many months before reaching a final hearing. The Civil Procedure Rules set out how to make a claim through the judicial system, which system to use and what procedures you need to undertake before beginning a claim. In addition, there are various other procedures which are recommended, each designed to encourage a settlement outside of court.

8.2.1 The Civil Procedure Rules

The Rt Hon Lord Woolf published a review of the civil justice system in June 1986. His findings were that the civil justice system was too slow, too costly and too complex. As a result of this review, legislation was made for the introduction of rules of court to be called the Civil Procedure Rules (CPR). The CPR came into force on 26 April 1999, replacing previous Rules of the Supreme Court and the County Court Rules. The CPR are divided into 79 sections called 'Parts' and each part is subdivided into 'rules'. It contains two schedules:

Schedule 1 contains various High Court rules (the old rules of the Supreme Court that are re-enacted with modifications). The TCC is part of the High Court.
Schedule 2 contains re-enacted County Court rules.

The CPR applies to the Civil Division of the Court of Appeal, the High Court and County Courts. Each new rule is supplemented by a practice direction which sets out in more detail the procedure which has to be followed. The CPR are available on the Court Service website at www.hmcourts-service.gov.uk. They are regularly updated by Practice Directions and updates to ensure their currency with law and legal practice.

The overriding objective is to deal with each case justly, which includes dealing with cases expeditiously, ensuring proportionality and that the parties are on an equal footing, limiting costs as far as possible and ensuring the appropriate allocation of the court's resources.

To achieve the goals, the central theme of the CPR was a fundamental transfer of the management and control of litigation from the litigants and their lawyers to the courts. The court is under a duty to further the overriding objective by actively managing cases. This altered the traditional role of the court away from merely adjudicating on whatever the parties presented.

8.2.2 Pre-action Protocols

The CPR introduced pre-action protocols to guide parties on what they should do before application to the court. There are several different protocols designed for different types of cases or industries. The most common one for the construction industry is the Pre-Action Protocol for Engineering and Construction Disputes. According to the Ministry of Justice's website, Justice, the objectives of pre-action conduct and protocols are to ensure that prior to commencement of proceedings, both parties 'have exchanged sufficient information to

- **a.** understand each other's position;
- **b.** make decisions about how to proceed;
- **c.** try to settle the issues without proceedings;
- **d.** consider a form of Alternative Dispute Resolution (ADR) to assist with settlement;
- **e.** support the efficient management of those proceedings; and
- **f.** reduce the costs of resolving the dispute'.[2]

The Pre-Action Protocol for Construction and Engineering Disputes 2nd edition (PAP) applies to all construction and engineering disputes (including professional negligence claims against architects, engineers and quantity surveyors). The PAP at 3.1.1 requires parties 'to exchange sufficient information about the proposed proceedings broadly to allow the parties to understand each other's position and make informed decisions about settlement and how to proceed; [and at] 3.1.2 to make appropriate attempts to resolve the matter without starting proceedings and, in particular, to consider the use of an appropriate form of ADR in order to do so'.[3]

8.2.3 Issuing Proceedings

After undertaking the PAP process, if matters have not been resolved the claimant must then apply to the court to begin proceedings, by completing a claim form. Claim forms and guidance notes to their completion can be found on the gov.uk website. In the Technology

---

2 https://www.justice.gov.uk/courts/procedure-rules/civil/rules/pd_pre-action_conduct (accessed 28 April 2025).

3 https://www.justice.gov.uk/courts/procedure-rules/civil/protocol/prot_ced (accessed 28 April 2025).

and Construction Court there are two options for claims: Part 7 or Part 8. Part 7 claims are for claims where the facts are in dispute and Part 8 are for when the parties agree the facts but disagree on the meaning of the law or the contract terms or even if there is disagreement as to whether a contract exists between the parties. The word 'Part' refers to it being part of the CPR. The completed form is then sent to the court with the requisite court fee. The court will stamp the form and return it. The claimant must serve that form (or a copy of it) to the defendant together with an acknowledgement of service form, notes for defendants (both available on the website) and their particulars of claim, which is a document which sets out all the arguments and facts that they wish to use in support of their claim. If they have followed the protocol, this will be similar to the contents of their letter before claim but may have been adjusted in respect of the defendant's response to that letter. The claimant must also send a completed certificate of service to the court to confirm that service has taken place.

The defendant has 14 days in which to acknowledge the claim and 28 days to file a response with the court. To acknowledge the claim, the defendant has to complete and return one of a choice of forms to the court. The form required depends on the response from the defendant. Their option is to either admit the claim and offer to pay, admit the claim but require time to pay, dispute the claim and want to submit a counterclaim for a specified amount or dispute the claim and submit a counterclaim for an unspecified amount. All the forms and explanations for their use are on the government website for courts sentencing and tribunals: https://www.gov.uk/government/publications/form-n9-response-pack. If the defendant does not respond within 3 months, the claimant may ask the court to find in their favour by completing an application form for application for judgement in default of filing an acknowledgment of service.[4]

8.2.4 Case Management Conference

If the defendant doesn't admit the claim in their response or suggest a suitable payment, the next stage is a case management conference (sometimes referred to as hearings). This will be arranged by the court and is a meeting with the judge to discuss a date for the hearing and how the case will be handled. The parties will be asked for the value of the claim, the costs incurred so far and any expert witnesses they wish to engage. The court may only allow one expert to provide evidence for both parties rather than one each. This will save costs. At this meeting the court will outline when parties must produce documents or other evidence and line up witnesses for the trial. Depending on the complexity of the case, there may be further meetings and /or a pre-trial review to check that everything is in place. The next stage would be the trial itself.

During case management, the TCC judge may recommend that parties undertake an early neutral evaluation (ENE) process (see the following text) and in some cases may order that parties do so even without their consent.

4 https://www.gov.uk/government/publications/form-adm13-application-for-judgment-in-default-of-filing-an-acknowledgment-of-service-andor-defence-or-collision-statement-of-case

8.2.5 Part 36 and Settlement

At any point during the process a party may offer to settle using the Part 36 settlement process. Known as Part 36 offers because the details are set out under Part 36 of the CPR. Either party can offer to settle the case for a sum of money. The defendant can offer to pay, or the claimant can offer to receive, a lower amount of money than the particulars of claim amount. The Part 36 offer is lodged with the court. Where a hearing results in the award of a sum lower than the offer sum, then the person who didn't accept that offer will have to pay all the other side's costs (and their own), even if they were victorious. The scheme is designed to encourage an earlier out of court settlement. If the Part 36 offer is accepted, the parties will ask the court to make a court order to bring it into effect.

8.2.6 Costs

In general, the 'loser' of the case will be ordered to pay the court costs and the associated legal costs of the other party (in addition to their own). However, the courts have the power to refuse the payment of all or some of the costs of a party who fails to engage in ADR. The County Court case of *Conway v Conway & Anor* [2024][5] highlighted the increased emphasis that courts are placing on parties' use of ADR when considering a cost order. In this case, it was the use of mediation. HHJ Mithani KC penalised the successful defendants for unreasonably refusing to mediate, with the defendant's costs being reduced by 25% as a result.

8.2.7 Enforcement and Appeals

Once a court order has been made, the parties must abide by it in a timely manner. If a party fails to do so, the other party may seek to have the court order enforced. There are various ways in which this will happen depending on what the order is for, but in general papers will need to be filed at the County Court. Details are set out in Practice Direction 70A and refer to Parts 70,71,72, 73 and 89.[6]

An appeal to a higher court may only usually be made relating to a matter of law. That is that a party contests that the judge(s) applied the law to their facts incorrectly. Matters of fact are decided by the first instance court and will only be overturned if new evidence comes to light which will make a material difference to the finding of fact or the judge in the lower court has made a significant error. An appeal from the County Court will be heard by the High Court (where the TCC sits); an appeal from the High Court will be heard by the Court of Appeal and an appeal from the Court of Appeal will be heard by the Supreme Court. Please see Chapter 1 for more information on the various courts and appeals systems.

---

5 *Conway v Conway & Anor* [2024] EW Misc 19 (CC).

6 https://www.justice.gov.uk/courts/procedure-rules/civil/rules/part70/pd_part70#IDAMCIOC (accessed 29 April 2025).

8.2.8 Shorter Trials Scheme

Since 2015 (initially as a trial), the TCC has offered the Shorter Trials Scheme (STS). STS offers quicker access to trials of no more than 4 days and is most suitable, therefore, for time-sensitive cases of moderate complexity requiring little evidence or disclosure where damages cost caps are not desirable. The Scheme, which aims to 'achieve short and earlier trials for business related litigation, at a reasonable and proportionate cost'[7] is available in the Chancery Division (including the Patents and Companies Courts), the Commercial, London Circuit Commercial and Technology and Construction Courts in the Rolls Building, which is a court in London.

8.2.9 Pros and Cons of Litigation

There is a clear advantage of getting a definitive answer in law, particularly for issues that are complex, either legally or factually. There is a logical appeal process, and the judgment can be enforced reasonably simply. However, on the downside, it can take several years to get to court and during that time parties are paying lawyers, using time of their executives and staff in managing the case, and often unable to continue work on site, so it can be extremely expensive. As court proceedings are a matter of public record, the details of the dispute will be public knowledge. It can be bad for business if a company is frequently in court – people don't like to do business with companies which they suspect are overly litigious.

8.3 Alternative Dispute Resolution

As the court system is time consuming and, therefore, costly and has been designed to encourage parties to reach their own agreements on disputes, there are lots of alternative forms of dispute resolution available. Commonly referred to as ADR. They range from the very formal methods, such as arbitration to the very informal methods, such as negotiation between the parties. Arbitration and adjudication are the formal methods, because they are regulated by Acts of Parliament and usually adopt a formal procedure. Although the arbitrator or adjudicator, respectively, will decide on how the process will be managed, there are rules set out in the Arbitration Act and the Scheme for Construction Contracts Regulations 1998. All other ADR methods are described as informal because the parties decide how they will run, sometimes with the help of professionals, but there is no formalised process.

8.3.1 Arbitration

Arbitration is a formal method of ADR which, in England and Wales, is governed by the Arbitration Act 1996 (soon to be amended by the Arbitration Act 2025). It is the settlement of a dispute by a technically competent expert, an arbitrator. In construction

---

7 Courts and Tribunals Judiciary (2015), *Short and Flexible Trial Procedures Pilot Schemes Announcement*, page 1.

cases, the arbitrator is likely to be knowledgeable about most construction related disputes. Most construction arbitrators will have previously been professionals from the industry, such as surveyors, commercial managers or construction project managers or they come from a legal background, having worked in the field of construction law and therefore will have a good understanding of the complexities involved in construction disputes.

Whilst arbitration is an option for all disputes it is generally only a preferred option if there is an arbitration clause in the contract(s) between the parties. This isn't a legal requirement, but a practical one. Without details of how the process will work or how the arbitrator will be chosen, it may be difficult to agree on all those details whilst already in dispute.

8.3.1.1 The Arbitration Act 1996

The Arbitration Act 1996 (as amended by the Arbitration Act 2025, see the following text) governs arbitration in the UK. It was drafted to be user-friendly, providing that there is no need for parties to engage lawyers to go through the process. However, as the process, like litigation is adversarial, requiring both parties to put their arguments forward for evaluation, most parties do choose to engage lawyers, and therefore companies feel pressured into employing lawyers so that they are not disadvantaged. The Act gives the arbitrators powers to award costs (S61)[8] and makes the award enforceable in the same way as a court judgment (S66).[9]

8.3.1.2 The Arbitration Act 2025

The Arbitration Act 2025 gained Royal Assent on 24 February 2025 and amends the Arbitration Act 1996. At the time of writing, the Act had not yet come into force. The Act is hoped to streamline the processes by introducing summary dismissal powers enabling dismissal of claims, defences or issues with 'no real prospect of success' (section 39A[10]). It is hoped that dismissing such claims will speed up the process and consequently reduce the time taken and therefore client costs.

According to Eversheds Sutherland, the changes made to the 1996 Act might further encourage parties to use arbitration as a reasonable alternative to Court either for final determination of a dispute or where the HGCRA does not apply to some or all of the work (e.g. power, water or chemical related projects). Arbitration may certainly provide more flexibility (and lower cost) than the TCC for disputes in England and Wales'.[11]

The new Act also limits the court's powers where jurisdiction has been challenged by one of the parties. By jurisdiction it means the power of the arbitrator to answer the question and may include arguments that the legal jurisdiction is incorrect or that the arbitrator

8 S61 The Arbitration Act 1996.

9 S66 The Arbitration Act 1996.

10 S39A Arbitration Act 1996 (as amended).

11 Eversheds Sutherland (2025) *What impact, if any, will the new Arbitration Act have on the construction industry?* found at: https://www.eversheds-sutherland.com/en/united-kingdom/insights/the-new-arbitration-act-on-the-construction-industry#:~:text=Whilst%20arbitration%20remains%20a%20popular%20method%20of%20dispute,means%20the%20process%20is%20lengthy%2C%20costly%20and%20complicated (accessed 2 May 2025).

chosen isn't the correct choice for the dispute as previously agreed by the parties in their contract. The existing power of a court under S67[12] to re-hear arguments or hear new arguments on the issue is to be withdrawn by the new Act. The court will only be able to consider arguments that were considered at the arbitration tribunal, thus reducing the time and costs incurred. It is hoped that this will make the UK arbitration process more attractive for use on international projects.

8.3.1.3 Choosing an Arbitrator

Arbitration uses technically competent professionals from the industry with knowledge of both appropriate law and the more technical/physical aspects of construction. Disputes can vary from purely legal, the meaning of a contract term, to the very technical, such as whether the workmanship is of an appropriate standard, or a method of construction is safe and, quite often, a combination of issues. It is, therefore, usual for a contract which proposes arbitration as a dispute method to have a list of arbitrators for various types of incidences or to have a designated institution to appoint an arbitrator to the parties. By way of example, the Joint Contracts Tribunal contract suggests that the President or a Vice-President of one of the following institutions should appoint an arbitrator: Royal Institute of British Architects, The Royal Institution of Chartered Surveyors, Chartered Institute of Arbitrators, or another institution agreed by the parties in the contract particulars.[13]

8.3.1.4 Procedure

After the appointment of the arbitrator, the arbitrator will call a preliminary meeting of parties to discuss the arbitration requirements, such as deadlines for evidence and documentation and how the process will run. The JCT uses the Construction Industry Model Arbitration Rules published from time to time, as also recommended by the Society of Construction Arbitrators.[14] The process may sometimes be governed by the contract between the parties but is usually determined by the arbitrator themselves.

There is usually a hearing to present the arguments, in a similar way to court proceedings, but for more simple cases the arbitrator may request arguments in writing. The arbitrator will decide the outcome and their decision is known as an award. The process can take as long as 18 months; however, the Society of Construction Arbitrators has drawn up rules to allow for a 100 day arbitration process[15] in order to speed up the process and, as a consequence, reduce costs.

8.3.1.5 Enforcement and Costs

Section 66 of the Arbitration Act 1996 provides that the arbitrators award will be enforced as if it were a court judgment, so the same security of enforcement exists for arbitration as for litigation.

---

12 S67 Arbitration Act 1996.

13 Clause 9.1.5 Contact Particulars, The Joint Contract Tribunal Standard Building Contract with Quantities 2024.

14 *Ibid* and https://www.constructionarbitrators.org/rules/cimar (accessed 7 May 2025).

15 https://www.constructionarbitrators.org/rules/100-day (accessed 7 May 2025).

The Act allows for the award to be challenged (appealed) through the courts on limited grounds:

1. where the jurisdiction of the arbitrator (S67) has been questioned. This challenge has been limited further by the 2025 act (see earlier);
2. where there has been serious irregularity in the procedure (S68). This is usually something like procedural unfairness or something which goes against natural justice; and
3. finally, S69 considers points of law, which are claims that the arbitrator did not apply the law correctly.

The arbitrator can make an award for costs under S61, which means that they can determine who will pay the costs. This usually follows the event – loser pays the costs, but it doesn't have to be that way if the arbitrator thinks a party has inflated costs, etc. It should be noted that liability for fees of arbitrators is joint and several (S28), so where a losing party is unable or unwilling to pay the other party will be liable for the whole of the arbitrator's costs. It is not a matter of paying just their half.

8.3.1.6 Pros and Cons of Arbitration

The plus points of arbitration are that the parties get a definitive answer from an expert in the field, it is a shorter process than litigation proceedings, and the award can be enforced in the courts. The process is also confidential between the parties and the arbitrator, unlike litigation which is always a matter of public record. However, the process is adversarial, pitching parties against each other rather than seeking mutual solution; litigation-type procedures have been adopted, including the practice of hiring lawyers and therefore it can be very expensive and with an average 18-month-long process.

8.3.2 Adjudication

Adjudication is a similar form of dispute resolution to arbitration. It is a quick and simple method of dispute resolution by an independent party. In the construction industry, it is a statutory right to all parties to a construction contract,[16] if their contract falls within the definition of a construction contract under section 104 of the Housing Grants Construction and Regeneration Act 1996 (HGCRA) (see Chapter 3). It does not apply to contracts with residential occupiers; that is, individuals having construction work undertaken to their primary dwelling.[17] That is not to say that domestic contracts cannot be decided at adjudication, but that there is no legal right for them to do so. If a domestic party requests adjudication, the contractor may refuse.

Under the HGCRA, the parties may make their own agreement of how to run their adjudication within their contract; however, if there is no agreement in the contract then the HGCRA implies that adjudication process from the Scheme for Construction Contracts Regulations (England and Wales) Regulations 1998 (The Scheme) will apply. Many of the standard form contracts simply state that the Scheme for Construction Contracts will be used.

16 S108 Housing Grant Construction and Regeneration Act 1996.
17 S106 Housing Grants Construction and Regeneration Act 1996.

8.3.2.1 History Behind Statutory Adjudication

Adjudication exists in other industries and jurisdictions but was used infrequently in construction disputes until the advent of statutory adjudication arrived with the HGCRA. Prior to this, there had been a considerable number of litigation cases, which were costly and time consuming, not just to those involved but for the taxpayer covering the costs of court proceedings and with a reduction in gross domestic product due to lower construction output. Often the most harshly impacted were sub-contractors whose work was put on hold until the dispute was resolved. Many of these subcontracting companies end up in liquidation. This was confirmed by a joint government and industry commissioned report produced by Lord Latham in 1994 entitled 'Constructing the Team',[18] but more commonly referred to as The Latham Report. The enactment of the HGCRA was as a direct result of the report which asked 'is it true that the construction industry is riddled with disputes?'

8.3.2.2 The Scheme for Construction Contracts

The Scheme provides a speedy method for settling disputes with a timetable of only 28 days, unless parties agree to extend it by up to 14 days. The adjudicator has a free hand on how to conduct proceedings which could be with written or oral submissions. The adjudicator's decision, like in arbitration, is known as an award.

8.3.2.3 Enforcement and Perceived Issues

The award is legally binding at the time of issue and must be abided by. There is no direct appeal of the award, but a party who is unhappy with the outcome can commence alternative ADR or litigation.

Awards made by the adjudicators will be enforced by the courts at summary judgement. A summary judgment is a judgement by a court for one party against another based on a matter of law, without a hearing (summarily). All that is required is for the party to produce the Award documentation to court for their confirmation that the award is legitimate. The court will not consider any facts or findings of the adjudicator. Initially, losing parties would try to overturn awards in courts but with little success. Awards were enforced even where the adjudicator had made an error.[19] The adjudicator in *Bouygues v Dahl-Jennsen*[20] made incorrect calculations but the court enforced the award at summary judgment, despite the error. This is because at summary judgment hearings, the court only considers validity of the award, not the decision itself. In *Bloor Construction (UK) Ltd v Bowmer & Kirkland (London) Ltd*[21], His Honour Justice Toulmin CMG QC ruled that an adjudicator can alter their decision to correct an error arising from an accidental slip or omission. This became known as the 'slip rule'. The rule was confirmed in *Edmund Nuttall Ltd v Sevenoaks District Council.*[22]

---

18 D. Cahill and M.-C. Puybaraud, 'Constructing the Team: The Latham Report (1994),' (2008), https://doi.org/10.1002/9780470758526.ch11.

19 *Bouygues UK Limited v Dahl-Jensen UK Limited* [2000] 2 TCLR 308.

20 Ibid.

21 [2000] BLR 314.

22 [2002] HT 00 119.

> "...in the absence of a specific agreement by the parties to the contrary, there is to be implied into the agreement for adjudication the power of the adjudicator to correct an error arising from an accidental slip or omission...provided this is done within a reasonable time and without prejudicing the other party:"

The enforcement without investigation led to adjudication being described as an on the spot fine because the courts will enforce it, even if it is wrong. In *Carillion v Devenport*[23] Justice Jackson referred to adjudication as 'pay now, argue later' explaining that unless there is a demonstration of procedural unfairness, even an award which has misinterpreted the law would still be enforced by the court. He went on to say that it is very rare that an adjudication award will not be enforced.

Whilst procedural unfairness is rare, there have been instances of adjudicators helping one side[24] by using an argument which was not actually submitted by the party concerned but was a better argument than the one which they had put forward. An adjudicator, like a Judge and an arbitrator may only consider the arguments put forward by the parties and not substitute any other law or argument which they think applies. Similarly, in *Discain v Opecprime*[25] it was found that the adjudicator had made phone calls to one side to clarify their argument but had not allowed the other side the same opportunity.

8.3.2.4 Smash and Grab Adjudications

One of the most common uses of adjudication is payment disputes and enforcement of the HGCRA payment rules. As enforcement at summary judgement is almost guaranteed, some construction firms started to use adjudication as a means of obtaining higher payments than deserved due to payless notices being issued incorrectly by contract administrators. The term relates to contractors applying to adjudication immediately where a pay less notice isn't issued correctly by the employer, even though they know that if one were to be issued correctly, the payment would be legitimately reduced.

The adjudicator must find for the contractor even where the employer has a legitimate right to withhold payment (e.g. for abatement for poor workmanship), because the HGCRA requires a pay less notice in the correct format and doesn't look at the merits of the payment itself. The judiciary has mixed views on its use.

Justice Coulson, in his final case for the Technical and Construction Court, made it clear that he disliked the practice and that he hoped it would soon end. 'A pay less notice will be construed by reference to its background, in order to see how a reasonable recipient would have understood it. The court will be unimpressed by nice points of textual analysis, or arguments which seek to condemn the notice on an artificial or contrived basis. One way of testing to see whether the contents of the notice are adequate is to see if the notice provides an adequate agenda for a dispute...'. He went on to say '.... I do not consider that the conclusions which I have reached strike at the heart of the adjudication system. On the contrary, I believe that it will strengthen the system, because it will reduce the number

---

23 *Carillion Construction Limited v Devonport Royal Dockyard* [2005] EWCA Civ 1358.

24 *Balfour Beatty Construction Ltd v Mayor and Burgesses of London Borough of Lambeth* [2002] EWHC 597 (TCC).

25 *Discain Project Services Ltd v Opecprime Developments Ltd* [2001] EWHC Tech 450.

of 'smash and grab' claims which, in my view, have brought adjudication into a certain amount of disrepute'.[26]

However, the system is still used by contractors to insist upon payment of a notified sum to protect and preserve cash flow in the short to medium term. It usually arises in the absence of a notice to pay less or of a certificate. As one of Latham's aims was to ensure cashflow and to protect the solvency of contracting parties, it doesn't seem as though the courts will go further in trying to reduce its use.

8.3.2.5 Can Adjudication Awards by Appealed?

The short answer is no. As you have seen earlier, an adjudication award will be enforced even where the adjudicator has made an error. The only time the awards will not be enforced at summary judgment is if there is evidence of procedural unfairness or the adjudicator did not have the jurisdiction to answer the question. This could occur in a situation where parties ask for a decision on one aspect of their dispute, but the adjudicator finds on an issue which the parties did not raise. In that situation the parties did not give the adjudicator the power (jurisdiction) to answer that question so the award cannot be enforced.

The only way to 'appeal' the award is to start fresh proceedings on the matter at arbitration or litigation. The award stands until otherwise overturned by arbitration or litigation, which is why an adjudication award is described as an interim award. The Latham Report envisaged a method of dispute resolution that would ensure that parties returned to site as soon as possible. This is why Jackson J described it as 'pay now, argue later'.[27] Of course, in most cases, the award is a final decision, but there is the 'risk' that the other party may decide at a later stage to re-open the dispute in other proceedings.

In *Harlow & Milner Ltd v Mrs Linda Teasdale*,[28] Mrs Teasdale tried to stop the enforcement of an award against her because she had already begun arbitration proceedings on the matter. Mrs Teasdale had used her pension savings to purchase some investment properties which she intended to renovate and then let to provide her with an income. Mrs Teasdale had applied to the local council for a grant to meet some of the renovation costs; however, her application failed, which left her with insufficient funds to meet the payment due to Harlow and Milner. HHJ Coulson QC observed that:

> ... [this case]...illustrates the clear but sometimes harsh consequences of the system of construction adjudication introduced by the Housing Grants Construction and Regeneration Act 1996.[29]

Note that whilst Mrs Teasdale is an individual, the construction contract did come under the HGCRA because the properties concerned were not occupied (or to be occupied) by her.

8.3.2.6 Costs

In general, each party will meet their own costs and the loser is not expected to pay the winner's costs, unless the parties have agreed to such a term within the contract. The rates

26 *S&T (UK) Limited v Grove Developments* Limited [2018] EWCA Civ 2448.
27 *Carillion Construction Limited v Devonport Royal Dockyard* [2005] EWCA Civ 1358.
28 [2006] EWHC 1708 (TCC).
29 *Harlow & Milner Ltd v Mrs Linda Teasdale* [2006] EWHC 1708 (TCC).

charged by adjudicators are similar to those charged by arbitrators, but as the process is considerably quicker the overall bill is considerably lower.

8.3.2.7 Pros and Cons of Adjudication

Adjudication is by far the quickest and cheapest of the formal dispute resolutions. Parties can return to the project more quickly, keeping the economy running and achieving an award which can be enforced. Like arbitration, the adjudication process is confidential between the parties and the adjudicator, unlike litigation which is always a matter of public record. Of course, if a party uses summary judgement to enforce the award, that judgment will be on record, but the details of the dispute will not.

On the negative side, the other party may open up the matter again at a later stage by arbitration or litigation and the award will be enforced even if incorrect. That said, the chances of mistake are quite low given that most cases concern payment under the HGCR which are often quite straightforward; however, for more complex disputes it may be better to use arbitration or litigation where aspects can be considered in much more detail, to avoid a mistake due to the quick 28 day turnaround time.

8.3.3 Informal Alternative Dispute Resolution

Informal dispute resolution can be as simple as having a phone conversation or flipping a coin. The methods by which parties make their agreement are entirely left to them, as are the rules relating to how they undertake their chosen method of resolution. Following are some of the more common and established methods, but, of course, there are many other options.

8.3.3.1 Negotiation

Negotiation is simply talking it through with the other side and agreeing on compromises to achieve a way forward. There needs to be some give and take from both sides in order to make it work. There is no set way of negotiating, so parties are free to agree a venue and timescale as they see fit. Negotiations don't have to be in person but could be by email, telephone or video calls. As negotiation doesn't involve third parties, there are no costs other than the costs of the time of the employees who are undertaking the negotiations. Of course, if there are technical differences, then it may be that negotiations require technical assistance. If so, who pays for that expert, or will the choice of the expert be part of the negotiations?

8.3.3.2 Mediation

At mediation, the parties hire an independent person (the mediator) to mediate between them. The mediator empowers the parties to make their own settlement on the issue(s) by using what is known as shuttle diplomacy. They will discuss issues with each of the parties and then help them to find common ground. The mediator can advise on the legal position if required but should always remain impartial. The government provides a guide to civil mediation at: https://www.gov.uk/guidance/a-guide-to-civil-mediation.

8.3.3.3 Conciliation

Conciliation is similar to mediation, in that a professional (this time a conciliator) is engaged to help the parties come to a resolution for their dispute. Unlike a mediator, the conciliator actively suggests ways forward to the parties and can make recommendations for resolution. Some contracts will agree that conciliation recommendations will be binding. For example, the Institute of Civil Engineers contracts have a clause which provides that where an approved conciliation procedure has been used, the recommendation will be binding 30 days after issue. Of course, binding refers to the matter being agreed as a contract. The matter of enforcement is not as simple (see the following text on pros and cons of informal methods).

8.3.3.4 Dispute Boards

Some of the standard form contracts (see 3.1.3 in Chapter 3) include provision for dispute advisory (sometimes adjudication) boards. They originated in FIDIC contracts but are now provided for in NEC4 and the JCT contracts. In addition, several institutions, such as Institute of Civil Engineers and The Chartered Institute of Arbitrators, provide rules for dispute boards which can be adopted.

The idea is that at any time a dispute arises the board is called upon to investigate and decide upon the outcome of the issue(s). Some of the boards are also called upon to address issues to avoid disputes arising. As the matter is internal between the parties, the costs are generally low and help to maintain the relationship between the parties. They are reasonably commonly used in other jurisdictions but less used in the UK due to the provision of statutory adjudication, which is often used for any dispute that falls within the remit of the HGCRA. A form of board, the Independent Dispute Avoidance Panel was successfully used during the construction phase of the London 2012 Olympics.

The contract will state which set of rules applies or set out how the boards are to be run and who will constitute the board. There is usually one or three people on the board, who will have been decided upon at the time of the contract agreement.

8.3.3.5 Early Neutral Evaluation

ENE is an evaluation at the early stages of a dispute by a neutral person with specialist knowledge and skills on the issue(s) under dispute. The evaluator is typically (but not always) a sitting or retired judge, a practising barrister, or practising solicitor. Parties seeking ENE but with no agreement as to their evaluator can approach institutions like the Chartered Institute of Arbitrators or the Centre of Effective Dispute Resolution for a recommendation. The evaluator will review the key facts, evidence and legal arguments and provide an opinion on how the case might be resolved if it proceeded to court. This opinion will highlight the strengths and weaknesses of arguments and therefore assist constructive negotiation between the parties. This evaluation is usually undertaken on a without prejudice basis and is non-binding. Without prejudice means without prejudice to any court proceedings, i.e. should the negotiations fail between the parties, the discussions at ENE cannot be disclosed to the court because anything discussed at ENE is confidential.

8.3.3.6 Pros and Cons of Informal Methods

There are many benefits to the use of informal methods of dispute resolution, not least being the speed and cost-effectiveness and that the proceedings are all confidential. One major consideration is how the resolution method may affect the relationship between the parties. All the formal methods are adversarial in nature, pitching the parties against each other with each party, usually through lawyers, having to argue their case, points of law and version of facts, which will inevitably cause ill feeling between the parties. The informal methods are non-adversarial and parties are encouraged to find a way forward together. Such informality may help to maintain or even strengthen relationships between the parties. Another benefit of their informality is that the solutions are not limited by contract law. Parties are free to agree on compromises or suggest amendments to other contracts between the parties which are separate from the contract under discussion.

Of course, the informality can be a negative, as there are few ways to enforce agreements made informally. Whilst a contract can be written, or become legally binding per the original contract, as is the case in ICE contracts with conciliation (discussed earlier), if a party breaches that new agreement, both parties are inevitably back at square one in relation to the original dispute. Similarly, the forums may not be appropriate for very complex technical matters of large projects with many interconnecting contracts and parties.

Index

Note: Page numbers in *italics* and **bold** refers to figures and tables respectively.

d

p

q

r

s